AMATEUR CINEMA

The publisher gratefully acknowledges the generous support of the Ahmanson Foundation Humanities Endowment Fund of the University of California Press Foundation.

The publisher also gratefully acknowledges the generous support of the Eric Papenfuse and Catherine Lawrence Endowment Fund in Film and Media Studies of the University of California Press Foundation.

Amateur Cinema

The Rise of North American
Moviemaking, 1923–1960

CHARLES TEPPERMAN

UNIVERSITY OF CALIFORNIA PRESS

University of California Press, one of the most distinguished university presses in the United States, enriches lives around the world by advancing scholarship in the humanities, social sciences, and natural sciences. Its activities are supported by the UC Press Foundation and by philanthropic contributions from individuals and institutions. For more information, visit www.ucpress.edu.

University of California Press
Oakland, California

© 2015 by The Regents of the University of California

Library of Congress Cataloging-in-Publication Data

Tepperman, Charles, 1974– author.
   Amateur cinema : the rise of North American moviemaking, 1923–1960 / Charles Tepperman.
      pages   cm
   Includes bibliographical references and index.
   ISBN 978-0-520-27985-8 (cloth : alk. paper)
   ISBN 978-0-520-27986-5 (pbk. : alk. paper)
   ISBN 978-0-520-95955-2 (ebook)
   1. Amateur films—Production and direction—North America—History—20th century. I. Title.
PN1995.8.T46 2015
791.43′3—dc23
                                           2014018278

24 23 22 21 20 19 18 17 16 15
10 9 8 7 6 5 4 3 2 1

For Lee and Laurel

Contents

List of Illustrations	ix
Acknowledgments	xi
Introduction	1

PART I. CONTEXTS OF AMATEUR CINEMA

1. Ciné-Prophecy: The Emergence of Amateur Cinema (1892–1927) — 17
2. Ciné-Community: The First Wave of Amateur Film Culture (1928–1945) — 44
3. Ciné-Engagement: Amateurs and Current Events — 79
4. Ciné-Technology: Machine Art for a Machine Age — 98
5. Ciné-Sincerity: Postwar Amateur Film Culture (1945–1960) — 133

PART II. MODES OF AMATEUR CINEMA

6. "Communicating a New Form of Knowledge": Amateur Chronicles of Family, Community, and Travel — 169
7. "The Amateur Takes Leadership": Amateur Film, Experimentation, and the Aesthetic Vanguard — 193
8. Mechanical Craftsmanship: Amateurs Making Practical Films — 217
9. Photoplaying Themselves: Amateur Fiction Films — 241

Conclusion	271
Appendix 1. Amateur Filmography	277
Appendix 2. A Preliminary Directory of Movie Clubs	285
Notes	293
Selected Bibliography	339
Index	349

Illustrations

FIGURES

1. From *Mag the Hag*, Hiram Percy Maxim, 1925 — 18
2. The first masthead and motto of *Amateur Movie Makers*, 1927 — 19
3. *Amateur Movie Makers'* "SWAPS" Amateur Film Exchange, 1926 — 40
4. A new motto for *Amateur Movie Makers*, 1927 — 43
5. The *Amateur Movies* face of *American Cinematographer*, 1937 — 47
6. Urgent: Where have you filmed? 1942 — 92
7. "Color Adventure Drama!!" 1940 — 106
8. The Fidelitone Dual-Turntable system, 1940 — 114
9. Eastman Kodak's three film widths, c. 1932 — 118
10. Advertisement for the Ciné-Kodak Special, 1933 — 120
11. From *San Francisco*, Tullio Pellegrini, 1955 — 125
12. From *Filmorama Travels*, Ron Doerring and George Ives, c. 1955 — 127
13. From *San Francisco*, Tullio Pellegrini, 1955 — 127
14. Advertisement for Nord 3-D converters, 1952 — 129
15. The masthead and motto of *Metro News*, 1954 — 138
16. Production still from *Julius Caesar*, David Bradley, 1951 — 145
17. From *Fairy Princess*, Margaret Conneely, 1956 — 163
18. Prize-winning filmmaker Margaret Conneely, 1956 — 164

19. From *Another Day*, Leslie Thatcher, 1934 — 181
20. From *Another Day*, Leslie Thatcher, 1934 — 181
21. From *Tombs of the Nobles*, John V. Hansen, 1931 — 190
22. From *The Fall of the House of Usher*, James Sibley Watson and Melville Webber, 1928 — 199
23. From *H₂O*, Ralph Steiner, 1929 — 202
24. From *Mr. Motorboat's Last Stand*, John Flory, 1933 — 210
25. From *The Eyes of Science*, James Sibley Watson and Melville Webber, 1931 — 226
26. Production still from *The Story of Bamba*, Ray Garner, 1939 — 236
27. Margaret Bourke-White and Charles Carbonaro during production of *We Are All Artists*, 1935 — 239
28. David Bradley shooting a film near Winnetka, Illinois, c. 1941 — 247
29. From *Peer Gynt*, David Bradley, 1941 — 249
30. From *Peer Gynt*, David Bradley, 1941 — 250
31. From *A Race for Ties*, Dorothea Mitchell, 1929 — 256
32. From *A Race for Ties*, Dorothea Mitchell, 1929 — 256
33. From *A Race for Ties*, Dorothea Mitchell, 1929 — 257
34. From *A Study in Reds*, Miriam Bennett, 1932 — 259
35. From *A Study in Reds*, Miriam Bennett, 1932 — 259
36. From *A Study in Reds*, Miriam Bennett, 1932 — 260
37. From *Her Heart's Desire*, Othon Goetz, 1949 — 262
38. From *Tarzan and the Rocky Gorge*, Robbins Barstow, 1936 — 263
39. From *Little Geezer*, Theodore Huff, 1932 — 267

TABLE

Ratio of record to story films, 1946–1950 — 191

Acknowledgments

I have had support from so many quarters that I can't hope to acknowledge all of them here. This book began as a dissertation at the University of Chicago, where Tom Gunning provided the perfect balance of freedom, encouragement, and inspiration that one would wish to have from an adviser. Jim Lastra and Jacqueline Stewart provided generous and careful commentary, and I am also grateful to Miriam Hansen and Yuri Tsivian for their advice, guidance, and support at key moments during my time at Chicago. More recently, I am grateful to Rick Prelinger and the anonymous readers for their many excellent suggestions, and to Mary Francis at the University of California Press for her encouragement—and especially patience—while I was completing this book. My sincere thanks to Kim Hogeland, Aimee Goggins, Rachel Berchten, Robin Whitaker, Cynthia Savage, and all of those who helped me through the book production process. The Social Sciences and Humanities Research Council of Canada supported the beginnings of this project, and University Research Grants Committee funds at the University of Calgary helped me complete it.

My work has benefited enormously from the generous assistance of many film archivists and scholars. Bill O'Farrell first introduced me to the worlds of film archives and amateur cinema, and I'm grateful to him for sharing both his vast knowledge and his infectious enthusiasm. Nancy Watrous, Michelle Puetz, Anne Wells, Andy Uhrich, Buckey Grimm, Kaveh Askari, Caitlin McGrath, Ariel Rogers, Ryan Shand, Snowden Becker, Rosemary Bergeron, David Pierce, Anke Mebold, Carolyn Faber, Melinda Stone, Dan Streible, Charles Acland, Haidee Wasson, John Gledhill, Stephen Tapert, and Dwight Swanson have shared my interests and assisted my search for amateur movies in many ways. Thanks also to the helpful staff at Library and Archives Canada, the Wisconsin Center for Film and Theatre Research, the Human Studies Film Archive (Daisy Njoku and Pam Wintle), the Northwestern University Archives, Northeast Historic Film (David Weiss and Karan Sheldon), the George Eastman House (Nancy Kauffman), the Library of Congress, the East Anglian Film Archive, the National Archives and Records Administration (Carrie Goeringer), and Lilly Library at Indiana University.

I owe an enormous debt to the amateur filmmakers who generously shared their films and experiences with me: Tom and Delores Backe, Robbins Barstow, Josephine Black, Fred Briggs, and Bill and Mary Ann Leeder and the gang at the South Side Cinema Club. Margaret Conneely, in particular, helped me in many ways. Her clever movies and playful spirit were an inspiration for my work; in sharing their films with me, Margaret and these other amateurs have given me a tremendous gift and more materials than could be included in this project.

At the University of Calgary, Jim Ellis, Brendan Kredell, and Dawn Johnston have been good friends and warm colleagues. My students have also provided assistance and fresh insights, especially Eric Becker and Sheena Manabat. Elsewhere, Michael Cheng, Charlie Keil, Gillian Roberts, Ken Eisenstein, Doron Galili, Oliver Gaycken, Christina Peterson, Andrew Johnston, and Theresa Scandiffio could always be relied on for stimulating conversation, encouragement, and good cheer, as could my friends at the Calgary Cinematheque. My family has offered both support and pleasant distraction while I was writing this work. I couldn't ask for better role models of hard work, professional accomplishment, and generosity than my parents. I'm grateful to my siblings for all of their encouragement, and to so many other supportive relatives cheering me on. Finally, I can't begin to enumerate the ways that Lee Carruthers has provided crucial assistance of all kinds during the writing of this book. I'm so fortunate to have a partner in life whom I also admire as a thinker and writer, and I'm grateful to Lee for encouraging me in my work while also challenging me to improve it. Laurel's arrival is more recent, but she has already offered a new perspective on nearly everything.

Part of chapter 3 was previously published as "Color Unlimited: Amateur Color Cinema in the 1930s," in *Color and the Moving Image*, edited by Simon Brown, Sarah Street and Liz Watkins (London: Routledge, 2012). Some material from chapter 6 appeared in "Uncovering Canada's Amateur Film Tradition: Leslie Thatcher's Films and Contexts," in *Cinephemera: Archives, Ephemeral Cinema and New Screen Histories in Canada*, edited by Zoë Druick and Gerda Cammaer (Montreal: McGill-Queen's University Press, 2014). A section of chapter 8 was previously published as "Mechanical Craftsmanship: Amateurs Making Practical Films," in *Useful Cinema*, edited by Charles Acland and Haidee Wasson (Durham, NC: Duke University Press, 2011).

Introduction

"Amateur" is a word which, in the Latin, meant "lover"; but today it has become a term like "Yankee" ("Amateur—Go Home"), hatched in criticism, by professionals who so little understand the value of the word or its meaning that they do honor it, and those of us who identify with it, most where they think to shame and disgrace in their usage of it.

Stan Brakhage, *"In Defense of Amateur"*[1]

This book explores the meaning of the "amateur" in film history and modern visual culture. In the middle decades of the twentieth century—the period that saw Hollywood's rise to dominance in the global film industry—a movement of amateur moviemakers created an alternative world of small-scale movie production and circulation. For Stan Brakhage, whose stature as a giant of American avant-garde filmmaking was already established when he made these remarks, identifying with the "amateur" might be seen as a way of describing his work's aesthetic incompatibility with commercial practices. For earlier amateur filmmakers, however, the "value" and "meaning" of their works remain an unresolved issue. To begin an evaluation of the aesthetic and social meaning of the amateur, this book investigates the first wave of amateur film culture in North America, between approximately 1923 and 1960. This was a period when being an amateur meant experimenting with all the possibilities that making movies outside Hollywood presented.

When we think about amateur cinema, it is perhaps the rough home movies of birthdays and family vacations that come first to mind. But the domain of amateur cinema is much more expansive than this and includes polished filmmaking as well. Advanced amateurs often moved far beyond the "point-and-shoot" aesthetic of home movies and distinguished their work through attention to the planning and finishing (pre- and postproduction) of their films. But these works are not merely pale imitations of professional film; rather, they retain traces of their amateur status in moments of accidental beauty or in deliberate choices of playful or intimate subject matter. Whether experimental, nonfiction, or short-subject narratives, amateur works are a species of film that reveals a creative response—with all the naïve optimism that suggests—available only outside the commercial marketplace. The films by "advanced" or "serious" amateurs discussed in this book are often expressively creative works with a complex relationship to other artistic practices. Produced outside academies of artistic taste and free from the profit-earning requirements of commercial media, these amateur films represent a mode of vernacular art making that scholars have only recently begun to examine.

This brief introduction sketches out the terrain of "the amateur," considering the development of this category, and the way the amateur has largely fallen through the cracks of film history and criticism. One goal of this book is to open up some space in which to productively discuss artworks by amateurs Brakhage might have defended: lovers of cinema who privileged the movie camera as a medium of reflection, a means for personal expression, or a way of becoming participants in modern visual culture. Beyond the boundaries of the institutions of high art and mass commercial culture there exists an enormous unmapped terrain for creative works and amateur expression. Today, this space includes the products of digital video, social networks, and other user-generated content. This book aims to illuminate the field of amateur media production by looking closely at the earliest surviving amateur films; in this way we can start developing an understanding of amateur moviemaking as a significant aesthetic and social practice.

WHAT IS AN AMATEUR?

It was a notion of the amateur as a productive and powerfully creative, but noncommercial, figure that Hiram Percy Maxim hoped to promote when he founded the Amateur Cinema League in 1926. In his inaugural editorial of *Amateur Movie Makers* magazine, he proclaimed a new era for the cinema, as well as a new kind of filmmaker. "When we analyze amateur cinematography," wrote Maxim, "we find it a very much broader affair than appears upon the surface. Instead of its being a form of light individual amusement, it is really an entirely new method of communication."[2]

Maxim's call to distinguish amateur cinematography from a form of light individual amusement is noteworthy here, but to understand the social significance of amateurism in the early twentieth century and its vexed relationship with both professional work and mass commercial culture, it is necessary to trace the development and historical meaning—and later the scholarly neglect—of the amateur.

The word *amateur* emerged in English use in the late eighteenth century, borrowed from the French language: "Amateur, in the Arts, is a foreign term introduced and now passing current amongst us, to denote a person understanding, and loving or practising the polite arts of painting, sculpture, or architecture, without any regard to pecuniary advantage."[3] This disregard of pecuniary advantage sets the amateur aside from a paid worker and signals the aristocratic origins of amateur activities. But over the course of the nineteenth century, many fields that had been the domain of serious amateurs (fields as diverse as biology, athletics, and photography) gradually became professionalized.[4] By the Progressive Era, professionals were assumed to be more proficient at their work than amateurs because they were trained in it, devoted more time to it, and could demand payment for it. Though professionalization was accompanied by policing the boundary between amateur and professional—in some cases through certification, in others simply through the disparagement of amateur efforts—a class of serious amateurs continued to grow in many fields. The rise of public education and popular presses furnished a modern, *non*aristocratic amateur public with access to recent discoveries and developments in their field of interest.[5]

By the turn of the twentieth century, the role of amateurs in American society had become a contentious issue. In his 1904 article "The Amateur Spirit," American essayist Bliss Perry itemized the amateur economists, sociologists, preachers, and critics of art and literature "who have plenty of zeal, but no knowledge of standards, no anchorage in principles." In contrast to these amateurs, dilettantes, and dabblers, "the real workaday progress, the solid irretraceable advance in any art or profession, has commonly been made by the professional."[6] But as Perry knew, modernity and scientific specialization also challenged the possibility of living a balanced life. And despite his acknowledgment of the more productive qualities of the professional, Perry's article was really a plea to temper American professionalization with the amateur spirit: "The cultivated amateur, who touches life on many sides, perceives that the professional is apt to approach life from one side only. . . . Your famous expert, as you suddenly discover, is but a segment of a man,—overdeveloped in one direction, atrophied in all others. His expertness, his professional functioning, so to speak, is of indispensable value to society, but he himself remains an unsocial member of the body politic. He has become a machine,—as Emerson declared so long ago, 'a thinker, not a man thinking.'" The creativity of the amateur could temper and balance the atrophy of human qualities brought on by modern specialization. At stake for Perry was nothing less than remaining human in industrial mass society: "The personal enthusiasm, the individual initiative, the boundless zest, of the American amateur must penetrate, illuminate, idealize, the brute force, the irresistibly on-sweeping mass, of our vast industrial democracy."[7] Perry suggests that a merging of the spirit of the amateur with professional scientific method was already appearing in 1904. "There are here and there amateurs without amateurishness, professionals untainted by professionalism," Perry noted, and attributes this mix to a sort of "human curiosity and eagerness, which are the best endowment of the amateur."[8] Amateur moviemakers likely had this balance in mind when, some years later, they fused together a creative hobby with the technological sophistication needed to master cinematography, editing, and storytelling. Hiram Percy Maxim was clearly a firm believer in this set of tenets, as he promoted a kind of knowledgeable, but also feeling and thoughtful, amateur pursuit. Amateur filmmaking might therefore be seen as a defense against the atrophy of human qualities, particularly the creative qualities that were put at risk by an institutionalized mode of modern mass entertainment that produced films according to industrial logic and positioned viewers as increasingly passive consumers of media.

Beyond Perry's humanistic defense of the amateur, the steady flow of new communication technologies also provided a more systemic challenge to a culture of efficient specialization and commodified expertise. Modern media technologies—from typewriters and telephones to movies and the radio—provided a means for people to gain new kinds of expertise and, as Maxim reminds us, to engage in "new forms of communication." Mass media, as Walter Benjamin noted, turns everybody into a kind of expert (but an *amateur* or "quasi-expert"), and this was particularly the case with movies.[9] Consumer culture and media technologies may act on society as a mass, but they also provide the means for small-scale and amateur responses that invert the commercial values of expertise and productivity. "The distinction between author and public is about to lose its axiomatic character," Benjamin writes. "At any moment, the reader is ready to become a writer." And the film spectator is ready to become a filmmaker.

Despite the broad potential for amateur expression suggested by Benjamin, the work of amateurs has received scant attention in humanities scholarship. Histories of photography and self-taught art reveal that amateurism is at antipodes with high art institutions, a victim of the academies of artistic taste and training, and the pejorative connotations of the word *amateur*. Some historical accounts of photography have traced the role of amateurs, but in these studies the amateur designation is usually associated with technical or aesthetic lack of accomplishment. For many "elite" amateurs, like Alfred

Stieglitz, the designation of "amateur" was applied only because photography had not yet proven itself as an artistic medium or established a "photographic academy" and was dropped once the amateur reached standards of professional or artistic quality.[10] More common in scholarly literature is the dismissive use of *amateur* to refer to bourgeois, "middlebrow" pursuits—exactly the "light individual amusement" Maxim wished to distinguish it from. In this vein, Pierre Bourdieu argues that amateur photography isn't the fulfillment of a creative desire so much as the performance of a social role; it is a "middlebrow" hobby that participates in and reinforces rituals of social status and accomplishment. In his study of French amateur photographers, class hierarchies are neatly mapped onto hierarchies of taste and aesthetic sophistication. For Bourdieu, when amateur photographers make aesthetic choices, they are merely "the poor man's aestheticism" and evidence of their class standing; amateur photography isn't so much a medium of expression as it is a means of social "up-classing."[11]

One area of art history that has made space for artworks outside conventional canons of taste is the recent scholarship concerned with "self-taught" art. Though the comparison might seem unlikely (for reasons of class or cultural capital) there are some obvious similarities between amateurs and folk artists (one kind of self-taught artist). For example, we can understand both kinds of artists as offering individual aesthetic responses to the everyday that are produced and circulated outside commercial or high art institutions. But where folk artists have produced works that appealed to local cultures and longstanding traditions (even if reinvented in the twentieth century), amateur filmmakers were generally middle-class and urban (or suburban), and the media were technological rather than purely manual.[12] So while different from folk art in significant ways, amateur films reside in a similar blind spot of art criticism and aesthetic theory. The more general category of self-taught art opens up a conceptual space within which works of evident aesthetic interest, produced outside high-art traditions, can be considered. Cultural anthropologists such as Michael Owen Jones insist instead on a more quotidian understanding of aesthetic taste, thus narrowing the gap between specialized and self-taught artistic knowledge: "All of us are self-taught artists," Jones writes, when we "strive to perfect form in some of the endeavors in which we engage because of the sensory pleasure and intellectual satisfaction of doing so."[13] This category provides a necessary corrective to art criticism that adheres too much to established hierarchies of aesthetic taste and genius and is an important amendment to theories of "middlebrow" culture that overlook creative production in favor of consumption or undervalue aesthetic qualities altogether.

Amateur movies have received salutary attention from scholars, but this research has generally focused on the domestic characteristics of *home* movies (with emphasis on their locus of both production and consumption) and neglected other forms and contexts of amateur filmmaking. Anthropologists have long considered homemade media as forms of "folk material culture," examining how the structure and content of domestic snapshots and films reveal a "symbolically created world."[14] In a similar vein, social historians and film scholars have "mined" home movies for traces of submerged, marginalized, and unofficial histories.[15] In her pioneering work on amateur filmmaking, Patricia R. Zimmermann persuasively argues for the amateur movie's capacity to challenge received narratives of film history and aesthetics but notes that amateur media have rarely lived up to this subversive potential. Instead, she finds home movies to be weakly complicit adherents to bourgeois film culture and finds amateur cinema discourse as "an adjunct and promoter of Hollywood."[16] Like many studies, Zimmermann's work focuses primarily on unedited home movies and rough travel footage and tends to reduce all amateur work to the aesthetic simplicity of "home movies." This scholarship has tended to overlook or diminish the aesthetic complexity and cultural significance of the polished films made by serious amateurs. Advanced amateur films differ from home movies in ways that require further attention: though both are produced outside professional filmmaking contexts using mass-marketed small-gauge film formats (16mm and 8mm film rather than professional 35mm film), films by advanced amateurs employ more polished filming and editing techniques and feature elements of narrative or thematic continuity. And while home movies are generally produced as private records of family and friends, more advanced amateurs have had a wider group of potential viewers and viewing contexts in mind.[17]

A recent surge of interest in amateur, small-gauge, nontheatrical, and other kinds of "ephemeral" films sought to correct these oversights and introduced considerable nuance (through focused case studies) to our account of nonmainstream filmmaking.[18] For example, amateur film culture beyond the domestic sphere gained more specific attention in Melinda Stone's research into local amateur movie clubs in the 1950s and '60s, which uses the San Diego movie club as a case study.[19] Jan-Christopher Horak's anthology, *Lovers of Cinema*, offers a lens for considering the aesthetic complexity of amateur filmmakers, providing a selection of case studies about early American avant-garde filmmakers, many of whom (Robert Florey, Theodore Huff, Melville Webber, and James Sibley Watson, to name a few) were also active in amateur circles.[20] Finally, independent historian

Alan Kattelle's suggestive book about amateur film is primarily concerned with the development of amateur film technology but also devotes significant attention to amateur clubs and the careers of successful amateur filmmakers.[21] Kattelle has also published a master-list of the Amateur Cinema League's annual "Ten Best" competition winners from 1930 to 1994, along with a brief introduction to that organization.[22] These materials were the first to document the extent of serious amateur filmmaking and provided much of the inspiration for this book.

Recent scholarship on early cinema and the cinema's public dimensions provides additional coordinates for this study. The amateur mode, like that of early cinema, situated itself within a context of shifting forms of technological communication and modern challenges to the experience of human perception. Maxim's announcement of a new future for cinema may by 1926 have seemed somewhat old hat in this respect, as he touched on themes that had been connected to cinema since its earliest years, including the utopian promise of modern communication technologies and the privileged, even magical, place of moving images among them. Like early cinema, amateur film invoked both new aesthetic forms and utopian possibilities. The amateur film's characteristics, however, were not predominantly new; its technology was reminiscent of the about-to-become obsolete silent film, and its silence or rough synch sound estranged amateur films from reality. Amateur cinema also reestablished movies as a valid terrain for individual people to work as aesthetic pioneers, mechanical tinkers, and showmen long after classical Hollywood had banished these roles from its industrial mode of production and exhibition. Among amateur filmmakers, clubs, and circuits some of the central features of the cinema's attractions—such as technical showmanship mixed with visual display—would reappear. Indeed, amateur films also returned to many of the subjects and genres of early cinema, such as actualities, travelogues, trick film, and short subjects. Amateur cinema appears to share a surprising amount, in both subject matter and visual rhetoric, with films of the cinema's first two decades.

But also important to note is that the relationship of amateur film to mainstream entertainment was very different from that of the early cinema. Unlike early cinema, which was exploited as a popular novelty and commercial entertainment, amateur film emerged as a largely noncommercial entertainment. As Tom Gunning points out, "The cinema of attractions does not disappear with the dominance of narrative, but rather goes underground, both into certain avant-garde practices and as a component of narrative films, more evident in some genres (e.g., the musical) than others."[23] Gunning's account draws our attention to some of the primal appeal of early film and its continued relevance for other kinds of filmmaking: the fascination with motion, pleasures of visual curiosity, and the magical plenitude of mechanical reproduction. While experimental film has revisited many of these "primal" elements (and shows a recurring fascination with early cinema), they are also privileged in amateur filmmaking. Indeed, it is the amateur film's preoccupation with both the past and present of film culture that marks it as a self-conscious aesthetic form, practiced by a self-taught community. Amateur films are rarely instances of powerful novelty, but they remain curious objects, reflecting a fascination with the world and its visual reproduction.

Beyond its significance as an alternative aesthetic practice, a history of amateur cinema also calls attention to a range of issues around alternative film exhibition and participatory modes of film spectatorship. While early movie exhibition was quickly integrated into variety entertainment and then its own theatrical forms, amateur film in North America emerged and persisted in an emphatically *non*theatrical context. These nontheatrical and amateur film cultures offer sites for examining the self-conscious reception and negotiation of moving images and the influence that these media have on other kinds of creative expression. Indeed, amateur cinema is a kind of vernacular film culture that invited reflection, appropriation and the manipulation of dominant Hollywood film styles in the form of both creative reinterpretation and alternate modes of reception. In this way, a study of amateur cinema builds on the concept of "vernacular modernism" developed by Miriam Hansen, as amateur works provide us with films and exhibition circumstances that existed in playful and self-reflexive counterpoint to the subjects and structured viewing publics produced by mainstream Hollywood film.[24]

Amateur activities during the twentieth century presented a Janus-faced companion to technological innovation and professionalization. Much as Walter Benjamin prophesied a radical democratization of culture as a result of mass reproduction technologies, we can see today that every effort to professionalize new areas of technology brings a flood of *non*professional expressions of that technology. While clearly consumers of commercial culture and technology, amateurs provide through their films a more complex response to modern life than simple commodity fetishism. Nor was the appeal of amateur film strictly socially determined (as either folk or middlebrow), though its means of production often ensured some combination of estranging qualities (particularly in the late 1920s and early '30s). Modern society demanded a self-taught artist capable of adapting, taking up new technologies, and adopting new traditions in mass culture; the amateur answered that demand, using new technological materials like motion pictures to express his or her response to these modern conditions. While definitions of *amateur* were subject to debate and revision over the period of this study, the amateur we are concerned with here was a figure who participated in a film culture outside the commercial mainstream and developed "advanced" skills in film production. These coordinates provide starting points for this study of amateur film, positioning the works by amateurs as a twentieth-century vernacular aesthetic expression that developed at the intersection of popular culture, modernism, and new technology.

AMATEUR CINEMA AND THE PRAGMATIC IMAGINATION

In this book I argue that amateur cinema—by which I mean *advanced* amateur filmmaking and the culture that emerged around it—is crucial to our understanding of media practices in the twentieth (and twenty-first) century. Although amateur cinema has generally been dismissed as a middlebrow culture, it is precisely this "middleness"—or is it, rather, aesthetic and cultural *centrality*?—that demands further explanation. In contrast to accounts that depict middlebrow pursuits as "second-order aestheticism" or mere consumption, this study illuminates a terrain of constantly changing ideological, aesthetic, and technological complexity, much like the situation we inhabit today. Amateur moviemakers in the mid-twentieth century were the first group to embrace this new media situation, and their fascinating films convey the excitement and creative possibility of becoming independent media experimenters and producers.

I approach the phenomenon of amateur cinema with two specific goals in mind: first, to sketch out the *contexts* of amateur film culture; and, second, to articulate the broad *aesthetic and stylistic tendencies* of amateur films themselves. Part 1 of this book provides an examination of the different historical contexts that amateur cinema emerged and flourished within as a large-scale activity from the 1930s through the 1950s. This facet of the study offers a chronological account of amateur film culture, including the emergence of major organizations like the Amateur Cinema League (ACL), the development of movie clubs and contests, and the way shifting technologies and current events affected these developments. It examines why the practice of amateur filmmaking emerged as it did, its relationship with other aesthetic practices of the moment (such as classical Hollywood cinema, early nonfiction or avant-garde practices, and the rise of alternate exhibition and ciné-club circuits). This period is delineated by the introduction of

16mm film in 1923 and the emergence of film schools and underground cinema in the late 1950s, two factors that significantly changed the terrain and future direction of amateur cinema.

While drawing on the growing body of scholarship about amateur media, this book is based in archival documents, films, and other primary literature, which illuminate amateur films and filmmaking. This project examines motion pictures from over a dozen archives and private collections, along with the unpublished documents that accompanied them; small-run newsletters from local movie clubs also provided richly detailed information. I also draw extensively on more widely available magazines that were geared to amateur filmmaking, such as the Amateur Cinema League's monthly magazine *Movie Makers* (1926–54) and the regular amateur section of *American Cinematographer* (1930–50s). These magazines contain articles that advised amateurs on technical, creative, and organizational matters and maintained a tone of constant encouragement to the reader-filmmaker. Other magazines published regular columns for amateurs, such as *Photoplay* (starting in 1927) and the *Journal of the Photographic Society of America* (1947). In addition to these popular magazines, books about amateur filmmaking proliferated during the period; such books and magazines provide important guides to understanding how amateurs developed technical proficiency while also developing their own style. Moreover, an examination of these primary texts helps inform and complement a close analysis of amateur films.

A study that attends to amateur cinema according to its own qualities must examine the films themselves. The process of locating the amateur films discussed in this book has involved textual research and archival detective work and has drawn on existing scholarship (especially on early American avant-garde film), guidance from archivists and scholars, and the generous assistance of participants in the amateur film world. Alan Kattelle's publication of the annual Ten Best lists from 1930 to 1994 pointed to the enormous gap in understanding this field presented; beginning from his list of more than six hundred films, I started the process of tracking down extant prize-winning films from the Amateur Cinema League period (1930–54). A handful of familiar names on the list (such as Watson and Webber, Theodor Huff, Budge and Judith Crawley) provided a starting point. From here, I searched archival databases and inquired directly to archivists, who were often able to point to films that they recognized as relevant or noteworthy but that didn't fall into established film categories. My biggest stroke of research luck came when, following Melinda Stone's lead, I started attending meetings of a local amateur movie club, Chicago's

South Side Cinema Club. I was soon introduced to the Chicago amateur film luminary Margaret Conneely, who at age ninety provided a living memory of the later parts of the era I was investigating. Margaret shared her large collection of amateur films and documents with me (subsequently donated to the Chicago Film Archives), among which were several award-winning films, including her own playful and accomplished works. She also put me in touch with several surviving amateurs and award winners, some of whom had their own caches of significant films; it became clear that Kattelle's list was just the tip of the iceberg, so my search was extended to include other organizations and contests.

Part 2 of the book provides analyses of a selection of these extant films from aesthetic and formal perspectives, as well as a discussion of their prominent modes and styles. This part of the book elucidates amateur filmmaking as a practice with its own genres and conventions and places these films within larger modes of amateur film production (chronicle, experimental, practical, and photoplay films). Most of the films discussed here were included among the ACL's annual Ten Best film lists, so I also consider the criteria by which award-winning amateur films were judged "the best." Focusing on award-winning films does not mean that these are the most interesting films produced by amateurs, any more than the Academy Awards (which were, coincidentally, established just a few months after the ACL) are a reflection of the best films of their kind, but award-winning films can help to reveal the qualities that a particular community of filmmakers, in this case amateurs, prize most highly. This discussion of prize-winning films is balanced and extended by looking at the other self-identified (if not prize-winning) amateur films that can also be found scattered in archives and private collections. Fewer than 10 percent of the Ten Best award winners and honorable mentions are known to be extant. This book's appendix 1 provides a filmography of extant amateur films, their archival locations, and links to online videos clips where available. Some of these films have been preserved by archives, which are increasingly attentive to the "orphaned" films that have historically been overlooked. The preservation of these films may bring them greater legitimacy and public recognition than they received when first produced, but they still retain traces of their amateur origins in their textual and contextual properties.

Ultimately, I argue that these two aspects of amateur film—contexts and stylistic tendencies—are profoundly intertwined, as historical, technological, and artistic contexts influenced the aesthetic forms through which amateurs approached the task of filmmaking. A final coordinate that provides useful tools for considering these interconnected issues of technology, aesthetics, and public life is the intellectual tradition of American pragmatism. At its most superficial level, amateur filmmaking can be seen as a "pragmatic" activity that combined creative pleasure with the camera's practical recording function and reinforced the value of *learning* (creative and practical skills) through *doing*. But there are compelling reasons for considering amateur filmmaking in light of the American pragmatic philosophical tradition.[25] Like pragmatism's resistance to a priori theories, amateur film discourse eschewed predetermined forms for both aesthetic production and social organization; instead, it established open structures that allowed for the emergence of idiosyncratic but functional aesthetic and social formations that were the products of practice, problem solving, and experimentation. Pragmatic writers also frequently espoused a pluralistic philosophy that was echoed in amateur discourse's promotion of liberal democracy as well as their disavowal of dogmatic ideologies. And like John Dewey, one of pragmatism's principal figures, amateur filmmakers sought out ways of resolving the conflict in modern life between quotidian and aesthetic experiences.

I propose in part 2 of this book that amateur filmmakers, and the Amateur Cinema League in particular, operated within a mode that we might call a "pragmatic imagination." This term points to the ways in which amateur films represent a *working through* of the relationships between creativity and technology, between individual and collective experience, and between local contingencies and the commercial aesthetics of mass media. In contrast to this amateur pragmatic imagination, we might posit a "commercial imagination," which produces works according to principles of market value, or a "theoretical imagination," which produces artworks based on a priori theories of aesthetic form or academies of taste. Each of these imaginative modes has produced both masterpieces and banal works; the point in proposing such a typology—and in illuminating the amateur's place within it—is not to provide an evaluative system but to give form and definition to the middle category of creative work and experience, a category that has thus far been characterized as either chaotic or passively derivative. Instead, the pragmatic imagination can be seen as a mode of thoughtful media reception and creative production that has constituted an enormous but neglected segment of media spectatorship in the twentieth century—a sort of enveloping "dark matter" that makes up the pervasive substance of media experience but somehow evades scholarly description. Drawing on ideas from pragmatism to illuminate amateur films and film culture helps us to break out of a reductive consideration of middle-class leisure and middlebrow culture. Rather than dismissing the activities in these categories as an easily reduced calculus of taste and commodity consumption, pragmatic writers can help us to see amateurs as participants in a more complex terrain of social and creative struggles. My objective here is to bring to light the amateur's multifaceted, contradictory, and even playful responses to a set of widely experienced conditions of modern life.

Since amateur film continued to flourish after the 1950s, gaining in popularity with the introduction of Super 8mm film in the 1960s, the work of making sense of the amateur is just beginning. Today, anyone with access to an inexpensive digital camera, a computer, and an Internet connection can produce and share his or her own short films. But these recent digital developments follow a long tradition of technological advance—from 16mm and Super 8 film to consumer video and camcorders—which has repeatedly promised to fulfill the cinema's utopian potential for democratic expression, a potential proclaimed since the earliest years of moving pictures. But what are we to make of the creative products of amateur moving-image technologies? And how we are to understand their aesthetic and social significance? This book proposes that the discursive and aesthetic qualities of amateur filmmaking between 1923 and 1960 can provide us with crucial insight into American society's collective visual imagination during the mid-twentieth century. And perhaps even more than commercial works, amateur film can illuminate the tension between modern mass society and individual creative experience.

PART I

Contexts of Amateur Cinema

1 Ciné-Prophecy

The Emergence of Amateur Cinema (1892–1927)

> O wad some Power the giftie gie us
> To see oursels as ithers see us!
> It wad frae monie a blunder free us
> An' foolish notion:
> What airs in dress an gait wad lea'e us,
> An' ev'n devotion!
>
> **Robert Burns,** *from "To a Louse"*

Mag the Hag, a playful send-up of the social-melodrama movie, is one of the oldest surviving amateur films. Produced in 1925 and featuring a group of boarding-school girls in Connecticut, this "dripping melodrama" recounts the tale of Percy Proudfoot, "the aimless scion of a wealthy city family, [who] finds happiness in the pure love of a simple country girl, much to the chagrin of his aristocratic sister." Although typical of later amateur films, which borrowed elements from commercial cinema and blended them with clever tricks and rough technique, *Mag the Hag* is fascinating in its own right. In the film we see Percy (played by a woman in drag) out driving in his enormous motor-car in the country, where he encounters "Mag the Hag," a mysterious old crone. As thanks for a small act of assistance, Mag uses her magical talisman to repair Percy's car after it breaks down and then loans him the talisman so that he can make his sister approve of his country sweetheart, Peg. Back home, Percy uses the talisman to perform a series of tricks (achieved through stop-action photography), transforming a loaf of bread into an enormous phallic squash, a doll into a live cat, and then finally—and triumphantly—transforming the modestly dressed Peg into a stylish flapper (figure 1). Convinced at last, Percy's sister gives her approval to the romance, and Percy and his newly fashionable Peg enjoy a long kiss to end the film.

Mag the Hag provides tantalizing clues about the implications of amateur film at the moment of its arrival in the mid-1920s. Stylistically, the film appears unremarkable, relying primarily on long shots from a fixed

Figure 1. Country sweetheart Peg is transformed into a stylish flapper. *Mag the Hag* (Hiram Percy Maxim, 1925). Courtesy Northeast Historic Film, Maxim Collection.

camera position, with few camera movements or cuts (except for the Georges Méliès–like transformations). The most visually striking moments of the film are also those that seem to threaten it as a diegetic space, such as when a bird flits across the frame or a cat wanders through the foreground and grooms itself. In these moments *Mag the Hag* recalls some of the very earliest motion pictures, which appealed to many viewers less for their ostensible subject matter (a baby eating breakfast, for example) than their unintended details (the visible effects of the wind on foliage).

At the level of the film's symbolic economy we find a similar preoccupation with eruptions of uncertainty in daily experience, here expressed as encounters between the city and the country or between modernity (Percy's car) and ancient magic (the talisman). But although these seem like predictable oppositions, what is striking about *Mag the Hag* is the way these oppositions are complicated, perhaps even undone, by the magic of the talisman and the magic of the camera. First used to repair the broken-down motorcar, the talisman is later used as the on-screen motivation for the camera's tricks—tricks that braid together the fulfillment of technological, sexual, and romantic wishes.[1] In the amateur's hands the cinema becomes a modern talisman designed for both the *making up* and the *making over* of a range of different types of desire: from the transformation of social status and sexual longing, to the amelioration of the old with the new, to a playful

Figure 2. The Amateur Cinema League's first motto. *Amateur Movie Makers*, March 1927, 3. Courtesy Media History Digital Library.

intercourse between everyday life and commercial culture. In its juxtapositioning of old and new, country and city, mysterious talisman and modern automobile, *Mag the Hag* offers us a glimpse of the tensions that informed the emergence of amateur film culture in the mid-1920s.

Indeed, the "magic" of the movie camera was understood to be an appealing feature of 16mm amateur film equipment when it first appeared in the 1920s: "The motion picture is a kind of magic," one Kodak advertisement proclaimed. "And the real magician is the camera."[2] But another facet of cinema's transformative capabilities was hinted at by the phrase the Amateur Cinema League chose as its motto in 1926: "To see ourselves as others see us." This line, an apparent allusion to Robbie Burns's poem "To a Louse," appeared on the masthead (and frequently elsewhere) in the organization's *Amateur Movie Makers* magazine during its first year (figure 2). On one hand, we can read this slogan as a fairly straightforward play on the representational capacity of amateur moving pictures: they give us the ability to put ourselves in pictures and to make a visual spectacle of ourselves.[3] On the other hand, the transformation of social, romantic, and aesthetic desires in *Mag the Hag*—which was produced by the ACL's founder, Hiram Percy Maxim—suggests more complex implications for the motto. One of these is perhaps the desire that the movies would provide amateurs with a reflective medium through which they could envision themselves in different ways. Pragmatic philosopher William James observed, "A man has as many social selves as there are individuals who recognize him and carry an image of him in their mind."[4] Through the cinema, amateurs could experiment with different ways of seeing their social selves: as creative individuals, members of a social organization, and masters or directors of their experiences of modernity and mass consumer culture.

Coupled with this vision of amateur film as a self-reflective medium was a similar aspiration for both the Amateur Cinema League and its monthly *Amateur Movie Makers* magazine. In fact, the desire to establish a coherent amateur film culture is evident in ACL president Hiram Percy Maxim's very first editorial, published in December 1926: "With this first issue of our magazine a nebulous idea becomes a tangible reality. Amateur cinematography becomes organized."[5] Like casting a spell, the magazine promised to transform amateur cinema from nebulous and chaotic blundering to a tangible and productive order. But as an analogy for the self-representation of amateur filmmakers in their new magazine, this motto—"to see ourselves as other sees us"—is somewhat problematic. During its first year of publication *Amateur Movie Makers* revealed a range of different kinds of film amateurs, aesthetic philosophies, and amateur interests. From its inception, the Amateur Cinema League appealed to a more diverse constituency than simply the affluent camera hobbyist. And over the course of its first year, the community of film amateurs rapidly expanded in terms of both its social composition and its vision of the movie amateur. In 1927, a movie amateur might have been a cinematographer or an actor, an affluent traveler with a camera or a member of a collective company, a fan of popular films or a critic determined to elevate the art form. Considering how many different kinds of amateurs there were, the ACL's motto perhaps reveals more of a wish for coherence than its actual realization. In short, to see the amateur as represented in the first year of this magazine is to see his multiple and fragmented nature. Because of the many perspectives reflected in *Amateur Movie Makers*, amateur film continued to be a somewhat nebulous idea in which different visions of cinema and its amateur future were presented and contested.

This chapter examines the emergence of amateur film culture in the mid-1920s, in particular, around the founding and first years of the Amateur Cinema League. Guiding this examination is a consideration of the amateur as seen in the multifaceted reflection of the *Amateur Movie Makers* magazine. Maxim and the editors of this magazine would return often, over the years, to its significance as a crucial venue for presenting the face of amateur movies and the ACL. Indeed, the magazine was the organization's principal medium of contact with both its membership and the public. The ACL did not organize local chapters of the league, preferring instead to provide assistance to anybody who wished to form a movie club and then affiliate it with the ACL. Similarly, the ACL decided that it would not hold annual conventions to bring together its membership. So it is really in the pages of *Amateur Movie Makers* that we can find the virtual meetings of the membership, in the published articles, different topics, and, later, letters to the editor. As writers in the magazine worked to situate amateur film in current artistic and amateur practices, they also tried to legitimize their organization in a variety of different ways. Some writers proposed manifestos of amateur film aesthetics, while others foregrounded the amateur film's overlap with other arts and hobbies, and still others positioned amateurism as a form of film spectatorship. What is clear from examining this first year of organized amateur film activity is that the culture can't be subsumed (or dismissed) under one activity, social group, or aesthetic philosophy. The heterogeneous writings in *Amateur Movie Makers* reflect this complexity and shed light on the discursive coordinates of the amateur's pragmatic imagination.

THE AMATEUR IMPULSE

The Amateur Cinema League was formed at a meeting at the New York Hotel Biltmore in July 1926, but its technological and aesthetic precursors go back to a much earlier time. For Hiram Percy Maxim, the affluent inventor and entrepreneur who organized the meeting, amateur cinema was a "new art," "an entirely new method of communication," and a new "national sport." Though their efforts to organize nonprofessional filmmakers on a national (and international) level were certainly new, much of what intrigued these amateurs about cinema was not.[6] In fact, a direct link between early film and amateur efforts was provided in the person of Alexander Black, the early cinema pioneer who attended and spoke at the ACL's first meeting. Described in one account of this meeting as "the inventor of the first photoplay," Black was a showman who mixed lectures and stories with images, usually in the form of projected slides.[7] Black became popular during the 1890s for offering middle-class audiences uplifting—but modern and visual—entertainment at respectable venues like the Brooklyn Institute of Arts and Sciences. Coincidentally, one of Black's most successful illustrated lectures was called "Ourselves as Others See Us" and featured instantaneous photography and hidden camera work.[8] Black's presence at the founding of the ACL and his shared fascination with self-reflection provide a tangible link between the amateurs and the earliest moments of film history.

The promise of amateur film, as both a memorial and a visual curiosity, had existed since the invention of motion pictures. The desire to halt time by capturing "living portraits" of a loved one in lifelike motion was explored by Étienne-Jules Marey's assistant Georges Demeny as early as 1892. During the promotion of his Phonoscope, Demeny said, "How many people would be happy if they could only see once again the features of someone now dead. The future will see the replacement of motionless photographs, frozen in their frames, with animated portraits that can be brought to life at the turn of a handle."⁹ Demeny shared his idea with Louis and August Lumière, the inventors of the Cinematograph, who had a similar interest in putting images of family and everyday life into motion. The Lumière brothers saw motion pictures as a logical development from their production of instantaneous photographic emulsions for amateurs, and Tom Gunning suggests that the Cinematograph was more than likely intended for the same market. Motion picture photography was consistent with the amateur's fascination with stopping time through instantaneous photography, but motion also marked a significant aesthetic shift that made it appealing for more than just family portraits. Indeed, Gunning argues, "The reproduction of movement transformed daily life into a spectacle by endowing it with technological novelty and new thresholds of representation."¹⁰ The mass popularity of motion pictures, however, quickly forced the Lumière brothers to reconfigure their invention toward commercial exhibition.¹¹ Although preserving images of family and capturing the spontaneous motions of everyday life mark two persistent impulses toward amateur filmmaking, they remained largely unfulfilled until the 1920s.

The invention of 16mm reversal film in 1923 provided the crucial precondition for the emergence of an amateur film culture in North America, reducing the cost of amateur filmmaking to less than a quarter of professional 35mm production. But even though 16mm film was almost certainly the decisive development leading to widespread amateur filmmaking, there were some important technological precursors that foreshadowed its invention and the emergent amateur film culture. During the 1910s both Pathé and Kodak introduced nonflammable safety film formats for home and other nontheatrical use. The Edison Home Kinetoscope (22mm film) and Pathéscope (or Pathé Kok in France, a 28mm format) were primarily used for presenting films, but the latter format was also adopted by a handful of amateur and nonprofessional filmmakers.¹² A 1919 magazine article, "Cinematography, a New Art for Amateurs," touted the aesthetic, educational, and domestic promise of movies, such as those that could be captured on 28mm: "The new Art not only affords an expression of artistic feeling, but allows cinematographers to see themselves as others see them in their home as well as elsewhere, while as an educator it has no equal."[13] The impulse toward both artistic production and aesthetic self-representation in this article (promoting the Pathéscope) clearly foreshadowed the ACL's development. Though the 28mm format presented a less expensive (and dangerous) format than 35mm film, it was still a costly medium that was marketed primarily to the very rich.[14]

Before the arrival of 16mm film, the high cost of film production was specifically identified as a hindrance to the development of experimental and amateur film movements in the United States. As early as 1921, critics were asking why a "Little Movie" movement had not emerged in the United States to present the kind of experimental (and often amateur-based) expression that had succeeded in the Little Theatre movement. But as Robert Allerton Parker wrote, in his review of Charles Sheeler and Paul Strand's short experimental film *Manhatta* (which was produced on 35mm), the problem with a Little Movie movement was that "the expense would be enormous and the profits small."[15] The appearance on the market of 16mm film in 1923 provided a solution to this problem that many amateurs seized upon. But the ACL would later point out that even if smaller-gauge film equipment made the medium accessible to more people, a handful of amateurs still worked in 35mm: "Amateurs," they wrote, "are not classified in millimeters."[16] Even though the 16mm reversal film format was a crucial condition in the popularization of amateur and home movie-making, its appearance simply fulfilled a long-standing link between amateurs and moving pictures. The arrival of 16mm film equipment in 1923 and the formation of the Amateur Cinema League just a few years later provided an opportunity for the history of cinema to begin anew and to follow a once-"forgotten future" of moving pictures.[17]

THE AESTHETIC HORIZON OF AMATEUR FILM CULTURE

Of course by 1926 cinema had already developed a history of its own, and it was in the context of this history and other contemporaneous developments in the arts that the ACL attempted to situate its new "sport." This effort took a variety of different forms and provided several different avenues along which amateur film would develop. Some proponents, such as Maxim, envisaged film as an amateur broadcasting medium, in effect doing for the eye what amateur radio had done for the ear. Other writers, such as the ACL managing director Roy Winton, hoped that amateurs would help to elevate the status of movies as an art form by instilling in them elements of taste and aesthetic sophistication. Still others saw amateur movies as an opportunity for participatory expression (as in community theatre) or a way of channeling their enjoyment of popular commercial films. Each of these visions reveals a different facet of the way film amateurs saw themselves, and taken together they constituted a rich and sometimes contradictory horizon of possibilities for amateur film culture. The very matter of what film amateurs *do*—whether they take moving pictures, act in amateur productions, or simply "love movies"—seemed to be an open question during the ACL's early years.

One aspect of filmmaking that appealed to many amateurs was the steady stream of new technologies, gadgets, and tools to learn about. Because Hiram Percy Maxim was the founder and first president of the ACL, his vision for the film amateur was prominently positioned in early issues *Amateur Movie Makers*, and it drew, in large part, from his involvement in amateur radio. Maxim's interest in radio was not atypical among amateurs, and neither was his propensity for mechanical or engineering tasks. In some ways driven by advertising and the commodification of hobbies, this interest in tinkering and gadgetry also permitted amateurs to see themselves as creator-inventors of modern devices and stories, sharing in the "magic" of icons like Thomas Edison, the "Wizard of Menlo Park." Maxim was himself an inventor; son of the inventor of one of the first machine guns, Maxim studied acoustics at MIT and invented one of the first gun silencers.[18] One profile describes Maxim's amateurism largely in terms of his "characteristic curiosity for scientific information," suggesting the combination of enthusiasm and scientific rigor that Bliss Perry believed to be essential to the American amateur.[19]

Despite his singular dedication to amateur cinema, Hiram Percy Maxim had, in fact, been engaged in the commercial motion picture business even before he helped organized the Amateur Cinema League. Some five years before the ACL was founded, in 1921, Maxim wrote a screenplay, which was produced by Fox and directed by J. Searle Dawley. *A Virgin Paradise* featured Pearl White and, according to Maxim, "started out to be an example of the tremendous amount one must learn in order keep one's place in modern civilization. A young woman of the best ancestry grows up in savagery and has to learn *everything*."[20] Maxim's experience with the commercial film industry—including his trajectory from professional involvement to amateur status—was anomalous among amateurs. But his screenplay, with its fantasy of unlearning and relearning aspects of civilized life, is a suggestive metaphor for the amateur filmmaker. Amateurs used the cinema as a tool for a pragmatic reimagining of their relationships to art, technology, and mass culture.

Maxim had founded the Amateur Radio Relay League in 1915, and his vision for film in some ways echoed Thomas Edison's predictions of a synthesis of audio and visual technologies.[21] Maxim predicted a time when home movies would be conveyed over great distances through radio waves: "You are going to see the day when radio-transmitted colored motion pictures will be shown not only in theatres, but in your own homes." The appeal for Maxim in this was not simply the domestication of these technologies but also their potential use as media for long-distance personal communication and international understanding: "Mr. Maxim believes that the day is not far distant when amateur moviemakers will be exchanging films with the same great ease and enjoyment as the amateur radio operator now communicates with his distant friends."[22] Perhaps only with the recent emergence of Internet video sharing on social networks is Maxim's prediction starting to be fulfilled. But it shows that for Maxim, amateur movie technology was one among many new communication technologies that could reproduce and transmit sound and images across space and into homes.[23] This vision of cinema as a universal language haunts Maxim's writings and perhaps provided some of the motivation for his prominent role in organizing amateurs into an association that would bring people together in strictly mediated ways: through the ACL's magazine, to begin with, but also later and more importantly through its film exchange.

Though Maxim also identified the aesthetic benefits of an amateur film culture—namely, its autonomy from the demands of commerce—Roy Winton, the ACL's managing director, explored this area in the most detail. Winton's background was not in the film industry or any closely related field. Before being invited by Maxim to organize the ACL in 1926, Winton had worked as a reporter, an army officer (from 1906 to 1921), and finally a "field representative" of the National Recreation Association. Winton presented a vision of the film amateur as both a creative individual and an arbiter of film taste. Winton suggested (somewhat strategically) that the amateur film, as a personal art form, posed no threat to the commercial film industry. Whereas the commercial cinema had been successful in producing popular works, "the most striking thing the amateur can do in motion pictures," Winton writes, "is to personalize their application." In an address to the National Board of Review of Motion Pictures, Winton clarified many basic questions of amateur filmmaking, including the meaning of the word *amateur* itself: "The amateur is simply a 'lover of the arts' or of some particular art.... In the Amateur Cinema League we are trying to get back to the original meaning of the word 'amateur.' We want to be classed as lovers of cinematography and the art of the photoplay. We may or may not be practitioners. We may or may not press buttons or crank cameras or write scenarios or direct or act before the screen. But we do claim to be lovers of the eighth art."[24] Winton argues that what marks amateurs is not their craft or skill but their devotion to the medium and its development. His suggestion that film amateurs don't have to be filmmakers or actors or be in *any* way connected with film production, so long as they are cinephiles, is surprising, but it might explain the effort in the first year of *Amateur Movie Makers* to include not only articles on technique for amateurs but also reviews of films and profiles of filmmakers, perhaps designed to encourage more sophisticated viewing practices. Even someone who didn't have a camera could participate in the ACL's mission.

But while the inclusion of movie lovers was essential to the Amateur Cinema League, the exercising of aesthetic judgment in filmmaking is what remained a central goal of the organization. In this, Winton drew upon screenwriter and journalist Ralph Block's vision of a film amateur who would help refine the language of cinema. Writing in 1921, Block argued that "movies" as a popular art had not yet had the opportunity to benefit from a "fine art" patronage: "fine arts, as distinguished from the popular arts are not supported by the great crowds of human beings. They are aristocratic in their environment; they are nourished by the few, and made for them."[25] Block claimed that "the fine art of motion pictures" would need both creative artists *and* a refined audience before it could flourish. Winton's theory of the film amateur clearly echoed Ralph Block's call for an "aristocratic" intervention in the movies. In one article, Winton suggests, "The art of cinema, failing a disciplining patronage, must look to its amateurs who are both artists and patrons." Refining this idea further, Winton writes, "The amateur brings the understanding of the artists without the artist's urge of bread-winning; he brings the detachment of the patron without the patron's direct power of discipline. From the amateur photoplay maker can come a broad standard for this art, a standard not necessarily 'high brow' and not inevitably puerile, but a standard brought into being, as all worthwhile standards are, by a non-professional, on the one hand, and on the other, something more than a casual interest in the thing being evaluated."[26] Freed from the demands of commerce, film amateurs could exercise aesthetic standards that had been lacking in film and in this way propel the cinema toward becoming a more sophisticated and aesthetically complex art form.

But along with Winton's plea for a more "conservative standard of taste" also came an appeal for a kind of experimentalism in amateur film: "The amateur can become the Twentieth Century patron. The Maecenas of the

Movies will come from the non-professional experimentalists of the Little Cinema." Winton notes that "the amateur is an experimentalist" and "an aesthetic refiner." Because amateurs weren't bound to produce marketable films they were free to explore aesthetic discoveries more thoroughly than commercial producers. The amateur, Winton suggests, "has brought beauty from serviceability. . . . there are esthetic possibilities that the amateur will exploit for their beauty and not for their profits." Block's argument for a trained, even aristocratic, environment for motion pictures was also inflected with modernist influences and experimentation: "Experiments in the style of the narrative, comparable to modern experiments in pure form in the other arts, must await a producer free to take advantage of every scope the art offers, without any limitation by a crowd looking only for fairy-tales."[27] This kind of modernist experimentation (and other "experimental" poses) would flourish among amateurs in the late 1920s and early '30s and will be discussed in detail in chapter 7.

For Block and Winton, along with many other commentators, the most appropriate model for an amateur film culture that was both aesthetically restraining and experimental was the Little Theatre movement. By the time the ACL was founded, the idea of a Little Movie movement, analogous to Little Theatre, had been circulating already for several years.[28] The Little Theatre movement had transformed the shape of American theatre in the first two decades of the twentieth century and emerged from a desire to develop a theatre that explored creative and aesthetic possibilities that had been ignored by the commercial theatre. Like the Little Theatre movement, amateur film culture attended to and modeled some of its activities on the more daring modernist aesthetic developments of European theatre or cinema. One ACL contributor expanded on this possibility for amateur film: "One only needs to glance back through the history of the Little Theatre movement to see how genuine a contribution the amateurs can bring to art."[29] And, like the Little Theatre it was the potential for amateur, or "small," work to influence commercial or larger-scale artistic trends that appealed to some proponents of "little movies": "The apparatus is cheap, the use of it is cheaper, the opportunities for experiment are priceless, and the sincere and studied work that would undoubtedly come from such uncommercial experiments would feed the screen as the stage has been fed." This role for amateur cinema, as an area of experimentation unfettered by commercial concerns, is one of the strongest and most consistent defenses presented for amateurism. In this sense, the noncommercial, unmarketable aspect of amateurism was understood as a virtue, not a vice. But as Dorothy Chansky writes, the experimentalism that accompanied

Little Theatre was tempered by more conservative impulses: "Like other reform movements in the era, the Little Theatre movement had contradictory strains; it included forward-looking activism and modernist aesthetics as well as skepticism, nativism, elitism, and nostalgia, sometimes within the same production company or publication."[30] Even though experimentalism was often used as an aesthetic justification for amateur film culture, experimental films represented a fairly small segment of all films made by ACL members. But with these aspirations and contradictions in tow, the ACL clearly hoped to use the example of Little Theatre as a way of legitimizing the aesthetic position of the amateur film.

Writers like Winton also—and almost paradoxically—distinguished the potential Little Movies from the theatre by emphasizing the applied and industrial applications of amateur filmmaking. Though the focus of Winton's writing was often on the personal application of amateur filmmaking, from his attention to amateur industrial, scientific, educational, and religious filmmaking we can glean that this personal application and experimentation could also have a practical use. "The amateur," writes Winston, "is placing at the disposition of all those who have to do with the complex problems of human relations in industry, in education, in recreation, in religion, and in daily life as a whole, a new factor which they can use with all the variations suitable to their personal desires."[31] In some ways, we can see this inclusion of industrial, educational, and religious films as an effort to cast as wide a net for potential ACL membership as possible. In each of these areas, filmmakers had been "experimenting" with different ways of using film, outside the commercial industry, since the mid-1910s. But because this group included producers of films for professional purposes (educational, business, religious), it is hard to see how we can think of them as belonging to the category of amateur filmmakers. Certainly, part of the justification for doing so relates to the group's use of amateur equipment, and they also worked outside a professional production context. But the practical amateur certainly appears to be of a radically different kind from the film amateur as an aesthetic patron.

One way of bridging the gap between artistic and applied amateur filmmaking can be found in a profile about photographer Edward Steichen in the July 1927 issue of *Amateur Movie Makers*. The article portrays Steichen as a solitary, experimenting artist, a person trained in art but someone who took up photography on his own and developed his own skills. Particularly striking is the emphasis placed on industrialism and modern technology as influences on his photographic aesthetic.[32] The author also emphasizes Steichen's practicality: "He can best be described as a man of contradictions. He is an artist and a dreamer. Yet he is a hard worker, a shrewd craftsman, and a firm believer that there is nothing on earth without interest if you are attracted to it."[33] This mix of creativity and hard work appealed, no doubt, to the editors of *Amateur Movie Makers* and perhaps to certain segments of the amateur filmmaking public more generally. For the class of practical professionals who pursued filmmaking with a great deal of seriousness, this idea of the "practical artist" must have seemed an appealing contradiction and one for which they sought artist role models like Steichen.

In these different visions of amateur film and in the interrelationships suggested between film and other media, we see an aesthetic horizon for amateur film culture that was both rich in possibility and filled with contradictions. This is not just the question of whether film was best thought of as a medium of broadcasting or a new art form; nor is it simply the tension between popular film, conservative taste, and experimentation; nor, finally, is the position of amateur film complicated by its comparison to amateur activities in radio, theatre, and photography. Though writers like Winton and Maxim offer strong visions and potential directions for the amateur, ultimately Winton suggests that it was up to individuals, not the ACL, to decide which aesthetic and social directions amateur moviemaking would pursue: "We hope to do our part in guiding that power so that it will be productive of good to individuals and to society. We do not feel any responsibility, as an organization, for the social consequences of personalizing this new force." If this seems like a betrayal of the ACL's goal of making amateur film "tangible," Winton suggests that the principal purpose of the ACL was "to render the amateur camera man and the motion picture amateur more self-conscious, in the scientific sense of the term, and more effective in bringing his contribution to the eighth art." Winton's version of the ACL was an organization that provided a helpful spark or sounding board for amateurs. The league could give them a venue for new ideas and help them to think pragmatically about their work, without imposing on them any one of the many possible visions for amateur film; the ACL, Winton writes, will do as "the American people always do, it will make up its mind as it goes along."[34]

THE AMATEUR AS CINEPHILE

The cinema, more than any other art form, received the most attention in *Amateur Movie Makers* as a central influence on amateur film culture and aesthetics. The emergence of an amateur film culture in the mid-1920s corresponded chronologically with the appearance in major American cities of the first art-film repertory cinemas. Haidee Wasson notes that about nineteen "little" movie theaters had appeared in major American cities by 1927, "exhibiting old and new European, old American, amateur, experimental and feature films."[35] But what constituted the cinema and what kinds of films—popular or the emerging European art films—were worthy of praise and emulation were contested issues in *Amateur Movie Makers*. On one hand film amateurs were often fans of popular cinema and played with their stylistic and generic conventions, as Hiram Percy Maxim did in his "dripping melodrama" *Mag the Hag*. On the other hand, some critics (like Winton) tacitly criticized popular film and advocated a more refined American cinema. *Amateur Movie Makers* addressed a wide range of intellectual, independent, and popular films during its first years. Though European films provided some of the aesthetic inspiration in the magazine's pages, more often it was American independent producers, like Robert Flaherty, who were profiled in depth. Finally, the mode of criticism that became a regular feature of the magazine was one that attended to formal innovations and stylistic features removed from the context of their films—in a way refashioning a mode of film spectatorship into a mode of production.

The pages of *Amateur Movie Makers* made frequent reference to successful filmmakers and their relationship to amateur production or advice for amateurs. But none of these filmmakers received more admiration than Robert Flaherty, whom we might think of as the amateur who "made good." An interview called "Filming with Flaherty: From Arctic to Antipodes with the Famous Amateur Who Made *Nanook* and *Moana*" presented the filmmaker as the embodied spirit and inspiration of the amateur moviemaker. The article also situated Flaherty's work in terms of travel filming, one of the most popular genres among amateurs, and the subject of the May 1927 special issue, in which the interview appeared. The author Mina Brownstein reinforces this dual emphasis on amateurism and travel filming throughout the article. With regard to Flaherty's amateur classification, Brownstein elevates him as a model amateur film artist:

> Robert Flaherty, mining engineer by profession, and moving picture experimentalist by inclination, has, in the last ten years, attained an enviable position as one of the freshest directing personalities in the moving picture field. His training as an engineer did not touch on the intricacies of experimental photography. And now that he is equipped as directing and filming expert, it is because an amateur has become professional through personal experience. He proves in actuality what moving picture enthusiasts, Ralph Block on one end, and Gilbert Seldes

on the other, have claimed in theory; that originality and strength, artistry and sincerity will most certainly come into moving pictures through the work of amateurs, who are disinterested commercially, and who feel the same sense of intimacy with their cameras that painters feel with their tubes and brushes.[36]

This description emphasizes the twinned qualities that Flaherty presents—a practical and trained engineer on the one hand and an artistic and sincere filmmaker on the other. We might understand the term *experimentalist* to combine some elements of each of these qualities. As has been pointed out, mechanical tinkering or engineering was a common interest among many early amateurs and though these skills were not specifically geared toward experimental photography in Flaherty's case, they inform the idea of what an experiment might be and how a practical filmmaker might approach it. Specifically, Brownstein might have had Flaherty's well-publicized problems of (and ingenious solutions for) filming in Arctic conditions in mind.

Brownstein's article explores Flaherty's aesthetic approach to filmmaking, including his well-known pictorial romanticism in filming nonindustrial cultures. Though Flaherty acknowledges the skillful nature of artistic films like *The Cabinet of Dr. Caligari* (Robert Wiene, 1920), he says that he does "not believe in synthetic filming." And while he regarded the synthetic, expressionist movies of the moment as a degeneration of film art, he believed using the camera merely to reproduce life was equally unsatisfactory: "When he utters in his soft, Celtic voice, 'The camera is a super-eye, detecting nuances of feeling and motion, capturing rhythm like music,' one senses immediately a knowledge of the possibilities of the camera which very few possess."[37] Though Flaherty refers to this kind of filmmaking as "ethnological," Brownstein is quick to sidestep such a seemingly dry and scientific label, emphasizing instead Flaherty's focus on the camera's super-eye and the sensitivity displayed by Flaherty in employing this tool.

While reinforcing Flaherty's status as an amateur, Brownstein also offers him up as a model of the travel filmmaker who made creative films of exotic locales but also (and perhaps more important for readers who couldn't travel so much) a "camera poem" of New York: "For this unique producer, himself an amateur in the best sense of the term, who has heretofore wandered to the far corners of the earth to record with eye of truth and beauty the lives of strange peoples, is now engaged in attempting a 'camera poem' of New York City, which is to be a sort of architectural lyric where people will be used only incidentally, as part of the background."[38] This opens up the possibility of thinking of a travelogue as a kind of film that could be made even out of close or familiar places, so long as it recorded with "the eye of truth and beauty." The film referred to is likely *24 Dollar Island;* Flaherty's New York film is a negotiation of modern urban culture (the city) by a filmmaker whose interests had primarily been of the exotic, the folk, the ancient cultures. In this way, amateur ethnography is brought from the realm of traditional exploration to the amateur modern filmmaker.

At its close, the interview reinforces Flaherty's status as an amateur, at the same time linking the North American amateur movement to appreciation of his films in France (the Théâtre du Vieux-Colombier) and Germany. But the article downplays any sense of Flaherty as a remote or eccentric artist: "Having no formal training in moving picture technique to handicap him with rules about plot and approach, Mr. Flaherty feels himself fortunate. He is free to putter about with his instrument, taking his spoiled films as proof of his unspoiled originality."[39] In this portrait, Brownstein presents a figure that any amateur could relate to and develop his or her craft in a similar, almost instinctive way. Like a new filmmaker, Flaherty used his interest and instinct as creative guides, and like those of a new filmmaker his efforts sometimes resulted in spoiled films, which in the context of *Amateur Movie Makers* were a demonstration not of his lack of skill but of his "unspoiled originality."

Several similar articles appeared in *Amateur Movie Makers* to profile films and filmmakers that were thought to share certain characteristics with the amateur oeuvre. In many cases, these films were quasi-ethnographic works about exotic foreign spaces, but some of them treated American locales as exotic and deserving of ethnographic attention as well. Merriam Cooper and Ernest Schoedsack were profiled in July 1927 following the successful reception of their *Chang*. In the article "Are Elephants Art?" the author interviews the directors and, once again, points to the popular nonfiction film's particular relevance for amateur efforts. An article by Karl Brown, about his independent commercial film *Stark Love* (1927), appeared in the June issue of *Amateur Movie Makers* and recalls some of the issues raised by Flaherty's approach. Brown remarks on the amateur actors and the harsh conditions of filming in the southern mountains of the United States, which necessitated some very basic (i.e., nonstudio) production techniques. This article demonstrates that the travelogue was understood to be a natural genre of the amateur filmmaker and that exotic or primitive "Others"—with all of the racism and cultural superiority those terms imply—could be found as close as the backwoods of the American South. We will return to these issues in chapter 6, which discusses amateur travelogues and ethnographic film in more detail.

While the growth of an audience for art and travel films in the United States provided some context for the emergence of amateur filmmaking, their attention to specific qualities of films in release (both artistic *and* popular) provided a significant tool for study. This attention can be observed in the column "Critical Focusing: Reviews to Aid the Amateur," which first appeared in the May 1927 issue of *Amateur Movie Makers*. Sometimes credited to the *New Republic* film critic Evelyn Gerstein, the column provided brief reviews of commercial films. Its approach to film criticism was almost completely formal in orientation, focusing on issues like camera movement, editing, use of intertitles, unorthodox narrative strategies, and the like. "Designed to increase the fun and facility of making amateur motion picture plays," the column abandoned "all of the customary methods of photoplay reviewers." Discarding plot synopses and reports about the screen personalities, it discussed instead the "directors, cameramen and technicians, the skill, and sometimes genius, all of whom is the direct concern of the amateur who aspires to match, and, sometimes, may surpass their achievements."[40] Also, the column was not necessarily as concerned with the "best" films of the moment so much as the ones that had moments of visual interest: "There is so frequently a moment of inspiration in the most insipid films, that we will not close our columns in advance to the most banal of pot-boilers nor the cheapest 'quickies,' lest we miss something of intrinsic worth which the amateur might develop."[41] This willingness to watch films for their moments of visual interest, or formal punctures, rather than for their overall plot or narrative quality is almost modernist in its orientation; in this approach, spectatorship is a fragmented experience that eschews narrative realism or coherence. Ultimately this critical practice was still framed by a productive goal, giving amateur filmmakers ideas about technique and film style. In this sense, film reception took on an active aspect: the amateur's position as both an active spectator and a potential filmmaker suggested that stylistic and narrative elements derived from the dominant film-producing institution might later be placed in the service of amateur, localized, and therefore vernacular filmmaking practices.[42]

In each issue, "Critical Focusing" presented short discussions about some of the interesting elements of recent films, often touching on films that have since been canonized as the most significant of the late silent era. Films reviewed in this manner include *Sunrise* (F.W. Murnau, 1927) for its "third dimension" (or "stereoscopic" depth of space); *Seventh Heaven* (Frank Borzage, 1927) for its "use of moving camera"; and *Secrets of a Soul* (G.W. Pabst, 1926) for its technique in "filming a dream." In many cases, these comments seem designed simply to prompt the amateur's creative thinking process, but in some cases they suggest specific ways the amateur might take up (or had already taken up) such techniques. Regarding Fritz Lang's *Metropolis* (1927), the author remarks upon the film's use of miniature models, which "made possible an impression of immensity and bizarreness." And, as if to assure amateurs that such an effect was not beyond their means, the author notes, "The amateur might well consider the possibilities of this method, which in amateur production has been so well handled by the Little Screen Players of Boston." Similarly, Sergei Eisenstein's *Potemkin* (1925) is praised for its "cutting" and "tempo": "The manner in which the various scenes are cut, one into the other, reveals new fields for the amateur to conquer with his own productions."[43] These are interesting insights showing, at least, that these films were a part of an intellectual culture that hoped to refine amateurs' taste and influence their filmmaking and perhaps even suggesting how amateurs might have viewed films in a productive way.

"Critical Focusing" drew the amateur's attention to interesting ways of presenting narrative and visual material, while also providing a more general aesthetic observation of trends in current cinema. Some of these brief reviews made specific suggestions about how materials in a film could be adopted by amateurs (such as the use of news reel footage), but more often they seem to have been intended to broaden the amateur's film vocabulary, suggesting many interesting ways of presenting visual material: "Study of the photographic excellence of this picture," the author says of *The Night of Love* (George Fitzmaurice, 1927), "will repay the amateur. This picture and *Flesh and the Devil* [Clarence Brown, 1926] represent two of the outstanding achievements for the year in artistic photography."[44] These observations offered a way for amateurs to become more aware (or self-conscious, as Winton hoped?) of their aesthetic choices. The column also suggested ways that amateurs might stage and edit their films more creatively. For example, a review of Cecil B. DeMille's *King of Kings* (1927) noted how paintings could be used as aesthetic guides for amateur filmmakers. Noteworthy in the film is "the use of famous biblical paintings as the basis of many scenes.... The method, simply employed, can be followed by amateurs to secure interesting and effective results, if paintings which harmonize with the scene to be depicted are chosen as guides."[45] Such a suggestion might have helped amateurs to solve problems of film composition in light of familiar paintings—or at least have proposed that such options were open to them. In some cases "realism" and the expressive use of composition in depth were specifically praised, such as in the review of *The Way of All Flesh* (Victor Fleming, 1927): "Its amazing power rests wholly on the fidelity of its naturalistic detail, on the saliency of its characterizations and the subtle use of the camera. Still another instance of the ability of the cinema to portray realism even more effectively than the novel."[46] On another occasion, the use of framing to expand a depth of field was examined in Michael Curtiz's *Moon of Israel* (1924); here, the author notes "a novel use of foreground obstacles to give greater depth to the scenes" and in this way suggest a "third dimension" in the image.[47] But the use of deep space composition was not a statement of aesthetic preference so much as one direction that filmmakers could take. Similar praise was offered to films that were less concerned with realism but made interesting uses of creative cutting, or multiple exposure, or even animation. The column didn't promote a single definition of film art so much as it promoted a range of multiple possibilities.

Though "Critical Focusing" largely dealt with commercial films, it also recognized filmmakers whose origins lay in amateur or independent work. Dudley Murphy (of *Ballet Mécanique* fame [along with codirector Fernand Léger, 1924]) received special attention as one who had started out as an amateur but then moved into commercial work as a "special camera man." His use of double and triple exposure in the crystal gazing sequence of *The Loves of Sunya* (Albert Parker, 1927) was particularly praised: "With amazing rapidity he has catapulted his camera through space, gathering in half glimpsed and distorted images of objects to augment the unreality of the scenes, to suggest the wildness of a dream, its incoherence and crazy rhythms."[48] Similar references to Murphy's work in a column about Clarence Badger's *Man Power* (1927) praised the film's depiction of machines and objects:

> An almost sinister beauty will be found in such a mundane object as a motor tractor under artistic cinematic treatment, as illustrated in the scenes of this picture where a huge tractor is driven through a sea of mud in a rainstorm.... Professionals are now awakened to the abstract beauty of machines as film subjects, and it is interesting to note that the pioneering work in this field was largely the work of amateurs, as exemplified by Dudley Murphy whose *Ballet Mécanique* proved a stepping-stone to an important place for him in the professional industry, which his talents will undoubtedly enrich.[49]

For this reviewer, the sinister and abstract quality of machines was a theme that amateurs could easily access and one that earlier amateurs, like Dudley Murphy, had possibly even pioneered. Moreover, the author's familiarity with Murphy's filmography and praise of his experimental work imply that *Ballet Mécanique* had received some attention in the United States.

Reviews also focused on how amateurs might learn specific and practical skills from professional films. This kind of learning is thematized in the film *High Hat* (James Creelman, 1927), a "movie burlesque" in which "many secrets of professional picture making are revealed," making it "a particularly helpful picture for the study of amateurs."[50] Of particular interest for the amateur in this film are the "tricks" used to create special effects: "Among the methods revealed are the stunts by which the professionals simulate rainstorms, and snowstorms, and also the use of models for miniature work and of moving backgrounds are well illustrated." In addition to these oblique lessons, the column also on occasion identified certain techniques from films that were then treated in one of the magazine's technical advice pages:

> Probably the finest stereoscopic effects yet secured on the screen, and achieved without mechanical devices are to be viewed in *Sunrise*. In the first scene in which the "man from the country" crosses the fields to keep a rendezvous with the "woman from the city," the stereoscopic effect of trees and fences is uncanny. These effects were secured by the double means of keeping the camera constantly in motion and by proper lighting, with backgrounds fairly dark and mellow light in the middle foreground. The bearing of camera motion on the illusion of three dimensions is covered more fully in *The Clinic* in this issue.[51]

In this way, we can see how the reception of films becomes transformed into a production practice; the magazine hoped to train amateurs to be more sophisticated viewers of films and to see professional films as providing cues for their own creative style and technique. This even included animation work, such as the animated insects designed by W. Starewitsch for *Youthful Ecstasy*. A double-page spread of images in the magazine describes how Starewitsch's animated film was made and noting that the film suggests "a world of filming possibilities for Fall and Winter evenings.... Clever amateurs can work out delightful little playlets with similar tiny puppets of their own manufacture."[52] How many amateurs took up this challenge is hard to know; amateur Claymation and other kinds of stop-motion work seem to be a rarity among extant amateur films.

The aesthetic philosophy of *Amateur Movie Makers* might be described as an enthusiasm with the range of expressive and stylistic options that were open to the medium of film and thus to film amateurs. The pages of *Amateur Movie Makers* were attentive to European experiments with film style and expressed a hope for the increase in the popularity of little cinemas in the United States. But filmmakers like Flaherty, who were able to infuse their travel films with pathos and expressive touches, were also praised, particularly when they found new ways of turning familiar spaces (the city or the local countryside) into sites for amateur ethnographic filming. Finally, *Amateur Movie Makers'* attention to film influences was exemplified in "Critical Focusing," in which visual techniques and stylistic devices were atomized from their original context; here elements of European art films were presented side by side with popular American films. The result was a mode of spectatorship that proposed a radical equivalence between formal techniques and visual styles and that might best be compared to an encyclopedia or periodic table for film experimenters.

THE AMATEUR MOVIE(MAKING) PUBLIC

As we have seen, an image of the amateur filmmaker in 1927 was nebulous and fragmented, reflecting multiple social selves. Since amateur filmmaking began as a pastime of the very rich, the pages of *Amateur Movie Makers* contain many references to high-class leisure activities, including world travel, hunting, and country vacations. But there were also articles for more middle-class amateurs who formed clubs or worked on films in more modest ways. And then there were references to younger classes of filmmakers who worked in small experimental collectives (like Lewis Jacobs's Philadelphia Movie Crafters) and in groups of college students. *Amateur Movie Makers* defined the moviemaking class inclusively while still reinforcing certain parts of its original (and financially sustaining) community: the rich. Acknowledging those groups who were not discussed in *Amateur Movie Makers*, most notably nonwhite racial and ethnic groups, is also crucial. While African Americans were not restricted from membership in the ACL, there is scant evidence of nonwhite amateurs as a part of this community.[53] We might consider the scarcity of nonwhite filmmakers in the ACL in light of evidence that some—such as James and Eloyce Gist—made elaborate amateur productions outside the organization.[54] Even if the ACL did have a neutral attitude toward race (i.e., instead of neither prohibiting nor encouraging nonwhite members), local clubs may have exercised their own membership policies and, like many other kinds of social organizations during the midcentury, admitted or excluded members on the basis of local (and often reactionary) attitudes toward race, nationality, or ethnicity. Still, the amateur movie public can be tracked according to the different clubs that are discussed and reported, as well as the different (commercial, if alternative) exhibition venues that are discussed in the magazine. Finally, one of the central goals of *Amateur Movie Makers* was to coordinate a film exchange among members of the ACL.

Several articles in the first year of *Amateur Movie Makers* provided advice for starting an amateur movie club. Hiram Percy Maxim (writing under the pseudonym Dr. Kinema) noted that local circumstances prevented any one-size-fits-all approach but suggested a model for identifying filmmakers through equipment dealers and the ACL and then inviting them to an organizational meeting. At the first meeting, Maxim recommended showing at least "one good" amateur film and then allowing the dealer to demonstrate some equipment before discussing the organization of the club. He recommended about two meetings a month to begin with, each of which would involve the showing of members' films and presentations on technical topics.[55] The viewing and critiquing of amateur films was at the center of this kind of meeting (in a way very different from the emphasis on exhibition of professional or art films in ciné-clubs in France), and Maxim noted that clubs should "have a number of films shown at each meeting so that everyone in the club can have a chance to get his films criticized." These strategies would provide a basic structure for movie clubs over the next three decades, with a range of variations that are discussed in subsequent chapters.

From its earliest issues, *Amateur Movie Makers* published a regular column detailing the local happenings of amateur filmmakers and eventually established a new section devoted specifically to amateur clubs. The first column of this department included a list of twenty-one "already organized" movie clubs and another list of about a dozen clubs in the process of being organized.[56] This section of the magazine provided different visions of the social and aesthetic organization of movie clubs. In some cases they were defined in terms of members of a city's social elite and required hefty membership dues.[57] Young people and college student groups made up another large category of amateur filmmakers; how big a group the college student amateur filmmakers were is unclear, but evidently it was big enough to prompt some people to voice their concern that amateur filmmaking would encourage young people's fantasies of going to Hollywood.[58] But profiles of movie clubs who claimed more "democratic" membership policies were also included. One of these was the Little Screen Players of Boston, an amateur filmmaking club established in 1923 as a utopian model of communal filmmaking. Though the club was organized by members with some professional film experience, its more general ranks were relatively diverse in their background:

> What is most notable about the organization is its membership. Until now, much of the news about amateurs has included the usual footnote about college students, aesthetic critics, and undiscovered geniuses who

are going to capitalize the letter "A" in "art." Here is a group among whom it is possible to pick the average man and woman, the stenographer, school teacher, clerk, civil engineer, photographer and storekeeper. The members of the Little Screen Players are ordinary folk whose time is not their own. They give up all their Sundays and holidays, once crammed with picnics and card parties, to be hustled about and shouted to by their director. They pay a dollar a month for the privilege. . . . If the moving pictures have so far been called the most democratic of the arts, they might also develop, in the future, as the most communal of the arts.[59]

Brownstein differentiates between the amateurs hoping to become successful artists and the "truer" amateurs who pursued the activity for fun, as a hobby, while drawing their livelihood from another source. But the club also retained a professional dimension. Herbert Lang, the club's founder and principal film director, hoped to "combine the perfection of the professional with the freshness of the non-professional."[60] Lang (who had worked in a film studio) and a handful of others with technical experience provided the professional technique in the club's productions. They shot their film productions (*It*, 1925) on 35mm film and on at least one occasion rented out a film studio for a day in order to have access to professional lighting and sets. This profile of the club demonstrates that that amateur film culture included a variety of different amateurs—amateur filmmakers and amateur actors, as well as amateur critics and cinephiles.

One of the most successful groups of mid-1920s might also draw our attention to the influence of commercial motives in amateur filmmaking. The Rochester Community Players were a group that produced a number of films, including one, called *Fly Low Jack and the Game*, directed by Marion Gleason.[61] Though *Amateur Movie Makers* describes Rochester as "the Kodak City," it doesn't note the professional connection to the filming. But as Dwight Swanson points out, the film's camera operators were Harris Tuttle and Allan Mogensen, two Kodak employees who were instrumental in the development of the 16mm amateur camera technology. In *Amateur Movie Makers*, Gleason herself was given a great deal of credit as the production's director (though it was not entirely complimentary: "The Community Players' movie is rather a pretentious affair; and yet the making of it was simplicity itself").[62] *Fly Low Jack and the Game* included sensational elements like an airplane crash and a polo game and was subsequently part of a traveling program of 16mm amateur films and professional features circulated in the American Midwest by Kodak, for promotional purposes.[63]

One of the long-lasting functions of the Amateur Cinema League was the extended distribution of amateur films by initiating an amateur film

- - S W A P S - -
Our Amateur Film Exchange

> **AMATEUR FILMS AVAILABLE FOR EXCHANGE**
>
> One of the chief functions of the Amateur Cinema League is to establish a safe and workable amateur film exchange. This will not be undertaken until a procedure has been worked in such a fashion as to insure absolutely safe transportation and return of valuable films.
>
> The League desires to have a list of films which their owners are willing to exchange under conditions of absolute safety. Will you not send such a list to the editor of AMATEUR MOVIE MAKERS as soon as possible?

Figure 3. The Amateur Cinema League's early effort to create an amateur film exchange took the form of their monthly "SWAPS" column. *Amateur Movie Makers,* December 1926, 25. Courtesy Media History Digital Library.

exchange among members. In the ACL's first years, this exchange took the form of a column called "SWAPS," which listed members with films they were willing to circulate to other members (figure 3). Maxim himself was the first to provide a list of the films he was willing to share with other amateurs, and his list gives us a glimpse of the eclectic mix of subjects that early amateurs captured on film: "Fishing Trip," "Development of an Old Farmhouse into a Country Home," "Field Day, 1925 at Dobbs," "European Trip," "Winter in Connecticut," "Mag the Hag," "Log of the 'Sea Gull'" (a motor boat), and "Summer in Connecticut." Maxim's list was joined by another Hartford amateur's films, which included travelogues of Europe and Bermuda. From this first list of amateur films, we can see the upper-class subject matter that made up both the topics of the films and the rest of the filmmakers' leisure hours. The film selections in "SWAPS" often settle on these kinds of film subjects, but even as the demographic makeup of the ACL shifted over time (as equipment became more affordable, and movies were made by members of lower socioeconomic groups), many of the principal genres presented in this list—travelogue, documentary, scenic, narrative short—remained central to amateur filmmakers.[64]

The end of 1927 predicted new directions for amateur competitions that would eventually lead to the ACL Ten Best lists. "We all learn by example," wrote the "Amateur Clubs" columnist (probably Arthur Gale), "by comparison, and by competition. So all amateur clubs are urged to conduct cine contests.... If each club will undertake an amateur cine contest, the foundation will be laid for an eventual national and international cine salon which will establish amateur cinematography on a firm footing as an authentic and definite art."[65] So the role of ciné-clubs was eventually to allow amateurs to improve their filmmaking skills through comparison and competition. As later chapters will show, this function became a central aspect of organized amateur film culture.

HERALDING THE MOTION PICTURE OF TOMORROW

In addition to showing the horizon of influences and historical relationships suggested above, *Amateur Movie Makers* also shows us some of the specific advice in filmmaking techniques and composition directed toward amateurs. Lessons about particular film topics (using titles, making animated sequences, etc.) appeared along with detailed instructions and schematics. The adaptation of stories (whether short fictions or actual events such as travels) also played an important role in the aesthetic advice provided by the magazine. *Amateur Movie Makers* regularly published model scenarios and scripts that amateurs could try to shoot; it also later published short stories along with their adaptation into shooting script form. But despite these practical tips and this advice, the dimensions of an amateur filmmaking aesthetic were constantly undergoing processes of explication, analysis, and revision during the ACL's first years.

Amateur Movie Makers encouraged amateurs to approach their filmmaking with some basic aesthetic guidelines in order to ensure viewable films. How-to manuals and prewritten scenarios for amateurs grew rapidly in number during the late 1920s. Advertisements and reviews of manuals for amateurs, available for purchase from the ACL, were common in the magazine.[66] Some of the advice articles published in the magazine were technical in nature (learn about exposure, color filters), but the most emphatic (and clichéd among amateurs) were probably the regular cautions against rapid panning. Hiram Percy Maxim (again writing as "Dr. Kinema") touches on this in his column "Perils of Panoraming," which encouraged amateur filmmakers to reflect more on the technique they use in taking films and to save their audiences the pain of viewing their roughest material: "In a fit of temporary enthusiasm," Dr. Kinema writes, "one might be led to take them; but to show them, and ask respectable people with sensitive eyes and dispositions to look at them, was criminal."[67] In addition to establishing basic levels of skill and stylistic clarity, Maxim also discouraged the sense (popular for many years) that amateur films of this rough quality might be presented—because showing such rough films gave amateurs as a group a bad name.

In a similar vein, the question of what made a film interesting was discussed in *Amateur Movie Makers*, both in articles about amateur technique and in reviews of commercial films. In one article, a young amateur named Marion Kerr discussed the "shock" of discovering that her most recent eight-hundred-foot travelogue reel lacked interest for both herself and other people when projected: "It was such a great disappointment," she wrote, "that I fell to analyzing the film in detail, in the hopes that I might locate where the weakness lay."[68] This impulse to analyze and critique not just the technique of a film but also the more profound question of what moves people about amateur films is striking. Kerr found that it was not a lack of continuity (which her film had), or of people (because some of her more successful films lacked people), or of "a compelling idea" that hindered her film. Rather, she concluded that her film was uninteresting because she "had taken too many scenes that did not inherently APPEAL." Kerr points to one particular scene in her film, of a little girl and a puppy, which generated the most interest from her audience, even though it was overexposed. "And yet," she asks, "what is there about an ordinary puppy jumping about that is interesting? There is something interesting, however, and I call it 'appeal.' The clumsy, enthusiastic, silly actions of a little puppy dog appeals [sic] to us and we say it is interesting." Kerr's conclusion here is certainly clumsy, somewhat circular, and does little to explain to us what appeal really is.[69] But her attempt to figure it out is interesting for its dismissal of the usual elements that were commonly considered as criteria for successful (amateur) films: continuity and technical proficiency. Kerr's other example of images that appeal seem at first rather simplistic but are perhaps not so straightforward: "It is pictures of the people in the audience. They will look at them over and over again, hour on end, sitting bolt upright in their chairs with their eyes glistening. There need be no special action. Just the normal motions of ordinary life are enough to set an audience into spasms, if the pictures are of themselves." Is this pure narcissism? Or is this kind of self-recognition another element of the "attraction" of

Figure 4. *Amateur Movie Makers* sports a new motto. *Amateur Movie Makers,* June 1927, 3. Courtesy Media History Digital Library.

the moving image? These questions remind us of the first images of the Lumière family, the fascination with seeing a person represented, and the ACL's first motto: "To See Ourselves as Others See Us."

While Kerr's article, and the motto itself, offers some insight into how the founding amateurs saw themselves and the desired quality of their films, the phrase turned out to be short-lived in the publication. By its June 1927 issue, *Amateur Movie Makers* sported a redesigned masthead with the phrase "Heralding the Motion Picture of Tomorrow" replacing Burns's line (figure 4). Had something changed among people's vision for amateur film? As 1927 drew to a close, *Amateur Movie Makers* reflected on the ACL's progress, and Arthur Gale announced the arrival of (yet another) new epoch of amateur cinematography: "The wide sale of personal and home movie equipment marked the first phase; it brought amateur possibility to motion pictures. The formation of the Amateur Cinema League marked the second phase; it established amateur consciousness in motion pictures. ... Now, the local clubs, that are appearing like magic all over the six continents and the islands of the seas, are turning amateur effort into a useful social and civic medium to realize vast future possibilities of cooperative amateur cinematography."[70] By the end of the first year of *Amateur Movie Makers* a new spell had been cast, this one transforming the energies of local movie clubs worldwide into a force for useful social and civic activity. While the magic of amateur film culture, as well as the transformations in an alternative public, film spectatorship, and a developing film aesthetic, had seduced the amateurs during their first year, they were now asked to look away from their own multifaceted reflection and toward the motion picture of tomorrow.

2 Ciné-Community

The First Wave of Amateur Film Culture (1928–1945)

> Regarding the importance of the amateur motion picture movement, people are now coming to realize that this activity which is sweeping the country is more than a craze. They are beginning to understand that in the future of the amateur cinema movement lies the real hope of progress in the art of the silent screen.
>
> **William J. Shannon,** *"Amateur Movie Clubs—What They Offer"*[1]

The 1930s were the heyday of amateur film culture. This was the heroic period of amateur filmmaking, when "the amateur" could be an artist, an aficionado, a documentarian, an educator, or simply a hobbyist making carefully crafted films about his or her own family. As the epigram for this chapter indicates, by the 1930s amateur cinema had become a widespread and popular activity. Building on the foundations established by the Amateur Cinema League, amateur film culture expanded rapidly and continued to advance claims to its social and aesthetic significance. But just as the initial image of the amateur filmmaker that emerged in the 1920s was a multifaceted one, the amateur movement that grew and matured during the 1930s had many different, and sometimes contradictory, aspects.

Amateur moviemaking was not a coherent film "movement," but it did have some consistent features and prominent organizations and figures. Much as the Amateur Cinema League had proclaimed the arrival of the amateur in the late 1920s, *American Cinematographer*—published in Hollywood by the American Society of Cinematographers—joined the scene in the 1930s and played a significant role in shaping discourse around amateur cinema. *American Cinematographer* catered to an amateur audience for much of the decade and invites an analysis of the complex relationship between amateurs and professionals, as well as between independents and industry workers, during this period. Another significant role played by major publications was in the organization of national and international movie contests, the first of which was launched by *Photoplay* magazine in 1928. Annual movie contests proliferated over the course of the decade and provide a valuable barometer of amateur accomplishments, as well as the discourse and taste cultures that surrounded them. But the amateur cinema community was characterized by more than large magazines and international organizations. Most amateurs had their most immediate network of colleagues at the local level in movie clubs. Local amateur movie clubs proliferated rapidly in the 1930s, appearing in North American cities large and small. The role that these clubs played in amateur filmmaking was significant but could also be quite varied. Though these groups often received guidance from larger organizations or publications—like the ACL or *American Cinematographer*—they also developed in response to local conditions and the inclinations of their members. While film production was the primary activity of amateur clubs, amateurs also developed new networks and venues for the exhibition of noncommercial films. An examination of a particular exhibition context during the 1930s—the Little Movie parties, which spanned the decade—will serve as a way of exploring some of the key exhibition contexts and concerns of the amateur world during this period.

This chapter traces the culture of amateur filmmaking during the 1930s and through World War II. Examining the emergence and expansion of amateur filmmaking as an organized activity permits us to see the cultural role of motion pictures in North America in a new light, compared with traditional film histories. Amateur film culture was participatory in ways that commercial, Hollywood film culture did not easily permit (except as fan culture). After World War II, many of these qualities of amateurism would persist, but in a more muted form, as experimental, documentary, and educational filmmaking came to occupy more distinct fields of filmmaking endeavor. For the 1930s, however, being an amateur meant exploring all those filmmaking possibilities that were ignored by Hollywood.

AMERICAN CINEMATOGRAPHER: PROFESSIONALS AND AMATEURS

> "to serve in a practical way all who use motion picture cameras, either for business or for pleasure."
>
> *American Cinematographer*[2]

In May 1929 *American Cinematographer*'s new editor announced the creation of a new department in the magazine: "Because of the increased demand for cinematographic knowledge, the magazine is widening its scope to include the vast field of the AMATEUR cinematographer."[3] *American*

Cinematographer might seem a strange venue to discover a burgeoning support for amateur filmmaking culture. First published by the American Society of Cinematographers in 1920, the magazine was established to supply cameramen in Hollywood with technical developments and to hasten the professionalization of the field of cinematography.[4] But it was precisely this publication, and its closed professional society, that provided one of the principal venues supporting amateur moviemaking and film culture during the 1930s. While the magazine's inclusion of amateur activities may have been intended to broaden its general readership and subsidize the magazine's more specialized, professional content, this does not diminish the valuable trace of amateur film culture provided in its pages over the course of nearly three decades. The volume of amateur content in *American Cinematographer* increased rapidly during the 1930s, and for more than a decade the publication sustained a balance between amateur and professional content. Starting in 1929, the magazine's front cover included a line under its title specifying the magazine's audience: "A Publication for Professionals and Amateurs." In 1932, *American Cinematographer* expanded its amateur content into a monthly "amateur section." By 1934, the "Amateur Movies" section appeared with its own, second cover, separating it from the professional section, thus creating a "reversible" magazine, which could be placed on newsstands as either *American Cinematographer* or as *Amateur Movies*, depending on how it was folded (figure 5).[5] We see here a Janus-faced image of the publication that is useful both for the portrait of amateur culture that it helps flesh out and also for the illuminating portrait of Hollywood that its coverage of amateurs reveals. The amateur materials in *American Cinematographer* shed light on the *mutual*—not just a one-way—attraction between Hollywood and nonprofessional moviemakers. In contrast to fortifying a monolithic and hermetically sealed industry, *American Cinematographer* points to a more porous industry culture that was open to the different creative and technological influences presented by amateurs, whose freedom from industry constraints was often remarked on in the magazine. In general, *American Cinematographer* promoted amateur film culture in three ways: through technical instruction and expert advice, through the organization of annual movie contests, and finally by supporting and publicizing the growing network of local amateur movie clubs. And all of this was promoted from the center of the film industry in Hollywood, taking full advantage of the status and glamour that location provided.

Capitalizing on the magazine's base among professional industry workers, much of *American Cinematographer*'s content for amateurs was

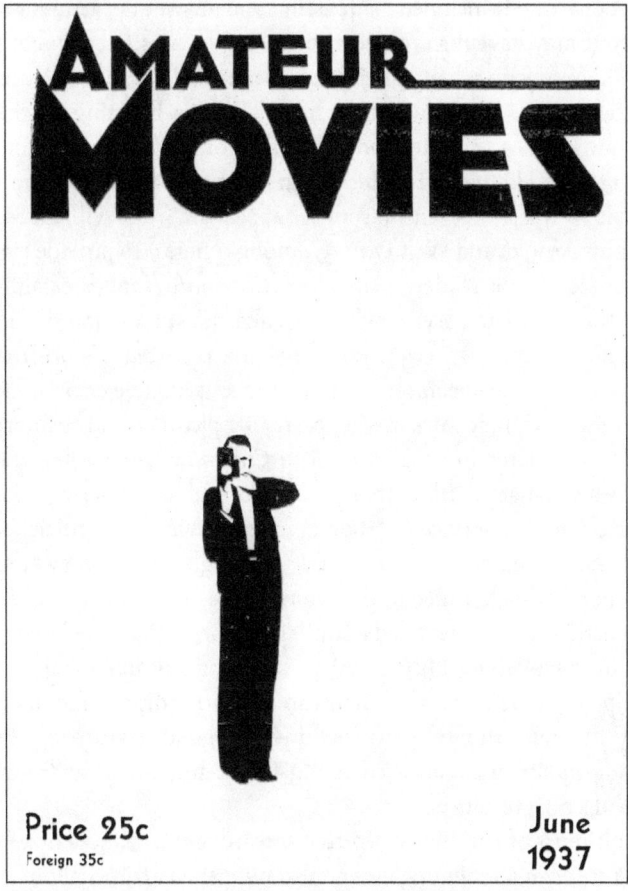

Figure 5. After 1934 *American Cinematographer* became a "reversible" magazine, with a separate cover for its amateur section. *American Cinematographer,* June 1937.

technical in nature and designed to appeal to advanced amateurs interested in technique, equipment, and gadgetry. Advertisements urged amateur readers to "Keep Step with the Professionals by Reading the Technical Cinematic Magazine of the Motion Picture Industry."[6] Typical articles provided advice for overcoming the most common faults in amateur films, and while the problems identified were similar to those in other guides for amateurs, *American Cinematographer*'s advice carried with it the authority of professional technique.[7] Reinforcing this authority was the access to Hollywood industry experts the publication provided. The magazine's amateur department included "a question and answer department in which the amateur may have his problems solved by the master cinematographers whose skill and genius have placed American-made motion pictures at the top of the world's motion picture ladder."[8] This bridging of the divide between amateurs and professionals was laid out as a unique characteristic of the magazine. Hollywood professionals did indeed respond to the amateur moviemakers' questions, with responses appearing from William Stull, Karl Struss, John Arnold, and Walt Disney, among others.[9] To provide even more specific advice to its readers, *American Cinematographer* established an amateur film criticism service, which invited the submission of films for a professional critique. By 1932, the magazine reported, "More than 1200 amateur pictures have been sent in to us for constructive criticism and suggestions as to how their work on that particular picture could be improved."[10] Nearly a decade later, in 1941, *American Cinematographer* began publishing reviews of amateur films that it had received and described the magazine's long-standing service of "individualized review and criticism of amateur movies by members of the A.S.C."[11] Though these review "members" were not generally identified in the same way respondents to amateur questions were, their service retained a similar authority. Published reviews were selected in cases where "little tricks" from long professional experience could help amateurs in areas such as camerawork, editing, and direction. In this way amateur film reviews became a regular feature of *American Cinematographer* and appeared alongside commentary and reviews of Hollywood's own products.

Though most of the advice directed toward amateurs was of a technical nature, *American Cinematographer* also published articles about film aesthetics for both amateurs and professionals. During the mid-1930s, the magazine presented a series of articles by J. Belmar Hall, instructor in the nascent Department of Cinema at University of Southern California. On topics such as "the art director in 16mm," "what is composition in cinema?," and "editing is really an art," Hall draws on comparisons with other art forms—painting, music, architecture, and so forth—to alert the amateur filmmaker's attention to particular dimensions of film form.[12] Similarly, Max Liszt, a director working with the politically oriented New Film Group, wrote a series of introductory articles about montage around the same time, starting with "Just What Is 'Montage' Anyway?"[13] Amateurs also benefited from articles about film aesthetics that were directed more to a professional readership, including introductions and glossaries of technical terms as well as reviews of contemporary commercial films and commentaries about film style.[14] These articles were a mainstay of the magazine, featuring many written by cinematographers. *Citizen Kane*, for example, was immediately recognized as an aesthetically significant film and was featured in several articles, including one by its cinematographer, Gregg Toland.[15] The proximity of amateur activities to professional Hollywood craftsmanship was especially poignant in those issues of the magazine that praised the Academy Award–winning cinematographers of each year.[16] *American Cinematographer* published articles about, for, and by professional and acclaimed cinematographers, thus framing the amateur section of the magazine as related or aspirational simply by virtue of its proximity.

Despite this proximity, the precise nature of the relationship between amateurs and professionals was sometimes ambiguous, and the distinctions among different classes of filmmakers and their delimitations were a recurring preoccupation in the publication. William Stull, who was a regular contributor to the amateur department and later became the magazine's general editor, wrote in 1929, "In almost all sports there are recognized three great classes: novices, amateurs, and professionals," but when it comes to photography "one is either an amateur—a blundering novice, or a professional—and perfect." Still points out the injustice of this dichotomy to "advanced amateurs" who had "so perfected their art that they could take place beside the greatest of professionals, if they chose, but prefer to follow their art merely for the love of it rather than for profit."[17] In this definition, the true amateur was every bit as skilled as the professional but made a choice to pursue his or her art for love rather than profit. Stull also widened the gap between amateurs and novices, whom he describes as "snapshotters": "They are the ones who have not yet passed the 'you-press-the-button-we-do-the-rest' stage—the ones who have not yet become conscious of the vast, unexplored world of new experiences awaiting them in the realm of true amateurism." In contrast to these beginners, the realm of "true amateurism" was characterized by "growing attention to little details of technique; the birth of a spirit of inquiry; the conscious expenditure of thought on the business of taking pictures—the change from a picture-*taker* to a picture-*maker*." This important distinction describes the amateur's skill in an active ("making") way and foregrounds the skills that help accomplish picture making, including exposure, composition, subjects, action, and angles. Many articles for amateurs in *American Cinematographer* elucidated these skills and provided instruction for those who wished to move from the position of snapshotter to that of advanced amateur.

No doubt amateur filmmakers got a charge out of reading material for them alongside specialized or laudatory material for professionals. But what did professionals think about the amateur section? Was it simply another arm of the industry's public relations operation? Or did amateurism represent a space for film "play," free from industry pressures, commercial strictures, and orders from studio bosses? A partial answer to these questions comes in the form of a series of articles about "professional amateurs." These profiles were written to take advantage of the magazine's access to industry workers and stars, but author William Stull cast them in terms of a recurring preoccupation with amateur status: "With the development of the motion picture industry there has arisen an entirely new class of photographic amateur. Formerly," Stull continued, "one was either an amateur or a professional. The division was sharply defined, and there was no middle ground. But today, the motion picture has brought forth a new being—the professional amateur; men and women whose lives are spent in the production of cinematic entertainment for the world, but who also find in amateur cinematography the same absorbing interest that other amateurs do." With this, Stull tied amateurs and professionals closely together in ways that might be inspirational or even titillating to amateurs who aspired to become professional or who sought proximity to Hollywood's craftsmanship and glamour. Stull also notes the range of different interests among "professional amateurs"; while industrial filmmaking was praised for its high quality, professional technique, and sharp business acumen, the amateur sphere was more tailored to individual interests and preferences.[18] Ostensibly the amateur realm was where industry personnel were able to express themselves in motion pictures and to link motion pictures to their personal lives, interests, and artistic expressions in ways that were more intimate, perhaps even more authentic.

Articles in this series profiled a range of directors and actors, beginning with Fred Niblo, director of popular films like *The Mark of Zorro* (1920), *Blood and Sand* (1922), and *Ben-Hur* (1925). Niblo is presented as an amateur still photographer who later moved into motion pictures, where he learned how to become a producer and travelogue lecturer, which eventually led to working as a director for Thomas Ince. So Niblo's story was not only a tale of a successful Hollywood director who continued to shoot amateur films in his leisure time (travel and family pictures, primarily) but also an inspirational tale of his rise from amateur to professional. Other "professional amateurs" profiled included the actress Mary Astor, who, according to the article, had a longstanding interest in knowing what goes on on the other side of the camera (unlike many other actresses, Stull suggests).[19] The professional cinematographer John Arnold was also revealed to enjoy making 16mm "gag" films as well as experimenting with trick effects that he planned to adapt to professional shooting.[20] In his profile, Cecil DeMille discusses his use of an amateur camera to film fishing trips and notes how amateur movies mark the similarities among people: "Of course, when it comes to such personal films, I suppose we all make about the same sort of pictures. Whatever our business, we all have families, and friends, and pets, and we like to record them and their pleasures in the same way."[21] While praising these universal themes of amateur films, DeMille was less favorably disposed to their recurring technical flaws, and he warned amateurs against using too many unusual camera angles in unmotivated ways. He also encouraged careful organization and distribution of labor in amateur production: "My advice to the amateur is to learn this lesson from the professional; to make Organization, Specialization, and Cooperation his watchwords if he would successfully produce his own photoplays."[22] As DeMille's comments suggest, a consistent theme of these professional amateur profiles was the trajectory from simple "family snapshots" to more complexly and accomplished amateur films. These accounts shared in the publication's general project of elevating amateur film technique above that of the novice.[23]

American Cinematographer's goal of distinguishing advanced amateurs from mere snapshotters culminated in a drive to find a new designation for serious nonprofessional filmmakers. "YOU ARE NOT AN AMATEUR," a 1933 advertisement announced, "You are a CINEPHOTOGRAPHER . . . CINEGRAPHER or CINEGRAPHIST or have you a better name."[24] While *American Cinematographer* had earlier differentiated between snapshotter novices and the more advanced amateurs that were their target audience, here the magazine explicitly stated its discomfort with the pejorative connotations of *amateur*: "We want to get away from using the word Amateur in our publication. We feel there is a sort of stigma to it in connection with the intelligent user of the Cine Camera. . . . he has reached out further. . . . he is no longer the amateur that the popular conception of that word implies."[25] In contrast to these meanings, *American Cinematographer* wanted to focus on the more advanced nonprofessionals; evidently, *amateur* was a term that just wasn't able to shake its stigma and was especially out of place in a professional industry publication. After conducting its mail-in vote, *American Cinematographer* announced the winning moniker, *cinephotographer*.[26] The magazine put the term into use right away in a profile of Clark Gable's forays into 16mm filming.[27] Surely *American Cinematographer* was fueling amateurs' anxiety about their relationship to novices and professionals with this fixation on naming. But in any case, the term *cinephotographer* did not catch on, and the publication soon returned to using the more familiar—and contested—designation of *amateur*.

Despite the publication's preoccupation with subtle gradations among amateurs and occasional movement up the ranks, a schema that placed amateurism as a point in the development toward professional filmmaking was not uniformly endorsed by contributors.[28] To discourage amateurs from harboring illusions of breaking into studio filmmaking, some authors pointed out stark distinctions between the two classes: "Cinematography as practiced by the studio cinematographer and amateur are two utterly different chapters," the author notes. "Their sole connection is the common celluloid ribbon. The most proficient amateur in the land is still the veriest beginner at studio cinematography. A deft letter-writer is not necessarily an accomplished playwright."[29] This is a harsh dismissal of ambitious amateurs, especially given *American Cinematographer*'s frequent emphasis on the connections and commonalities between advanced amateurs and professionals; here the vast distance between the two classes is emphasized. The article closes by noting the unemployment of cinematographers in Hollywood, underscoring the scarcity of work, even for professionals. *American Cinematographer* was ultimately an instrument of a professional organization and an industrial hierarchy that had a clear message to amateurs: keep out!

Eventually, *American Cinematographer* established a new way of reinforcing this hierarchy, announcing in 1936 the creation of "a junior society for the amateur": "THE SOCIETY OF AMATEUR CINEMATOGRAPHERS."[30] Like the ASC, the amateur organization would also be exclusive, and members would have to be somewhat accomplished filmmakers. Membership requirements included possession of a movie camera and a portfolio of films that were reviewed for quality by a board of ASC members. The benefits of membership included status ("a sign of achievement"), social networking, and expert advice: paid membership in the society included a subscription to *American Cinematographer* and access to its library of amateur films. Plans were also described for the creation of a special status of "fellowships" in the society for particularly accomplished filmmakers, and the goal of creating member branches of the society in different cities was also announced. Subsequent reports announced the quick growth of the new amateur branch of the ASC and applications for membership beyond the United States.[31] Over the course of 1937 and 1938 *American Cinematographer* contained few references to the organization, but the designation "SAC" did appear alongside a few award-winning amateur filmmakers' names. The organization received very little specific comment in the pages of the magazine, though, so how it functioned isn't clear.[32] Beyond these traces, however, little can be gleaned about the activities of the Society of Amateur Cinematographers.

Some years later, in 1945, on the twenty-fifth anniversary of the American Society of Cinematographers, the president of the organization noted the entry of amateurs to the contents of its publication:

> In 1929 the magazine, recognizing the need for imparting technical information to the rapidly increasing number of home movie makers, started publishing articles slanted towards the amateur, with particular emphasis on the advanced amateur. Then an entirely new group of readers came into existence. Amateurs by the thousands began reading the magazine because nowhere else could they find instructive articles written for them by professional motion picture cameramen; men who gave of their rich experience to help the amateur make better amateur films. The magazine has solved the problems of untold numbers of home movie makers who could find their answers nowhere else.[33]

No doubt this inclusion of amateur activities and events, starting in the 1930s, furnished *American Cinematographer* with a broader readership and higher advertising revenues. But it also simultaneously helped cement a category of "advanced amateurs" who made accomplished short films, forming a robust culture during that decade.

AMATEUR MOVIE CONTESTS

Movie contests played an important role in the development and expansion of North American amateur film culture during the 1920s and '30s. Contests relating to cinema had been part of popular culture for nearly two decades already, with fan publications providing the main venue for contests ranging from naming the new art form ("the photoplay") in 1910 to screenplay-writing contests in later years.[34] Contests geared specifically toward amateur filmmakers emerged in the late 1920s and provided a way of motivating amateur activity and assessing its accomplishments. Amateur movie contests flourished in the 1930s and far beyond, continuing today to be a principal way for amateurs to show off their polished films. The Amateur Cinema League grasped the significance of competitions early, but its first foray into the field in 1927 was a contest not for filmmaking but for scenario writing. Announced in July 1927, the scenario contest was a modest affair by later standards, with a winner proclaimed just two months later.[35] As *Amateur Movie Makers* had predicted in 1927, local movie clubs would eventually become a major venue for movie contests. But larger national and international competitions popularized the practice more widely and established high standards of evaluation. What follows is a brief examination of three competitions that were significant to the rise of American amateur movie culture in the 1930s.

PHOTOPLAY

It wasn't *Amateur Movie Makers* but rather *Photoplay Magazine* that held the first major amateur movie contest. Primarily a Hollywood fan magazine, *Photoplay* launched its own regular column on amateur filmmaking in 1927; over the course of two and a half years and two major movie contests, *Photoplay* was a major advocate for the amateur movement. Like other proponents, *Photoplay* proposed amateur filmmaking as a domain for the kind of small-scale filmmaking and experimentation that was impossible in Hollywood's industrial system. *Photoplay* promoted a vision of the amateur film movement that would develop into a Little Cinema art form parallel to the recent Little Theatre, which had transformed the American stage. The publication announced the $2,000 Amateur Movie Contest in April 1927 to support these goals by promoting the production of higher-quality amateur filmmaking that involved planning, editing, and polished work. This was articulated in terms of the trajectory of "the progress of the amateur cinematographer" both individually and as a category of filmmaking.[36] Supporting these objectives, *Photoplay* published numerous columns with technical and creative advice, along with an abundance of encouragement in the form of quotations from celebrity amateur filmmakers and proponents (H.L. Mencken, Ralph Barton, Robert Flaherty, Francis X. Bushman, Lon Chaney, and D.W. Griffith among them). Open to all nonprofessional filmmakers, in all formats (35mm, 16mm, 9.5mm), and across a range of possible topics, the contest emphasized "ingenuity, imagination and mechanical dexterity" as the key criteria by which films would be judged. The content of *Photoplay*'s amateur column supported this wide-ranging terrain for possible filmmaking. Among the stories featured were those about Watson and Webber's experimental production of *The Fall of the House of Usher* as well as more typical family and vacation films.

The winning films, announced in June 1928, were divided along film-gauge lines (35mm, 16mm, 9.5mm) and covered a range of different materials. The Amateur Cinema League played a major role in the contest's judging, with Hiram Percy Maxim serving on the award jury alongside film exhibitor Samuel "Roxy" Rothapfel and photographer Nickolas Muray. The winner of each division and a "special award" winner each received a five-hundred-dollar prize, and several were also named as honorable mentions. The winning films included a fictional seriocomedy produced by a movie club (35mm), a film of a quail hunt by a retired businessman (16mm), a study of the St. Louis Zoo (9.5mm), and a visualization of Thomas Hood's poem "The Dream of Eugene Aram" (special award). Brief descriptions of each film emphasized qualities like excellent photography, smooth continuity, and strong acting (where applicable). Evidently, *Photoplay* also arranged for a small number of screenings of these films, including at least one in New York. Even before the winning films were announced, a screening of the best films was being arranged for "leading New York motion picture critics and amateur enthusiasts." *Photoplay* hoped these films would "reveal, for the first time, a comprehensive view of *the amateur film movement*. All the better films of the contest will be presented and it is hoped that the showing will be a pioneer landmark in the progress of amateur cinematography" (italics mine).[37] The winner of the 35mm division was later shown to several Hollywood executives, resulting in a five-year contract with Fox for the film's director, Russell Ervin. So beyond receiving the cash prize and the public recognition, winners of the *Photoplay* contest could expect some possibility of an entrée to Hollywood.[38]

Movie Makers touted the contest as a major milestone in the amateur movement and planned a careful study of the winning films. From this they hoped to identify a "yardstick to measure amateur effort ... a sort of Amateur Standard by which [the amateur] can judge his own film."[39] Following the conclusion of the *Photoplay* contest, Roy Winton published an editorial in *Amateur Movie Makers* about its significance. Highlighting the fact that two ACL members were among the prize winners, the editorial emphasized the value of amateur filmmaking as a domain for aesthetic experimentation. "If our amateurs can produce films of simple scope, of subtlety, of cinematic quality," he wrote, "and if they try to get as far away as possible from the professional in subject matter and as close to him as possible in workmanlike technique, the eighth art will hasten forward." Closely connected to these goals was the establishment of little cinemas for the presentation of amateur movies: "If amateurs can produce artistic films," Winton proposed, "there is little doubt that the rapidly increasing number of Little Cinemas or Little Picture Houses will give these films to the public. Not only will the amateurs find remuneration enough to cover a part of their expenses in film experimentation, but they will also find a channel through which their experiments may be distributed."[40] In terms of their vision of the amateur's role in advancing film art, *Photoplay* and the ACL seemed to be closely aligned.

Photoplay's second amateur movie contest followed the philosophy that Winton and the ACL had laid out, emphasizing amateurs' experimental role in particular. In its announcement of the contest, the magazine noted two of its appeals: the opportunity for being discovered by Hollywood, as Ervin had been, and the potential for expanding film art through experimentation. The winning films would once again be presented to Hollywood's film executives, *Photoplay* reported, thus creating the possibility that this contest's winners, like Ervin, might find themselves turned professional. But there was also much the amateur could bring to Hollywood, including a fresh perspective and experimental attitude: "The great difficulty has been to provide a bridge to span the gap between the amateur movie experimenter and the professional studio. *Photoplay's* contest is that bridge."[41] This image of *Photoplay* as a "bridge" between amateur and professional was repeated many times in the several months the contest ran (it closed in March 1929, and winning entries were announced in November of that year) and foreshadowed the relationship between amateurs and professionals that *American Cinematographer* would soon seek to reinforce. Furthermore, "experimentation" was one way the amateur's particular vocation was articulated for this contest: "*Photoplay* launched its first contest with a very definite purpose. *Photoplay* wanted to make amateurs everywhere familiar with the whole job of picture making, from shooting to cutting and editing. It wanted amateurs to experiment."[42] And experimentation would indeed be rewarded in the second contest's prize selections.

The judges for the second contest included Hollywood director King Vidor, Wilson Barrett (secretary of the National Board of Review), and *Photoplay* magazine's editor and publisher, James Quirk. These were joined by two representatives from the ACL (board vice president Stephen Voorhees and managing director Roy Winton). Maxim opted to become a contestant in the competition instead of returning as judge.[43] The contest was heavily promoted by the ACL and in *Movie Makers*, which announced a goal of doubling entries from league members over the previous contest: "The Amateur Cinema League urges its members to send entries. These contests are dignified, the judges are men who understand amateur movies, the prizes are suitable and the renown which comes to winners is the amateur's best payment for effort."[44] Characterizing the contest as dignified points to a concern that magazine-sponsored contests were frequently frivolous or silly; in its effort to advance the development of amateur film aesthetics, the ACL endorsed *Photoplay's* contest as exceptional and worthwhile. Perhaps partly as a result of this endorsement, *Photoplay* reported a significant increase in the number and quality of films over the first contest.

The winning films in the second *Photoplay* contest were announced in November 1929 and emphasized the unconventional qualities of the top prize-winning films. In the photoplay (or "dramatic") division, the five-hundred-dollar winner was a 16mm film, *Three Episodes*, which depicted "what passes in the mind of a dying soldier in a shell hole in Flanders. The three memories flashing back to the suffering doughboy were well done and the film as a whole disclosed the best sense of cinematics revealed by any contender in this division."[45] In the nondramatic category, Ralph Steiner's abstract 35mm film about water, H_2O, won top honors. Hiram Percy Maxim won third prize in the same category for his 16mm film, *The Sea*, a poetic but much more conventional visualization of water and water activities. Maxim also received an honorable mention for his scenic film *Summer*. But little can be said of the other prize winners, since their descriptions in the magazine are so brief.[46] After this concluding column about the contest's prize winners, *Photoplay*'s amateur film department disappeared. The publication appears to have ceded its amateur movie coverage to *Movie Makers* and turned over its contests to the ACL. Or at least the ACL used the experience it gained from the two *Photoplay* contests as it launched its first contest with its 1930 Ten Best list.

MOVIE MAKERS: THE TEN BEST

Each year, starting in 1930 and running until the ACL's demise in 1954, *Movie Makers* magazine selected ten films, along with several honorable mentions, for annual recognition. Though most of these films are now lost, their descriptions, printed in *Movie Makers*, provide valuable information about a vast corpus of amateur filmmaking.[47] These lists acted as annual evaluations of the progress and development of amateur filmmaking and serve as indications of the ACL's shifting critical norms and aesthetic aspirations for the medium. But there were some key differences between the selection criteria used for the Ten Best lists that *Movie Makers* presented annually and those used for other contests. Indeed the Ten Best list was initially not framed as a *contest* at all but was merely a *recognition* of notable and memorable films that had been viewed by the *Movie Makers* staff over the course of the year. Over the next two and a half decades, the annual Ten Best list did become more formally and officially framed as a contest, but the organizers always retained a somewhat flexible and pragmatic approach to their assessment of the best amateur filmmaking work.

Since its inception, the ACL had encouraged amateurs to send their films to the league's head office for analysis, commentary, and advice. The selection of the annual Ten Best films was taken from the films that had been sent into the ACL headquarters in the previous year. In 1930, choosing the films for the first Ten Best list was described as an "informal" selection "made by the staff of *Movie Makers* from all of the amateur films which have been seen at the headquarters of the Amateur Cinema League during the year."[48] In framing the Ten Best in this way, the ACL created a competition without many of the logistical difficulties that go along with running a major contest—rules, entry deadlines, categories, and selection criteria. Instead, *Movie Makers* described the criteria and judging of the films in more general terms:

> The selection of these ten best amateur pictures was based upon a consideration of technical quality, continuity excellence and subject matter interest. In some cases special qualities and experimental effort were given particular weight. The films chosen represent a wide range of amateur filming activities although, in order to leave the selection as free as possible, no formal classifications were made. The actual filming date was not considered and the ten best films were chosen from those that came to League headquarters during the past year whether they were actually made during the preceding year or slightly earlier.[49]

As indicated here, the films selected in the first year include a range of different types of filmmaking, from nature study and scenic films to travel films, medical/scientific record films, a theatre adaptation, and photoplay fictional films. And while most of these films were American in origin, the list also included a photoplay produced by a "Siamese" *(sic)* amateur. In this way, amateur filmmaking could be seen as international, not only in subject matter (travel films and the like), but also in terms of the films' countries of origin. Among the films listed as the first year's Ten Best and three honorable mentions, only one—*The Forgotten Frontier*—is known to be extant. Described by *Movie Makers* as "the most ambitious welfare film yet produced by an amateur," the film documents and dramatizes the activities of a nursing service in the Kentucky mountains.

Further distinguishing the *Movie Makers* selections of the best amateur movies was the relatively detailed recognition that each film received. Unlike the *Photoplay* contest, in which descriptions of each winning film amounted to only a line or two in the magazine, *Movie Makers* devoted a full paragraph to describing each film's merits. In this way, *Movie Makers* demonstrated its commitment to filmmaking as well as to the analysis of the films. For the upcoming year, *Movie Makers* invited amateurs to send in their films for commentary and future selection among the Ten Best: "With the appearance of this article, the period of this selection of next year's ten best amateur films is automatically opened. All amateur films sent to the League for screening are eligible."[50] Nonmembers were encouraged to send in their films for commentary and criticism "as a sample of League service" as well as consideration for the Ten Best list. This way of framing the Ten Best lists promoted ACL membership and services as including more than involvement in a specific contest. The following year, the selection of the Ten Best and honorable mentions for 1931 indicated that the recognized films were "chosen from nearly a thousand different amateur subjects."[51] Evidently there was no shortage of films sent to the ACL headquarters for commentary and consideration.

The selections of the ten best amateur films proceeded in this vein for many years, though how the contest was framed went through some shifts over time. In May 1932, an editorial urged ACL members to experiment more with their filmmaking and to submit their experiments for consideration in the contest. An experimental approach to filmmaking was useful for amateurs, because it didn't require special equipment or elaborate production techniques: "Mental energy, inventiveness and the capacity of seeing old things in a new way must come from the experimenter and he cannot borrow them or buy them. MOVIE MAKERS wants you to make these experiments and to send them in for us to see, as we determine upon the ten best films for 1932."[52] In response to this call, on the Ten Best lists for 1932 and 1933 were several films that were notable for their aesthetic experimentation, including ones that are now recognized as significant early American avant-garde works, by Watson and Webber, Henwar Rodakiewicz, Theodore Huff, and John Flory. More generally, the annual lists commented upon the steady development of the amateur field. In 1932 the Ten Best announcement noted that "the subjects [were] more specialized than formerly," a change that was evaluated as a mark of the field's evolution: "As an avocation matures, a larger number of people will specialize in some particular phase."[53]

For the Amateur Cinema League, the Ten Best selections quickly became a barometer of the progress of the amateur cinema movement, and by the mid 1930s, its level of technical and creative accomplishment was evidently quite advanced. In some years this resulted in a marked increase in the number of films that employed new technologies (such as Kodacolor film) or experimental aesthetic approaches. The 1934 a Ten Best editorial reported that a new level of technical proficiency in amateur films could be assumed: "It may truly be said that personal movie makers are able to express what they will in their chosen medium, so far as technical capacity is concerned, and that which they have willed to say is decidedly worth saying.... Capacity now may be taken for granted, leaving the future annual Ten Best selections to be made upon the basis of universal distinction and cinematic superiority."[54] The claim that their technique was relatively transparent is surprising given our received sense of amateur movies as necessarily rough and clumsy. But in this the ACL aligned technical accomplishment not with

Hollywood studio standards but with the necessary means for conveying sincerity of expression of the kind found in the work of independent filmmakers like Robert Flaherty.

Beginning in 1935, *Movie Makers* began using *nontheatrical* as a designation for its field of filmmaking. Previous years had announced the Ten Best *amateur* films, but the 1935 announcement touted "the Ten Best Non Theatrical Films of the year."[55] We see a shift here, though one that was disguised as continuity, in the framing of an amateur field of activity. The following year presented a clarification, the "New Ten Best," and a new mapping of the amateur field, in the annual listing's attempt to differentiate between different categories of filmmaker: those who made films with their own funds and those who received some kind of payment for their films. Henceforth, the Ten Best selection was to be divided between seven "personally made" pictures in the "General Class" and three films from the "Special Class": "Under this new plan of selecting the Ten Best, the productions which fall into the Special class will be *all those for which the maker has received compensation from a client at any time previous to the official closing of the year's competition.*"[56] The inclusion of films that received some kind of compensation vexes our understanding of the concept of "amateur." But it was a distinction that made sense in the mid-1930s, when the broad oppositions in film production were theatrical and nontheatrical films, with Hollywood reigning supreme over the former and "amateur" movies providing an umbrella designation for all manner of the latter. Following World War II and the emergence of some distinctly *no*namateur manifestations of nontheatrical filmmaking, this special category was eliminated, and in 1948 the Ten Best once again included all amateur films.[57]

Not until 1937 did the ACL finally establish a top honor for their annual Ten Best selection. In that year, the Hiram Percy Maxim Memorial Award was established to recognize the top film in the General Class of the year.[58] The first recipient of the prize was Hamilton Jones's film *Western Holiday*. The film was praised in *Movie Makers* for its "cinematic thrills" and "those sequences in which competence becomes artistry and technique rises to inspiration." Such thrills were evidently present in Jones's film in the form of a spectacular Mount Robson sunrise captured on Kodachrome, intelligent editing, and impressive dual turntable accompaniment that included lip-synchronized sound. Jones produced the film to use as part of his work as a lecturer promoting vacationing in Canada. So although Jones worked as a professional lecturer and promoter, his filmmaking work was considered "amateur"; it belonged to the General Class of the competition because the film was produced "entirely at his own expense and not for compensation from a client. It is a part of his professional equipment." Perhaps this is a somewhat murky distinction, but Jones's film was still to be understood as an outstanding independent, artisanal production, not a professional or industrial one.

In 1945, the ACL's managing director, Roy Winton, clarified the long-standing practices used for selecting each year's list. In his article "Choosing the Ten Best," Winton contrasted the ACL's approach to other contests, which employed different categories, used a formal scoring system, and awarded material prizes. "We wanted to set up a standard that would call forth from filmers their best efforts of all kinds and that would demand from our staff a real judgment and analysis."[59] It was this act of judgment and analysis that Winton claimed had to be left free from the constraints of categorization and formal systems: "We rejected certain contest methods that, in our opinion, would award honors for less than the best effort and that—we felt that this point was very important—might enable a staff, in years to come, to evade real critical responsibility and to let averages and categories determine selection."[60] For Winton the standards upheld by the Ten Best selections rested with the ACL staff's interest in identifying, comparing, and debating the particular merits of individual amateur films. This process is indication of both the organization's pragmatic approach to promoting amateur filmmaking progress and also their commitment to criticism and analysis as inherently intertwined with film production. The Ten Best selections were, after all, the product of the ACL's film consultation service that was available to members, and making better pictures was central to both the organization and the competition's mission. This annual activity would continue until the ACL dissolved in 1954.

AMERICAN CINEMATOGRAPHER

American Cinematographer organized contests for amateur filmmakers throughout the 1930s and then again, after a hiatus of several years, in the early 1950s. These contests capitalized on the magazine's proximity to the Hollywood film industry, as its amateur content more generally did, and often evaluated amateur work in relation to commercial film's stylistic norms. Its first contest was announced in October 1931, with awards presented the following year in December 1932. The judging committee for the inaugural contest was announced with considerable fanfare, and the list was made up primarily of cinematographers (members of the ASC) but also of Hollywood directors (DeMille, Clarence Brown), actors (Clark Gable, Leslie Howard, Conrad Nagel, Joan Crawford, Irene Dunne), film editors, and critics. Major authors and screenwriters would be part of the judging committee, as would the production heads of the major studios of Hollywood. In subsequent years, the judges of the contests received less attention, but in this first version, the opportunity to have one's films seen and evaluated by the cream of Hollywood's studio system was emphasized. Unlike the competition for *Movie Makers'* Ten Best lists, the *American Cinematographer* contest had detailed rules and judging criteria. There were thirteen categories for the certificate awards, and the evaluation system used for the top prizes in the contest involved elaborate balloting and many weeks to complete.[61] As William Stull related, "The final determinations of the winners of the contest has proved an intricate bit of mathematics ... giving separate ratings for photography, composition, direction, production technique, story, titles, editing, acting and entertainment value." Stull noted that poor editing was the most common fault of the amateur films submitted, especially the tendency to repeat particular scenes several times, showing slight variations of angle and exposure, when only one shot would have sufficed.[62] Judges also appeared somewhat skeptical of amateur experimental efforts: "As one of the more ultra-impressionistic films was projected, Clarence Brown was overheard to remark, anent a series of weird angle shots, 'Maybe I'm wrong, but a crooked camera is still a crooked camera to me!'"[63] Even though Henwar Rodakiewicz received a "certificate" first award for his photography of *Portrait of a Young Man,* and Theodore Huff was commended for his *Little Geezer,* there was no special category for experimental work, and experimental aspects were not commented upon favorably in *American Cinematographer.*[64] On the other hand, travel films were praised highly for the attractive "locations" they provided; with these films measured according to their technical achievement, the amateur was at a disadvantage, but in terms of mobility, he had an advantage over the professional.

The top prize in the contest went to a three-reel film called *Tarzan Jr.* (William A. Palmer and Ernest W. Page), which was filmed at a boys' summer camp.[65] According to one article, it was a film "many of the judges felt would have been worthy of showing in any theatre. The acting, direction, story and handling as a whole was considered equal to many a professional comedy." That the contest's top prize went to a group of teenage filmmakers is telling and privileges a certain kind of amateur: the youthful, energetic, and imitative kind. This is not the amateur whose filmmaking marked a sphere of activity distinct from Hollywood but one that was decisively related to Hollywood: a fan text, the work of young "textual poachers," to use Henry Jenkins's term. Even the *Jr.* of the title asserts an unthreatening relationship of kin to the Hollywood industry that inspired it and evaluated the contest entries. This evaluation suggests that the jury was more impressed by a film that imitated Hollywood films (as a form of flattery) than one that challenged it. Second place went to the Japanese amateur Tatsuichi Okamoto for *Lullaby,* one of his many award-winning amateur films produced during the decade. Okamoto's films were much admired for their photography and composition: "Many regarded his photography as the finest that had every been put on motion picture film." Third place went to *I'd Be Delighted To!,* which relates a story of a romantic dinner entirely through shots of hands and feet.[66] In *American Cinematographer* the prize-winning films did not receive extensive description or commentary of the sort that appeared for the ACL's Ten Best winners; just a line or two was written about each. Following the contest, the prize-winning films were circulated widely both in North America and beyond. For example, a screening of these films in Kansas City reportedly drew nine hundred spectators.[67] *American Cinematographer* reported on a number of screenings of *Lullaby,* including one in the Bell and Howell exhibit at the Chicago Century of Progress Fair.[68] The films also traveled to Europe, where they were seen in amateur venues in France and the United Kingdom.[69] Evidently, *American Cinematographer* did an effective job in circulating their award-wining films and in doing so became an important part of the amateur nontheatrical distribution circuit (like the ACL's member film library).

American Cinematographer repeated its annual competition throughout most of the decade, advertising the contest in advance, touting the prize winners in the magazine, and duplicating some of the prize-winning pictures for distribution among nontheatrical amateur movie clubs. As a demonstration of the expanding significance of the amateur film contest, *American Cinematographer* reprinted a 1935 *Time* magazine article about the amateur prize winners, with the headline "Amateur Movie Contest Now BIG NEWS."[70] The number, as well as the quality, of entries fluctuated somewhat from year to year, showing a steady increase during the middle of the decade but then some decline toward the end of the 1930s. Many of the winners in the competition were repeat competitors, so evidently some well-known and accomplished amateurs emerged (perhaps even an amateur "star system"). The 1935 contest also included, for the first time, a number of sound accompaniments for the competition films and initiated annual articles by William Stull describing the musical scores for the prize-winning films.[71] By 1936 the publication was touting the contest's global appeal, claiming, "The American Society of Cinematographers' Amateur Movie Makers Contest has become the most famous cinematographic competition in the world. Each year entries arrive from every country on the globe that has earnest devotees of the substandard cine camera."[72] Moreover, the publication claimed a higher standard of filmmaking than any other international competition: "It is generally conceded by the advanced amateur that an honorable mention in the *American Cinematographer* contest is equal to the highest honors in many other competitions," the magazine claimed.[73] These standards were ostensibly upheld by the objective nature of contest's judging, which privileged matters of photographic technique over those of content or originality. But even though the publication touted "more entries than any other contest throughout the world" to support its claim as the "most outstanding movie contest in the world," by the following year (1938) *American Cinematographer* was reporting only sixty entries in the competition.[74]

The winners of *American Cinematographer* contests included both people who were close to the magazine's base of operations in Hollywood and many filmmakers from much farther afield. Several different countries were represented in the contest's first year of submissions, including England, Australia, Japan, Holland, Korea, Catalonia, South Africa, Italy, Belgium, France, and all parts of the United States. "Of the foreign countries," William Stull noted, "Japan had the largest representation, with nearly a dozen entries. Some of them were the finest combinations of perfect technique and sheer cinematic artistry that I have ever viewed."[75] The prize winners were mostly men, but not exclusively; Ruth Stuart of Manchester won a Gold Medal in the travel film category in the 1933 contest and then the top prize in the 1936 contest, for her film *Doomsday*.[76] Stuart's technical skill and editing sense were offered as evidence of her qualifications as a successful filmmaker, but comments in the magazine still framed her abilities as transgressive of an "unwritten law."

The 1938 contest would prove to be the last *American Cinematographer* amateur movie contest until the 1950s. The publication reported that forty-five subjects were submitted to the contest, a decrease from the previous year's sixty, and the winner was James Sherlock's *Nation Builders*, the second top prize in a row for this Australian amateur.[77] In total, twenty-five films received either a prize or honorable mention—more than half of the films submitted!—so we might conclude that the termination of the contest was the result of the decline in submissions. Had the standards for the contest become so high that they discouraged more middling amateurs from participating? There was no *American Cinematographer* Amateur Motion Picture competition in 1939 and no note explaining the discontinuation of the contest. December 1938 was also the last month of a separate "Amateur Movie" section in *American Cinematographer*. Starting in January 1939 amateur articles were mixed in among the rest of the publication's content dealing with professional film matters. Coverage of amateur activities continued to be extensive in *American Cinematographer* for nearly two decades, but the suspension of its annual contest at least symbolically brought to a close the publication's Janus face, with two covers for two distinct groups of readers.

MOVIE CLUBS AND AMATEUR COLLECTIVITY

While many amateurs belonged to international organizations like the Amateur Cinema League or read magazines like *Movie Makers* or *American Cinematographer*, local movie clubs were the primary way that people formed and participated in communities of other filmmakers. Local clubs provided a way for them to come together, view one another's films, and discuss the challenges and pleasures of their hobby. Amateur movie clubs were articulated in a variety of different ways: in some cases they were characterized by locale (a city, a neighborhood, or factory plant); in other cases they were defined by format (the "eights" clubs, which emerged for 8mm filmmakers) or specific attitude toward their work (movie "crafters," for example); some groups were even formed around the age or ethnicity of the participants (high school groups or Jewish amateur film societies).[78] From the outset, organizations like the Amateur Cinema League supported the formation of local clubs for the good of both individual experience and the amateur "movement" at large. However, the ACL left local movie clubs free to determine their own membership policies, so there is no doubt that exclusionary policies and racial segregation appeared among organized amateur moviemakers, as it did in many other aspects of American life during this time.[79] While determining the precise number of amateur movie clubs is difficult, the Amateur Cinema League provided some indications of their rapid expansion in number at the beginning of the 1930s. A 1933 *Movie Makers* article tracks the rise in number of ACL member clubs from 13 in 1927 to 173 in 1930.[80] Reports on amateur movie club activities appeared in the monthly "Amateur Clubs" column of *Movie Makers* and included a range of information about local productions, club governance and meetings, films exhibited, and competitions organized. *American Cinematographer* also presented a regular column called "Amateur Club Activities," which summarized local club meetings and presentations and especially highlighted clubs that were working on films to submit to the magazine's amateur movie contest.[81] From these reports, as well as local movie club newsletters and other ephemeral documents, we can trace some of the most frequent activities and interesting variations of local clubs. (Appendix 2 provides a partial directory of these clubs.)

Reports in *Movie Makers* provided a detailed account of activities in the northeastern United States, where officers of the ACL often appeared as members or speakers. New York's Metropolitan Motion Picture Club was, according to these reports, one of the largest and most significant clubs in the United States. The club's directors included well-known writers and producers of nontheatrical films, such as Raymond Ditmars (producer of nature documentaries), Carl Louis Gregory (author and cinematographer), and Herbert C. McKay (author of several amateur guides and columns).[82] Attendance at MMPC meetings was routinely reported to be in the hundreds.[83] *American Cinematographer*, on the other hand, favored news about movie clubs from Los Angeles and elsewhere in Southern California, as William Stull and the editors Charles VerHalen and George Blaisdell were regular visitors to clubs in these areas. Los Angeles and other Southern California clubs were also often visited by industry experts, such as a professional makeup artist from the Max Factor company and the professional cinematographer Dan Clark, ASC.[84] An active group, the Los Angeles Amateur Cine Club organized "a monthly contest giving prizes for the best 400-ft or less picture submitted to the membership."[85] According to these reports, the attendance at Los Angeles Amateur Cine Club meetings averaged around a hundred people during the mid-1930s.[86] The movie club environment helped advance the skills and high standards that the amateur movement sought to attain. Later in the decade, the Los Angeles Cinema Club promoted the venue as ideal for instruction and discussion that could help advanced amateurs improve their work: "The cinema club affords opportunities for comparison and discussion of each member's results with his associates and can contribute very much to improving the composition of the amateur."[87] According to the author, some amateurs liked to learn theoretically and so enjoyed lectures at club meetings, whereas others preferred to learn experimentally by trying out different technical approaches.[88] Self-criticism was a key element, but individuals benefited from attending club meetings and listening to other members' comments.

The Toronto Amateur Movie Club provides a valuable case study of the formation and activities of a club in a midsized city. Its inaugural meeting was held at the Royal York Hotel on December 12, 1934, and was attended by approximately two hundred people. The organizers "had learned that there were three hundred owners of cine equipment in the City of Toronto and suburbs, and felt that there were great possibilities for an amateur movie club in Toronto."[89] Founded to support local amateur filmmakers and enthusiasts, the club was originally divided into two sections, one section to deal with "cine" (cinematography) or technical issues, the other to produce and screen amateur "photoplays." Award-winning amateur Leslie Thatcher was the first vice president of the club and participated in its activities in a variety of ways, including writing the club's first group film production and organizing demonstrations of film equipment by local dealers. By 1937, when its official membership had reached ninety-one people, the club was leasing its own quarters, which satisfied at least some of the following needs: "a club room available for use at all times—an editing bench—storage facilities for unedited films—titling tables—dark-room—developing tanks and racks—photographic books—bridge table for a quiet game of bridge—social evenings such as dances and movie evenings of some outstanding pictures—office space and editorial offices for which we are sadly in need—and a permanent address."[90]

It is difficult to say how typical this kind of club facility was during the 1930s; there was a great deal of variation across movie clubs, with some contributing to shared space and equipment while others were simply a means of connecting amateurs to one another through meetings and screenings. The Toronto Amateur Movie Club also published a newsletter, *Shots and Angles*, which reveals multiple facets of amateur filmmaking work during this period. The club's activities focused primarily on three subjects: the technical improvement of films, the production and presentation of members' travel films, and the group production of short fictional films. The newsletter could also present philosophical ruminations about amateur filmmaking, such as one article that foregrounded the filmmaker's creative or personal imprint on his films: "It is indeed, one of the strongest lures of our hobby that a man can stamp his personality on his film so definitely and vitally that it is, in effect, a picture of his own mind—his own thoughts—and his own reactions to the place and circumstances he sets out to depict."[91] Evidently, amateur nonfiction filmmaking was not just an act of reproducing the visible world; it also included the possibility of filtering and presenting an interpreted vision of the world.

As new technologies arrived in the form of 8mm film stock, movie clubs were formed to focus on the specific challenges and techniques the new gauge entailed. In 1934, a new Los Angeles club devoted to 8mm film production was organized under the direction of Claude Cadarette and Randolph B. Clardy ("winner of the American Cinematography prize for photography and scenario in the 1933 Amateur contest"). The activities this club engaged in were similar to other ambitious clubs, including "instructive talks and criticisms; exchange of film with other eight millimeter clubs; prize contests every two months and a grand yearly contest; a club production each year."[92] By 1937, the club had grown from fourteen to seventy members, and membership was closed in the interest of maintaining a manageable size.[93] The *American Cinematographer* writer William Stull was an "honorary member" of the club, and he showed his own films there (including a Kodachrome reel about railroads). Clubs such as the Los Angeles 8mm Club point to strong interest in 8mm amateur filmmaking among the public during the 1930s. Even with its membership capped at seventy, attendance at its meetings and film screenings could run into the hundreds, such as a screening of *American Cinematographer* contest winners in 1938, which drew 280 spectators.[94]

Even people who worked at movie studios established their own movie clubs, as was the case with the Paramount Club. This "young and thriving" group was made up of "non-photographic workers in the Paramount Studio."[95] In one sense, this club was the same as the groups organized at factories and other large companies, though the proximity to expertise at the studios made this a somewhat special case.[96] Employees at Columbia Studios also formed an amateur movie club in the late 1930s.[97] This group, Columbia Cub Productions, avoided any conflict with "amateur status" through a strict policy of "assigning no one to do that with which he is familiar—writer may hold reflector by cannot work on script." According to the group's president, it was formed in 1936 and quickly made a first production called *Lucky Piece*; by 1938 the club had organized into units so as to involve all (approximately) fifty members in ongoing production projects.[98] The club's unit system was elaborate and in some ways mimicked the production units of a major studio: three complete and autonomous minor units competed to feed productions into the major, or "A," unit, which made more accomplished films. The club seemed designed to satisfy film studio workers who had an interest in participating in smaller film productions, over which they could feel a greater sense of personal contribution and accomplishment. And even though this appeared to be a highly structured club—with production units and clearly delineated roles—it is perhaps only an accentuated version of the many clubs that tried to accomplish the same things when producing films collectively. Further, it demonstrates that even people who worked in the film industry were able to identify opportunities for creative expression in amateur filmmaking that were not satisfied by contributing (professionally) to major studio productions. From the outside, amateurs might think that working at a major studio would satisfy all of their filmmaking aspirations, but in fact individual creative aspirations (whether professional, artistic, or merely playful) evidently still survived within the studio.

The group film productions that movie clubs organized could take a variety of different forms. Some were fiction films, whereas others documented local events. Similarly, the organization of such productions varied from place to place, with some clubs alternating key creative roles (director, writer, actors) and others devising more collective production methods or inventing new ways of coordinating film productions to accommodate multiple cameras and moviemakers at the same time. Fiction films were often produced by a club subcommittee or spearheaded by a particularly experienced amateur. The production models for these clubs were multiple, drawing on film studio production, community theatre practices, and other kinds of club activities. *American Cinematographer* compared the production capacity of movie clubs with that of film studios, pointing out the particular importance of careful organization. "Organized as many [amateurs] are into clubs," the author notes, "they have a producing power in their field that makes them almost equal to a completed unit in one of the largest studios. Mass activity, many have discovered, is bringing them pictures that would be utterly impossible for the average amateur to procure. Not only subjects that are wide in their scope, but a variation of viewpoints to compare the whole that is startling to many of them in the completed pictures."[99] The Los Angeles Cine Club, for example, made a film of the 1932 Summer Olympics, filming the events from multiple angles and eventually editing some ten thousand feet of exposed film down to a finished work. The Portland Cine Club, on the other hand, planned a film about car touring through Oregon that its members could contribute to over the course of their summer holiday travels.[100] There are many other examples of amateur movie clubs undertaking the filming of local special events. For example, the Chicago Cinema Club coordinated its efforts to film the 1933 Chicago World's Fair.[101] Similarly, 1939 saw the production of several films produced by movie clubs across Canada, chronicling the royal visit. The creation of separate production units could also include different and more diverse kinds of members, including nonfilmmakers with amateur theatre or writing skills: "Is there any reason, then, why every cinematographers' club should not admit writers, actors, artists and carpenters to membership as well as movicam hobbyists?"[102]

Some movie clubs became well known for their production of scenario films. For instance, after the Long Beach (CA) Cinema Club was founded in 1937, it made more than half a dozen scenario films, four of them feature length, in the ensuing four years. The distribution of labor on these club productions went against the grain of a typical production unit that employed specialized roles and only one cameraman. Instead of having "an official Club cinematographer" the club facilitated multiple filmers:

> All of us who want to film the picture may—and our recent productions have been lensed by as many as seventeen 16mm. and 8mm. cameras simultaneously. Needless to say, there's some rivalry between the members as to which of the various versions of each story is best! Since each member is free to choose his own camera-angles, to shoot or to ignore any given scenes, and to edit and title his film as he may choose, the different picturizations of the same story and action show a remarkable range of originality and treatment.[103]

So rather than competing for the prized role of director or cameraman, each of the members could play director and cameraman and then edit their scenarios into different versions of the same one. The club started out with about seventy members but by 1941 had deliberately limited its size to fifty members.

Amateur movie clubs often organized contests and presented thematic programs of films in order to promote film production. Annual film contests were a regular part of most clubs and provided motivation for amateurs to complete and improve their work. Where possible, external judges with expertise in filmmaking made the winning selections, as in a contest organized by the Los Angeles 8mm Club, which was judged by three members of the American Society of Cinematographers.[104] In New York and environs, ACL directors and staff were often part of the contest juries.[105] While local contests could be very straightforward, they were also sometimes subdivided into different categories: novices, experienced filmmakers, story films, family films, and so on. Some clubs organized special contests among women members to encourage more production.[106] While the majority of active filmmakers were men, this was not an exclusively masculine domain, and many women succeeded as filmmakers during this era. Women's participation in amateur clubs included working individually on films, collectively with other members, and—perhaps more often than male members of the club—supporting the social activities of the group. Local club competitions were often coordinated with regional circuits of amateur club exhibition, so that clubs could swap one another's award-winning films for viewing. In some cases this led to regional film contests between rival clubs. The most prestigious awards, however, were those given out by international contests, such as the ACL's annual Ten Best, and the annual contest held by *American Cinematographer*.

Amateur movie clubs also appeared in school settings, especially in the form of high school photoplay clubs. Young people made up a large segment of amateur moviemakers, so it is not surprising that amateur movie clubs' membership could be delineated by age, as well as locale. Often these clubs began as film appreciation clubs but then explored production projects such as school newsreels. This was the way the New Haven High School's club developed. Two years after their initial formation, they were screening their 16mm newsreel of school events, *Hillhouse Highlights*, before students and other guests.[107] These clubs evidence the close links that were understood to exist between the appreciation of film as a new cultural form (which was being explored in a range of different educational settings during the 1930s) and experiments with film production. The organization of high school movie clubs could take different forms, with an ACL veteran moviemaker serving as the club's unofficial technical adviser, as in the case of the New Haven High School group. In other cases, film production was undertaken as part of a more pedagogically considered plan: "It is generally agreed that a high school movie club may function along three lines: (1) assist in the visual education program of the school; (2) develop critical judgment of the varied aspects of theatrical films; (3) provide outlets for the artistic and creative impulse of its members."[108]

During his well-known film education lectures at New York University during the 1930s, Professor Frederick Thrasher encouraged this set of associations. His course—offered to public school teachers for professional development credit—included production experience that would help when establishing these clubs.[109] And while economic austerity might have discouraged such activities during the Depression, amateur magazines publicized ways of organizing film production on the cheap. A 1937 article called "High School Films without Subsidy" outlines how a high school movie club was able to operate without any (or at least much) money; this was achieved through cooperation with a local camera shop, the sale of "shares" to pay for film, and an admission charge for the screening of the completed film.[110]

Amateur cooperative production was also organized along political lines. In Los Angeles, the New Film Group produced a topical reel called *Lives Wasted* in 1936. The film was about "a crippled World War veteran looking backward from the present in review of those events which brought him to his position of poverty and despair."[111] The New Film Group was an affiliate of the New York–based Film and Photo League, which might seem to strain the category of amateur filmmaking; filmmakers associated with the Film and Photo League were more likely to identify themselves as cultural workers than middle-class hobbyists. However, these categories could be quite porous, because amateur moviemakers were explicitly invited to participate in Film and Photo League activities: "The Film and Photo League, a small group organized in New York City, will welcome hearing from substandard movie makers in the metropolitan area interested in working on this type of serious film production."[112] Even though we might identify tensions between the Film and Photo League's avowedly political approach to filmmaking and the Amateur Cinema League's more apolitical stance, both groups seemed to recognize the common terrain they occupied. Amateur movie clubs present a range of interpretations of the pleasures and functions of this kind of group activity: from primarily social activities to effective emulations of professional film units, amateur group film production adopted many guises.

Over the course of the 1930s amateur movie clubs emerged in a variety of different forms and locations. While most movie clubs were new organizations, some expanded upon existing still-photography clubs. For example, the Boston South Shore Camera Club evidently "became so enthused that it decided to establish a movie section of this club and endeavor to make a picture for the 1933 competition."[113] There were also instances when clubs from the same region came together to compound their communities, such as the Amateur Cine Clubs of Southern California, which in 1941 held aggregated meetings of clubs from Los Angeles, Long Beach, Pasadena, Alhambra, Santa Monica, Santa Anna, and others. According to reports, four hundred people attended, and Charles G. Clarke, ASC, was main speaker, on the topic of lighting.[114] Later, similar aggregate meetings of movie clubs would be organized in Chicago and New York. Reaching even further in their broadening of an amateur community was a radio-broadcasted movie club in the 1930s. *Columbia's Camera Club* was the name of a regular Monday radio broadcast in 1939 by Columbia Broadcasting System, from its studio in Hollywood.[115] Though tracing detailed information about this club's activities is difficult, they evidently included discussions about both still and moving photography, attracted some fifty-five hundred virtual members, and expanded the scope of amateur club activities as far as the range of Columbia's airwaves.

Beyond North America, amateur movie clubs proliferated around the world during the 1930s, providing venues for the production and international circulation of both noncommercial films and discourses. News of distant movie clubs was reported in *Movie Makers*, helping to support the ACL's claim to its international relevance, and while studiously ignoring its North American competitors at the Amateur Cinema League, *American*

Cinematographer reported on foreign amateur movie organizations, such as the recently formed Institute of Amateur Cinematography in England in 1933.[116] The growth of pan-European movie contests in the 1930s was also noted; the first of these contests was held in Brussels, in 1931, Holland was in charge of the second contest in 1932, and France would conduct the Third International Contest to be held in Paris in December 1933.[117] One account of international amateurs from the mid-1930s identified activities in Britain, France, and Germany as the most significant, lauding the activities in these countries, especially their contests, clubs, and publications, which evidenced a robust European moviemaking culture.[118] Even farther afield, Australian amateurs were also active during the 1930s, reporting their activities to U.S.-based publications. Often the prize-winning films from local or national competitions appeared as entries in international amateur movie contests based in the United States or the United Kingdom, as with James Sherlock's films, which were frequent winners in the *American Cinematographer* contests.[119] Asian counties also participated in the international production and circulation of amateur movies during the period. Japan was particularly active in amateur movie activities and in 1937 hosted an international movie contest, sponsored by Prince Yamashina of the Japanese imperial family.[120] *American Cinematographer* noted, "It was the considered opinion of the judges that Japanese photography and general camera work are fully up to the best international standards, but that in cutting and editing the films from abroad on the whole were superior."[121] Here, international movie competitions provided an opportunity for comparing both skills and characteristic styles. This contest also suggests at least some form of "camera diplomacy": using amateur movies as a form of cultural exchange and international communication. Amateur movie clubs also appeared in India, as one 1937 report attests of the newly formed Amateur Cine Society of Bombay. The announcement included news about a new competition for Indian amateurs.[122] Such international activities were a frequent part of the "Amateur Clubs" column in *Movie Makers*, appearing alongside club news from much closer to home. Even though the emphasis of major amateur organizations like the ACL or *American Cinematographer*'s column was on North American (primarily U.S.) activities, creating international networks of amateurs was seen as an important part of the culture, echoing Maxim's early utopian call for international "intercommunication." This was a vision of cinema's circulation around the globe that relied less on Hollywood's increasing global hegemony and more on smaller-scale networks among amateurs, clubs, and their larger international organizations.

AMATEUR MOVIE EXHIBITION

In addition to their role as production hubs for films, amateur movie clubs were also significant nontheatrical exhibition venues. The 1930s witnessed a remarkable rise in nontheatrical film exhibition of all kinds and in the public exhibition of amateur films in particular. The principal venue for screening amateur films was local movie clubs, which routinely presented programs of the members' own films, but movie clubs also showed nonamateur works, and amateur works could circulate far beyond their own filmmakers' clubs. Amateur cinema was part of a field of alternative film venues that emerged in the 1920s and '30s. As noted in chapter 1, amateur movie culture had been one of the constituencies interested in the emergence of commercial "little cinemas" in the United States in the late 1920s. In a similar vein, in 1933 two film societies devoted to artistic, foreign, and classic American films emerged in New York. Both the Film Forum and the Film Society featured organizers and participants who were also active in alternative and amateur film culture; both organizations launched ambitious regular screening programs in January 1933 but survived for only a period of months.[123] Throughout this period, amateur film exhibition was a significant aspect of the nontheatrical film field. Typical movie clubs included the presentation of members' films as part of their regular meetings. In some cases, this activity was even mandated, as was the case with the Mount Kisco Cinemats, which had a "long established policy of 'compulsory' presentations of films by each of the members in rotation."[124] This, along with regular contests, was designed both to encourage members to be more productive filmmakers and to facilitate the exchange of advice, salient technical information, and creative suggestions.

Beyond their regular screenings, some movie clubs also organized special presentations of their members' award-winning or topical films. A Chicago club, for example, organized annual special screenings of amateur films related to medicine and dentistry that were produced by its club members. The Fourth Annual Doctors' and Dentists' Night in 1936 drew more than two hundred audience members: "Among the films screened were personally produced clinical pictures by Doctors."[125] Later in the decade, clubs organized movie nights for members and guests, such as the New York 8mm Club's second annual guest night in 1940, which was attended by over 150 people.[126] Magazines like *American Cinematographer* and *Movie Makers* provided extensive reporting on the programs and presentations of movie clubs. One 1939 article about a Minneapolis movie party recounts the successful preparation and presentation of a screening that was eventually attended by more than six hundred people.[127] In Orange,

New Jersey, the amateur club gave a special presentation of award-winning films in its own "little theatre."[128] By billing their presentations as "guest nights" and "movie parties," amateur movie clubs established a new kind of film screening that straddled the lines between private and public film presentations—open to the public but resolutely noncommercial, amateur film exhibition marked a new development in North American film culture.

Inspiration via film presentations could come from elsewhere as well. While the emphasis of amateur movie clubs may have been primarily on the presentation and discussion of their members' films, they also showed films from other clubs and sources. One of the principal external sources of amateur movies during this period was the ACL film library, available to clubs that held membership in the league. As early as 1927 *Amateur Movie Makers* magazine coordinated film exchanges through its SWAPS column. Over the next three years, the organization established a more centralized collection. According to *Movie Makers*, "These films are available to any amateur movie club, entirely without charge or obligation, and the clubs are urged to make use of the service, as the library includes many of the outstanding amateur photoplays and club productions of this country as well as some of the finest work of individual amateurs. A club may have a list of films in the library upon application."[129] Over the years, winners of the ACL's annual Ten Best film competition were added to this library, and it became an important collection of independent and experimental films of the era. Affiliated movie clubs made extensive use of the library, and in this way the Cinema League established an amateur film distribution circuit. In 1933, *Movie Makers* even toured a package of its prize-winning films from the ACL library through the United Kingdom, thus extending this distribution circuit even farther. These films included H_2O, *The Telltale Heart, Wild Rice, I'd Be Delighted To!, The Fall of the House of Usher*, and *Celestial Closeups*.[130] *American Cinematographer* also circulated programs of award-winning films from its annual contests.

Amateur clubs sometimes presented professional films alongside their amateur works, drawing on films available from other sources serving nontheatrical exhibition contexts. Some of these sources advertised in magazines, and *Movie Makers* compiled a regular column titled "Featured Releases," "for the convenience of readers in guiding them to library films, announced in this issue." The range of different companies and offerings was quite broad, though it did not include other major nontheatrical distributors, such as the YMCA.[131] Government films were also shown at some movie clubs, such as a screening of U.S. government documentaries organized by the Long Beach club, including *The River, Power and the*

Land, and *The Plow That Broke the Plains,* with cinematographer Floyd Crosby in attendance, along with an audience of a thousand people.[132] These screenings show the linking and overlapping worlds of amateur and nontheatrical film exhibition; in the aspects of both film content and exhibition context, amateurs were significant participants in and contributors to alternative film culture in the 1930s.

In the early 1930s local movie clubs were the principal venue for viewing amateur films, but some film screenings were also organized outside of official club activities, as amateurs sought out new niches for exhibiting alternative films. New York insurance broker and amateur filmmaker Duncan MacD. Little organized his first movie party for a small group of friends in 1929; he repeated the event annually for over a decade, eventually forging cooperative relationships with institutions such as Columbia University to enhance the screening further. In 1937 the Little show was branded "The Amateur Cinema—Successor to the Snapshot" and was the first program to be selected by jury and held outside the Littles' home, at the Salle des Artistes in New York. The movement from private to public film culture became enhanced further in 1938; after the success of the 1937 show, Columbia University's Division of Film Study offered to sponsor the program as part of its "Motion Picture Parade," and it was presented in April 1938. The program included eight amateur films from as many different countries, in most cases films that were winners of national or international movie contests. The International Amateur Movie Show (as described in the *New York Times*) included films from Japan, Australia, Germany, Canada, Scotland, England, Czechoslovakia, and the United States; Little also presented a separate program of American amateur films. The 1939 event marked yet another expansion of the movie party format, and its attendance swelled to five hundred people. Titled the Tenth Annual Movie Party and International Show of Amateur Motion Pictures, the movie party combined the domestic and international aspects that had been presented separately the year before.

As the collaboration with Columbia and at least the nominal participation of the Museum of Modern Art (jury member Mack Gorham was identified with the MoMA Film Library) suggest, Little's activities in the late 1930s overlapped with other efforts in film education at the time. As Haidee Wasson argues, MoMA had established its film library in 1935 and, through its acquisition, distribution, and exhibition of films, gradually helped to establish a historical cannon of film art and a discursive apparatus for supporting its appreciation.[133] And Dana Polan notes that by the late 1930s both Columbia and NYU (along with other universities) had made significant forays into film study, forays that often involved at least some attention to the activities of amateur cinema.[134] Little understood the rise of his annual movie parties to be a part of this dialogue around film appreciation and study (as well as supporting amateur production). While the place of amateurs in this terrain was by no means clear, it was a goal of Little's movie parties to help articulate it more clearly. Little cites the aesthetic development of film as a particular reason for holding the movie parties: "The cinema is still in a 'growing' state, and the amateur cinema is free to roam where it desires. These Parties of ours can act as a 'testing ground' to see how it is developing and what reaction the 'lay public' has to our efforts."[135] If MoMA's collection focused on tracing the historical trajectory of film art, amateur activities were more concerned with the latest in noncommercial production. But the strong presence of international amateur films in Little's parties also suggests another important role for amateur films, which he articulated in terms of a kind of global fellowship. Like Maxim had before, Little forecasts a time when films would easily cross borders, and people would communicate easily at a distance. So along with claims about its aesthetic significance, amateur cinema was also seen as an important medium for international cultural exchange. Seen in this way, the movie parties were a way of connecting (in a semipublic way) to other people and places while bypassing the depersonalizing effects of mass culture.

The Eleventh Annual International Show of Amateur Motion Pictures in 1940—which appears to have been the last of the Little Movie parties—announced no fewer than six presentations of the program, from its preview and full presentation in New York to a tour of clubs and universities in New England. Little positioned it as a kind of amateur Academy Awards and simultaneously clarified the role that he felt the movie parties played in the film world: "As the scope of these Shows has become enlarged, so also has grown a definite desire that there can be provided a 'recognized screen' upon which can be exhibited the worthwhile results of Amateur Film Producers, whoever and wherever they may be, thus assuring these producers an opportunity that more persons may see their work, than just the home circle and nearby friends, and that this 'recognized screen' may offer those interested the opportunity of seeing the worth-while amateur efforts from near at hand and far away."[136]

Little's comments once again forge a close link between amateur creative works and international fellowship. The effect of the spreading world war on the program was evident: even though the printed program acknowledged the assistance of other international organizations, the program of films was, for the first time in several years, exclusively American made.

There is no evidence of any movie parties after 1940. No doubt the global war—even before America's direct involvement—made them impossible to sustain. The war also challenged two of the more utopian aspirations that proponents of amateur cinema had promoted during the 1930s: its place on the vanguard of film aesthetics and its role in spreading international fellowship. With the onset of war these objectives were for the time being either irrelevant (in the former case) or naïve (in the latter). In wartime, amateur film, like most things, served the war effort, and afterward its domain and objectives were somewhat more modest in scope. During the 1930s, however, Little's annual movie parties mapped a trajectory from private soiree to public presentation and in so doing shed light on amateur cinema's aspiration for a broader artistic and cultural significance.

3 Ciné-Engagement

Amateurs and Current Events

> Personal filmers are so absorbed in the practical phases of their hobby that they would be surprised, not to say embarrassed, if they were told that they are trusted guardians of one of the world's great social values, the right of free, individual self expression. Yet this is entirely true.
>
> **"A Free Art,"** *Movie Makers*[1]

As the opening epigraph suggests, there is something unlikely about linking amateur moviemaking to social values and, by extension, to the current events that challenge such values.[2] Despite this assumption, amateur film culture was responsive to major current events, such as the Great Depression and World War II in specific ways, offering predominantly middle-class, home-front views of these events. These were also events that shaped (and then reshaped) the discourse around amateur moviemaking. This was especially the case for World War II, as an amateur network that had grown increasingly international during the 1930s quickly felt the onset of this global conflict. Even before the United States entered the war in 1941, there was already keen awareness of the conflict, and Canada's earlier "mobilization" of amateurs to support the war effort was quickly followed in the United States once it had entered the conflict. Somewhere between the grandiose claims for the amateur's role as defender of the world's great social values and countervailing assertions that amateurs were a socially disengaged group, we find a middle ground where amateur film culture responded to current events in ways that were complex and contradictory.[3] This chapter traces some of those activities and discourses in order to sketch out amateur film culture's relationship to some of the current events and social crises of the 1930s and '40s.

A geographically and politically diverse group, amateurs held a range of different views on current events. Some amateurs participated in topical and socially committed filmmaking, while others treated their hobby of moviemaking as an escape from current events and political issues—part of a "culture of reassurance."[4] Often the positions identified here are fragmented and piecemeal, if not contradictory. What they seem to have in common, however, is a belief that amateur cinema was a new technology for engaging creatively with the world, whether that world was limited to a domestic sphere or expanded to include social and political realities of the time. Emerging at a time when intellectuals and artists voiced pessimism about American culture and expression, amateur moviemaking provided an alternative to the mass-produced culture of Hollywood and the conformity of other social groupings.[5] Even such hard-boiled realists as H. L. Mencken saw the promise in amateur moviemaking: "Soon or late the movie as an art will have to emancipate itself from the movie as a vast, machinelike, unimaginative, imbecile industry," he declared in 1927.[6] In this respect, amateur moviemaking offered a rare locus of cultural optimism in the face of social and political crises. Amateur filmmaking would repeatedly present opportunities for individual participation and intervention in social problems of the era, whether in the forms of documentation, advocacy, or creative diversion. Amateur discourse presented the hobby as simultaneously individual and socially significant. It was a modern means of communicating about and participating in many of the social contexts of the period. The task of this study is to examine in a nuanced way the different relationships to current events and popular culture that amateurs and amateur discourse created in order to illuminate the range of functions and desires amateur moviemaking satisfied (or promised to satisfy). During the 1930s, we can identify both deliberate engagement and explicit reluctance to engage with current events in amateur discourse. In particular, I examine the ways that amateur culture addressed the social and economic crisis of the Great Depression, and later the political conflicts that led up to World War II.

AMATEURS AND THE GREAT DEPRESSION

Amateur cinema was a hobby that required considerable financial resources for the purchase of film, cameras, and other equipment. But even under the catastrophic financial conditions of the 1930s, the ranks of amateur filmmakers swelled, responding both to the novelty and appeal of the hobby and to the amateur film industry's ability to adapt to the difficult times with cost-saving developments, such as the introduction of 8mm film in 1932. In the same year, the Amateur Cinema League announced its relative financial stability, noting an increase in advertising revenue, magazine sales, and new ACL members.[7] Here an acknowledgment of the tough financial conditions of the Depression coincided with the rising popularity of the organization and of amateur moviemaking more generally. Nevertheless, discussions about social circumstances appeared with some regularity in amateur discourse. Most specifically, this took the form of advice for planning a social welfare film in 1932: "The film is one of the best mediums possible in which to present social problems, to publicize relief plans or to ask for definite support for specific welfare programs."[8] In contexts where commissioning a professional film was not viable, amateur film production here provided an alternative. More typical commentaries included suggestions for how amateurs could make the most of their reduced means during the period. Magazine columnists noted that the Depression called for cutting back on holidays but that filming one's only vacation of the year could help extend its value.[9] In a similar vein, writers advised staying closer to home for the holidays; rather than focusing on travel footage, this strategy resulted in images from closer to home: "An antidote for the 'depression blues' ... 'Get a movie camera and discover your own back yard.'"[10] The presumption that readers would still have jobs and holidays suggests a certain kind of readership, but the implication that nobody was unscathed by the Depression is significant.

Throughout the Depression but especially during its depths in 1932–33, *Movie Makers* used its monthly editorial column as a venue for commenting on the state of current economic and social conditions. Often these commentaries framed amateur moviemaking as a "sane" or even a socially responsible leisure activity. In one editorial, printed in October 1932, the anonymous author pointed to the signal importance of leisure activities in determining social attitudes: "Our social attitudes come from our recreations and our deliberately selected activities when we are not bread winners," the author claims.[11] In contrast to the excessive pleasures and luxuries of the 1920s, amateur movies presented a somewhat "saner pleasure," a pleasure that also has significant social functions: "Here is an employment for free time that has none of the connotations of Babylon and none of the vulgar expenditures for showy luxury that have obscured real recreational values since the World War." The author sees a broadening of the activity of amateur filmmaking that comes as a result of the inexpensive equipment made available, which demonstrates that filmmaking is not a leisure activity for conspicuous consumption. "Wealth," the author notes, "cannot make better movies than modest competence and, by now, the earlier restriction of movie making to moneyed amateurs has been removed. The field is now open to almost everybody that has a job—and more people are going to have jobs." The editorial marks amateur moviemaking as an increasingly democratic activity, which by 1932 was available to anyone with a job (because of the introduction of 8mm film). Moreover, inasmuch as the cinema had technological and creative qualities, it shared similar qualities with the "temper" of the age, which was creative and mechanical.

The following month, the political tenor of amateur discourse was presented even more explicitly in an editorial about the 1932 American election. Noting that although the editorial didn't concern filmmaking, it was addressed to filmers "because movie makers are members of an exceedingly important and vital group in the world of today, the group of responsible and conservative men and women upon whose judgment, probity and decision rests the solution of the world's problems."[12] The editorial proceeded with a discussion about the consequences of the upcoming American election, which was being watched around the world, seemingly promising "answers to the hopes" of many, although pointing in the "direction of untried experiments" for others. Rather than aligning specifically with either of these positions, the author urges a "responsible" response to the election. Regardless of who would win, the partisanship of the election must dissipate so that government could address the important problems; amateur moviemakers were part of this responsible group able to transcend the emotions of the election. Further, a new "duty" for the amateur moviemaker was proposed: "the difficult task of persuading the apathetic, when they are aroused, to look at governmental matters broadly and fairly and not narrowly and selfishly." The task here was to make a productive contribution to civic life; amateur moviemakers were not an apolitical group: they were citizens with a responsibility to their respective societies. The political position urged was a conservative and pragmatic one that encouraged engagement with political issues but not emotional or partisan agitation: "Responsible Americans will see to it that the United States neither sinks into an obstinate Bourbonism nor swings off at any wild or radical tangent."[13] According to this, moviemakers had an important social duty to direct others toward social responsibility and away from radical movements or purely emotional causes.[14]

The year 1933 brought new optimism both for the social and financial health of the country and for the hobby of amateur filmmaking more specifically. Part of this bright outlook stemmed from promising employment figures and a reduction in the costs of film equipment.[15] However, the Depression and its attendant social ills continued to be commented on in the coming months. An editorial on the effects of the Depression identified optimistic signs, such as the prospect of more Americans returning to work.[16] With the prospect of greater employment came hopes for the circumstances necessary to pursue amateur filmmaking—not just economic circumstances, but emotional ones as well: "The release from tragic fear and continual worry that will come with mounting employment will liberate the recreational urge of the whole world and we shall have a playtime, a season of merrymaking that we have not known for nearly half a decade." Amateur movie discourse foregrounded the necessarily playful nature of filmmaking but also positioned it as a socially valuable activity, when framed in a measured way: "Now, if ever, is the time for the advancement of sane recreation, among which movie making stands very high. Before 1929, amateur movies were adopted by rapidly increasing thousands and the depression has not melted those thousands to a dangerous degree."[17] Amateurs were called on to "serve as missionaries for a kind of leisure time occupation that is not only in itself entrancing but, as well, socially defensible and desirable." The language of public service was employed by amateur discourse, positioning moviemaking as a sensible amusement, not one that was wild or destructive: "Let all of us who know how movie making enriches and stabilizes living take care that we pass the gospel on."

During the mid-1930s, political issues began to eclipse the primarily financial problems of the Depression, at least in amateur publications. During this period, amateur discourse voiced concerns about "repression" and "regimentation" in a pragmatic fashion that resisted dogmatic affiliation or clear party lines. A 1934 editorial noted, "Not the least happy feature of personal movie making is found in the fact of its being an expressive and not a repressive occupation."[18] This opposition between expressive and repressive became a political (not just a creative) way of understanding amateur film discourse. The editorial observed the amateur filmmaker's relationship to more dogmatic positions as one of respite and resistance: "It is a relief to turn from the harsh, negative and forbidding picture of experiments in social regimentation to a field of human activity in which there is either expression or nothing. It is literally impossible to employ cinematography as an agent of repression, because the very nature of sensitized film requires that it shall first be aware, then record and, lastly, reproduce the scenes to which it is exposed." Here, the editorial's plea for free expression foreshadows a plea for free speech, which would not be extended to movies in the United States until after World War II. But the censorship of content was less egregious here than the regimentation of social order or thought, perhaps voicing resistance to certain New Deal policies. Amateurs were, according to the ACL, resistant to these forces because of their individual and pragmatic relationship to filmmaking: "Filming is the most democratic method of expression, because it does not require long training to acquire reasonable proficiency and is, therefore, admirably suited to the busy man who is not a trained writer, public speaker or artist. It is everybody's hobby." A subsequent concern with free expression appeared several months later in an editorial responding to the newly enacted Hollywood production code. The author criticized Hollywood for giving up free speech and praised amateur movies as the last space for such personal liberty in motion pictures. But aside from their freedom from commercial requirements and codes, the amateurs' advantage was "their right to say whatever they may wish to say on film, without the obligation to say it to advance a particular social or political idea. . . . They need neither be socially constructive, to please those who would remodel the existing state of things, nor seek that adroit blend of the commonplace and the spicy which has been so dependably certain a prescription for below the average Hollywood productions."[19] The resistance to regimentation returned in 1937 when the ACL president's editorial noted, "We want no regimentation of thought or of action," demanding again the flexibility of amateur cinema.[20]

A more neutral relationship to domestic politics was suggested by articles that proposed elections as promising subjects for filmmaking. One such article included a sample continuity script for an election film: "We are in the midst of an exciting presidential campaign, a unique and colorful national entertainment presented each four years for our amusement and edification."[21] Some filmmakers appear to have followed this advice: Joseph P. Hollywood's 1941 film *Democracy* offered a "Republican's-eye view" of the previous year's election.[22] The *American Cinematographer* reviewer of this film asks "why more amateurs don't try using their cameras as a means of expressing their views on public questions." He suggests that amateur films are a forceful means of expressing even abstract ideas. In the late 1930s amateur discourse often blended the "practical" or educational element of filmmaking with social content. This was the case with a film about sharecroppers produced by Alan S. Hacker in 1937: "Made to aid the Southern Tenant Farmers' Union, the production illustrates the agricultural despotism and destitution which have resulted in the formation of that group bargaining organization."[23] The goal of this film was to promote the organization of the Farmers' Union, indicating again a range of political positions occupied by amateur filmmakers.

Even as current events left an indelible mark on amateur discourse and activities, an impulse among amateurs to hold off the influence of current events from the hobby was also evident. One 1937 editorial remarked, "We are, as Virgil says, 'multa jactata'—greatly thrown about the by waves of circumstance. We hunt for familiar things in the kaleidoscope of our days. The machinery of civilization is so much about us that only with real effort can we turn to the ancient comfort of the seasons."²⁴ To this author it was only in nature and changing seasons that the amateur filmmaker could find shifts that escaped the social, political, and financial crises that had shaken recent years. "In spring a man is an artist, whether his expression is formal or purely personal," the anonymous author writes. Withdrawing from a social and political sphere, the amateur could also explore a world that was more personal or aesthetic.

AMATEURS AND WORLD WAR II

World War II would radically change the tenor of the amateur film movement of the 1930s, recasting the amateur's role in society and transforming the way 16mm film was used and understood. The amateur cinema world's response to the political and military tensions that led to World War II ranged from muted to explicit. Unambiguous anti-war filmmaking was not a common feature of amateur culture during the 1930s, but the New Film Group's *Lives Wasted* provides a significant example, as was discussed in chapter 2.²⁵ Reports of *Lives Wasted* appeared in both *Movie Makers* and *American Cinematographer*, and the film was shown at amateur movie clubs, among other venues. In a similar vein, Garrison Films, affiliated with the Photo League, advertised films for purchase or exhibition in *Movie Makers*, such as "*Dealers in Death*, a story of munitions."²⁶ More consistent across amateur discourse than these openly political works, however, was an assertion of the amateur's role as promoter of "international understanding" among different nations and peoples. Over the course of the 1930s, international exchange had become one of the pillars of amateur discourse. This was understood in terms of Maxim's initial prediction of intercommunication between peoples and countries facilitated by the exchange of amateur films among nations or of the depiction of different nations and peoples that were brought home via travel films. This international exchange via cinema was also encouraged through the major annual film contests held by the ACL and *American Cinematographer* during the 1930s, as well as special screenings like Duncan Little's movie parties, which encouraged the presentation of films from Europe, Asia, and elsewhere. The philosophy that accompanied this international understanding was typically anti-war, though as the discussion of the Great Depression suggests, the pragmatic orientation of amateur publications tended to avoid explicit political alignments. As World War II began, many of these pacifist and internationalist attitudes were displaced by support for the war effort and troops. The international orientation of amateur filmmaking returned somewhat after the war but never with the same utopian outlook that had been present during the 1930s.

As war seemed to be looming late in the decade, commentaries about the amateur filmmaker's relationship to it became more direct and explicit. The most pacifist of these was an editorial by the ACL managing director Roy Winton, penned in November 1938 and called "Can We Hate?" Himself a veteran of World War I, Winton responded with horror to the prospect of a new conflict in Europe: "Movie amateurs are civilized beings, and to them there is something supremely horrible in the concept of the world as a battleground.... That men, and the achievements of men, should be blasted into fragments offends and revolts their deepest convictions."[27] Winton anchored his beliefs in the principles of the ACL's founder, Hiram Percy Maxim, who "believed that personal movies would increase the capacity of men and nations to live together as rational beings and not savages. He held that whoever sees often, and in varied presentments, the ways of other lands will protest the attempts of politicians and saber rattling adventurers to regiment human beings into organized slaughter." This offers a clear articulation of the argument for amateur movies as a medium for promoting international understanding. Their effect on viewers was seen as that of elevating understanding and relations to a rational level and effecting the average people of different countries—not the elites or leaders—to resist calls for conflict between nations.

Winton extended the responsibility of amateurs even beyond this spread of international understanding, arguing that come war or peace, amateurs had an obligation to circulate images from abroad. This was not to be accomplished via propaganda—"because there again is regimentation"— but "by bringing back our individual reports from other lands we may visit, so that our friends may, because of our films, know a little more about what lies outside their own neighborhoods." In the case of war, this role was even more crucial, as the presentation of films from warring nations could remind viewers of the humanity of participants:

> We can constantly remind our audiences that, whatever may be the right or wrong of political situations, behind them all lies the simple and stupendous fact of humanity, of men and women who are as decent as we are, and as foolish as we are, badly or admirably led, following great or cheap ideals, just as we are led and follow. We can show these men and women and their works and daily lives, knowing that they will convey a message utterly at variance with the actions of the military machines of the countries where they live. This special task has great importance, because it is these men and women, living normal and peaceful lives, whose normal and peaceful outlook will eventually prevail in all conflicts.

Winton's argument provides a crystallization of amateur political pragmatism, opposing the regimentation of propaganda and instead providing images of everyday life. He recognizes the varied ways and arguments—both good and bad—that might propel nations into war but argues that the amateur's role is to provide an antidote to militaristic and one-dimensional thinking. It is a deeply humanist and pacifist argument that shows tremendous faith in the pathos evoked by images of daily life. "So, come peace, come war," Winton concludes, "let us not forget that we movie makers are special messengers of civilization, because we report the every day facts of one part of the world to another.... Our scenes may be lacking in excitement, but they bring the comfort of the commonplace, and the commonplace, in the long run, is the way of the angels." Winton, one of the most thoughtful articulators of amateur philosophy in the 1930s, staked the terrain of the commonplace as that of the amateurs. This resonated with ideas of the middleness of amateur moviemaking: primarily middle-class producers of images that are located between high art aspirations and low culture. Films of commonplace life—whether domestic situations or images chronicling life during travels—were concerned with the everydayness of experience, which, for Winton, made amateur cinema a medium of peaceful expression.

While Winton's editorial directly addressed the coming of war, other voices in amateur groups were more circumspect. In his 1938 annual editorial, the ACL president Stephen Voorhees articulated the strengths (and implicit limitations) of the ACL when he described the organization as "first of all, an educational institution. Whatever may be the purpose of our films, the League's concern with them is almost entirely one of methods."[28] By dismissing the content of films in favor of an interest in technique or method, Voorhees disavowed any particular role for amateur moviemakers in war or peace. Noting the variation around the world in different kinds of human dignity and freedoms, another author framed amateur moviemakers as defenders of these, though not necessarily in explicitly political terms: "There will very likely be no direct political discussion in amateur movies, but the things down underneath will be restated insistently. The family will be shown more vividly, the world of decent men will be recorded more impressively and the familiar commonplaces, that have gained a new importance in these troubled times, will be set forth as the great commonplaces of which civilization is built."[29] In presenting and circulating familiar commonplaces during a time of political turmoil, these images were understood to have a political valence, even if no political argument was explicitly stated in them. Here is a plea for a free society, one that is not bound up in militaristic or patriotic fervor.

Similar comments from amateur publications appeared in the following months, reinforcing the amateur's art of the commonplace. They often noted the generally peaceful quality of amateur movies, sometimes acting as a respite from current events. In some cases, amateurs were urged to record images of their favorite places now, during peacetime: "What has happened in Spain and in China is not impossible anywhere. There is no guarantee that the incredible insanity of war may not break out in any part of the world."[30] While not intentionally alarmist, the author notes, "If a few madmen in high places can make this globe over, as far is its civilization is concerned—and this seems possible, in spite of all that the mass of us can do to prevent it—these films will comfort us. They may even encourage us to rebuild what is left, according to an order and a more decent scheme of things." In this, amateurs could achieve a set of images different from commercial films providing an archive of the everyday: "The everyday things that, in the long run, are the important things; the emphasis on what is commonplace, as opposed to what is startling and sensational; the insistence that what the average man does is more vital that what a maniac on horseback may undo; let these be the subjects of some of our summer footage. We can make no greater contribution to the safety of an imperiled civilization."[31] In these prewar discussions, the role of the amateur was repeatedly aligned with pacifism and the common thread of everyday activities that were being threatened by mounting militarism.

However, amateur film discourse was rarely one-dimensional or dogmatic, and participants had a range of different ideas about how moviemaking intervened in political life and activities. Filmmakers who were settled in politically volatile locations sometimes avoided political topics altogether. Fred C. Ells, who won several prominent amateur contests over the course of the decade, reported in 1936 from Japan, where he lived and worked for an American company. In his long experience of work and travel overseas, Ells noted, he had always assiduously avoided film subjects that might be seen as politically volatile.[32] For Ells, political subjects were not desirable for filming, because they might ruin his professional life and spoil his hobby. Filmmaking could remain an apolitical activity: "In my own case, making a motion picture is a form of escape from the unchanging routine of the office, to a world where I can dream and create, make all my own decisions, work hard or procrastinate at my own sweet will." Later, after the beginning of World War II, Ells recounted his trials with Japanese censorship in the lead-up to hostilities between Japan and the United States.[33]

With the arrival of war in Europe came a restatement of the peaceful role of moviemaking as "one of the major influences for friendly international relations, because this activity enables one part of the world to see another part intimately."[34] ACL president Voorhees struck a similar note in his annual December letter. "We have only to keep a firm will not to let the friendly world of the home movie screen suffer a blackout. It is our task and our privilege to keep the channels open, so that friendship and understanding may have a path through time and so that this generation may look forward to tranquility for its children."[35] American amateur publications did indeed make an effort to keep channels of communication open with amateurs in countries that were already at war. One issue carried news of a Dutch filmmaker's offer to assist ACL members visiting Utrecht but then noted the Nazi invasion of Holland.[36] From Finland came a similar story in the form of a letter from a Finnish ACL member:

> I greatly regret to tell you that I cannot send my membership fee any more, because of the difficulty with exchange. This difficulty will last until the war ends. As you know, of course, the Russian bandit army attacked our dear, beautiful country, destroying our homes and making it quite impossible to continue to work regularly and to earn the bread for our families to eat. Things have fallen out badly with me. My home is damaged and my wife's health is broken. My work has been suspended. I had reserved the necessary funds to keep up my League membership and to buy a new camera, but now the possibility of doing this is past. . . . I thank you for the help I have got as a League member. I send my best regards. Some day, when this is all over (if I am still alive) I shall write again and, hopefully, pay my membership fee.[37]

This letter juxtaposes the hobby of filmmaking to the realities of war in especially stark ways. Though Americans were not yet part of the world war, these letters made them witnesses to the direct effect of war on their European contemporaries. American amateurs were already seeing their international network being dismantled and their dreams for international understanding with it.

From some corners came the hope that the war would be short-lived and pose only a brief interruption to film activities. The editor of *American Cinematographer* noted the wide range of publications that were still in operation, even in early 1941: "England, Germany, Australia, Holland, Switzerland, Japan, India and Sweden—all send one or more photographic and cinematographic publications, both professional and amateur, across this desk. The world may be at its neighbor's throats, but picture-making must go on!"[38] Particularly encouraging for the author was the lack of prowar and partisan propaganda in these magazines, which he took as a sign that amateur moviemaking would, after the war, "play a vital part in restoring the spirit of universal understanding and fellowship upon which, once peace is restored, we must all strive to build a new and happier world." This article suggests the sustained fantasy that the war would be just a brief interruption in normal activities—that even in warring countries, amateurs continued to pursue their hobbies, magazines continued to be published. But not all signs of international amateur culture were so neutral. In late 1941 *American Cinematographer* protested the evident partisanship of the European organization UNICA and its annual amateur contest.[39] According to the report, leaders of the UNICA 9th International Contest were German and Italian political figures, propagandists, and fascist youth group leaders: "To one accustomed to considering that amateur cinematography, like amateur hobbies and sports generally should be something free, wholly apart from political or governmental domination, such a statement as that seems revolting in the extreme." The United States, not yet in the war, sustained an idea of international understanding that characterized the moviemaking hobby through the 1920s and '30s. After the war, this would be less of a focus, as amateur moviemaking became more domestic (in both political and familial terms) and less interested in this kind of internationalist rhetoric: less utopian and more sincere.

On the eve of America's entry into the war, popularity for amateur filmmaking in the United States was extensive.[40] *Movie Makers* readers inquired about ways of supporting American national defense as early as 1940 and were advised to make films about their own country and their routine pleasures.[41] Movies about everyday life were recast as patriotic, because they presented images of what American military defenses should be reserved for. Editorials in *Movie Makers* continued to frame amateur filmmaking as a vehicle for peace: "To movie makers, those who take up the sword of conquest are barbarians and savages, no matter how much the invaders try to justify their actions. These savages deny the peaceful values that filmers and other artists believe to be the flowers of civilization and not the weeds of decadence, as the barbarians assert."[42] While American amateur production of wartime films was yet to come, various templates for moviemakers' participation in the war effort were provided by activities in other countries, long before December 1941. From Britain came reports of regular movie club meetings "carrying on" and producing amateur defense and instructional films on topics such air raid precautions and aircraft spotting.[43] Amateurs also remained active in Canada, producing films such as a melodrama called *Confusions of a Nazi Spy*, by the Movie Makers Club of Ottawa.[44] In Toronto, the war "[failed] to diminish the activities of the veteran Toronto Amateur Movie Club."[45] Defense filmmaking was already underway in the United States during 1941, as the commercial industry produced training and recruiting films for the army.⁴⁶ For amateurs, activities in the United States remained limited initially; in June 1941 one group reported using amateur cinematography as a way of conveying hometown news to troops in camps via amateur movies.⁴⁷ For some, comedy was the best approach, as in the amateur film *Mr. Hitler Never Loses*, a satirical documentary by Joseph P. Hollywood about the German invasion of Poland.⁴⁸ In a similarly lighthearted vein, some American soldiers waiting to be deployed made their own amateur films, such as *Our Hero*, a comedy filmed by members of the Naval Reserve Aviation Squadron.⁴⁹

With the American entry into the war, Hollywood's important role was immediately made apparent, especially in the Hollywood-based *American Cinematographer*, which followed the industry's wartime activities closely.⁵⁰ Less evident was the value of amateur and nontheatrical film. *Movie Makers* soon articulated the important role that amateurs could play in the war effort, spelling out the useful categories of amateur filmmaking explicitly: (1) civilian defense: to make or project training films; (2) American Red Cross: to make or show training films; and (3) United Service Organizations: to show films (amateur or rented) at USO clubs. In all three cases, amateurs were encouraged to volunteer their services individually or as a movie club unit; to help facilitate amateur production activity, *Movie Makers* included a volunteer form in their January 1942 issue.⁵¹ *American Cinematographer* was also quick to respond to readers' requests as to how to support the war effort and made its library of award-winning amateur films available for USO screenings.⁵² As amateurs rushed to produce films that would be helpful for the war effort, they had to be careful not to run afoul of new filming restrictions. According to one report, soon after the declaration of war, "two unsuspecting movie makers in Chicago were arrested by the city's police for taking pictures of a cloud of smoke billowing from a factory chimney."⁵³ Because the factory was a steel mill working on war orders, the incident provided a pretext for announcing prohibitions on filming military installations and bases; federal government buildings; railroad stations; public utilities; airports; docks, bridges, waterfront installations; and industrial plants working on war orders.⁵⁴ Conversely, amateurs were also called on by the government to provide information about any footage they had recently filmed outside the country: "If you have filmed or photographed OUTSIDE THE UNITED STATES, you are requested to answer the questionnaire on the opposite page, as a patriotic duty.... Report all photographs and transparencies, whatever their size. Quality is unimportant; subject matter is paramount" (figure 6).⁵⁵ Here, amateur movies filmed for personal interest became a potential source of valuable

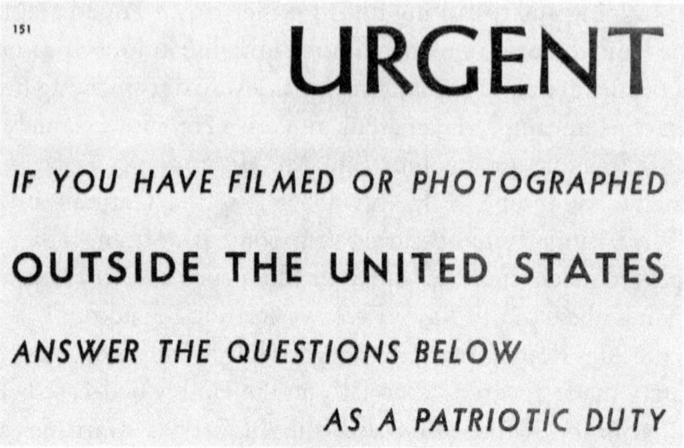

> **URGENT**
>
> *IF YOU HAVE FILMED OR PHOTOGRAPHED*
>
> **OUTSIDE THE UNITED STATES**
>
> *ANSWER THE QUESTIONS BELOW*
>
> *AS A PATRIOTIC DUTY*

Figure 6. Amateurs were called on to provide information about recent filming abroad. *Movie Makers,* April 1942, 151. Courtesy Media History Digital Library.

information for the war effort: images of foreign cities and towns that could be of strategic value to the American military as it went to war.

Amateurs quickly learned how to make films that supported home-front needs while also staying out of the way of the authorities and filming restrictions. California's Long Beach Cinema Club was particularly active in producing civil defense films. To be useful for these purposes, amateur films needed to be factual and authentic, as well as technically accomplished. "If you can't do a good job," one amateur noted, "don't attempt it; step aside and leave the field clear for somebody who can. Don't give America's really capable amateur filmers a black eye."[56] The Long Beach club's first civil defense film was funded by local businesses, and *American Cinematographer* published tips for defense productions, as well as a "bulletin board" to facilitate the circulation of equipment.[57] *Movie Makers* also articulated an amateur "call to service" in articles encouraging the production of Red Cross films. Roy Winton wrote, "Every Red Cross chapter has a story to tell. It will differ from the story that is told in a town in the next county.... The very fact that one place will meet standards differently from the way in which its neighbor meets them is one of the things that distinguishes American communities from the regimented populations of our enemies."[58] The magazine provided a template treatment for Red Cross films, which included intertitles, and the film's order of sequence, even down to shot transitions. Just as Red Cross organizations presented local variations on centrally established standards, amateurs were encouraged to make their own variation on a standardized film template.

The demand for amateur Red Cross films was also felt in Canada, where the Ottawa Cine Club produced a film called *The Tie That Binds* (1942). The film presents just the kind of home-front attempt to make a contribution to the war effort promoted by Winton. In the film, a young woman receives a letter about her brother's arrival in army, which prompts her to ask: "What can I do to help in this war?" The film's answer is to give blood, and it proceeds to show the process of the young woman and her father giving blood at the local Red Cross clinic. The entire procedure is shown, including medical examinations and long sequences in the clinic that explain all the parts of the process. Eventually, this vivid color film shows the actor actually giving blood. To provide drama, the film shows an alternation between shots of the woman at church and her injured brother resting in a hospital after Dieppe; it soon reveals that he is being treated with blood transfusions, and we can see that he will soon recover. The film ends with a sequence of shots showing the soldier walking down a snowy Ottawa street with a cane, returning home. When he sees from a sign in the window that the woman there gave blood, he is touched by her lifesaving contribution. This silent film is thirty minutes long and blends elements of fictional or dramatized scenes with process sequences at the Ottawa Blood Donor Service. Shot in 16mm color film, it is both a vivid and professional-looking production; indeed, it exemplifies both elements of the practical amateur genre (creative engagement with practical issues) and the wartime necessity of the moment. Of course, the film's silence is typical of the amateur practical film; even by the early 1940s, amateurs rarely had affordable and reliable sound equipment. This film was probably projected with a combination of recorded music and live, spoken commentary.

On the civilian front, the Amateur Cinema League continued to hold its annual Ten Best contests in 1942, noting that movies made for Red Cross or civil defense were eligible for the contest, because they were made without compensation.[59] In his annual letter to members, ACL president Voorhees praised amateurs for their contribution: "Movie makers have served. They have helped to locate films and pictures for the Office of Strategic Services; they have made movies of civilian defense activities and records of Red Cross chapters; they have shown training films in their communities, as volunteer projectionists. They have done much and they can, and will, do more."[60] These production activities continued throughout the war. Later, in 1944, *American Cinematographer* suggested a slightly different approach to the amateur's contribution to war efforts, proposing that clubs make films that are "a picture of life in your home town" to send overseas to servicemen.[61] At least one club appears to have followed this advice; for instance, the Syracuse Movie Makers was congratulated for taking pictures of the families of men serving in England and sending the films overseas.[62] In this way amateur movies adapted their domestic function and communicated images of family and home to soldiers far away. This function also showed a shift in the perceived value of amateur films over the course of the war, from an earlier local mobilization role to this later communication of personal images and message. No doubt this was an indication of the effect the war's duration had on family and local life; amateur movies could provide a visual complement to letters, newspapers, and other ways of communicating with distant loved ones.

Amateurs also supported the war effort via film exhibition, not just production. Early "practice blackouts" held in December 1941 resulted in many canceled movie club meetings, but news from England, about the "shelter shows" held there, provided encouragement and, again, models for North American club activities: "In England, 'Shelter Shows' of 16mm. movies are being held in air-raid shelters beneath railway arches, and in basements under city stores. Both professional and amateur films are being used."[63] American amateurs organized film screenings in a variety of different contexts, most commonly in order to raise money for the USO or other patriotic causes: "Many of our own clubs, especially the older and more established ones, have in their libraries and the libraries of their members an invaluable collection of outstanding amateur-made films which the public might well be glad to pay to see."[64] Amateurs provided films and projection equipment for shows at nearby army camps, which were particularly interested in showing 16mm films about foreign countries for visual education programs.[65] By the middle of the war, *American Cinematographer* was reporting an increase in this kind of film exhibition:

> An increasing number of amateur movie clubs all over the country are putting on movie shows for service-men—sometimes in big camps and metropolitan USO Centers, and sometimes individually, to small, isolated groups like barrage-balloon, searchlight and anti-aircraft gun squads whose duty prevents leaving their posts except at long intervals, and which are too small to be reached by the regularly organized entertainment services. These patriotic movie-makers are performing this very necessary service on their own time, using their own projectors, gas, tires and films—the latter they have often purchased with their own money.[66]

As the war created restrictions on materials and travel, some amateurs proposed forming a national association of movie clubs to coordinate clubs, film exchange, and defense filming activities, as well as annual conventions and other social gatherings after the war was over.⁶⁷ *American Cinematographer* assisted by offering to list films available for exchange among clubs and by promoting the idea of creating a national amateur film exchange in order to pool equipment and talent for making civil defense films and for the actual exchange of films.⁶⁸

While some clubs considered ceasing their activities during the war, amateur publications encouraged them to stay active. Of course many members of amateur movie clubs went to serve in the war, and *American Cinematographer* suggested that amateurs in military service should have club dues waived during the war.⁶⁹ *American Cinematographer* was one of the publications that encouraged clubs to stay as active as possible:

> With gasoline rationing coming on in previously unrationed parts of the country, and rationing or restrictions on film, lamps and other moviemaking necessities, we've heard that some clubs are considering disbanding "for duration." As we see it, there's no need for that. Of course filming opportunities are going to be restricted by wartime curtailments—but there will be no restrictions on a Club's opportunities for service and fellowship. Indeed, the amateur movie-maker has a priceless opportunity to serve his country and his community today, and he can emerge from this war a more useful citizen than he has bothered to be before.... [Every] club, anywhere, will find opportunities—constructive projects to keep their members together and active in a useful way—if they'll only look for them!⁷⁰

It is difficult to judge how many movie clubs suspended their activities during the war. But certainly publications like *Movie Makers* and *American Cinematographer* continued carrying news and providing support for movie clubs throughout the war.⁷¹ They facilitated film exchanges between clubs and also circulated prize-winning films from their own individual annual contests.⁷² Wartime travel restrictions meant less social contact among amateur clubs, but the Indianapolis Movie Club responded to this situation by making a movie to introduce itself to other clubs and included this along with films listed as part of the *American Cinematographer*'s club film exchange program.⁷³ As a result of the various restrictions and the lower membership during the war, some amateur movie clubs had difficulty staying in operation. In one case the St. Louis club worked to solve its financial problems, which resulted from low membership dues, by giving a public show with old-time atmosphere and charging admission. Half of the program was made up of old films, half was new amateur works; the event was accompanied by a piano player and presented with period costumes.⁷⁴ These wartime activities evidence the amateur's effort to be involved in supporting troop and home-front activities. Through this hobby they also no doubt hoped to provide temporary respite from the horrific current events of the day.

POSTWAR RECOVERY

The end of the war brought with it significant shifts in the professionalization of the 16mm film format, as well as a broadened appreciation of nontheatrical film more generally. In certain respects this represented a move away from amateur spheres of activities as both government and film industry recognized the important role 16mm film had played during the war. But amateur movie clubs had been—and for a time continued to be—instrumental in shifting the way people understood noncommercial cinema. What was distinct about an amateur attitude was the broad accessibility of participation, especially since 8mm film had been introduced. One commentator noted in 1945 that in the past fifteen years movie clubs had moved from merely social clubs to educational venues, with talks on specialized topics, and now included members from all walks of life: "from the gas station operators to aircraft executives meeting on common ground to discuss their filming results."[75] Here was a model for noncommercial film that was integrated with the everyday lives of its participants, as opposed to the separation that professional moviemaking created between filmers and their subjects.

Closely following the end of the war came the Amateur Cinema League's twentieth anniversary and with it an occasion for looking back over the previous two decades. While the ACL's mandate had focused on the production of films as a leisure activity, Roy Winton's long recollection included some reflections on the organization's relationship to current events. This relationship was, once again, considered in light of the contrast between dogmatic and pragmatic attitudes: "Many times in the past twenty years, when something has been proposed by zealous but remorseless idealists, we at headquarters have had to reject the project because it would not, as far as we could see, bring about any increase of pleasure. Since our constitution was so definite about the pursuit of happiness, we have felt that regimentations that might well have produced better films and made them more serviceable to worthy social ends would not square with the concept of happiness which our constitution has advanced."[76] Here is an acknowledgement that amateur cinema could have been more socially engaged and could have produced films for more valuable social purposes, but that this is not what the ACL was founded to do. Winton poses fascism as the main danger for the regimentation of amateur filmmaking:

In the full swing of the late Fascist era in Europe, some Italians and, soon afterward, some Spaniards developed most ambitious projects for systematizing and controlling personal filming internationally. Because of its world standing, the League was asked to become a part of these totalitarian efforts. When we gave a blunt negative, we were assailed bitterly. Quite typically, the Germans were later so self assured that they went ahead with very little concern with what the League might think. All those disciplines of regimentation forgot the important factor of happiness. They are come to dust with their vast schemes and the League still goes forward, because it believes that, to free men, pleasure is a valid purpose.

What these projects for systematizing and controlling personal filming might have been remains unclear. But for the Amateur Cinema League and (North) American amateurs, moviemaking had remained a primarily individual activity. Though moviemakers produced films to support the war effort, amateurs did so voluntarily. While freedom and pleasure, as organizing principles, did not preclude amateur reflections on and responses to current events, these principles often made amateur films about current events idiosyncratic and individual in nature.

4 Ciné-Technology
Machine Art for a Machine Age

From the electric lights, telephones, and automobiles that transformed experiences of time and space to the factories, typewriters, and automats that gave everyday life newly mechanized dimensions, people in the twentieth century had increasingly frequent and pervasive encounters with machines. Under these conditions, the emergence of devices like amateur movie cameras, which provided a newly mechanized means of individual expression, is not surprising. How better than making movies to renegotiate one's relationship to machines, to adapt their manipulation of time and space to individual ends, and to assert one's agency and experimental knowledge over the constantly expanding terrain of new technology? In a certain sense, there was no better way of being modern than to make one's own films. Paradoxically, making one's own films could also be a way of staving off the mass culture that typified modern life—to perpetuate traditions of home or community (or folk) art making and to create visions of contemporary life alternative to those of industrial entertainment. Investigating the history of amateur cinema requires a consideration of the particular characteristics, effects, and uses of film technology.

Amateur film technology is not deterministic, though there are some important distinctions and tendencies about its use, especially compared with commercial cinema and film technology. When we think about the commercial cinema, perhaps the seamless nature of its technological base is what comes most quickly to mind: its apparatus is made to appear invisible, and consistent, when not dazzling us with expensive or complex visual spectacle. Above all, professional technique is designed to present a polished, fully deliberate, and in-control aesthetic. Amateur film technology, on the other hand, is a story of nonstandardization in terms of gauge, image, and sound characteristics. This nonstandardization is the result of the development of new technologies but also the idiosyncratic and unstandardized use of existing technologies. The visual characteristics of amateur films can be quite varied in quality depending on the gauge used or whether they are in black and white or color. There are even different aspect ratios among amateur films and, later, widescreen amateur filmmaking. The sonic characteristics of amateur film (as they are both recorded and presented) can also be quite varied: though synchronized sound recording among amateurs lagged many years behind the commercial cinema, sound—both live and recorded—was a common element of amateur film presentation, employing voice, music, synch, nonsynch, live, and recorded sound. As a result of these many technological shifts and options—both visual and sonic—the surface of amateur film is not as smooth and consistent as professional film in terms of the technologies used or the techniques and skills applied.

Amateur cinema involved not just the story of new technological developments but also the pragmatic experimentation with different technologies. In some cases, this was a matter of adopting new technologies and exploring their limitations and potentials, as with film color. In film sound, experimentation took place both in recording format (wire, phonograph, mag) and presentation (recorded, live, chosen by filmmaker, chosen by presenter). What was significant about this was the attitude of experimentation that amateurs, and amateur discourse, frequently adopted. Amateur cinema provided opportunities for individuals to engage productively with machines and to adapt the use of these machines to individual—expressive, artistic, familial—objectives. Amateur images come from a variety of different formats but are still able to produce works that record and, more important, creatively shape recorded events. While less polished than professional film, some of the pleasure of amateur works came from their evident and ingenious use of low-tech or consumer-grade technologies. Amateurs negotiated these limitations, the "economy of means" of amateur filmmaking, in a variety of different ways: some foregrounded the limitations, while others worked to accomplish as much of the seamless polish of professional filmmaking as the technology would permit. But in order to make sense of amateur cinema in both aesthetic and cultural terms, we must trace some of the significant developments and shifts in the technology used by amateur filmmakers. This chapter surveys some of the key technologies and their uses by amateurs during the period from 1930 to 1960, focusing in particular on discussion and developments in film color, sound, and gauge. In addition to these major categories there is also a range of smaller areas of development and technological experimentation by amateurs. Taken together, amateurs' relationship to technology was multifaceted, encompassing both discourses of technical proficiency, novelty, and heterogeneous experimentation and bricolage.

AMATEUR FILM COLOR

Color filmmaking had played an important role in the Amateur Cinema League's prognostications for motion pictures from its founding in 1926 onward. In the first issue of *Amateur Movie Makers* magazine, Hiram Percy Maxim predicted a time when color motion pictures would be transmitted like the radio and would permit the home viewing and exchange of color films by people around the world.[1] While Maxim's vision of personal color broadcasting would have to wait until the arrival of the Internet, the magazine also published articles about how amateurs could employ existing color techniques, such as tinting and hand painting.[2] Compared with professionals, however, amateurs did have a privileged relationship to color filmmaking. While early small-gauge film was black and white, "natural" color processes came into widespread use more quickly among amateurs than 35mm color film did among professionals. The arrival of Kodacolor film in 1928 marked a significant—if primarily symbolic—development for amateur filmmaking. Appearing at a time when the transition to synchronized sound occupied commercial filmmaking, the arrival of Kodacolor marked a distinct path for amateurs. For over a decade, from 1928 until the end of the 1930s, amateur filmmakers explored color film aesthetics, first with Kodacolor and later with the much-improved Kodachrome process, introduced in 1935. An editorial titled "Color Unlimited," published in 1935, articulated the amateur's position in explicit terms: "While sound movies were a definite product of the theatrical motion picture industry, it is indisputable that a wide use of color movies has been a specific product of personal filming.... Amateurs are several jumps ahead in the intelligent use of color in cinematography, because their employment of it has been so extensive. As amateur sound has been aided by Hollywood pathfinding, so can amateurs extend to their professional friends a helping hand in this new color field which will rapidly engage Hollywood's interest."[3] Though mute, amateur films would be claimed as the terrain for continued development of film aesthetics, understood as essentially a visual art form, now with the addition of color.[4]

When the 16mm Kodacolor film process was introduced to the American market, it was greeted by *Movie Makers* magazine with a great deal of excitement. An editorial touted the significance of Kodacolor as an expressly amateur innovation, developed and marketed just for them: "[By] the very fact of his existence in large numbers, the amateur has been responsible for the development of a new kind of color photography in motion pictures."[5] Kodacolor also promised new aesthetic possibilities for amateur filmmakers. "Here is something that is their very own," the editorial pronounced. "From their comments upon it, their experiments with it, and their suggestions concerning its betterment and expansion will come the brilliant future for it that MOVIE MAKERS confidently expects." With the arrival of Kodacolor came a new aesthetic terrain for amateur filmmakers to experiment with and explore. The introduction of Kodacolor was a timely arrival for amateurs, corresponding with discussions about the fate of film art with the coming of sound. By the end of the 1920s, popular film was shifting away from the artistic achievements and style of the silent era. Roy Winton, managing director of the ACL, noted in 1930 that this shift presented an opportunity for the amateur: "The events of the last two years in the professional movie world have put the movie amateur in a very novel position. To put it bluntly, the commercial producers have gone out of the movie business into the stage entertainment business and their present product of talking movies is fare not for the devotees of movie art but for patrons of stage entertainment. The movie amateur is the inheritor of the silent films."[6] Winton's remarks reproduce what has become the canonical account of the transition from silent to sound film aesthetics: if silent film embodied a young art of plastic movement, sound film appeared to be becoming little more than a handmaid of stage drama. And whereas commercial silent films made extensive use of color effects like tinting and toning, the arrival of synchronized sound put an end to these techniques. Aside from a handful of two-strip Technicolor films released during this period, early sound cinema was black and white. Color filmmaking presented a unique opportunity for amateurs to develop silent film style further, and in a new direction, in contrast to commercial cinema's increasingly stage-bound style. But what did amateurs *do* with color cinema, and how did they advance new directions for film art?

Developed by Kodak specifically for 16mm amateur use, Kodacolor was an additive, lenticular process. In an additive process, the presentation of color is not intrinsic to the film stock's photochemistry but is the result of a system of filters attached to the camera in filming and the projector in exhibition. Kodacolor film stock also employed miniscule lenses embossed directly onto the base of the film stock. To the naked eye, a strip of developed Kodacolor film is monochrome in appearance, and when projected without the appropriate filter it is indistinguishable from black-and-white film except for the presence of fine vertical stripes. When projected through the appropriate red-, green-, and blue-striped Kodacolor filter, however, the embossed lenses on the film combine the three hues to reproduce the appearance of natural color. Writers expounded the values of the color system for travel films, and even Hollywood cinematographers called it "a natural-color process far more perfect than anything available to the professional."[7] Despite the excitement with which amateurs greeted Kodacolor, the format was not as user-friendly and easily adopted as originally touted. The use of filters and embossed film stock created problems with obtaining correct exposure, as it required very bright lighting conditions. As a result, Kodacolor was most commonly used by amateurs for exterior filming. And although Kodacolor equipment was adapted in 1933 to function in more diverse lighting conditions, including indoor shooting, the format still required more careful calculation of exposure than many amateurs were prepared to accommodate.[8] Articles written to convince amateurs that filming in Kodacolor was "worth the trouble" betray a general acknowledgment that the format was not widely embraced. Though Kodacolor was technologically capable of producing strikingly colorful images and providing home moviemakers with greater realism in their personal or travel records, its technical challenges appear to have dissuaded most casual filmers from adopting its use.[9]

But some amateurs persevered with more thorough explorations of Kodacolor's possibilities. The more successful attempts to use Kodacolor can be found in the ACL's annual Ten Best amateur film contests.[10] To trace along purely statistical lines, these lists reveal that only one Kodacolor film received an award in 1930 and 1931, two both in 1932 and in 1933, and three in 1934. One of these Kodacolor award winners was the retired engineer and avid film hobbyist John Hansen. Before turning to color filmmaking, Hansen had already demonstrated his skill as a filmmaker with his 1931 black-and-white travel film about Egypt, *Tombs of the Nobles*, which was named one of the Ten Best of that year. In 1932, Hansen turned to color filmmaking with the reel *Studies in Blue and Chartres Cathedral*. Described in its award citation as a "cerulean cinema achievement," the film was evidently both a travelogue and a meditation on the use of color in amateur filmmaking.[11] In a similar vein, Hansen's next award-winning Kodacolor film, *Venice* (1934), also explored color cinema's capacity for presenting an older art form. Like a typical amateur travel film, *Venice* chronicles some of the city's attractions and artworks, but according to its description in *Movie Makers* Hansen's treatment of Andrea del Sarto's mosaics at St. Marks "exemplifies in a new way the amazing versatility of the amateur color medium in the hands of a master craftsman."[12] In this account, it is not just Hansen's technical skill in capturing the mosaics under unfavorable lighting conditions that marks him a "master craftsman"; it is also his sensitivity to the original artwork's texture and tonality and his use of this work to explore Kodacolor's expressive range. The *Movie Makers* award citations repeatedly compared Hansen and other filmmakers to the great artists of other media, not just for their reproduction of those other artists' artworks, but also for recognizing and mastering Kodacolor's range of aesthetic expressions in personal motion pictures.

If Hansen's color films seem primarily concerned with the faithful reproduction of artworks from other media, we can shed further light on his aesthetic objectives by examining the articles he wrote about Kodacolor filming for *Movie Makers* magazine from 1932 to 1934. In these articles, Hansen notes the broad range of potential subjects for color filmmaking, a range that far exceeds "personal, flower and sunset opportunities."[13] In addition to these familiar topics, he also suggests some subjects that might be otherwise overlooked: "Even the big cities of America overflow with subjects worthy of color delineation. The dull everyday street scene is brightened with painted vehicles." In this context, color filming could be just as much a strategy for refreshing one's view of familiar places as a presentation of the distant or the exotic. Indeed, Hansen's articles seem more concerned with color filmmaking that pursues primarily aesthetic goals than with films about specific subjects, and to this end he proposes strategies for improving color perception and productive experimentation arguing, "Attention may be directed to a sadly neglected branch of cinematography, namely, experimentation with light and composition."[14] Hansen's award-winning films used artworks like stained glass and mosaics as starting points for color experimentation. In his advice to other amateurs, however, he proposes everyday ways for filmmakers to attune their eye to color. Hansen outlines exercises for training one's perception of light and color under different circumstances, such as the observation of different shades of blue sky visible on a bright morning, the variations in tint and intensity of hue of a flower seen from different angles. "Through this procedure," Hansen writes, "in a short time will be acquired a new sense of light appreciation which will be found most helpful later on in selecting special subjects and choosing the right camera position for bringing out desired details and combinations in color values, rarely seen by the average person."[15] Here, Hansen suggests how attentiveness to light and color lead to a keener perception of these qualities and productively direct the composition of a film.

In another article, Hansen draws on this sharpened color perception to encourage the use of "transmitted light," or light that has visibly passed through another substance, in color filming. Hansen suggests, "[Transmitted] light and color rendition can be woven into striking and fascinating compositions. . . . Closeups of translucent orchids or the large petals of other flowers are obvious possibilities."[16] Hansen doesn't mention the effect of filming light transmitted through stained glass, as in his film of Chartres Cathedral, in which there is no use of reflected light in the interior scenes at all. But he suggests a number of other natural sources for filming transmitted light, such as the foliage of trees, particularly during fall, when they change color and produce something like a natural stained-glass effect. For Hansen, effective color composition passed along to viewers an experience of the light and color of even quotidian objects that many people overlook. In this way, color filmmaking could be seen as enhancing and expanding the amateur filmmaker's *and* the viewer's sensorium, attuning them to new ways of seeing the world, from familiar subjects like family, to defamiliarized settings like the city, to compositions of pure light and hue. But this result could be accomplished only through technical skill and pragmatic experimentation with the medium. For advanced amateurs like Hansen, Kodacolor presented many more possibilities for creative color filming than were generally acknowledged and explored among amateurs.

Although some amateurs did experiment with Kodacolor, not until the arrival of 16mm Kodachrome film in 1935 did amateur filmmaking cement its advantage over professional filmmaking in the area of color moviemaking. The Kodachrome subtractive color process required no special filters for filming and projection and marked a major advance for amateur filmmakers in terms of its ease of use and vividness of results. Indeed, according to *American Cinematographer*, "many connected with the motion picture profession in Hollywood hail it as even better than Technicolor."[17] Because Kodachrome film stock employed a "reversal" developing process, through which the same reel exposed in-camera became a projectable film print, it was not adaptable to the commercial industry's requirements of mass reproducibility. Among amateurs, however, anyone could now produce high-quality natural color images, especially once 16mm Kodachrome was followed in 1936 by Kodachrome 8mm film stock.[18] *Movie Makers* magazine heralded the arrival of the new film process with its usual hyperbole: "The year 1935 will be marked in the history of personal movies as that in which the era of unlimited color filming began."[19] This time *Movie Makers'* hyperbole was matched by Kodachrome's rapid and broad acceptance among amateurs. But the editorial also points out the important role that users of Kodacolor had played: "They have made the pioneer experiments in bringing color movies up to the status of accepted art. Their efforts and discoveries have erected a basic esthetic philosophy about color filming that is as applicable to the less limited new conditions as it is to the older."[20] Whether it was due to these "pioneer experiments" or not, Kodachrome films were quick to appear on the annual Ten Best lists. While 1934's Ten Best list included only three Kodacolor films, already in 1935 five Kodachrome films were listed among the Ten Best and honorable mentions. In 1936, this number more than doubled to eleven, and by 1937, less than three years after its introduction, more color films were listed than black-and-white films. This trend would continue through to the end of the decade. Among amateurs, Kodachrome filming was quickly associated with travel and exploration. Films of exotic journeys around the world or even just to America's color-named national parks (Yellowstone) were perfect ways of highlighting the amateur film's colorful attributes.[21] Some locales even published advertisements that promoted color cinematography as a special draw for tourism, as was the case with the Virginia Conservation Commission: "Color Adventure Drama!! Capture them all with your Camera in Old Virginia" (figure 7).[22]

Though understood to be a significant advance in color filmmaking technology and ease of use, shooting in Kodachrome still required careful measuring of exposure levels in order to ensure best results. While the process did not require the complex system of filters and processing that Kodacolor necessitated, amateurs still noted the adjustments and mistakes that accompanied changing over to the new format. Maxim tells of his own failure to obtain good quality Kodachrome images the first time he used it during a trip to Gaspé, with no exposure meter.[23] Despite these preliminary problems, color filmmaking rapidly became a normal practice among amateurs, and by the end of the 1930s, even an award-winning film's use of color was not always remarked upon.[24] John Hansen continued making noteworthy color films, but because he became a director of the ACL in 1936 he was no longer eligible for awards. Hansen made the transition to Kodachrome with ease and gained further attention for his film *Denmark in Color* (1937), which was widely shown in Europe and the United States.[25] So well-known was Hansen for his use of color that he was even the subject of a gently satirical film called *Dabblin' in Moods*, produced by his own Washington, D.C., movie club:

> The film is an amusing impersonation of the Hansen cine manner, but with results entirely different from those of the famous original. Mood

Figure 7. Tourist bureaus, like Virginia's, promoted their scenery for color filming. *Movie Makers,* May 1940, 235. Courtesy Media History Digital Library.

Indigo croons a title, to be followed by a deep blue underexposure. Mood Pastel claims its running mate, to give way to nearly blank overexposure. The Mood Inverted piques your interest, then discloses a debacle of scenes spliced wrong side up. The Mood Dynamic promises a masterpiece, only to perpetrate as dizzy and delirious a sequence of "pans" and tilts as ever struck a silver screen. The first definite burlesque of a distinctive cine style, *Dabblin' In Moods* strikes us both as a lot of fun and some sort of milepost in the progress of amateur movies.[26]

In its presentation of over- and underexposure, sloppy editing, and haphazard camera movement, the film offers a tongue-in-cheek primer of common amateur mistakes. The satirical slant of this film also highlights Hansen's own reputation for expressive and experimental color use at the opposite end of the amateur spectrum.

The appearance of Kodacolor and Kodachrome coincided approximately with the novelty of commercial production in two- and three-strip Technicolor, respectively. Both Kodacolor and two-strip Technicolor can be seen as imperfect technologies but still important steps along the path of color development toward the eventual perfection of amateur and professional color in Kodachrome and three-strip Technicolor, respectively. But what distinguished amateur from professional color filming was exclusivity; while Technicolor filming represented a very small portion of commercial output, Kodachrome was available to all amateur filmmakers. As a result, color filmmaking was widespread among amateurs from the 1930s to the 1950s, even as it remained a relative rarity or special feature for commercial films. Some observers even declared Kodachrome superior to Technicolor, and one article used the first three-strip Technicolor feature film, *Becky Sharp* (1935), as a demonstration of what to avoid when shooting in Kodachrome. The author is critical of *Becky Sharp* because of its use of bright, clashing colors that distract from the main action and characters. Instead, he encouraged amateurs to shoot lighter shades, lighter colors, and pastels rather than primary colors. He warns, "Too much color will tire one very quickly . . . too much clashing of eye interest."[27] Historian Neil Harris describes the rise of color filmmaking in terms of its movement toward natural effects; while earlier Technicolor films (like *Becky Sharp*) exploited color for its own sake, as this novelty wore off color use became naturalized, and commercial color filming was considered successful.[28] Among amateurs, naturalized color use was the starting point: exterior shooting, natural light, documenting the color of nature and travel. Some amateurs' push beyond this natural way of thinking about color to experiment with its aesthetic and perceptual qualities was therefore significant. There was, no doubt, much more room for color experimentation among amateurs than in commercial Technicolor production.

The Amateur Cinema League *did* continue to promote experimentation in color use, pushing its aesthetic development still further. In 1935, ACL president Hiram Percy Maxim predicted an ongoing link between color film and experimentation when he wrote, "[Color] comes at the same time that a modernistic tendency appears among us. Shots made at unusual angles and shots made under unique lighting conditions seem to be driving the shot taken from the conventional point of view and with standard lighting into the limbo of the old fashioned. This modernistic tendency will unquestionably cross breed with color."[29] Looking into the latter half of the 1930s, we can observe the results of this crossbreeding with an experimental impulse in a little more detail.[30] Films that emphasized unnaturalistic color use were particularly noted. For example, one Ten Best winner, *These Bloomin' Plants* (1936), treated the familiar color subject of flowers but this time through time-lapse photography: "Through this device of time condensation, buds are seen bursting open before one's eyes, often in cascades of beauty which vividly suggest fireworks against a night sky."[31] As this description suggests, the effect of color combined with time-lapse filming here denaturalizes a familiar image, so blooming flowers take on the appearance of fireworks. Writers and amateur filmmakers also drew on metaphorical associations between cinema and the other arts in order to describe some of the ways the medium exceeded a purely naturalistic recording of reality. In this vein, Robert Kehoe's award-winning *Chromatic Rhapsody* (1939) used a musical metaphor to organize, and render more expressive, scenic footage of autumn foliage: "This beautiful picture can only be described as a scenic—a scenic held together rather tenuously by editing to create a symphonic arrangement of color and to associated scenes with the seasons."[32] In this description we see further indications of how amateurs used color film in order to push aesthetic exploration of the medium and familiar surroundings further. While these films may seem to be a far cry from the pure modernist abstractions of Oskar Fischinger, for example, they are still experiments with the purely graphical dimensions of color cinema. Like Hansen's advice in his articles, a blend of the experimental and the pragmatic is here: Kehoe's film appears from this description to push beyond the typical amateur scenic through both its musical analogy and the filmmaker's careful color composition and skillful exposure of the Kodachrome stock.

The peak of Kodachrome's "novelty phase" came in 1939, in the form of Kodak's Great Hall of Color at the New York World's Fair. The display produced "an astounding effect of combined projection of Kodachrome slides, upon a screen one hundred and eighty seven feet long and twenty-two feet high," and promoted Kodachrome's still and motion picture uses at the fair for over a year. The display was designed to foreground the dramatic color effects of the process and their particular domestic setting, employing "two model living rooms, in one of which home movies will be projected in color, and in the other of which color 'stills' will be shown."[33] Some months later, *Movie Makers* applauded Kodak's display as "the most important photographic show that the world has ever seen": "This magnificent demonstration of Kodachrome will be remembered longest for its sheer beauty and for its power of transporting the beholder, by an enveloping dome of many hued magic, into a new world that is made up of the familiar things of life, but that is more than they are."[34] What is noteworthy here is color's power to transport the beholder and to imbue the familiar things in life with magical qualities. While this description certainly encapsulates the goals of mass advertising strategies in the twentieth century, it also signals some of the aesthetic power of color cinematography that was delivered into amateur hands with Kodachrome film.

Kodachrome filmmaking persisted for decades—and indeed was discontinued as a process supported by Kodak only in 2010—a testament to its striking visual quality and longevity. For amateurs, however, its novelty as an aspect of film aesthetics to be explored dissolved with the appearance of World War II. After the war, color filmmaking became simply one of a range of options for amateurs to exploit creatively. Hollywood's increasing use of color film through the 1950s gradually eroded the Kodachrome user's special status. No doubt many amateurs continued to explore color film's creative possibilities, but perhaps more often they took it for granted as one of the typical components of filmmaking. In 1955, Nadine Pizzo sought to reinvigorate color's use among amateurs, suggesting, "The average amateur is un-instructed and inexperienced in this usage of color."[35] Pizzo's critique implied a dominant mode of natural color aesthetics rather than a stylized or aesthetically self-aware one. At the end of the 1950s and in the 1960s, however, the "value" of color as a marker of creative filmmaking became further complicated with the appearance of black and white, low-budget, independent filmmaking. Color filmmaking perhaps came to signify another way that amateur movies had become aesthetically conservative.

As with other amateur technologies, the use of color was by no means uniform. Many amateurs continued to make films on black-and-white film stock. This can partly be attributed to its lower cost, but we might also identify aesthetic causes, such as an appeal to the Hollywood black-and-white film style (i.e., film noir). Even after the arrival of natural color processes, such as Kodacolor and Kodachrome, amateur filmmakers experimented with home tinting and toning processes.[36] Instructions for amateur color tinting and toning can be found in advice columns as late as 1949.[37] So even during the era of Kodacolor and Kodachrome, otherwise obsolete techniques still persisted in amateur circles. While color filmmaking provides an instance in which amateurs were technologically advanced, compared with professional filmmaking, amateur circles still provided a repository for historical, even obsolete, film techniques and technologies.

AMATEUR FILM SOUND

Silent films, as the cliché goes, were never really silent; they always had some manner of sound accompaniment, whether a piano, an organ, or a full orchestra in a movie palace. This observation requires some qualification for a consideration of sound in amateur moviemaking. Amateur film culture emerged in the late 1920s at the same moment that talkies were arriving in movie theatres. As amateurs began organizing clubs and promoting the advancement of amateur filmmaking as a distinct, noncommercial art form, the arrival of synchronized sound in commercial films signaled a strong distinction between the industry and the medium of amateur cinema. In this context, amateurs were declared the inheritors of silent film art and champions of the further development of film aesthetics. The amateur use of sound between the 1920s and 1960 was highly varied. During most of this period, like the commercial film's silent era, the films themselves lacked synchronized sound tracks; it was only in the 1950s that magnetic tape allowed for widespread synchronized sound among amateurs. Prior to that, amateur films were shown in silence, with spoken accompaniment, or with a range of different nonsynchronous recorded sound accompaniments. While most of the amateur films that survive today suggest—in the absence of any visible sound track—a mute presentation, historical accounts propose much more varied and heterogeneous practices.

Avant-garde filmmaking was one area of amateur work that saw deliberate and experimental uses of sound accompaniment. Abstract music was seen as the companion art form for abstract filmmaking. Ralph Steiner's abstract films, for example, were presented in 1931 with specially composed modernist music by Colin McPhee and Marc Blitzstein.[38] The composer of music to be presented with H_2O and *Mechanical Principles*, Colin McPhee, wrote, "It has been prophesied ... that the sonorous film, the film with specialized musical accompaniment, would give music a new lease on life.... In collaboration with Steiner, we have tried to produce an integral whole whose two component parts, film and music, might stand alone.... They are parallel creations in two different media." McPhee suggests that the film would help modern music, which "has become terribly erudite and more than ever difficult for the average ear to derive pleasure from," to find a wider appeal. Blitzstein's accompaniment for *Surf and Seaweed* was made up of a suite in six short movements: "The music attempts to provide a setting for the film; it is sometimes descriptive, sometimes direct."[39]

More typical amateur films from this period often included intertitles but were frequently accompanied by live spoken narration during exhibition. As a format that was often presented to small audiences at movie clubs or private homes and generally with a filmmaker present, spoken accompaniment could take either scripted or informal form. In either case spoken narration limited the possibilities of wider distribution for amateur films. If they required spoken explanation of some kind—clarifying the locations or actions in a travelogue, for example, or reading a poem that the film illustrated—this dimension was difficult to circulate beyond the filmmaker's presence. Manufacturers of home movie equipment responded almost immediately to the arrival of sound in commercial filmmaking by bringing a range of different home equipment to the market. DeVry marketed an early 16mm projector with a turntable system in 1928, and other machines soon followed, often releasing 16mm reduction prints of commercial films with accompanying sound-on-discs. In this way, commercial "talkies" could be viewed at home as early as 1928; sound-on-disc projection systems were marketed for 16mm and later 8mm through the 1940s. Sound-on-film projectors for 16mm were first marketed to home audiences in 1932, but early models were very expensive and flawed; the slower speed of 16mm film passing through the projector compared with 35mm posed a significant technical hurdle for engineers.[40] Sound-on-film projection was not widely available for 8mm until the 1950s.

Despite these opportunities for projecting commercial sound films at home, the use of sound with amateur-made films took slightly longer to appear and employed a variety of different strategies.[41] Early systems presented a range of problems in terms of both fidelity and sound synchronization, but by 1931 functioning systems for recording and presenting sound were available for amateur use. One writer remarked on the development of sound-on-disc systems from the vantage point of 1933:

> Several years have elapsed since the first sound on disc synchronizer appeared on the sixteen millimeter market.... It was not long before the amateur projectionist, with his customary discrimination, declined to accept "scratchies" and called for a combined disc and projector outfit that would deliver sound results at least approximately approaching the perfection that amateur motion picture photography had then attained. The sound synchronized, non-professional motion picture became an accomplished fact, having no drawbacks that must be overlooked simply because the idea was a novelty.[42]

By 1933 the technical problems of both sound-on-disc and sound-on-film recording ostensibly had been solved.[43] At least one amateur club, the Cinema League of Philadelphia, announced the production of its first sound film, *To Om by Omnibus,* that year.[44] The picture was made with the new RCA Victor 16mm outfit, which recorded optical sound on film. Such productions as these were rare, however, as sound equipment continued through the 1930s to be too costly for most amateurs.[45] For those who wanted the seamless presentation of a postsynchronized sound track without purchasing the equipment themselves, commercial services offered to put optical sound tracks on amateur films. "Sound on your films is not the expensive luxury it may seem," explained one service. "You may be spending as much now for a first class job of professional titling. You may even be spending more for a sound-on-disc recording if you take into account all the costs incurred. The advantages of recording sound-on-film are obvious enough: assurance of perfect synchronization, easier projecting, no deterioration of sound quality resulting from continual use, more pleasure and satisfaction for you and your audience."[46] How many amateurs availed themselves of these services is unclear, but often sound accompaniment was of interest precisely for the technical challenges it posed to advanced amateur moviemakers and required them to overcome.

A more common sound accompaniment strategy that emerged in the 1930s and survived well into the postwar era was the use of dual-turntable systems to perform and "mix" music and sound effects during a screening. In 1934, *American Cinematographer* contributor (and later editor) William Stull compared the amateur use of nonsynchronized sound with that of commercial theatres during the transition to talkies:

> The amateur of today is in virtually the position of the professional showman of six or seven years ago. At that time, it will be recalled, sound suddenly appeared. Sound—of any kind—became a desirable feature of any programme. Yet the regular "Vitaphone" and "Movietone" equipment . . . was almost prohibitively expensive. Therefore many exhibitors continued to play silent pictures, providing musical accompaniments and sound-effects by non-synchronous reproducers. This was done by using two turntables, each equipped with an electric pick-up, and feeding into a common amplifying and reproducing system; a "fader" was included, by which sonic lap-dissolves could be made from one record to another, with the volume of the piece being played diminishing as the volume of the succeeding piece increased. Many theatres built up sizable libraries of sound-effects records, using both the 33⅓ R.P.M. sound-and-broadcast record and the 78 R.P.M. commercial phonograph records. In due time, as synchronous sound-equipment became more economically available, the theatre men added it, or, in some cases, adapted their non-synchronous equipment to synchronous reproduction.
> The amateur can well do the same.[47]

Compared with the costly synchronous sound recording systems available to amateurs, recorded music and sound effects were widely available and presented a more inexpensive option for sound accompaniment. "Therefore," Stull concluded, "the most practical thing at the moment would appear to be the use of non-synchronous disc-recorded accompaniments and sound-effects, graduating from this to experiments with synchronous disc recording and reproduction, and eventually, to the use of a complete sound-on-film installation when such becomes really practical for amateur use."[48] From the mid-1930s on, articles that described dual-turntable sound accompaniment occurred with increasing frequency in publications for amateurs.[49]

This use of recorded music and sound effects is significant for its positioning of amateur filmmakers as recyclers and repurposes of commercial media. William Stull was also a record collector, and beginning in 1935 he published an annual article that recommended specific recorded musical accompaniments (or scores) for the *American Cinematographer* contest prize-winning films.[50] Stull himself presented these films at the LA Cinema Club, and when no musical accompaniment was specified by the filmmaker, he presented them with his own arrangement using a double-turntable system. When *American Cinematographer* loaned these prize-winning films to amateur movie clubs around the United States, Stull hoped that at least some clubs would show the films with his scores. This was possible because of the generally wide availability of musical recordings. One goal here was to create sound accompaniments that would be transferrable to other locations. It is also clear from writings in amateur publications that recorded, nonsynchronous sound was understood to provide an aesthetic enhancement to a film and also to enliven its presentation. "The music must fit the film," one *Movie Makers* author writes, "and on how well the mood of the music matches the spirit of the cine sequences, that it accompanies, depends the success of the combination." Tips for creating cue sheets were provided, along with lists of classical works and suggestions about the effect of choosing different instrumentations.[51]

The dual-turntable system of sound accompaniment also allowed amateurs to explore a new area of technical gadgetry. Responding to the demand from amateurs, portable dual-turntable systems were advertised to them in the late 1930s. One ad touted: "Add thrilling sound to your movies! Fidelitone dual turntable: a perfected, portable, flexible sound unit, priced for the amateur field. Join the hundreds of enthusiastic movie makers who are complementing their films with dual turntable sound effects, background music and speech" (figure 8).[52] But some amateurs preferred instead to create or modify their own custom equipment. Prize-winning amateur filmmaker Hamilton Jones published an article describing his use of the system in 1934 and later experimented with using even three and four turntable

Figure 8. Dual-turntable systems provided a popular option for nonsynch sound accompaniment. *Movie Makers*, February 1940, 81. Courtesy Media History Digital Library.

pickups to achieve smoother sound mixing: "It is placed midway between the two turntables and allows a wide variation of effects. A record may be repeated without a break by using the two pickups at one time on the same record, fading out with one and in with the other. It is also much easier to achieve apparent synchronization with a sound effect record if the second pickup is used. Mr. Jones is said to have used a fourth pickup for some of his amazing and well known efforts at adding sound and music to his pictures."[53]

Another amateur, Ormal Sprungman, emphasized both the reliability and fun involved in performing dual-turntable sound for presentations. "Some moviemakers would have us believe," he writes, "that the dual turntable, grinding out sound and music with disc, is lowbrow entertainment, and only a stepping stone to the perfection supposedly reached by the more refined sound-on-film. The truth of the matter is that double turntables can produce music far superior to the celluloid product, even varying background music with each performance, without worrying about the disastrous consequences of a sound film break. Take it from a carload of amateurs the country over, it's a lot more difficult, yet a peck more fun, playing with turntables stuff than tinkering with celluloid recorded sound."[54]

Implied in Sprungman's comments are both a technical savvy and a sense of the entertainment value provided by presenting recorded music.

In this vein we can see, finally, that the dual-turntable system of sound accompaniment also contributed to an apparatus of amateur film exhibition showmanship. Duncan MacD. Little foregrounded the curated (i.e., carefully selected) use of recorded sound to accompany the films shown at his movie parties.[55] The live mixing of recorded music and sound effects was also supplemented by narration, spoken over a microphone. So here the additional equipment, amplification system, and skillful presentation of different sounds along with the films elevated the amateur exhibition from informal (and relatively unskillful) home exhibition to an impressive performance fit for public consumption. Carefully crafted and executed sound accompaniment was another way that "advanced amateurs" distinguished their films and film exhibitions from home movie snapshooters, on one hand, while also developing an artistic practice that was distinct from (canned, standardized) commercial film exhibition, on the other.

While the presentation of nonsynchronous sound with films was most common, some amateurs continued experimenting with sound recording and synchronization systems. For example, Los Angeles amateur Randolph Clardy developed his own system for synchronizing 8mm film along with synchronously recorded dialogue on disc.[56] Most often, though, amateur experiments involved postdubbing sound onto silent-produced films.[57] One member of Washington's Capital Eights club demonstrated this approach at a club meeting: "Equipment owned by William L. Cook, ACL, was used in the demonstration, which involved the recording on a disc of the unrehearsed commentary of Fred Au on his own Christmas film. The record thus cut was immediately played back in accompaniment.[58] In this manner, it was possible to preserve any postrecorded commentary or music for a film. Later some amateurs recorded their dual-turntable music and narration score onto a single disc, in a way, completing the film by recording a "master track" out of the multiple tracks that made up a dual-turntable accompaniment.[59] But even when amateurs were able to accomplish some measure of satisfactory synchronization, these early sound-on-disc efforts were not easily transportable from one location and projector to another. *American Cinematographer* critic Edward Pyle remarked on this problem in his effort to evaluate an amateur film for readers of the magazine. Pyle had particular difficulties synchronizing the projector speed with the turntable and recommended just using silent titles for amateur films. Using different equipment made "accurate synchronization . . . next to impossible," he wrote.[60] Various solutions to these synch problems were attempted throughout the 1940s, including a "stroboscopic sensor" to keep record and image in synch.[61] These difficulties with sound accompaniment provide some justification for the persistent encouragement amateurs received for including clear explanatory titles in their films. As late as 1947, *Movie Makers* published articles proposing techniques for effective intertitle use.[62]

After World War II, amateurs began experimenting with magnetic recording systems, first on wire, but soon on magnetic tape. Like the previous sound-on-disc approaches, magnetic sound was initially understood to operate as a nonsynchronous accompaniment, produced by a distinct piece of equipment on which sound and narration had been previously recorded.[63] Very quickly, however, the possibility of an apparatus that would produce a recordable magnetic track right on the film were being discussed.[64] It wasn't until 1952 that magnetic sound recording became accessible enough to be widely adopted by amateurs: "The big news these days for amateur movie makers is the recent introduction of a practical method of recording magnetic sound on 16mm home movie films. It means an end to discs, phonograph records, magnetic wire and tape, of dual turntables and stroboscopes—all of which progressive amateurs have dealt with in recent years in an attempt to provide synchronized sound for their movies. Now two developments make synchronized sound possible for every 16mm filmer: (1) sound striped movie film, and (2) 16mm magnetic recorder-projectors."[65] In order to add a magnetic sound track to their 16mm films, amateurs needed to have a magnetic tape, or "stripe," affixed to their silent film at a laboratory and then use the 16mm magnetic projector-recorder to record the sound track on the film. This system of recording using a magnetic stripe and projector would be common practice for amateur filmmakers for several decades. Adding sound to older 16mm films also became possible by sending them to a lab for magnetic striping. Magnetic sound tracks provided an immediate and popular way of adding a synchronized sound accompaniment to amateur films, and amateurs quickly adopted it. The 1953 ACL Ten Best contest noted an increase in the number of entries that included recorded sound but also remarked on the need to improve its technical quality.[66]

While some element of sound had become common in amateur films, the technologies and stylistic strategies used remained quite diverse. Technologies that were commonly used in the 1950s included dual turntable, magnetic wire, and magnetic sound on film. And found among the different strategies for presenting sound were nonsynchronized musical accompaniment, combinations of music and synchronized sounds, and live-recorded and synch-sound dialogue. This was a period of tremendous stylistic and technological diversity in amateur film sound, and its significance was not overlooked by amateurs: "Just as sound, in the middle twenties, changed the aspect and destiny of professional motion pictures, so it has today with amateur movies. Sound is now an important adjunct to an increasing number of amateur films."[67] However, as amateur movie critic George Cushman noted, this created problems for amateur movie contests seeking a consistent criteria for quality work. Cushman proposed that sound quality and synchronization not become criteria for judging because of the limitations of amateur equipment. Instead he suggested ways of considering how sound was coordinated with the image, what it added to the picture, and whether a full range of it (music, dialogue, effects) was used. In these ways, amateur contests attempted to reward the stylistic and creative accomplishments in film sound over pure technical mastery or access to more expensive equipment.

THE MEASURE OF AMATEUR FILM: FILM GAUGE

Amateur film technology was defined more by the narrow gauge of its film stock than any other feature. The introduction of 16mm film equipment in 1923 created a viable film production and exhibition alternative to the professional—and highly flammable—35mm-gauge film. But even though the 16mm film format was the most significant film gauge in terms of the emergence of an amateur film culture in the 1920s, its status within the amateur and nontheatrical film worlds shifted considerably between 1923 and the end of the 1950s. Further complicating the role of 16mm was the introduction of various competing film gauges, especially 8mm in 1932.[68] This section examines the emergence of the 8mm film format and the transformation of 16mm from an amateur to professional gauge (figure 9).

While 16mm film certainly enabled the widespread emergence of home film exhibition and amateur film production, it was still a relatively expensive format requiring costly equipment and film stock. Kodak's first Ciné-Kodak outfit (consisting of camera, projector, tripod, and screen) was marketed for $335 in 1923, slightly more than a Model-T Ford automobile; the camera alone was available for $125.[69] The 8mm film format was introduced in 1932 as a less expensive and more widely accessible system and was quickly embraced by amateurs: "With the introduction of a new method for making amateur movies inexpensively . . . a barrier is removed that has prevented numbers of persons, in the past, from taking up this absorbing human activity."[70] An advertisement for the new 8mm system claimed, "The new Ciné-Kodak at $29.50 cuts film cost nearly ⅔ . . . . For those who want movie making at the least possible cost . . . [8mm] makes

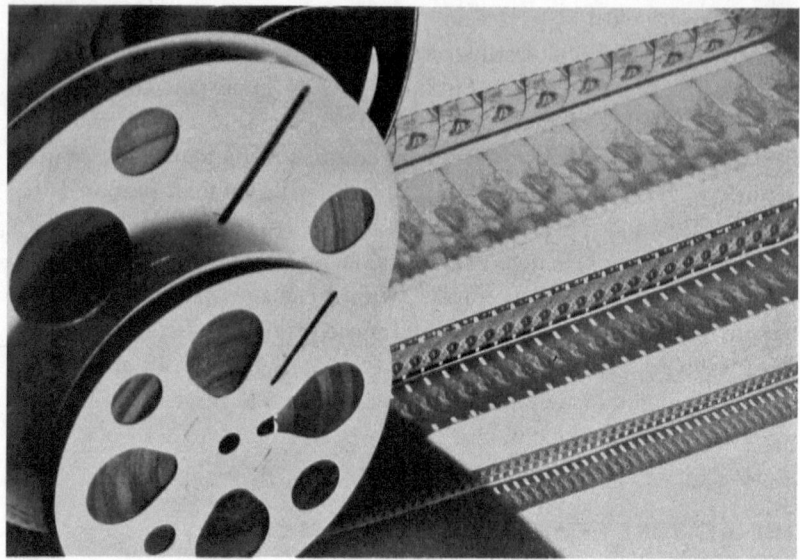

Figure 9. Eastman Kodak's three film widths, circa 1932: the professional 35mm and the amateur 16mm and 8mm gauges. *Movie Makers*, October 1932, 440. Courtesy Media History Digital Library.

every foot of film go four times as far."[71] The 8mm film format accomplished this reduction in cost by using much less film; the camera was loaded with a reel of film that was 16mm wide, but it exposed only half of the film at a time; then the reel was flipped over and the other half exposed. The film was split down the center during processing and spliced together at one end, thus producing an 8mm ribbon of film.

The 8mm format was rapidly adopted by amateurs and acclaimed by both amateurs and professionals alike. The format was admired not only for its low cost but also for the small size and the ease of use of its equipment.[72] *American Cinematographer* posted reviews of the 8mm format by industry professionals such as cinematographer Arthur C. Miller, whose only complaint was the 8mm camera's lack of an adequate viewfinder and an accurate footage counter.[73] The 8mm format was also marketed for easier use than 16mm, thus initiating a gap between the technological sophistication of 8mm and 16mm filmmakers. In *American Cinematographer*, William Stull praised the new 8mm system, not only for its reduction in cost, but also because it was a photographic instrument more suited to the requirements of the majority of those who wanted to make rudimentary films of home life:

[The new Cine-8 system] will open the doors to hundreds of thousands who could not otherwise afford to make movies, and through this renewed impetus to the film and camera business, inevitably result in great benefits to the established 16mm system as the medium of the semi-professional, the scientist and the advanced amateurs, for the snapshooter, now that 8 mm, with its lower cost and even greater simplicity is available, will hardly trouble with 16mm. And that is entirely as it should be, for present-day 16mm apparatus is high-quality, precision machinery, and as badly wasted in the hands of a calloused snapshooter as would be a Graflex. . . .

. . . although many cinematographers fail to realize it, the best of modern 16mm apparatus will enable one to do almost anything professional 35mm cameras can—and do some things (such as color cinematography) vastly better than is possible professionally.[74]

While the 16mm format had initiated a divide in filmmaking activities between professional (35mm) and nonprofessional (16mm), the arrival of 8mm served to further subdivide the universe of film producers. The new tripartite division saw 8mm as the true amateur format, 16mm as an intermediate system for use by advanced amateurs and semiprofessional filmmakers, and 35mm as Hollywood's theatrical format.[75]

A significant development in 16mm filming occurred the following year and served to reinforce its elevated technical status. This was the introduction of the 16mm Ciné-Kodak Special camera, designed to be fully customizable for "professional" filmmaking (figure 10). Features on the Special (priced at $375 for the camera alone) included variable shutter, direct focusing, more powerful spring motor, and interchangeable film magazines.[76] *American Cinematographer* called the Ciné-Kodak Special "a 16mm. camera of maximum versatility" that would "have a mighty strong appeal to advanced amateur motion picture makers, to clubs, engineers, manufacturers, doctors, laboratory technicians and that class of cinematographers having use for 16mm. equipment with a professional camera's range of abilities."[77] As this article suggests, the camera's technological sophistication was understood to appeal to advanced amateur filmmakers. But observers also noted the ways in which a "professional" 16mm camera could open up the format to new kinds of uses, including "an hitherto untouched field—that of the professional makers of 16mm. productions for commercial or industrial use. These have heretofore been forced either to use simple amateur equipment, or to make their picture with professional 35mm. 'release-prints.'"[78] Here, the 16mm format was seen to be maturing into a quasi-professional format, though it would take over a decade and World War II for this change to come about fully.

Figure 10. Providing a new range of technical features on a 16mm camera, the Ciné-Kodak Special was marketed to professionals and advanced amateurs. *Movie Makers*, November 1933, 484. Courtesy Media History Digital Library.

Among amateurs, the "professional" qualities of the new 16mm camera were understood in a different way, as a means of expanding the realm of the amateur, nontheatrical film field, now on an equal technical footing with 35mm film. An author in *Movie Makers* noted, "Anything that can be filmed on 35mm. width can now be made on 16mm. and everything that is produced on 16mm. film can be projected satisfactorily for medium sized audiences.... Subject only to the limitation of audience size, 16mm. filming can accomplish all that 35mm. filming can accomplish with the exception of sound recording. A further definite advantage is offered in the lesser cost of 16mm. raw film."[79] Advanced amateurs were thus unshackled from the earlier limitations of the 16mm format, and their range of activity would expand considerably: "Experimenters will discover in 16mm. movies many new things, just as Dr. Watson and Mr. Webber, working as amateurs in 35mm., discovered them in that medium. The whole motion picture technique will be carried forward by these experiments and, more and more, amateurs will lead, while professionals follow."[80] The Ciné-Kodak Special, like Kodacolor, was seen as a new technology that would allow amateurs to pursue new directions for both film production and film art. Over the course of the 1930s and '40s advanced amateurs worked in both

8mm and 16mm formats. Discussions in amateur publications, however, reveal that there was a certain degree of status-consciousness about format. In general, advanced amateurs produced more challenging works on 16mm or moved to that format when they had achieved a certain degree of technical accomplishment on 8mm.

The 1930s saw a gradual increase in professional uses of 16mm film. Beyond the introduction of the Ciné-Kodak Special in 1933, advances in 16mm projector illumination and optical sound track reproduction made it possible by 1936 to show 16mm to larger audiences in larger spaces.[81] These advances made 16mm film useful for nontheatrical exhibition far beyond home amateur uses; it was becoming a bona fide industrial medium, no longer designed only for amateurs, as evidenced by its increased use in educational and governmental exhibition.[82] By the early 1940s, 16mm film was being used even in Hollywood for studio preproduction tasks, such as location scouting and set décor color testing.[83] An additional shift came in the early 1940s with the arrival of a new generation of professional 16mm cameras, expanded use of films for business purposes, and finally an important wartime role for the small-gauge format. Bell and Howell introduced a professional 16mm camera in 1941; designed along the same lines as their studio 35mm equipment, it was intended for professional production use.[84] And in response to the increased use of 16mm for business and industrial filmmaking, *American Cinematographer* initiated a new column in 1941 called "16mm Business Movies," which reviewed new films in that field.[85] The inaugural column noted, "Sixteen millimeter commercial filming has long since outgrown the experimental stage and become a legitimate and highly-specialized field of professional cinematography. The technicians in this field stand definitely apart from both the 16mm. amateur and from their 35mm. professional fellows." Companies such as Coronet Pictures, which produced 16mm industrial and educational films in studios, were pointed to as evidence of this trend.[86]

By far the most dramatic move toward professionalizing 16mm film production came as a result of its wartime uses. The American government used 16mm films to instruct soldiers, document military activities, and inform and entertain audiences in both civilian and military settings.[87] The editor of *American Cinematographer* remarked in 1942, "As America's participation in the war increases, it is interesting to note the parallel increase in the use of 16mm. motion pictures by governmental agencies, civil and military alike."[88] Later the same year, the publication reinforced its position on the rise of the format: "We believe that 16mm. is very much the coming thing in professional cinematography—even in many phases of studio production. And we want our readers to be ready for it when it comes."[89] Subsequent articles during the war focused on 16mm production techniques and postwar possibilities in industrial and educational filming. Even as these areas promised expanded and professionalized 16mm film production, they sometimes acknowledged the amateur's role in developing these fields: "It was the amateur who innocently pointed out to the industrialist and the educator the economic method with which to impress the mind of the observer through the medium of 16mm. film."[90] This author gives amateurs credit for discovering the nontheatrical fields of 16mm informational film production and exhibition, fields that would soon become booming areas of postwar professional film production.[91] Popular writer Terry Ramsaye proposed that the 16mm format had flourished during the war: "These days of war find the sixteen millimeter motion picture come of age. It is functioning alongside its thirty five millimeter progenitor in every field and, the while, moves toward the extension of the service of the camera and screen into a greater, broader career than the standard film will ever achieve. . . . The sixteen millimeter film has achieved professional status without losing its amateur standing."[92] Ramsaye noted that 16mm film had demonstrated its value through use in numerous specialized and nontheatrical contexts: "It is the film of universal service." And while the format would continue to have creative value and amateur uses, its future uses were clearly also much expanded. As early as 1943, editors and manufacturers were anticipating the end of the war and the boom in amateur film equipment that would follow.[93]

The conclusion of the war brought the rapid professionalization of 16mm that had been promised. By December 1945, newsreel companies were announcing a move to 16mm for production, blowing up only the final edited reels to 35mm for theatrical exhibition.[94] In 1946, Mitchell introduced a new professional, studio-grade 16mm film camera that was designed to be compatible with other professional camera equipment and to ease the professionals' shift to the smaller format.[95] The professional use of 16mm film expanded over the next decade. The availability and widespread adoption of Arriflex cameras in North America during the 1950s were particularly significant for the emergence of 16mm direct and independent cinema movements, creating aesthetic uses of 16mm film that redefined new, *non*amateur alternatives to the Hollywood commercial mode of production. While the professionalization of 16mm film production was much proclaimed and applauded—especially by *American Cinematographer*—during the postwar years, *Movie Makers* warned against having expectations that were too great for the medium. No doubt the 16mm film had come far since 1923, but could it fulfill the burden of expectations that were being placed on it in 1947?[96] While praising 16mm film's ability to present incidents and events, as well as arousing emotions, the author cautioned:

> As the child of 1923 comes into the maturity of 1947, those who have watched over its youth hope that the new paths to which it is urged will be those in which its effectiveness can really operate and that it will not be called upon to accomplish those things for which it is not designed. We can best serve the future of the general film if we do not claim too much for it. It can best serve, if we who know its limitations make them clear to the great number of people who are looking to it for miracles.

In this the amateur reasserted a kind of authority over the postwar "general film"—the increasingly professionalized 16mm educational and industrial film.

Despite this change of status, many advanced amateurs continued using the 16mm format, and many defended its place in the amateur toolbox. Countering what was by the late 1940s a self-evident interpretation of the changed status of 16mm, one *Movie Makers* editorial refuted a deterministic way of thinking about film gauge: "It has been foolishly asserted that 16mm movies have become a kind of in-between professional width, leaving only 8mm to real amateur pleasure." The author argued that despite the emergence of semiprofessional "practical filmmakers," 16mm was still primarily an amateur format: "There is no reason for the amateur to feel unimportant, or to let his filming for fun be looked upon with kindly indulgence. By the very weight of his numbers he is the most important factor in 8mm and 16mm movie making. For the fun of it still remains the most compelling urge towards personal filming. And what fine fun it is!"[97] This plea defended the amateurs' claim on 16mm in terms of their greater numbers as producers of films and consumers of 16mm film equipment. And despite its increasing professionalization, 16mm remained a format for the most advanced and accomplished amateurs. Even in the 1950s, a larger proportion of prize-winning films in amateur contests were shot on 16mm. *Movie Makers* attributed this to 8mm's relative youth and pointed out in 1949 that the format was gaining adherence among advanced amateurs.

But even a few years later, the proportion of 16mm award winners was the direct inverse of the proportion of 16mm film users among amateurs in general. A 1953 article proposed that in the United States, amateur movie makers using 8mm outnumbered 16mm movie makers three to one; the ratio among ACL honors, however, was still the reverse of this. The article suggested that this was because many ACL members started with 8mm but then switched to 16mm as they became more accomplished filmers, which is why the ACL remained a predominantly 16mm organization.[98] The format of advanced amateurs would remain 16mm through the 1970s, even as 8mm cameras become more advanced. In 1957 a number of new "pro" features on 8mm cameras were introduced, including through-the-lens focusing; a dismountable lens system; and single-frame exposure. According to John Forbes, writing in *American Cinematographer*, these new features would "put 8mm camera on par with the sixteens [and] usher in a new era of movie making for serious cine filmers."[99]

WIDESCREEN AND 3-D AMATEUR FILMMAKING

Amateur filmmakers explored a variety of other technological developments including 3-D and widescreen filmmaking. In 1953, just as CinemaScope was arriving in commercial theatres, Bell and Howell launched a parallel technology for 16mm widescreen films.[100] Widescreen films seem to challenge the sense we have of amateur films as small-screen presentations. What was widescreen's appeal to amateurs, and how did it share space with the new living-room images being presented on television? A 1955 *Popular Science* article provides one account of the relationship between the theatrical widescreen and the amateur widescreen experience. Comparing a friend's home movies with a theatrical CinemaScope exhibition, the author was critical: "After the wide-screen movie we had just seen, his square projections looked flat and lifeless. I frankly said so. 'Yes, I know,' my friend agreed. 'If I could only get on my film what I actually see while I'm shooting—that would be something!'"[101] To be able to film what was actually seen while shooting was the promise of amateur widescreen cinematography like the Filmorama system discussed in this article. It offered an advance on the limitations of arbitrarily narrow frame size and a broadening of the amateur's point of view that would result in a seemingly less mediated reproduction of the world.

The Bell and Howell Filmorama system was joined by a handful of other new widescreen systems, some of which also worked on 8mm film (such as Vitascope, from Holland). An anamorphic system, Filmorama used the same lens on both camera for filming and projector for playback to create an image with a 2.68:1 aspect ratio, greater even than CinemaScope, one report boasted. From the outset, promoters of amateur widescreen film suggested the technology offered an immersive experience comparable to 3-D; when shown with a curved screen and using stereophonic (or three-dimensional) sound, the technology could create "a strong sense of depth and participation in the scene ... without the need to wear special viewing

Figure 11. Amateurs exploited Filmorama's wide aspect ratio by showing grand vistas, traveling shots, and sometimes both at once. *San Francisco* (Tullio Pellegrini, 1955). Frame capture from the Internet Archive (https://archive.org).

glasses, as for 3-D movies."[102] The *Popular Science* article noted, "Not only do you get wide pictures on the screen, but you actually get a sense of three dimensions."[103] Initially the format was geared toward large-scale, nontheatrical uses of 16mm exhibition, but it also included amateurs in its target audience.[104] *Popular Science* emphasized the value of widescreen films even for living room presentation, where one would expect a smaller screen and correspondingly a less immersive experience.[105] Perhaps the function of widescreen amateur movies was more compositional than immersive, permitting amateurs to film what they actually saw when shooting.

We can shed some light on this by examining how amateurs used the technology in three extant Filmorama movies. The first film, by the Italian American amateur Tullio Pellegrini, is a 16mm Filmorama travelogue of San Francisco in 1955 that employs a conventional structure and makes emphatic use of the widescreen equipment. The film's use of traveling car shots, or updated phantom rides, heightens our sense of being in motion, much like early Cinerama films (figure 11). This is no rough home movie; it is a very polished travelogue and was shown before an audience of five hundred amateurs at a Bay Area amateur screening the year it was produced. Two other surviving films are by a Kenosha amateur named Ron Doerring, who shot and edited them with a friend (George Ives) in the mid-1950s. *Filmorama Travels* is a compilation of travel footage from American tourist sights and natural vistas. Like Pellegrini's film it employs a car-mounted camera to create a phantom-ride effect. The final film, *Susie Steps Out*, diverges slightly from the travel genre and instead chronicles a little girl's visit to a local amusement park. If travel footage seems the most logical use of amateur widescreen, *Susie Steps Out* marries this tendency with glimpses of the everyday. It is a widescreen film for a family subject that uses the widescreen effect to create sight and editing gags but ultimately turns the camera away from the ride and toward the family spectacle.

This admittedly small sample of films suggests some additional tendencies of amateur widescreen filmmaking. First, these amateurs made deliberate but aggressive use of the phantom-ride technique, perhaps because it was a way of capturing a powerful sensory experience even on the relatively smaller screens amateur films would be projected on. Second, compositions emphasize the depth of space being explored, and winding patterns are particularly prominent. Third, there are compositional juxtapositions and even jokes in these films: from a panoramic view of the mountain horizon and a distant train to a graphic match with hot dogs on a BBQ; widescreen could make an impressively long spectacle of even the most banal sight or the smallest fish (figure 12). Amateurs like Doerring and Pellegrini developed strategies for maximizing compositions in terms of both width and depth of space. And despite the polished surface of these films, they are still open to the moments of contingency we expect from amateur movies, as when the camera's look is returned by curious onlookers (figure 13).

Not all commentators were fans of widescreen film, whether amateur or professional. In *Movie Makers*, the arrival of CinemaScope at the professional level was greeted with concern about the emergence of a more static cinema. When the Filmorama system was evaluated in the September 1953 issue of *Movie Makers*, it was dismissed as a fad, the latest in a line of widescreen attempts, dating back to a Ciné-Panor anamorphic system that was marketed to amateurs in 1931 but quickly faded from view. Widescreen filmmaking, however, would continue to attract a small but devoted amateur following. Doerring later became a member of the U.K.-based Widescreen Association, which was first formed in 1964 and established an American chapter in the early 1970s.[106] Arriving at a time when TV was also challenging the home movie's hegemony of moving images in the living room, widescreen movies created a more powerful feeling of immersion in amateur motion pictures. Was this an epic vision of family life or a complex inversion of mainstream cinema? Perhaps a consideration of 3-D amateur filmmaking will shed additional light on this.

Like widescreen filmmaking, stereoscopic, or 3-D, filmmaking first appeared among amateurs during the 1930s. In 1937, amateurs such as J. Kinney Moore were already adapting their amateur 16mm equipment to achieve three-dimensional effects: "'Stereoscopic motion pictures—movies

Figure 12. *Above:* What a big fish! By juxtaposing panoramic views with closer shots, amateurs created amusing uses of the widescreen format. *Filmorama Travels* (Ron Doerring and George Ives, c. 1955). Courtesy Chicago Film Archives, Ron Doerring Collection. **Figure 13.** Amateur widescreen films could still include moments of contingency, as when the camera's look is returned. *San Francisco* (Tullio Pellegrini, 1955). Frame capture from the Internet Archive (https://archive.org).

in which a real illusion of the missing 'third dimension' of depth is given— have received the attention of many researchers, professional and amateur. Some of their schemes have worked; others have not. But the goal of producing moving pictures which will give a scene the same roundness and depth the eye perceives continues to hold endless fascination."[107] According to this article, Moore was able to mechanically synchronize the exposure on two 16mm Ciné-Kodak Specials for filming and similarly synch two projectors for exhibition through polarized filters. The result, when viewed through the appropriate special glasses, was described as an "amazing impression of reality." In a similar vein, the California eye doctor and amateur filmmaker Dr. O.E. Ghrist adapted his 8mm cameras and projectors to achieve 3-D pictures as well.[108] Because the principle of producing 3-D films was relatively rudimentary, amateurs with the inclination and extra equipment necessary were able to create films with stereoscopic effects. In this way, amateurs explored different perceptual possibilities in motion pictures.

Although the war seems to have stalled further growth of amateur 3-D experimentation, a resurgence came in the early 1950s, coinciding with the boom in commercial 3-D filmmaking. The March 1953 issue of *American Cinematographer* was a special issue dedicated to 3-D and widescreen film, and it included an examination of recent amateur equipment designed to achieve these effects at home. Over the course of the year, three companies—Bolex, Nord, and Elgeet—marketed attachments that adapted amateur cameras and projectors for 3-D use (figure 14). These commercially available 3-D attachments usually took the form of special lens attachments that produced two images side-by-side on each frame of 16mm film.[109] So taken with 3-D was *American Cinematographer* that it organized a special 3-D 16mm film festival in March 1954. Not exactly a film contest, this festival showed 3-D films from both amateur and professional 16mm producers who employed these new attachments. While many were impressed with the results, they objected to the "narrow" images that these 16mm systems produced: "In the Bolex, Elgeet and Nord systems, the twin pictures—that is, the right and left eye images—are on one film, side by side, instead of on two separate film as in most 35mm systems. Because of this physical arrangement, the format of the 16mm 3-D picture on the screen is different than in theatrical films. The picture has a vertical instead of the conventional horizontal rectangular picture."[110] So as commercial cinema was exploiting a wider screen, amateur 3-D film was narrowed in dimensions. The author concludes, "For many in the Festival audience, the 'narrow' picture was an objectionable feature."

While it is unclear how widespread amateur use of this 3-D equipment was (no films are known to be extant), it seems to have been less popular even than the widescreen gadgets like Filmorama. But the two deserve to be examined side by side because of their broadening of the scope of amateur image making. Amateur interest in 3-D filmmaking was an updating of interest in an older technology: stereoscopic photography. In this sense, it participated in what Thomas Elsaesser proposes as an alternative genealogy of cinema: "the long battle of stereoscopic vision versus monocular vision."[111] Elsaesser points to the popularity of stereoscopic imagery through the nineteenth century but argues that this was repressed in the

Figure 14. Companies marketed attachments to adapt 16mm equipment for 3-D filming and projection. *Movie Makers*, January 1952, 25. Courtesy Media History Digital Library.

twentieth century with the growing popularity of cinema, resurfacing only occasionally in avant-garde filmmaking. I would extend this genealogy to propose that stereoscopic imaging persisted in amateur circles throughout the twentieth century. While amateurs adapted the mass medium of cinema to the living room and other small-scale contexts, they also extended the parlor fascination with stereo photography to organized amateur contexts, in which "Stereo or 3D photography" continues to be a contest category for amateur photographers to this day.[112] Seen in this light, 3-D films were firmly within an amateur terrain during the 1950s, drawing on a combined interest in photographic stereoscopy and DIY film tinkering.

TELEVISION

In many cases, amateurs also developed their own gadgets or customized film equipment. Amateurs were consistently interested in producing new "tricks" using their camera and its technology, whether through manipulation of frame rate (fast/slow motion, time lapse, animation), superimposition, or other special effects.[113] The arrival of television provided another locus of amateur curiosity, primarily as a venue for exhibiting amateur films but also for other purposes. In 1940 *Movie Makers* reported what it claimed was "the honor of presenting on a television program the first 16mm amateur motion picture complete with narrative, sound effects and music via the dual turntable."[114] According to the report, Frederick Beach, of the magazine's staff, presented his "popular railroad study, *Roundhouse to Roadbed*, with the half hour program being put on the air through W2XBS, the television unit of the National Broadcasting Company in New York City." As television expanded across the United States after World War II, further opportunities for broadcasting amateur work were proposed. These included semiprofessional news filming of local events, which some predicted would be in high demand: "Special production technique, developed by and in turn developing an entire new film industry, are prophesied by this pioneer in video picture programs. Will there be openings for the advanced and able amateur?"[115] As with 16mm film, filming for television became a topic that vexed the relationship between a broadening field of professional filmmaking and a new medium that might be open to opportunities for amateurs. On one hand, *American Cinematographer* noted the many opportunities for professional cinematographers there; on the other, television was also posited as one of the few possible access points for advanced amateurs wishing to become professionals.[116] Indeed, some amateurs were able to find an exhibition venue on their local television station. This could take the form of specialized documentary content, as with an eight-minute amateur film called *Pablito's Playground,* which was televised by a local station in San Francisco. The film presents documentary observations of the daily life of a Yucatán boy, Jaime, whom a pair of amateur filmmakers dubbed Pablito for their filming of him during a visit to Mexico.[117] Toward the end of the 1950s some explored the possibility of televising a regular program of amateur short films: "Too often it is assumed that home movies record only travels, birthdays, weddings, and children of the family, and therefore are limited to a small personal audience of family and friends. The Amateur Film Festival intends to disprove this view by showing to the public the creative work to be found in the amateur film field."[118] The program promised to present amateur films along with a panel discussion and interviews with filmmakers. While it isn't clear if this program ever got off the ground, other local and later community television became loci of amateur, small-scale, community-based media exhibition.

While television exhibition promised to expose amateur films to larger audiences, amateurs also used their film equipment to record and preserve television broadcasts. In some cases these recordings were framed as film chronicles of particular televised events, such as an amateur's film of a prize fight: "The original plan had been to invite a number of friends to watch the Louis-Conn fight, second edition. This innocent idea soon graduated into a plan for filming the guests as they arrived, got settled and reacted to the fight. Interspersed through this footage were to be shots of the fight itself."[119] This is a hybrid film that follows some conventions of an amateur filmed event (i.e., a travel film that includes some staged actions), combined with a film of a live television broadcast. More typical were suggestions that amateurs might use film as a way of capturing and replaying live TV content: "With the tremendous expansion of television broadcast activities during the past year, and the increasing volume of receiving sets sold—especially in the eastern seaboard and Pacific coast states—amateur movie makers will undoubtedly attempt to make films of various newsworthy telecasts directly from the television receiving screen."[120]

While filming off TV presented some technical challenges, including low image quality and flicker, amateurs experimented with ways of overcoming these challenges. This idea of creating a library of TV shows using amateur film equipment reappeared a number of times over the next decade.[121] While this kind of off-air recording would not become a typical part of home media practice until the VCR era in the 1980s, it is fascinating to see the impulse for this kind of "remediation" of broadcast TV foreshadowed so persistently in the 1940s and '50s. Even at these early stages, television was seen as continuous with film-based home media viewing and making. Forecasting this video age further were articles that appeared in the 1950s concerning the development of videotape technology. But the fulfillment of these efforts was acknowledged to be many years in the future.[122]

In these discussions about amateur cinema's reception and the incorporation of television into its media practice, we note again the unique characteristics of film (it is a medium for preserving images, as opposed to TV's ephemeral live broadcast) as well as its particular uses (programmed and made by amateurs, not on somebody else's schedule). We also note amateurs' interest in exploring new media technologies and integrating them into their filmmaking and viewing practices. How did TV change amateur filmmaking? Motion pictures became more ubiquitous: most people had them in their homes with televisions. But control over motion pictures, in terms of both making and viewing, could still be accomplished only with amateur film technologies. Many amateurs also suggested, however, that television was at least partly responsible for a reduction in amateur movie club activity in the United States during the 1950s. Evidently, some of the novelty of domestic motion pictures was gone, replaced by a new era of electronic home entertainment technology. The transformation of amateur moviemaking and culture during the post–World War II years up to 1960 is the subject of the next chapter.

5 Ciné-Sincerity
Postwar Amateur Film Culture (1945–1960)

> In less than a generation, an ever increasing army of amateurs has successfully mastered every fundamental technique of the craft, has imaginatively explored every subject under the shining sun. *More* people will do both of these things in the years to come. But it is hard to see how they can do them much better. Amateur movie makers of the first quarter century have written a creative record of which they may well be proud.
>
> **James W. Moore,** *"The Amateur: 1923–1950"*[1]

Between the end of World War II and 1960 amateurs continued to produce striking films, witnessing a growth, if anything, in the popularity of their hobby. But even as writers in *Movie Makers* noted with pride both the success of "the general film"—referring to the nascent industry of professional 16mm educational, industrial, and documentary production—and the growing market for home movie equipment, amateur discourse struggled to locate the amateur's position in what was no longer a new and wide-open field of small-gauge film production. What had seemed in the 1930s to be an amateur "movement," spurred by utopian attitudes about free expression and international communication, had lost its coherence and momentum. For some writers, amateur moviemaking had come of age and was therefore even better equipped to bring about the amelioration of international conflicts, as well as the pragmatic alignment of individual creativity with modern technology. But the postwar era also witnessed significant changes that forced a reconsideration of the field of amateur filmmaking. The first change was internal, as advanced amateurs produced increasingly polished films that were further away in technique than ever from the beginners and snapshooters who occupied the lower ranks of amateur activity. On the other hand, the expansion in professional, small-gauge film production effected a different set of changes around the terrain that amateur filmmakers could lay claim to. The 16mm film had played an important role in educational and informational propaganda during World

War II, and the postwar era witnessed a rapid expansion and professionalization of the 16mm field. The postwar era also saw the emergence of independent and avant-garde cinema communities that were increasingly separate from the amateur world. As these distinct small-gauge film cultures—educational, chronicle, experimental—emerged after World War II, amateur discourse faced the daunting tasks of supporting the accomplished work of experienced amateurs, attracting novice filmmakers to their fold, and rearticulating the identity of amateur film culture in new circumstances. No longer the inheritors of silent film aesthetics or the vanguard for film artistic activities, amateur moviemakers occupied a more populous and in some ways contested terrain.

This chapter traces the changes and challenges to amateur film culture following World War II until the end of the 1950s. During this period, amateur movie clubs experienced a brief resurgence before facing new challenges to membership. The new television viewing habits that came after the war, as well as the demands of the baby boom, clearly competed with the hobby. But changes to the amateur ethos were more difficult to pinpoint after the war. After World War II, amateur movie contests proliferated anew: The Amateur Cinema League continued its annual contest of the Ten Best amateur films, and *American Cinematographer* also returned, briefly, to the world of amateur competitions with contests in 1950, 1951, and 1952. The Photographic Society of America also began holding annual film contests.[2] Amateur movie contests after the war had to adapt to the rising proficiency and semiprofessional status of 16mm filmmakers. While some contests chose to reconfigure their terms in order to appeal more to novices, others sought out amateur, and later student, film production at the highest levels of technical proficiency. Tracing these different tensions in amateur movie contests reveals some of the significant debates and shifts in tone around amateur filmmaking between 1945 and 1960. North American amateur movie culture frequently turned to flourishing international, primarily European, models for higher standards and avenues for revitalization. But even while doing so, amateur filmmaking turned ever more domestic in its scope, focusing on the domestic family as a subject for filmmaking and strengthening the social bonds of the amateur family through changes in the structure of clubs and national organizations.

AMATEUR MOVIE CLUBS

Between 1945 and 1960 amateur movie clubs experienced growth and revitalization but also tensions resulting from the different interests and skill levels of their members. As amateur moviemaking grew in the 1950s, so too did movie clubs and their networks proliferate, especially in major cities like Los Angeles and Chicago. During this period, amateur movie clubs provided important venues for coordinating a variety of amateur activities, including film production and exhibition, competitions, and social activities. After World War II, movie clubs quickly returned to their full prewar activity, thanks in part to returning club members who had been engaged in military service during the war. Clubs welcomed home returning soldiers and military personnel and also opened their doors to new members. The period saw frequent presentations of wartime materials and reminiscences of soldiers, such as a 1946 talk at the Los Angeles Cinema Club by member Lt. Gaetano Faillace, who had served as an official photographer with General MacArthur in the Pacific campaign.[3] As examples of what must have been a somewhat common occurrence, the New York 8mm Club presented V-E Day films shot by a member, and the San Francisco Cinema Club showed a film called *Japan after VJ Day*.[4] In addition to welcoming these returning members, many clubs also set aside part of their meeting times to give introductory talks about filmmaking for newcomers, such as the Utah Cine Arts Club's "lecture on the fundamentals of movie making."[5] Many clubs also introduced contests specifically for novice moviemakers.[6] As *Movie Makers* reported, "Movie clubs all over the country are reporting increased attendance and stimulated interest. With club activities lessened in the war years, pent up enthusiasm is bursting forth like blossoms in the spring."[7] Discussions about the best way of organizing movie clubs and their production activities reappeared in magazines, along with encouragement for showing amateur films borrowed from other clubs or the ACL film library.[8]

Movie clubs returned to various activities that combined socializing with filmmaking and rapidly expanded their networks to include other clubs nearby. In 1946, for example, several Wisconsin movie clubs jointly held a "movie picnic"; in this way, local amateur moviemaking networks were expanded to a larger regional scope.[9] The same was the case in other regions, such as the Southern California regional meetings. In September 1947, the LA Cinema Club held its first amateur film exposition, which drew almost a thousand amateurs from Southern California movie clubs.[10] The expo included equipment displays, social activities, and a film competition in the form of the "Club Challenge Cup," which was won by Clarence Aldrich's *The Farmer's Daughter*, representing the Long Beach Cinema Club. In Chicago, there were many different clubs in and around the city; in 1944, three of these clubs formed the Associated Amateur Cinema Clubs of

Chicago. By 1952 the association had expanded to include twelve clubs, mostly Chicago and suburban but also including Kenosha, Wisconsin. It also organized an annual convention of Chicago's amateurs for a day of screenings and informative talks and workshops. This association held an annual contest, which crowned the best of each club's own contest winners.[11] This network for amateur movie clubs also led to an informal circuit for the exchange of amateur films, as clubs hosted one another for screenings nights.

The immediate postwar years also saw a flourishing of amateur film screenings in the form of gala and special themed events. For example, the 1946 New York Metropolitan Motion Picture Club's thirteenth annual gala screening at Hunter College reported over seven hundred in attendance and in subsequent years expanded to include screenings on successive evenings.[12] Films shown included the most successful amateur films from national and local club sources, and the gala also provided the first public screening in the New York area of the Maxim and Ten Best winners.[13] Movie clubs also presented special themed film exhibitions, such as silent movie and "Nickelodeon Nights." Between reels in film presentations such as *The Great Train Robbery*, clubs presented glass slides and live piano music. These screenings targeted a general audience, with the design of drawing new members to the club.[14] This event reinforces our sense of an affinity between amateur cinema and early film history in two ways. First, it positioned the amateur club as an exhibition venue appropriate for historical programming and indeed any noncommercial film fare. Second, it reaffirmed amateurs' interest in an earlier and more pared down kind of film production; this was consistent with postwar amateur film productions that were throwbacks to early cinema genres and themes, such as Clarence Aldrich's Keystone comedy tribute film *The Farmer's Daughter*.

But many move clubs were not able to recover from the disruption of the war or to sustain the momentum that came quickly after it. By the late 1940s, advice started appearing in amateur publications for "the ailing movie club." One author suggested that this lack of success was the result of an insufficient spread of responsibility around the group so that "too few do too much."[15] More generally, the problem of diverging interests among club members was seen as a significant challenge; the range of different interests and possible goals that could be incorporated into an amateur movie club included:

1. learning the fundamentals of movie making
2. improving amateurs' techniques

3. screening their films for constructive criticism
4. presenting their films publicly in the club and elsewhere
5. observing the results other beginners were achieving
6. seeing the very best in nontheatrical filming
7. keeping abreast of new techniques and new equipment
8. enjoying social contacts in the pursuit of their hobby[16]

These activities can be broadly categorized in terms of *learning* film production, the *exhibition* of nonmainstream films; and the *social networking* of people interested in film. But commentators frequently noted that these activities were often at odds with one another: "It is obvious that only a few members are likely to be interested in all of the phases of membership activity. It is also recognized that some of them make movies, others find pleasure only in viewing them, while still others are primarily gadgeteers or technicians." While club leaders worked to fulfill the promise of amateur clubs, the many different functions expected of the organization often led to frustration and disengagement.

As amateur movie activities in the United States struggled, the scene there was compared unfavorably with the situation in Europe. Addressing the issue of declining American movie club participation in 1951, *American Cinematographer* asked, "Have US amateur movie makers lost their way on the road to today's most rewarding hobby?" Pointing to television as a possible competitor, the author draws comparisons between the American situation and amateur activities in France and Britain: "There is considerable evidence that the American amateur has not kept pace with his European brothers. Whereas British and French ciné hobbyists returned to movie making with increased zeal following World War II, Americans—having been appreciably slowed in their activities during war years—never have gotten back into stride."[17] In contrast to the rapid and impressive growth in the amateur movement during the 1930s, the 1950s seemed to show a marked decline. In France, on the other hand, the excitement about the promise of amateur cinema recalled the earlier idealistic tracts that appeared in *Movie Makers* during the 1920s and '30s. French organizer Pierre Boyer wrote, "With the cine camera, every man can in accordance with his temperament reveal to us something of his personal philosophy, his reactions to life in the world and in society; he can take us inside his work and his activities; he can express in his own way, untrammeled by censorship or by commercial considerations, what he thinks, what he loves, and what he desires." Similarly robust amateur activity was identified in England, where

METRO NEWS

Published monthly by
METRO MOVIE CLUB
OF RIVER PARK, INC.
5100 NORTH FRANCISCO AVENUE
CHICAGO 25, ILLINOIS

OFFICERS

ANDREW C. GRAHAM, Pres.
FRANK BIEDKA, V. Pres.
CARL D. FRAZIER, Sec'y.
ARTHUR J. BARCAL, Treas.

Meetings every Wednesday at 8:30 p.m.
September to May inclusive

Edited by
MARGARET E. CONNEELY
5750 N. Meade Avenue

DIRECTORS

EDWARD W. DILLER
GEORGE R. IVES
AUGUST HENNINGER
EUGENE STITZ
ARTHUR H. ELLIOTT

"The aim of this club shall be to aid by mutual cooperation those interested in cinematography."

Figure 15. The Metro Movie Club framed itself as a moviemaking meritocracy that was affiliated with the major international organizations for advanced amateurs. *Metro News,* January 1954, 2. Courtesy Chicago Film Archives, Margaret Conneely Collection.

clubs often had limited membership in order to discourage "any but avid movie makers." In this way clubs were able to avoid "the deadweight of the 'social' member who comes to meetings to see pictures but rarely makes anything worthwhile to exhibit himself." The diagnosis of ailing American movie clubs was related precisely to this problem of too few active filmmakers and too many social members in the clubs. American movie clubs were urged to develop more collective production projects in order to specialize tasks and elevate the overall quality of the films produced.

Some amateurs responded to these criticisms by noting that, in fact, several groups of advanced amateurs were producing serious films in the United States.[18] People acknowledged the Long Beach Cinema Club as exceptional, and in Chicago the Metro Movie Club of River Park was the city's most active and award-winning club throughout the 1950s. In contrast to other cinema clubs, which met just twice a month, Metro held weekly meetings throughout the decade (figure 15). The club pitched itself as a middle-class club for serious amateurs: "Enthusiastic beginners and acknowledged experts, folks from all walks of life—doctors, lawyers, merchants, skilled tradesmen, businessmen, workmen, clerks—have been joining Metro Movie Club since 1936. They come from all parts of the city. They even come from outlying towns."[19] These members were prominent in regional and international organizations like the Amateur Cinema League and the Photographic Society of America and did well in regional, national, and international movie contests. So whereas the city's downtown Chicago Cinema Club had a membership that included some of the city's aristocracy, Metro framed itself as an amateur movie meritocracy. It was more oriented toward contests, polished filmmaking, and broader networks of amateurs. In 1960 a columnist for the national magazine *Photography* lauded Metro for being "a club that works," with the right focus on improving as filmmakers rather than just on the social dimension of moviemaking.[20]

The problem of finding larger audiences for amateur films remained a subject of discussion throughout the 1950s. "So long as the amateur works within the closed circle of his local club, almost entirely isolated from public opinion," the commentator Gordon Malthouse wrote, "the amateur film movement cannot easily grow in stature."[21] British clubs provided one model in which wider exhibition of amateur films was established, and prize-winning amateur films were regularly screened in larger venues for public consumption: "audiences of 600 are by no means uncommon." These screenings occurred in commercial theatres, causing amateurs to think about their audience more; they introduced films to the public, and the attendant publicity and printed program material also introduced the audience to the idea of amateur moviemaking. During the 1950s and beyond, large cities such as Chicago, New York, and Los Angeles routinely organized major screenings of amateur movies, but unlike the vision Malthouse presented, these didn't result in a generally broader public audience for amateur movies in North America. Along similar lines, a television show that would present amateur movie productions was proposed in the mid-1950s. The show's goal was to "offer the television audience an opportunity to recognize the talents of the amateur film maker in a new and unexplored manner."[22] It's not clear that this show was ever produced, but active amateur Margaret Conneely reported something like this in Chicago during the same period.[23] However, Hollywood continued to dominate the mainstream theatrical exhibition in the United States, and smaller circuits of artistic films emerged catering to those with more experimental tastes. Cinema 16, for example, was an exhibition forum for experimental films; its establishment in 1947 was announced in *Movie Makers* magazine, marking the links between amateur and experimental film fields, even as the latter became more autonomous.[24]

Despite concerns raised about the "deadweight of the 'social' member," amateur cinema in the United States became increasingly defined as a social, as opposed to an artistic, activity in the 1950s. The social aspects of clubs and amateur organizations underwent changes during the postwar years. The Amateur Cinema League continued to foreground its role as a "service" rather than "social" organization, noting that this was the reason it did not hold conventions. While this approach seemed successful during the 1930s, the postwar years witnessed a gradual move toward a more socially oriented hobby of filmmaking. Eventually, networks of amateur filmmakers both in regional settings and via events like the Photographic Society of America conventions resulted in a robust culture of filmmaking and socializing.

AMERICAN CINEMATOGRAPHER: AMATEURS, INDEPENDENTS, AND STUDENTS

American Cinematographer continued to publish regular content for amateur moviemakers during the postwar period. The publication was keenly aware of the postwar expansion of amateur moviemaking, as evidenced in an article that repeated Kodak's claim in 1948 that more than a million Americans were 8mm and 16mm camera users.[25] While articles and advice for amateurs were regular features of the magazine throughout most of the 1940s and '50s, its commitment to amateur status was increasingly ambivalent, often blurring the line between the amateur filmmaker and the nascent indie or "semiprofessional" filmmaker. Articles that would be helpful to semiprofessional or independent filmmakers expanded in number during this period, but the amount of attention paid to more typical amateurs fluctuated. As in the past, these articles presented a professional cinematography perspective on amateur activities, such as instructions for using three-point lighting on home movies.[26] In 1948, a new editor and format resulted in the clear "16mm and 8mm Section" but eliminated the reports of the "Among the Movie Clubs" column and generally reduced the quantity of amateur coverage in the magazine. The remaining attention to small-gauge film increasingly focused on industrial 16mm production and other profitable avenues for semiprofessionals.[27]

American Cinematographer announced a return of their annual contest a few years after the end of the war, but this return proved relatively short-lived as the contest struggled to find a successful measure of amateur filmmaking accomplishment. In 1949, the publication announced the "American Cinematographer Award: New Incentive for Amateur Movie Makers," which was designed to give exceptional amateur work wider recognition.[28] The prize was geared toward "the advanced or serious amateur movie maker, once a dub or snapshooter, but who has applied sound photographic principles and creative ability to his work, and in recent years has come up with 8mm. or 16mm. films that win prizes and are talked about." To build on the existing system of contests that was already well-established at most local movie clubs, the *American Cinematographer* invited movie clubs to select the best 8mm and 16mm films made by their members and submit them for consideration in the contest. Filmmakers who weren't members of a local club were permitted to submit films via a local club, which was given a quota for both member and nonmember film submissions. Notably, only American amateur moviemakers were eligible for entry in the contest. The contest was judged by several ASC members and notable professional cinematographers, including Arthur Miller, Charles Clarke, Hal Mohr, Charles Roscher, Ernest Haller, and Ray Rennahan. While touting the professional standard of the judges, the publication remained circumspect about distinctions between amateur and professional, noting, "None of [the advanced amateurs] labor under the delusion that Hollywood's studios hold promising jobs for them, if only their work could be shown to the right people there." Rather, the rewards for amateur accomplishment were more vague: "There are comparable satisfactions to be gained by those serious filmers providing there is ample incentive to pursue their chosen photographic hobby." While *American Cinematographer* would not promise access to the professional ranks, its contest was "the first important step towards creating world-wide recognition for the cinematographic abilities of America's outstanding amateur movie makers."[29]

By the time the winners of the *American Cinematographer* contest were announced in April 1950, the number of awards had increased from a single trophy to four awards (for best of color and black-and-white films in both 8mm and 16mm), which were accompanied by six additional certificates of merit and ten honorable mentions.[30] While most of the trophy prize-winning films were from traditional amateur cinema hotspots in the Northeast (especially Boston and New York City), one was from Seattle, and many of the certificate winners and honorable mentions were from very geographically diverse movie clubs: Oklahoma City, Los Angeles, Kansas City, Utah, Muskegon (Michigan), Canton, Atlanta, and Nashville, to name a few. This range of different American regions gives some indication of how widespread amateur moviemaking had become. The magazine also provided detailed descriptions of each award-winning film and lauded them collectively: "All have demonstrated a desire for serious accomplishments in film making and the contest committee believes their subsequent work will reflect considerable improvement."

Subsequent contests adjusted the rules to a more traditional format that permitted international entries and bypassed the system of club prescreening that had been used in 1950.[31] The 1951 contest presented its own Top Ten films, along with ten honorable mentions, thus closely matching the

ACL's longstanding format.[32] This second contest also provided some interesting statistics about its entries, noting that "over 51 percent had sound on film, on magnetic tape or on discs." Additionally, a third of the films submitted were produced on 8mm, but of these only one placed in the competition.[33] The high proportion of films with sound accompaniment (and even sound-on-film tracks) is indeed noteworthy. The low success rate for 8mm entries in the contest would tend to reinforce the argument that movie contests privileged more accomplished filmmakers who worked in the more expensive (and potentially semiprofessional) 16mm format. Some of the 1951 winners were repeat winners, but in general the winning filmmakers were less geographically diverse, with most winners located on either coast, plus winning entries from Mexico, Britain, and Italy.

The 1952 contest reinforced the sense that 8mm filmmakers were at a distinct disadvantage in the competition by emphasizing the contest's high technical criteria. The announcement for that competition highlighted the "professional" judgment criteria and focused on high-level advanced amateurs: "Only those films which display serious effort in the planning, photography and editing can receive consideration in the final judging."[34] When the winners of this 1952 contest were announced, it became clear that *American Cinematographer* had pitched its competition to the most advanced amateurs. This decision evidently came at the expense of the numbers of films entered, as the magazine reported, "While the volume of entries has decreased, the quality of the individual films is improving steadily."[35] One way this quality was identified was in the increased number of sound-on-film entries, which "indicates a more serious attitude on the part of amateurs making films for competitions." Winning films in the 1952 contest included many repeat filmmakers, and while the publication had previously emphasized the importance of club membership, profiles of winning filmmakers emphasized the individual work of amateurs.[36] The 1952 contest would prove to be *American Cinematographer*'s last annual competition, with its shift away from the significant role it had played in shaping amateur cinema over the previous decades. The following year, *American Cinematographer* announced a more specialized "festival" of amateur 3-D filmmaking, but an annual Ten Best list would not return to the pages of the magazine.

The blurred line between amateur and semiprofessional filmmaking could be found in a series of articles called "The Cinema Workshop," which started in July 1946 and outlined the various steps in film production and distribution. Appearing monthly for nearly two years, the series was explicitly geared toward the advanced amateur and semiprofessional filmmaker.[37]

From creative issues (the idea, script, direction) to more technical concerns (exterior shooting, sound cutting, and recording, etc.), each article in the series addressed filmmakers who had the degree of competence and opportunity necessary to make carefully crafted films. Particularly striking about this moment in nonindustrial filmmaking (especially on 16mm) was the new terrain and the potentially wider audience than had been available to amateurs during the 1930s. The concluding article spelled this out in dramatic form: "The outlook for the motion picture is a healthy one. Whether the producer is an advanced amateur making pictures for the amusement of himself and his friends, or a professional turning out commercial, industrial or educational films, he has every reason to expect a wider and more profitable market for his product."[38] More than at any time in the past, the gap between amateur and professional filmmaking appeared to be narrowing as the market for nontheatrical and independent films on 16mm expanded during the postwar years.[39]

The struggle between these two positions was also evident in articles that highlighted the distance between amateur and professional, on one hand, and those that blurred the distinctions, on the other. Among the former was Hollywood executive William Goetz, who emphasized the status of the professional: "Some people make the easy mistake of thinking that with a light meter, a measuring tape, a few charts, an operator and an assistant, anybody can be a good cameraman. . . . The cameramen have managed to keep themselves on a high professional plane."[40] And yet *American Cinematographer* was complicit in the belief that amateurs could attain some professional qualities, if not actual professional standing. The publication repeatedly emphasized the value of amateur study of professional films and techniques: "The only difference between an amateur motion picture and a professional one, someone has said, is in the photography. Somewhere between the two are films of varying quality, depending upon the knowledge and the skill of the photographer. The serious movie amateur, of course, strives to achieve a professional quality in his photography—the quality he sees in motion pictures on theatre screens."[41] Amateurs who studied professional techniques and honed their craft could aspire to professional results. And while the professional side of things was characterized by greater specialization than ever before, amateurs' success in that terrain was not unheard of.[42] A profile of the "number one movie amateur," Ralph Gray, for example, remarked on his many awards from amateur contests but also noted that some of his footage had been purchased by MGM.[43] A more vivid success story was presented in the form of David Bradley, whose teenage amateur films won recognition from the ACL in the early

1940s, and after completing an amateur feature of *Julius Caesar* (1951), he received a contract with MGM. Herb Lightman noted the exceptional nature of Bradley's situation: "Here, as a result of his extraordinary 16mm movie making talents, he has achieved a goal sought by countless non-professional film makers which few, indeed, attain. For among the nation's seemingly talented cine filmers, very few possess the imagination and the initiative necessary to the production of mature theatrical films. Bradley's case proves there are exceptions, of course, and that recognition of non-professionals by Hollywood *is* possible."[44] Lightman goes on to describe Bradley's *Julius Caesar* as a "thoroughly professional production," but here "professional" was evidently defined as carefully planned and executed. All of the personnel, except Charlton Heston (who had appeared in Bradley's earlier amateur work), were amateur actors (figure 16).

The aspirational ambivalence of *American Cinematographer* was best exemplified in a pair of articles that appeared in the magazine in the mid-1950s. One article, titled "Amateurs Who Became 'Pros,'" identified the "exceptions" like Bradley. "Is there a place in the professional motion picture industry for the amateur movie maker with ability?" it asks. "Can the ambitious cine amateur hope to progress to the ranks of the professional cinematographer in the motion picture studios? These are questions that, if not outwardly expressed, at least exist in the minds of hundreds of serious 8mm and 16mm amateur movie makers. The answer is a qualified 'yes.'"[45] The qualification provided was that opportunities at Hollywood studios for amateurs were exceptionally rare. But in other kinds of filmmaking, such as industrial, educational, and television production, professional opportunities did indeed exist, and most of the examples provided in the article fell into this nontheatrical field. Driving home the point that the Hollywood studios were nearly inaccessible was a later article, which sought to respond to the many letters *American Cinematographer* had received, asking how to gain access to studio work. The author replies: why set the Hollywood studios as your goal? Proposing that studio cinematographers' jobs were "almost unattainable," he explains that the necessary experience included as much as twenty years of working as an assistant or camera operator before becoming a pro cinematographer assigned to feature films. In contrast were the opportunities that lay in the nontheatrical field of production: "There's a lot of work ahead of you if you have chosen cinematography as a career, but most of it will be found in those fields far removed from the Hollywood studios, where the competition is not so keen, where the pay probably is less, but where you have a greater chance for developing into a professional cinematographer as an individual."[46] Hollywood studios were

Figure 16. In a rare case of an amateur making the leap to Hollywood, David Bradley's amateur feature *Julius Caesar* won him a contract with MGM. *Julius Caesar* (David Bradley, 1951). Courtesy Lilly Library, Indiana University, Bloomington, Indiana.

as difficult to break into as always, but the fields of nontheatrical, industrial, and educational film production were the potential avenues for the professional advancement for amateurs, much as they had always been. What had changed since World War II was the professionalization of nontheatrical production, which was also much expanded thanks to the growth of educational film, TV production, and the gradual emergence of independent production.

The focus on increasingly polished and accomplished amateur movies pointed toward a mode of amateur "independent producers" who were skilled—almost to a professional degree—in making short polished films. Opportunities for such skilled amateurs existed in new areas of the motion picture profession, such as local newsreels and television news.[47] Professional cameramen who focused on these areas were sometimes profiled in *American Cinematographer* and in some cases presented some of the distinctions between prewar amateur and postwar independent or small-studio professional. For example, Earl Clark began as an amateur in the 1930s but by 1954 was working for the Associated Screen News studio in Montreal.[48] Similarly, travelogues were touted as a genre that invited semiprofessional productions and could elevate the amateur to professional standards.[49] Curiously, though, this kind of elevation was often described in terms of passion for the filmmaking craft, which had always typified the amateur field: "'How do you break into the field?' almost every new acquaintance who owns a 16mm camera asks anxiously. To which I always feel like saying, 'Love will find a way,' then back down because it sounds foolish. It's not, though. Nothing could be truer. For if you don't love movie making *passionately*, you're just not going to spend the hours required to produce a film with sufficient substance to make someone who doesn't know you from Adam want to spend *his* time and *his* money promoting it for you."[50] The amateur "lover of cinema" was still alive and well, even when increasingly finding a way to make money from filmmaking. This stands somewhat in contrast to the profiles of studio professionals that describe their long-toiling work as assistants while moving up the ranks to cinematographer.

By the mid-1950s, however, being an "independent" was also seen as an option for professionals moving in the opposite direction. "The rapidly developing field of independent production offers challenging opportunities for veteran major-lot cameramen," noted one article.[51] Here we find evidence of the unsettled terrain of professional filmmaking; previously, the professional was to be found in the Hollywood studios, in contrast to the amateurs and semipros, who were clearly on the outside. But with postwar realignment of the film industry (the result of divorcement, TV, 16mm industrial and educational film), there were many more opportunities for "professional" jobs outside studios. Contrasts between amateurs and pros were no longer identified as clearly once outside the studio; now there was lots of opportunity for work on comparatively small—if professional—productions.[52] Accompanying these shifts were the stories about long-standing studio cinematographers who started working as independents, which became a staple of the publication. Where *American Cinematographer* had long been a primarily Hollywood studio–oriented publication, now it also reported on small studio work in the industrial, educational, and religious filmmaking fields.⁵³

American Cinematographer's commentary on amateur cinema eventually spread beyond the United States and lamented the American decline in amateur accomplishment compared with that of other countries. In 1958, the magazine profiled the Cannes Festival International du Film Amateur, which was then in its eleventh year and received more than four hundred entries. Described as the "world's most important amateur film competition," the festival lasted for eleven days in September, and the films were screened at the Palais des Festivals theatre, which seated sixteen hundred.⁵⁴ Of the eighty films selected for showing in 1957, only three had been from the United States. The article focused on the Cannes festival as evidence of the serious nature of European versus American amateur filmmaking: "The amateur cinematographer in Europe takes his hobby more seriously than does his counterpart in the United Sates." The author credited active movie clubs, competitions, and more widespread opportunities for exhibiting amateur film as reasons for this discrepancy. The producers of successful European films were often amateur groups, though not necessarily clubs, which had increasingly been viewed as serving a primarily social function in the United States. The author noted that American amateurs exposed more film than the rest of the world but with less impressive results in terms of both filmmaking and exhibition. We see in this commentary *American Cinematographer*'s lament of the declining quality of American amateur filmmaking and a ceding of support for this activity to European groups. Over the 1950s and '60s, *American Cinematographer* would instead refocus its attention on nascent student filmmaking and preprofessional film contests.

Initially, stories about emerging film schools and student filmmakers were framed in a way similar to those about amateurs: as an alternative sphere from the professional studio cinematographer. A 1951 article highlighted the gap between student and studio filmmaking: "UCLA's student film makers have no illusions about crashing the gates of Hollywood studios. Most have set their sights on the tremendous future looming for educational, industrial and television motion picture production."⁵⁵ By 1953, however, an article profiled a 16mm USC production that won the Screen Producers Guild Intercollegiate Film Award, and USC was described as "the best equipped year-around university film production workshop in America."⁵⁶ Evidently the magazine's commitment to professional filmmaking was clarified once there was a clear path of professionalization via film schools and less often from the amateur ranks. The end of special attention to amateurs occurred in January 1958, the last issue with the

"Amateur Cinematography" section; after that fewer amateur articles were run, and they were no longer "flagged" on the top of the page. By this time 16mm and independent filmmaking was firmly entrenched as a professional field in its own right, and while amateurs might follow a career trajectory that led to professional filmmaking, film schools were increasingly the preferred route.

THE AMATEUR CINEMA LEAGUE: RENAISSANCE AND DECLINE

On the occasion of the ACL's twentieth anniversary in 1946, the editor of *Movie Makers* remarked on the significant shifts in mood that had occurred in the intervening decades since its inception. The early years of the hobby were characterized as "an era of hope, of assurance that, if one contributed honestly to the commonweal, he would be rewarded as a normal byproduct of effort.... Security was something in which the aged might be interested—the youngsters were too confident to bother about it."[57] By contrast, the postwar era was characterized by a kind of fatigue, skepticism, and suspicion: "In twenty years most of that confidence has faded. Today, young and old men and women look about them and wonder how many more assaults will be made upon human endurance.... In an incredibly short time, humanity has tied itself into a Gordian knot of irresolution and suspicion." Despite the jubilation that marked the end of the war, this author recognized the marked difference in cultural mood that characterized the 1940s compared with the 1920s. As usual, *Movie Makers* responded optimistically to the cultural moment and predicted the significant role of amateur movies in rejuvenating cultural confidence, characterizing these movies as one of humanity's "greatest hopes": "The eighth art, come to maturity in two decades of social confusion, may be the new voice by which the old and weary world will be led into a fresh day. If this should be so, we who have served it will be greatly repaid." While this editorial was optimistic, its most significant aspect is its reflective acknowledgment of the changed spirit of amateur movie making. The 1940s, after the Great Depression and a world war, was leery of sweeping political, social, and aesthetic proclamations. The decade that followed would present the Amateur Cinema League with a variety of new challenges, most notably the challenge of reinventing itself for a new era and a new kind of amateur.

In the immediate postwar context, writers in *Movie Makers* recalled some of the early utopian claims for amateur cinema by looking outward at the international reach of amateur culture. Some writers pointed to amateur movies as crucial tools in the necessary intercommunication between authoritarian and democratic nations, in which motion pictures of everyday life could be used to spread international understanding once again. Amateur films had particular credibility, because "they are made not for entertainment or propaganda, but are the factual and intimate records which amateur filmers create."[58] While *Movie Makers* had always claimed an international reach, the postwar years carried with them communication between the ACL and amateur organizations like Great Britain's Institute of Amateur Cinematography, foreign movie competitions like the annual amateur festival at Cannes, and the international organization UNICA (Union International du Cinema d'Amateur). This Europe-based umbrella organization was established in 1938 and reemerged after World War II to coordinate amateur moviemaking activities around the world.[59]

Movie Makers also continued to promote a pragmatic approach to filmmaking, particularly a mode of mechanical craftsmanship. Explaining this position, a 1947 editorial proposed: "As every movie amateur knows, who has carried his cinematography beyond the casual stage, the most abiding satisfaction comes from a development of fine craftsmanship. This fact is one to be found in all superior human effort, but it is particularly vital in all effort which is creative, rather than repetitive and routine."[60] In an effort to puncture the more elitist associations with accomplished film technique, the author notes, "Actually, technique is nothing but craftsmanship—an intelligently worked out and effective way of doing something. The real joy that comes from it is that of the good worker, not that of the solemn pundit, mouthing strange words." All of this is accomplished following pragmatic means: "a thoughtful consideration of one's own trial and error," which "calls for a deal of thinking and doing." The author positions this as akin to sports, perhaps more than to traditional artistic activities: "Deciding what one will do, and then training the mind and the muscles to almost automatic performance, brings the same kind of coordinated power that we get from athletic activity. We enjoy the increase in our own effectiveness as well as the results which that effectiveness produces." Here, as in many other editorials, *Movie Makers* promoted a pragmatic, rather than a theoretical, approach to filmmaking. This approach was grounded in a practice of learning by doing and in learning craftsmanship so that the process itself carried with it as much pleasure—as in the play of music or sports—as the final product did. Nevertheless, such serious attention to craftsmanship may have been less appealing to casual filmmakers or beginners.

After the war, the Amateur Cinema League and *Movie Makers* made efforts to renew and revitalize their organization. Stephen Voorhees stepped down as president of the ACL in July 1947 and was replaced by the ACL veteran and long-serving vice president John V. Hansen.[61] An article in the August 1947 *Movie Makers* profiled Hansen's long career as an amateur filmmaker and his significant experiments with color films.[62] A few months later, *Movie Makers* renewed its appearance and formatting, evidently to appeal to a broader readership of new filmmakers. The magazine pledged to please its readers by addressing them in finer categories: "There are beginning filmers, average filmers and advanced filmers who make movies today. As far as we can, we shall present something of interest to each group."[63] In keeping with this approach, new symbols in some articles pointed out their particular applicability with the headings "The New Filmer" or "The Family Film." An editorial later explained the purpose of these new headings: "These captions are convenient guideposts to serve two very large groups of amateurs, groups large enough to merit special attention in every issue of the magazine.... We want them to know that *Movie Makers* considers them in planning every number for publication."[64] With these new labels and openness to a range of amateurs of different skill levels, *Movie Makers* refashioned itself. While the *Movie Makers* of the 1930s was concerned with pushing the limits of advanced amateur filmmaking across different kinds of nontheatrical activity, the new *Movie Makers* targeted a more general audience. The new "average" amateur was much closer to beginner status and much more concerned with family filming. Additionally, at least one amateur, the president of a club in Salina, Kansas, praised the new format of the magazine for a different reason: "Orchids to you on the change of pace in the make up of *Movie Makers*. Before I have always had the feeling that someone from 'New Yawk' was trying to look down their nose at we non-easterners, and it just didn't leave a feeling that was conducive to happiness. You have done much to improve the situation."[65] The letter suggests that the formatting changes marked *Movie Makers* as less geographically anchored and also less elitist. While *Movie Makers* had always made an effort to include coverage of amateurs and amateur clubs from outside the American Northeast, this writer suggests that it was still viewed as New York–centric in terms of geographical content or in its critical sophistication.

The terms and criteria for the ACL's annual Ten Best list also changed considerably after the war, largely the result of extensive debate about the different interpretations of "amateur" and what qualities amateur accomplishments should reflect. The magazine initiated a new column called "The Reader Writes" in 1947, which created a venue for displaying the different tensions and fractures among different categories of readers. Some writers debated the appropriateness of various aesthetic approaches in amateur filmmaking, in particular between "romantic versus realist" filmmaking.[66] Such exchanges showed that aesthetic attitudes among amateur filmmakers were by no means homogeneous. More fractious were debates about the material conditions of amateur filmmaking, such as one initiated by an Arkansas filmmaker. In a letter that appeared under the heading "How Amateur Is Amateur?" George F. Hartshorn announced that he would not be renewing his membership in the Amateur Cinema League: "The main reason that I decided to stop my membership is that I believe the Amateur Cinema League is no longer an *amateur* league. You have gone past your goal, 'the improvement of amateur films,' and have set your ideal on such a high pedestal that only the professionals can reach up to it."[67] Hartshorn complained that the standards that the organization set for amateur filmmaking were too high and that recent Maxim Award winners "had advantages no true amateur can have or ever expect to have." These advantages were most evident in terms of the 16mm equipment used to produce them: "Their films have been on 16mm film stock, which in itself lets out the 'little fellow' with his $10.00 8mm. camera, 8mm. black and white film and very little in extra equipment." For Hartshorn, the Amateur Cinema League no longer catered to the amateur level of film production, and their competitions had become dominated by semiprofessional filmmakers. Such debates over the status of 8mm versus 16mm film had occurred before, in the 1930s, but here the author reversed the previous rhetoric and positioned amateur aspirations lower: 8mm film production should be considered a different category of film production, as there was no point in aspiring to 16mm levels of accomplishment.[68]

Hartshorn's letter prompted a range of responses, which commented on differences between film formats, amateur standards, and the appropriate goals of an "amateur" organization and its publication. Most vocal were the winners of recent ACL awards, who objected to Hartshorn's suggestion that they were not "amateur" enough. Ralph Gray, winner of the Maxim Award for best amateur film in 1946, interrogated Hartshorn's complaints in a number of different ways, asking why an amateur couldn't make a fine film even with an inexpensive camera. He also noted that his own film was the product of more time than expense (Gray lived in Mexico because it was less expensive than the United States): "I collected sequences for over a year and a half, but the actual time spent at making movies was decidedly *less than three weeks*, at a total cost outside of Mexico City of about $8.00 (US) a day. Surely that is not a sign of 'great expense.'"[69]

Gray encouraged Hartshorn to continue participating in contests and aspiring to higher accomplishment. Another winner, Helen Welsh of Albany,

New York, noted that the expense of equipment should not be seen as a determining factor in amateur accomplishment: "I have seen perfectly appalling movies made with the most expensive camera on the market—and so, no doubt, have you."[70] For these award-winning amateurs, Hartshorn's complaints demonstrated a shortage of persistence more than funds.

Subsequent letters reinforced these sentiments and simultaneously provided a view into some of the professional and personal lives of the amateurs themselves. Al Morton, winner of an award, wrote, "Your assumption that I have plenty of time and money is completely wrong. I am a postman. Their salary, as you know, is only average; and yet out of it I support myself, my wife and the two daughters we have left at home. What filming I do has to be done on Sundays, holidays and during my fifteen days annual leave."[71] Morton previously shot on 8mm before shifting to 16mm. Francis Spoongle, of Alplaus, New York, wrote on behalf of himself and another Ten Best winner and friend: "Both of us work with 8mm film.... None of us has leisure, much money or artistic training. I am a welder and fabricator, working five to six days a week. Webber is an electrical engineer with General Electric, busy to the nth degree. We're just ordinary people. And yet we made the grade."[72] These letters present a varied sketch of amateurs, working in a range of different fields, many of them—as Spoongle suggests—quite distant from creative or camera work. Faced with these rejoinders, Hartshorn retreated to a simplified position: "The 8mm. film and equipment is the true *amateur* film and equipment. The fellow that can afford 16mm size usually can afford to buy and use extra equipment that will better his films."[73] Sixteen millimeter film had, at least in Hartshorn's mind, become naturalized as a professional format, and the equipment that went along with it and the films produced using it had correspondingly professional characteristics. While *Movie Makers* pointed out that 8mm film equipment was not really much less expensive, the perception of it as amateur grade compared with 16mm remained.

The conflict among these different kinds of amateurs was serious enough to warrant a response from the magazine's editor, who decried the emergence of "splinters" within the amateur filmmaking community.[74] For *Movie Makers* and the Amateur Cinema League, survival depended on reinforcing the commonalities of amateur filmmakers across differences of skill level and subject matter. But in the same editor's view, this seems to have become increasingly difficult in the late 1940s: "The Amateur Cinema League, and MOVIE MAKERS which it publishes, both believe in a broad proposition. We hold that amateur filmers will make some poor pictures, many average, an increasing number of good and a few great ones. They will make them on 8mm. or 16mm. film, as their desires and pocketbooks determine. They will make them in every part of a country—north, south, east and west. They will make them with much equipment or with little." Responding to issues of quality, film gauge, and region, the editorial attempted to reinforce the sense of commonality among amateurs and refuted claims of mistreatment. Speaking for the broad group of amateurs as a whole, the editor writes, "What they want from their hobby is pleasure and not politics. They do not want to manage, control or direct amateur movies—or other amateurs. They do not want anybody else to do it. They want—and it is certainly a reasonable wish—to get some fun and relaxation. The splinters spoil the fun." This editorial reveals the different tensions that were straining the Amateur Cinema League during the postwar era. The presence of these splinters and their acknowledgment by the ACL perhaps foreshadowed the decline of the league, which eventually folded a few years later, in 1954.

Perhaps responding to these splinters, the terms of the Ten Best contest were revised in 1948 (to eliminate sponsored films, which will be discussed further in chapter 8) and again in the early 1950s, when *Movie Makers* declared revised criteria for judging the Ten Best contest. These changes emphasized a particular attitude toward filmmaking: "What the judges seek first of all is sincerity—sincerity of camera work, film planning, editing, titling, and above all, creative movie imagination."[75] In this focus on sincerity, the contest marked a shift from the magazine's earlier emphasis on technical achievement and accomplishment: "For some years past our contest announcements have carried a statement almost identical to the one above. In it, however, there stood the word 'quality' in place of the present 'sincerity.'" In shifting from *quality* to *sincerity*, the ACL made a significant change in how it framed accomplished filmmaking (the Ten Best) and in how the organization should be viewed more generally. Tempering this shift by noting the high quality of contest entries, the league deemphasized technique as an objective in its own right: "What you have to say and the imagination with which to say it carry greater weight—with us, at least—than an empty perfection of mechanical photography." The shift in wording had a broader significance that we can identify in light of the debates and evident dissatisfaction that appeared in *Movie Makers* during the postwar era. But if the primary characteristic of amateur accomplishment had become understood as merely the display of technical quality, then this shift provides an indication of how far amateur culture had moved away from the clarity of the organization's creative mission when the movement was founded in the 1920s and flourished in the 1930s. In the 1930s, "quality" was not the only (or even the principal) criterion for judging films; it was often balanced against originality, experimentation, and other creative justifications. But while these objectives were offered in the 1920s and '30s in terms of new directions for film art, the postwar articulation pointed toward a less ambitious, and perhaps more accessible or middlebrow, understanding of amateur accomplishment. The postwar amateur's "sincerity" may have resulted in a continuation of the "amateur spirit," but it also reads here as only a faint echo of the original goals of amateur cinema and a concession to declining readership.

Movie Makers had always related amateur cinema to both commercial cinema and more small-scale artistic filmmaking in its pages; after the war, the balance between these shifted somewhat. *Movie Makers* continued to publish a column that drew lessons for amateur filmmakers from Hollywood movies, now called "Hints from Hollywood—Aids for the Amateur Cameraman, to Be Seen in Current Theatrical Films." From *Mr. Blandings Builds His Dream House*, for example, the column identified several ideas that amateurs could use for domestic comedies; and *Movie Makers* reported in 1949 on Red Skelton's amateur filmmaking activities a year before the comedian made his film about an amateur filmmaker, *Watch the Birdy*.[76] Conversely, the magazine's editorial staff and some of its readership still maintained an interest in experimental and nonmainstream artistic cinema. Some, like Paul R. Stout of Chicago requested that the magazine increase its coverage of artistic films that didn't play much beyond New York, "such as *Beauty and the Beast, Farrebique, The Stone Flower, Furia* and *The Raven*." In this respect, the magazine's base of publication in "New Yawk" was seen as an asset that should be taken advantage of.[77] However the editor's reply indicated that the omission of films that weren't in wide release was a deliberate strategy on the magazine's part; Stout's request for a return of columns such as "Reviews for the Cintelligenzia" that were found in the magazine in the 1930s went unheeded. Instead, *Movie Makers* presented brief news reports about Maya Deren, Cinema 16, and other similar figures, in this way informing interested readers of the expanding experimental film world.[78] *Movie Makers* faced new competition from publications such as *Film Comment* and *Hollywood Quarterly*, which were devoted more directly to the artistic, cultural, and experimental sides of filmmaking. *Movie Makers* ceded this terrain in order to refocus its attention on a narrowed definition of the amateur film world.

Movie Makers continued to trace the activities of previous winners in its regular monthly column called "Closeups—What Filmers Are Doing." The column also traces some of the occasional moves from amateur to professional ranks that occurred among its past members and contest winners. For example, Leslie Thatcher, a winner of a Ten Best prize and numerous *American Cinematographer* citations in the 1930s, was reported in 1949 to be "heading his own highly successful 16mm industrial film producing unit."[79] In a similar vein, *Movie Makers* noted the successful move to professional filmmaking made by Budge and Judith Crawley: "From the premier prize in amateur movies to the highest honor in Canadian professional educational film production is the capsule history of Judith and F. Radford Crawley, ACL, of Ottawa, Canada." This was a response to the Crawley's film *The Loon's Necklace*, which was lauded at the first Canadian Film Awards in 1949 and distributed in the United States by Encyclopedia Britannica Films.[80] From the Ten Best to the Canadian Film Awards, the Crawleys' trajectory signaled another success for prize-winning amateurs of the 1930s.

Amid this effort to balance some of the ACL's original goals with more recent developments, the postwar years saw the passing of the first generation of ACL leaders. Hiram Percy Maxim had died in 1937, and during the next decade a train of his successors and colleagues, including Stephen Voorhees, John Hansen, and Arthur Gale, left the ACL. It wasn't until 1949 and the death of Roy Winton, however, that the ACL announced the end of the first era. Winton had held the position of managing director of the ACL since it was founded in 1926, and he was responsible for establishing many of its organizational pillars and promoting its particular philosophy of amateur filmmaking.[81] The *Movie Makers* obituary presents a fascinating portrait of Winton, whose personal life was otherwise somewhat opaque:

> Those who knew Colonel Winton as an individual, rather than as an executive, will remember a gentleman of courtly charm and graciousness. He had majored in college in the Romance languages and he spoke both French and Spanish with fluency. His taste in art was catholic and informed, but stopped short of the extreme modernists. He was a member of the Grolier Club, a society of bibliophiles, and a founder of the Hajji Baba Club, a small and select group of Oriental rug collectors. But his real love among the arts was for music. He played a sensitive personal piano, favoring such composers as Richard Strauss, Schubert and the simpler Bach. He was for a decade a devoted member of the Metropolitan Opera Club.
>
> It has been remarked by many that Colonel Winton lived out of his era. If such was indeed the case, our era and the entire hobby of amateur motion pictures have been vastly the richer for it.[82]

From this account, Winton seems an unlikely figure to have directed the ACL for so long. Neither an avid amateur filmmaker himself nor a proponent of new technology and artistic forms, Winton's cultural conservatism reemphasizes the Amateur Cinema League's adherence to traditional culture and to a culture of reassurance more generally. An editorial about Winton remarked on his principled nature, which he imparted to filmmaking as an activity: "He believed, in the first place, in the decency and dignity of amateur filming. . . . In the subject matter of amateur pictures, he expected decency from the beginning, and, as the stature of amateur films grew with the years, he applauded their increasing dignity." And in relation to the politicization of the ACL, it notes, "He believed, finally, in the freedom of amateur filming. He regarded the hobby as a treasured and untrammeled medium of human expression."[83] Winton was evidently an adherent of a pragmatic attitude toward filmmaking, at least insofar as he opposed any restrictions being placed on it for some kinds of general principles. Instead, he favored a kind of freedom and breadth of communication supported by dignity and decency.

Following Winton's death, *Movie Makers* announced changes in staff and among the ACL's board members, heralding a "second generation" of the organization. Providing more historical continuity than renewal, James W. Moore, who had been associated with the magazine since 1929 and its editor since 1947, adopted the position of ACL managing director that Winton had held until his death.[84] Because of his decades-long association with *Movie Makers* and the ACL, Moore's changes to the organization were likely tempered by long-standing beliefs. Along with Moore came four new members of the ACL Board of Directors, still under John Hansen's presidency, who perhaps more than Moore, were representative of a second generation taking over the helm of the organization. An editorial contrasted the novelty of amateur movies when the organization was established in 1926 with the current situation: "Amateur movies today are as widespread and as much a part of American life as were still pictures after the advent of the Box Brownie. More than a million people make amateur movies today. Thus, if a hobby organization serving them is to remain healthy, these people must have a practical voice in its direction."[85] Emerging from a field of noncommercial, nontheatrical filmmaking and culture, amateur activity was defined apart from educational and industrial filming by the postwar era. If the number of amateur filmmakers had indeed grown significantly—to more than a million people—the field of activity had shrunk somewhat.

The ACL's second generation had more moderate goals and philosophical claims for the amateur motion picture than those of their predecessors. Rather than placing amateurs at the vanguard of silent film art and utopian intercommunication, *Movie Makers* suggested that even within the amateur's somewhat diminished terrain, films with "ideas" were still important. As it encouraged amateurs to move beyond mere snapshots, *Movie Makers* spurred amateurs to make films with a "point of view": "Shall we, with the magic of the movies, simply *record* something or shall we *say* something?"[86] The response to this rhetorical question was not encouraging, as the second generation of ACL leaders evidently struggled to find a second generation of members. In 1949, the outlook seemed promising when *Movie Makers* announced a renaissance in amateur movie activities. The publication noted a "35 percent increase in footage and a 73 percent increase in number of entries" to the Ten Best contest over that of the previous year.[87] But this surge in competition entries proved short-lived, and the following year the number was down considerably; entries in the Ten Best contest for 1950 dropped 43 percent from those for 1949. One editorial suggested that the rise of television viewing was at least partly responsible for this significant drop-off in amateur movie activities. The writer lamented that a greater number of people were falling for the passive recreation of television rather than the creative and energetic activity of moviemaking.[88] In 1954, the Amateur Cinema League was absorbed into the Photographic Society of America's Motion Picture Division. The cause of the Amateur Cinema League's demise in 1954 was likely the result of both gradual shifts in amateur film culture and more immediate financial problems. According to some reports, the ACL had been losing money for several years (since at least the end of World War II) and had been sustained only through private donations and wealthy patrons. Some suggested that the root cause of the ACL's insolvency was the cost of the organization's extensive member services, on one hand, and the reduction of income as more people became mere subscribers to *Movie Makers* rather than members in the league, on the other.[89] But a decline in the appeal of moviemaking, or indeed the relevance of an amateur pragmatic imagination, does not appear to have taken place. Just as the Amateur Cinema League was founded at a moment of optimism for both the unlimited aesthetic future of cinema and its potential as a force for pragmatically bridging inter- and intracommunication, its final years were marked by a continued confidence in the importance of amateur filmmaking.

THE PHOTOGRAPHIC SOCIETY OF AMERICA: AMATEURS MOVING AND STILL

The most important new organization for North American amateurs to emerge in the postwar years was the Photographic Society of America's

Motion Picture Division. Formed in 1934 from the Associated Camera Clubs of America, the PSA was devoted to "the promotion of the art and science of photography; research and dissemination of photographic knowledge; and promotion of photographic salons and exhibitions."[90] The Motion Picture Division of the PSA, however, was not formed until 1946, when it emerged as a rival organization of the ACL.[91] Moviemakers in the PSA found themselves among still photographers in several different divisions, including portrait, photojournalist, stereo, and slide, and some amateurs were active in more than one of these. The relationship between still and motion picture photographers could be contentious; even the founding MPD director, Harris Tuttle, noted the "radical" difference between the two media and suggested that "the very nature of motion picture photography makes it entirely different than still picture photography."[92] Despite these differences, Tuttle believed still photographers and moviemakers could learn from each other, and the *PSA Journal* sought out common ground in areas of composition and exposure.[93] Similarities were proposed between movie makers and slide producers, in particular, insofar as slide shows were also temporal and required narration, music, and editing.[94] Conversely, Hollywood was less significant as a point of reference for the PSA and its journal than was the case for *Movie Makers* or *American Cinematographer*. And unlike the ACL, the Photographic Society of America organized annual conferences that brought together society members in a major city for a few days per year for activities that balanced instruction, recreational image making, and socializing.

Like the ACL, the PSA acknowledged that many filmmakers who had started as amateurs could now be categorized as professional or semiprofessional filmmakers; most of the remaining amateurs were interested primarily in making home movies. Founding chairman of the PSA's Motion Picture Division (and former Kodak employee), Harris Tuttle pointed to three broad categories: "1. The beginner or snapshooter, who is interested mainly in family movies, sports, and vacation reels. 2. The more advanced amateur, who, in addition to filming the subjects listed above, also makes two or three other films a year which have continuity and are of general interest. 3. The advanced movie maker, who wants to produce something having entertainment value, every time he makes a picture."[95]

Tuttle suggested that in 1947, the first group probably represented 70 percent or more of all amateurs, the second group about 25 percent, and the third about 5 percent. The PSA's Motion Picture Division announced its interest in helping all three groups of amateurs, from basic technique for the first group, to tips on editing and continuity for the second group, to picture ideas and story materials with entertainment value for the third and most advanced group. In this, the PSA reflected goals similar to those of the ACL, which sought to broaden its readership during the postwar years to include more beginners.

In 1954, the Amateur Cinema League voted to merge with the Photographic Society of America, and approximately twenty-five hundred ACL members were absorbed into the society.[96] The Photographic Society was seen to be a more stable organization than the ACL for several reasons, most notably: it had a broader base of members (still- and moving-image amateurs), and its activities were more member-provided (in contrast to ACL's team of paid consultants).[97] Additionally, the PSA's regular monthly publication, the *PSA Journal*, was not available on newsstands, only to dues-paying members. Each division of the PSA (motion pictures, slides, portrait photography, etc.) circulated its own newsletters, which provided further contact with members. Though *Movie Makers* ceased publication in November 1954, the PSA welcomed ACL members with a promise to continue the annual Ten Best contests and expand the number of articles about movies in the journal. By the end of 1955, the Motion Picture Division of PSA had also established a film exchange system for coordinating film exchanges among clubs.[98] Beyond these features, ACL members would also have access to a larger organization that organized annual conventions and promoted face-to-face fellowship in a way the ACL had never emphasized.

Motion Picture Division's advice was only a small part of the *PSA Journal*, but a regular column was published in each issue, and eventually (starting in 1958) a separate movie section in the journal began.[99] Writer and editor George Cushman was the principal voice of moviemakers during the late 1950s, and he penned the journal's regular "Cinema Clinic" column from 1953 until the late 1970s.[100] Cushman's column promoted basic technical skill in moviemaking, but beyond this he emphasized the creative and artistic possibilities of amateur moviemaking. "It takes more than a technician to make a good motion picture," he wrote; "the amateur must be the whole team in one and must be both technician and artist."[101] In this sentiment, Cushman appeared to have support from many readers but not from organizers of movie club contests, which he regularly criticized for rewarding empty technical skill.[102] Cushman was also a vocal critic of movie clubs that catered to entertainment programming (just showing films) rather than instruction and constructive critique.[103] In addressing the difference between professionals and amateurs, Cushman wrote, "I think the whole difference between the amateur and the professional is that the professional knows how to use his equipment whereas the amateur is learning how to use it."[104] Cushman urged amateur clubs to take a more significant role in the education of filmmakers, by using mutual critique and regular programs of instruction.[105] He chastised movie club organizers that catered to those who were merely seeking "entertainment," at the expense of the members who joined hoping to improve their filmmaking.[106]

In addition to Cushman's columns, the *PSA Journal* published regular articles for moviemakers, and from these publications and the activities of the MPD, we can trace some of the key areas of discussion in the organization.[107] In a survey of MPD members, Cushman announced the general interests of the group as follows: (1) editing, (2) adding sound to films, (3) using color properly, (4) lighting, (5) titling, (6) preparing a script; and (7) doing trick photography.[108] Amateurs involved in the PSA also made amateur documentary and instructional films and even some semiprofessional nature films, but these were not a major part of their activities.[109] And though the PSA was a male-dominated organization, there were noteworthy exceptions to this, as in the case of the 1956 Ten Best awards, which included several women. As Cushman commented, "The fact that women cameramen, or must we say 'camerawomen' are beginning to get their share of the honors, indicates motion picture photography is not alone a man's world."[110] The judging of amateur films was a frequent topic of *PSA Journal* articles, as commentators proposed different methods for evaluating and encouraging strong amateur work.[111] One author noted the poor quality of most movie club contest entries and the generally low standard of technical quality; improving judging criteria was linked to club efforts to educate and promote higher standards.[112] Another author proposed a "merit system" for evaluating amateur film accomplishments, rather than one that created bad feelings among friends by ranking their works.[113] A separate section of the *PSA Journal* for moviemakers was finally established in 1958, with George Cushman acting as editor of the five-page section and calling on MPD members to submit articles.[114] The new column featured profiles of prominent amateur moviemakers—Esther Cook, Sal and Nadine Pizzo—and starting in 1959 monthly installments of a "course" in moviemaking. Cushman was the principal author of these lessons, and they were presented as lesson plans that movie clubs could use to enhance the educational content of their meetings.[115]

The "Cinema Clinic" column also continued to act as a sounding board for Cushman's own ideas—and those of his many correspondents—about the mission and activities of amateur moviemaking. In a column called "The All Time Best," Cushman reflected on the qualities of the most critically acclaimed professional films *(Potemkin, The Last Laugh, The Gold Rush)* and what these revealed about the amateur's relationship to film art: "Whereas the professional must keep an eye to the box office when making his films, must remember to give the audience what it wants and forget about true filmic form, the amateur has no such restrictions. If the amateur really understood the film art and wanted to create a masterpiece, there is nothing to stop him. The same raw film he uses on the record shots of his kids could just as well be used to turn out another *Gold Rush* or *Bicycle Thief*—films that need not be expensive to make."[116] For Cushman, the amateur's primary limitation was his or her lack of knowledge about film art: "He does not know that the art of films calls for telling a story by visual representations, by the ideological—and temporal—content of the shots, the meaning coming from the order of those shots." Cushman encouraged amateur filmmakers to study the great films and follow their example. Further, he suggested that movie audiences and contest judges needed to study these films as well in order to evaluate amateur film accomplishments beyond basic technique. Cushman proposed that some of these films would be presented at the next PSA convention; here we see a return to some of the earlier claims for the amateur's place in the vanguard of film art, but now the distance that had grown between amateurs and cinephile culture was emphasized.

In a similar vein, Cushman offered praise for a description of noncommercial filmmaking by Lewis Jacobs, which he felt applied to the amateur domain as well: "In opposition to the moribund aims and forms of the commercial film makers are those who believe in the movies as an art. Their objectives are not to 'entertain' but to reveal; not to mirror, but to explore; not to repeat, but to invent; not to reject esthetic standards, but to refresh and reshape them from the medium's own traditions and the current of life. To such film makers, movies are experimental by their very nature. The making of a film is a continuous process of discovery."[117] Cushman praised Jacobs's objective of creating films that reveal, explore, invent, and reshape, in contrast to what Cushman described as "postcard" amateur movies, which were technically proficient but little more. He writes, "If we in this Division, then, are really advanced in the art of movie making, why do we accept as noteworthy films which are little more than snapshots in motion—recordings which we should have discontinued by the time we had had our camera a year or two?" Cushman argued that an artistic use of the camera, rather than mere technical exercises, resulted in getting more out of the hobby.[118] To support this goal, subsequent articles by Cushman and others in the journal proposed experimental and creative approaches to amateur filmmaking.[119]

A highlight of PSA's main fall convention was the screening of the annual Ten Best winners.[120] Much like the ACL and *American Cinematographer* before it, PSA was engaged in a constant negotiation of inclusivity and restriction in its contests. The first post-ACL contest was called the 1955 PSA International Cinema Competition and placed no limitations at all on the amateur or professional status of its submissions, stipulating only that the films had to be on 8mm or 16mm.[121] The number of film entries was also reported each year, generally hovering around fifty during the late 1950s: "A total of 50 films were received in this year's contest [1956]. Of this number 38 were 16mm and 12 were 8mm."[122] The majority of the prizes were awarded to 16mm filmers, and as had been the case in the ACL, there was some friction between filmmakers working in 8mm and those in 16mm film. Cushman responded by arguing that while it was true that more advanced amateurs tended to work with 16mm, there was no reason why excellent results couldn't be accomplished on 8mm film.[123] In 1958, the contest was adjusted to create separate categories for filmmakers who produced films "without commission, assignment or order from any other person who makes the film" and for those who entered commissioned films. But the rules noted, in particular: "It is not the intention to exclude a film made by a 'professional' from entry in Class A provided it meets the requirements of Class A."[124]

In the late 1950s, the PSA created Ten Best screening programs to rent to local amateur clubs. Cushman noted that while the U.K. Ten Best selections received a theatrical screening and attracted much larger audiences when screened in Britain, he was skeptical about the prospects for a similar theatrical screening in the United States, where amateur film was an emphatically nontheatrical medium.[125] Although the Photographic Society of America presented a stable home for amateur moviemakers in the late 1950s, it also represented an additional withdrawal, of sorts, from the broader amateur terrain sought by both *Movie Makers* and *American Cinematographer*. At the end of the 1950s, advanced amateur moviemaking thrived within a robust network of local clubs and national organizations. But whereas the 1930s had presented an expanding movement and a capacious amateur field that included practical and experimental filmmaking, by the 1950s amateurs occupied a much smaller niche on the margins of film culture.

Chicago amateur Margaret Conneely presents a salutary, though not typical, example of the trajectory of postwar amateur filmmakers. Conneely bought her first (8mm) movie camera in 1949 to take home movies, but she soon joined the Metro Movie Club and by the mid-1950s was an active

Figure 17. *Fairy Princess* (Margaret Conneely, 1956) featured the filmmaker's niece and some clever stop-motion animation. Courtesy Chicago Film Archives, Margaret Conneely Collection.

participant in amateur culture on both a local and a national basis. As a filmmaker, Conneely's profile grew rapidly, and she soon made "the switch" to 16mm film after learning how to construct narrative films around her own children and extended family; her *Fairy Princess*, which featured her niece and some clever stop-motion animation, was named one of the PSA's 1956 Ten Best (figure 17).[126] She also became an active participant in club productions, one of which won an award at the Cannes International Festival of Amateur Film in 1956. Eventually Conneely helped found a specialized unit of advanced amateurs called Central Cinematographers, which met once a week to produce short narrative films. Conneely also made fund-raising films for local charities (such as the Women's and Children's Hospital and the Boy Scouts).[127] In addition to making films, which were screened around Chicago, Conneely was also an active participant in amateur culture, from editing her local club newsletter to organizing Chicago area amateur activities and contributing to ACL and PSA efforts to expand the hobby. Conneely even appeared on Chicago TV shows to speak about her hobby and wrote many newspaper and magazine articles promoting amateur moviemaking, including one for the *New York Times*.[128] Conneely's film interests continued to expand in surprising ways over the next three decades, as she became both a semiprofessional medical

Figure 18. Margaret Conneely, pictured with other members of Metro Movie Club (River Park, Chicago) in 1956, won awards locally and internationally for her films. Courtesy Chicago Film Archives, Margaret Conneely Collection.

cinematographer (for a Chicago medical school) and a promoter of creative and experimental filmmaking.

Conneely's involvement in the amateur movie world was more active and successful than that of most people, but it illustrates some important points. First, women—including those who had children and worked outside the home, as Conneely did—were active participants in the amateur movie world (figure 18). Though we associate women's amateur filmmaking primarily with domesticity, Conneely was one of many women who participated in amateur film culture to find a creative voice and an engaging world outside the home. Second, the range of Conneely's activities illustrates that amateur moviemaking was a robust and healthy activity in the 1950s and long after. But even as clubs and organizations proliferated during this period, the amateur movie world became somewhat more insular and removed from other spheres of film production than it was in earlier decades. Third, and finally, Conneely's engagement with film, like that of other amateurs, was multifaceted, crossing numerous media—8mm, 16mm, still and slide photography—and genres. From her own family chronicles, fund-raisers, and short fiction filmmaking to her promotion of experimental filmmaking and work as a medical cinematographer, Conneely's career spanned the range of different amateur film modes. A careful examination of these different modes—including their variations and broader significance—is the subject of this book's second part.

PART II

Modes of Amateur Cinema

6 "Communicating a New Form of Knowledge"
Amateur Chronicles of Family, Community, and Travel

In 1933, *Movie Makers* organized the Why I Film contest, which challenged its readers to submit letters explaining why they made amateur films. The winning letter came from Arthur Ewald of Cincinnati, who writes, "I make amateur movies because, engaged in the business of life, I have yet—who has not—learned some of its beauties but none of that art which transmutes their evanescence into tangible and communicable forms." With the movie camera, Ewald continues, "it is now within my power to preserve for memory the tangible forms of beauty, and I may relive at will those responses I wish through life to preserve, and may satisfy that deep longing which I and all men have to take friends into the good fellowship of happy hours."[1] Ewald's letter emphasizes the amateur's sensitivity to beauty as well as the cinema's ability to record and preserve his experience of encountering it. In a reflection on the contest submissions, the ACL managing director Roy Winton noted that as many people wrote about the aesthetic importance of amateur works as those who wrote about their more practical uses in recording family and travel:

> Family recording is the hardy perennial in the garden of film reasons and it is accompanied by other old favorites, such as travel filming and watching the development of children through films of them. The very large degree of artistic intention and planned artistic effort and the strong urge towards creative activity give genuine promise of results from amateur cinematography of a much more original and valuable kind than have ever come from professional producers. It is clear that personal movies have advanced from just another spare time occupation to the status of a conscious effort at expression in a new medium.[2]

These observations pose a challenge to our typical understanding of amateur family, community, and travel films as careless point-and-shoot home movies and dull travelogues. Instead, Winton's remarks reinforce the interconnectedness of the cinema's capacity for recording and aesthetically inflecting materials about everyday experience. We might conclude that motion pictures appealed to mid-twentieth-century amateurs on a number of different levels: in their recording capacity, their ability to shape and communicate everyday beauty, and through this communication the possibility of satisfying a desire for fellowship and the strengthening of social bonds.

To understand the relationships between creativity, everyday life, and cinema more thoroughly, this chapter explores amateur "chronicle films." Here I use the term *chronicle films* to designate a range of nonfiction film categories—variously referred to by amateurs as record, family, city, sport, community, and travel films—that shared a preoccupation with the aesthetic representation of the everyday. The term *chronicle* also resonates with the amateur filmmaker's place in a much longer tradition of recording events visually, a tradition that the amateurs themselves were fascinated by. The category of chronicle films is particularly foundational because, as Winton's remarks suggest, recording family, local events, and travel was understood to be a core function of amateur filmmaking. Many advanced amateurs worked with similar themes but presented them with greater attention to craft and technical sophistication. In doing so, these amateurs developed a significant relationship between their everyday lives and the new aesthetic and technological means of communication provided by the movie camera. Indeed the ACL's founder and first president, Hiram Percy Maxim, announced personal moving pictures as capable of "communicating a new form of knowledge" that could capture the grace of visual events in movement, record significant personal experiences, and allow amateurs to share these experiences with many others.

This chapter delineates the category of chronicle films by examining some exemplary works and considering the methods that amateurs used for shaping and transfiguring visual material. By examining the way amateurs understood their filmmaking to be working in a new visual language and by considering this new language's relationship to other kinds of media and art forms, this chapter also probes the claim that amateur movies somehow "communicated a new form of knowledge." Amateur discourse reflected a desire to refashion the relationships between social and aesthetic experience in modern life, and in this it often echoed John Dewey's idealistic writing about media and the public, particularly during the late 1920s and early '30s.[3] Part 2 of this book teases out some of these parallels between amateur film culture and American pragmatism to suggest a "pragmatic imagination," which shaped amateur filmmaking activities. And although the Great

Depression and World War II challenged the amateur's vision of a distinctly middle-class and pragmatic means of creative expression, this discourse returned to ascendancy during the postwar years and mingled once again with utopian claims for the amateur motion picture's capacity for bringing about mutual understanding, even on an international scale. To explore these claims, this chapter is divided into three sections: family, community, and travel films. Along the way, I will also consider some implications that this examination of chronicle films has for the history of nonfiction and documentary cinema. Like the early documentarian John Grierson, amateurs saw "the creative treatment of actuality" as a fascinating possibility for the cinema.

FAMILY CHRONICLE FILMS: *AT THE SANDPITS* (BUDGE CRAWLEY) AND *DUCK SOUP* (DELORES AND TIMOTHY LAWLER)

The impulse to record motion pictures of family and friends long predates the rise of amateur cinema. Histories of nonfiction film in particular locate important origins for this impulse in France during the 1890s. As noted in chapter 1, the Lumière brothers saw motion pictures as a logical development from their production of still photography emulsions for amateurs, and the Cinematograph was more than likely intended for the same market. But the mass popularity of motion pictures quickly forced the Lumière brothers to reconfigure their invention toward commercial exhibition. While preserving images of family and capturing the spontaneous motions of everyday life mark two persistent impulses in amateur filmmaking, they remained largely unfulfilled until the 1920s and the invention of 16mm film. In 1926, just three years after the commercial release of 16mm cameras and projectors, the Amateur Cinema League was founded and announced a new era of personal filmmaking. In the first issue of *Movie Makers* magazine, Hiram Percy Maxim presented a manifesto for amateur film that sketched out its closely intertwined aesthetic and social ambitions. He writes,

> Our civilization offers us today only the spoken word or the written word, as a means of communicating with each other. This word may be spoken to those within the sound of our voice, telephoned over a hired wire, mailed in a letter or telegraphed in dots and dashes. But no matter how transmitted it is still the spoken or written word. We are dumb as far as communicating such things as movement, action, grace, beauty and all that depends upon these things.
>
> The motion pictures communicate all of these . . .

And so, instead of amateur cinematography being merely a means of individual amusement, we have in it a means of communicating a new form of knowledge to our fellow beings,———be where they may upon the earth's surface.[4]

In this, Maxim emphasized amateur cinema's capacity to *communicate* visual information in new ways, in effect pointing to its *social* role. But he also noted its aesthetic qualities: "Amateur cinematography is a new art," he wrote. "It is different from every other art that was ever developed." Maxim posited an aesthetic means of communication in contrast to the Lumière brothers' interest in simply recording images of family; by 1926, it was possible to imagine a kind of filmmaking that drew from commercial film techniques in order to present personal subject matter in a creative and widely communicable form.

Contemporaneous with the appearance of the Amateur Cinema League was the publication of many books and articles guiding amateurs in their production of family films. The Rochester amateur Marion Gleason published a book, *Scenario Writing and Producing for the Amateur*, featuring the production of family films, which were understood by Gleason to be one of the principal interests of amateur filmmakers. In a 1932 article, Gleason promoted the carefully planned and executed production of family study films: "Now film studies of family and friends replace 'cine snaps.'"[5] She provides instructions for doing home movie portraits, posing, and similar activities, simultaneously demonstrating the emergent aesthetic dimension of family chronicle films. Another author, Sue Rice, promoted the cinema as a tool for both recording a child's facial expression and offering a gateway to the child's interior processes and concerns: "The movie camera [in contrast to still photographs], however, gathers all the child's thoughts as they are registered on his face, leading up to one big happy expression of understanding. In fact, the motion picture film is a medium for recording the action of child minds, and when studied on the screen, one may learn the secret of their thoughts, while at play, showing as it will the reactions to the various kinds of stories and toys which may be presented to it."[6] Here, the cinema goes far beyond a simple recording device for facial features and becomes a tool for recording and reflecting upon internal and psychological traits. These claims are consistent with Maxim's manifesto, which suggested that motion pictures could provide access to new kinds of visual knowledge. New amateur film technologies introduced in the early 1930s promised to allow for even more extensive documentation of family experiences and activities. The commercial release of Kodak's supersensitive, or "fast," panchromatic film permitted amateurs to engage in more extensive indoor filming, including filming restricted to the domestic space itself: "Those parts of the family film library, so long left blank, can now be easily filled with most important shots, for surely there is no site so productive of worthwhile films as the interior of the home." The author provided a sample scenario, *Baby Breaks Loose*, which narrativized an indoor domestic drama to create "an amusing domestic documentary film."[7] Here we can see how technological developments had specific effects on the possibility of producing domestic subjects within domestic spaces. We can also see the conflation of documentation with domestic semifictional scenarios. There is no contradiction in terms here; rather, family chronicle films allowed for the possibility of both amusement *and* documentation.

F.R. "Budge" Crawley's short film *At the Sandpits* (1933) provides an excellent example of this combination of amusement and documentation. *At the Sandpits* is perhaps Crawley's first completed work, produced when he was a teenager; Crawley went on to make many award-winning amateur films before turning professional in the 1940s as a producer of industrial films. Employing rapid cutting, trick photography, and imaginative scenarios, *At the Sandpits* conveys a strong sense of dynamic action in a short film about a family picnic. The film begins by showing the preparation of sandwiches for a picnic; after showing the meal in a few deft shots, the adults are seen relaxing, while the kids and pets, shot from extreme low angle in slow motion, run toward the sandpits. The film continues with short but carefully constructed sequences of the kids pretending to be buried alive in the sand, having a baseball game, and then returning home, tired. Finally, the film concludes with a strange dream sequence, employing trick photography, in which three girls appear decapitated behind a sheet. Though rough in many respects, Crawley's film combines the chronicling of a family event with a clear enthusiasm for the cinema's capacity for tricks and jokes and a definite interest in narrative technique. It recalls a *Movie Makers* article that promoted the use of dynamic montage as a way of reinvigorating familiar (and familial?) amateur film subjects: "Montage is a method of motion picture interpretation, a means whereby old movie subjects may be approached in a new way."[8] *At the Sandpits* demonstrates exactly this kind of interpretive chronicling; much more than merely recording the picnic, Crawley's film conveys the energy and playfulness of the afternoon.

Although this playfulness and aestheticization of family activities drew on montage techniques that originated in both Hollywood (Griffith) and the Soviet Union (Eisenstein), essays in *Movie Makers* announced amateur chronicle film as an emphatically middle-class activity, which placed this group at the center of both social and aesthetic standards. According to one 1934 editorial, the middle-class film amateur was important because she was a member of neither the fashionable upper class nor the fickle masses: "Not so expensive as to be a perquisite of the few and not so inexpensive as to be a temporary toy of heedless millions, amateur cinematography is a typical middle class hobby, with the safest foundation that a hobby can have—one built into the most solid and dependable factor of human society."[9] This statement is significant, not only for its declaration of the amateur as a middle-class figure, but also because of its allegiance to liberal, middle-class culture in the context of the Great Depression. In this, the editorial makes an emphatic defense of the social value of the middle class as well:

> True stability of human habits that have to do with avocations is reached only when the solid middle class of the world makes these habits its own. When this takes place, an avocation becomes a very logical mixture of recreation and practical application, which is precisely what has occurred with personal movies. As a leisure time activity, it ceases to have novelty and takes on the sureness of custom, which means that it is threaded into the fabric of day by day recreation; as a practical medium, it is turned to the service of more and more day by day needs. The middle class—upon whose preservation the whole structure of civilization depends—is serious, unexcitable, well grooved, unfickle, cautious, cheerful and intelligent. These are all qualities that an all too prevalent kind of present day critic condemns as unamusing, dull and uninspiring, but they are the qualities upon which anything must be based to achieve solidity and endurance. They are the qualities that have entered into personal filming and that will unquestionably make personal filming increasingly a part of human living. They do not prevent enjoyment and fun, as satirical critics allege. Rather they enrich enjoyment, by making that enjoyment natural and not neurotic.

Here, the editor makes a strenuous defense of the creative potential of the middle-class amateur and of the place of creative work alongside middle-class everyday life. Moviemaking was understood as a habitual activity and an art form that was woven into quotidian experience. This was an aesthetic and social position distinct from the radical alternatives that by 1934 were emerging from both left- and right-wing political movements and critics.

The creative possibilities available to family filmers were emphasized as a constant theme for amateurs well beyond the 1930s. As late as 1949, a *Movie Makers* article called "Got Any Ideas?" emphasized the importance of introducing a theme, or "point of view," into family films.[10] In contrast to simple home movie footage, family films by serious amateurs gave shape and structure to the personal relationships and quotidian events that they recorded. An exemplary case of this approach to filmmaking can be found in works by Delores and Timothy Lawler, who made several polished films of their family activities in the 1950s, even going so far as to frame their family events and relationships in semifictional narrative forms. Their film *Duck Soup*, in color with unsynchronized sound, was named the best amateur film of 1952 by *Movie Makers* magazine.

In addition to featuring the Lawler family, *Duck Soup* reimagines their domestic roles. The film chronicles a day in the life of the Lawlers but with a couple unusual twists. Father/Timothy, having suggested that taking care of five kids is no problem—or "duck soup"—is left by Mother/Delores to look after the kids and housework for the day. But even before we meet the Lawlers, the film introduces its two narrators, a pair of mice who provide a running voice-over commentary on the film's action and occasional rough-synch of lines of dialogue. (The two appear as cardboard cut-out silhouettes that look suspiciously like Mickey and Minnie Mouse.) "Since we're mice," one of them begins, "we get to see things that some people would give their right arm to see. Take, for instance, what happened one day at the Lawler's." From this playful introduction, the film cuts to a scene of Timothy and Delores in a living room; when Delores complains about how much house work she has, Timothy notices an article in the newspaper whose headline claims: "Inefficiency Is What Tires the Housewife." This provokes an argument between husband and wife while also providing the film's running ironic premise—that Timothy will attempt to bring a businesslike efficiency to the good natured but chaotic Lawler household.

The film's formal operations also show some influence of efficient narrative film technique. In this opening sequence and throughout the film, *Duck Soup* employs continuity editing principles: beginning from an initial close-up that provides a situating date and location on a newspaper masthead, we cut to an establishing shot of the room, then cut back to a closer shot of the newspaper article before establishing a shot/reverse-shot pattern between Timothy and Delores as they argue. Finally, when Timothy accepts Delores's challenge to take care of the kids and housework for a day, the mouse-narrator says, "Hey, kid, this we gotta see!" This opening scene shows that the film has clearly established narrative and formal structures, certainly a far cry from the rough "home movie." The film's playful tone presents us with a domestic comedy in the making, and it also immediately signals that it is not the kind of home movie we are used to.

But why does *Duck Soup* need this formal technique? Patricia Zimmermann argues that this kind of polished amateur film reflects little more than "slavish conformity to Hollywood narrative visual logic."[11] But *Duck Soup* doesn't hide its amateur status; from its rough unsynchronized sound track to its slightly hammy acting, there is no confusing it for a professional film. Rather, what we see here is an *adaptation* of commercial film conventions to somewhat personal purposes; after all, the Lawlers are making a film about their own family. But the film's technical proficiency—itself a coproduction of the husband and wife seen arguing in this opening scene—allows the Lawlers to imagine a version of their family in which conventional gender roles are overturned and patriarchal order is gently mocked. Here, the film's technical proficiency allows for role playing and fooling around with middle-class domestic identities.

In other ways the film's technique appears carefully adapted to the purposes of a family chronicle film. This is most evident in its frequent use of close-up shots of the children at various activities. For example, in one early scene of the family having a breakfast prepared by Timothy, the film departs from typical continuity editing by including individual close-up shots of each child in turn. This repeated use of close-up shots might seem out of place in a commercial Hollywood film of the same moment. But this stylistic approach is perfectly appropriate for *Duck Soup* when we think of the film as a kind of *family portrait in time* as well as a narrative. *Duck Soup* is a hybrid work: On one hand, it is narrativized and polished enough to present a playful meditation on domestic roles. But on the other hand, it is a record of the family itself and a self-aware document of both how they were at a particular moment and how they joined together to produce this film. In short, the technique employed by *Duck Soup* seems to be allowing the film to "*say* something," and not just "*record* something."[12] Aside from providing a means for the Lawlers to record and reflect upon their own family, the technical proficiency of *Duck Soup* also allowed this film to appeal to viewers without a direct connection to the family, such as members of a local movie club and other amateurs who saw the film after it circulated through the ACL library. In this circulation, *Duck Soup* retained its specificity as a Lawler family film, but more important it can be seen as one among very many amateur works about "the family" more generally. As a clever comedy about middle-class family and gender roles, *Duck Soup* evinces a greater self-awareness about the family than we might otherwise attribute to amateurs during this period. It even provides evidence of the middle-class wit and playfulness so strenuously defended by the earlier *Movie Makers* editorial.

When the movie is considered in this light, we can also understand some of the significance of "communication" in Maxim's manifesto. Maxim thought the ACL's broad scope for circulating personal and social experiences had epochal significance. He wrote, "It may not be too much to say that the organizing of amateur cinematography marks one of the greatest advances in general human education that has been made in modern times."[13] Maxim's manifesto echoed 1920s debates about media and the public. In his 1927 book *The Public and Its Problems*, philosopher John Dewey forecasts a time when modern modes of communication would catch up with the complex problems of modern society and develop "a great community" through "free and full intercommunication." "When the machine age has thus perfected its machinery," he writes, "it will be a *means* of life and not its despotic master."[14] Amateurs shared with Dewey certain pragmatic and utopian visions for how new communication technologies could reconnect community feelings that had crumbled under the social transformations of modernity (such as urbanization, industrialization, the rise of mass media). The cinema was understood as a technology that could help bring about such intercommunication. When *Duck Soup* is understood in this way, we can see it as a film that straddles the line between private and public, a film that presents a valuable form of *intra*communication (that is to say, for the family itself) and *inter*communication (a work meant to communicate an experience of family to a wider audience). The Amateur Cinema League and other amateur groups expressed this aspiration in many ways, both large and small, from editorials in *Movie Makers* to practical advice for amateurs and awards for their well-crafted films. An article written by Timothy Lawler about the making of *Duck Soup* reveals a specific instance of this practical advice. Lawler recounts an earlier occasion when he had sent a film to the ACL for commentary and received this critique from the ACL "continuity and club consultant" James Moore: "To date, where your filmmaking suffers is in the continuity or camera treatment aspects. These, especially the latter, are routine, dull and unimaginative.... Your scenes are invariably too long—an understandable weakness on the part of proud-father movie makers—but if you wish your films to have pace and interest for others too, they must be shortened."[15] In this we can see specifically how the ACL encouraged a film technique that appealed to both family and others too. By providing this specific technical advice, the ACL was also supporting its much larger claim about the positive social value of amateur movies. In encouraging filmmakers to refine their skills, the ACL hoped its members would make films that were able to reach far beyond the domestic confines of their subject matter and participate in a wider form of intercommunication.

COMMUNITY CHRONICLE FILMS: *ANOTHER DAY* (LESLIE THATCHER)

While family was their most frequent subject, many amateur filmmakers looked beyond their own domestic spaces to produce movies that chronicled local public events and surroundings. As they did with family films, amateurs drew from a variety of different aesthetic influences to creatively shape their filmed records of the world. In theory, the source material for this kind of filming was limitless, but in practice, amateurs returned to several common themes often, including local sporting events, urban spaces, and community parades and carnivals. Amateur publications routinely offered tips on how to go about this kind of filmmaking, such as this advice for amateurs trying to capture local sports events: "Just as the king's chronicler of old was privileged to see everything from the best point of vantage, the owner of a movie outfit and a reasonable amount of nerve is almost sure of a preferred position at the side line, if only he takes care to get acquainted with the players and to offer them, in return for the courtesy, a screening of the results at their convenience."[16] This advice provides a multidimensional view of the amateur: not only is the filmmaker recording an event for himself, but also as a member of a community he presents his film to the subjects and participants as well. This makes his position different from the commercial newsreel cameraman, who might offer little in return for the favor of filming an event. And for some amateurs, the idea of a king's chronicler was one they took literally: in May 1939, King George's visit to Canada resulted in a handful of amateur movie productions. In Toronto, members of the local amateur movie clubs banded together to produce *Toronto's Royal Day*, a Kodachrome chronicle of the king and queen's tour. In both their cooperative production method and their civic subject matter, these amateurs constituted a significant public film culture.[17]

World's fairs and similar pageants marked another important subject for amateur chronicles, mixing the appeal of simulated travel with quasi-ethnographic spectacles. The 1933 Chicago World's Fair combined modernist architecture with "national pageants" from around the world to provide a setting for amateurs to take colorful and exotic views without the requirement of leaving the United States. R. Fawn Mitchell, of the Chicago Cinema Club, advised amateurs on how to select the most appealing and significant aspects of the fair to film, emphasizing in particular the selection of striking visual elements: "First of all, we are struck by the colorful aspect of the Fair—the gala crowd, the modernist buildings and the colorings of these buildings which, even in daytime, are quite vivid. Therefore, probably we will plan to take some Kodacolor pictures."[18] Here, as in many points in the article, Mitchell remarks on the "modernist" aspects of the buildings, which was clearly part of the spirit of the fair and is returned to often in Mitchell's article. By contrast, Mitchell's article also recommended the filming of the various "national pageants" or "villages," which offered visitors an opportunity for recognizing and reflecting upon national differences: "Next to the Belgian Village is the Morocco Village, also enclosed in high walls; there one may see the direct antithesis of the European setting. Natives in their flowing robes and typical Moroccan architecture provide first class movie subjects. Further on in the Midway is a large Oriental Village also worthy of separate treatment." These villages provided fairgoers an opportunity to juxtapose the national styles and images of different cultures as simulated by the pageants and offered the amateur filmer the chance to make an exotic travelogue without leaving the city of Chicago. In both these villages and the films that were produced of them, Mitchell emphasized the importance of chronicling these impermanent simulations, such as the "Streets of Paris": "Here, if one is lucky enough to secure entrance, shots can be obtained of the personalities most active in the Fair's social life. These functions are as much a part of the Fair as the buildings themselves and as such are worthy of perpetuation."[19] While the village "captures" the atmosphere of Paris, the amateur moviemaker may capture and therefore "perpetuate" (that is to say, chronicle) the social events that happened in this hybrid Chicago-France social space.

Following on this theme of simulated spaces and captured images, amateurs were also directed to "Hollywood-at-the-Fair" to see how professional films were made and to make an amateur record of professional movie production. They were even permitted "to stage their own plays and receive expert professional assistance" on the movie lot. All of these displays not only provided dynamic subject matter for amateur films but also pointed toward aspects of modern aesthetics, mobility, and simulation inherent in motion picture chronicles themselves. In 1939, the ACL would express an even closer relationship with the New York World's Fair, publishing a special full-color issue of *Movie Makers*, which included maps, sunset schedules, and other filming advice. But nothing exemplified the connection between amateur cinema and worlds fairs better than their shared leadership; in 1939 the president of the ACL was Stephen Voorhees, a prominent architect and one of the principal designers of the New York World's Fair.[20]

Similar to their advice for family filming, magazine articles about community movie production encouraged amateurs to follow their natural curiosity in filming events and places around them but urged them to organize and shape their footage. In one case Jay Leyda argued that "actuality" films were the preferred and perhaps even philosophically appropriate subjects for amateurs. Not only were subjects available everywhere, but making films from nonfictional material, he suggested, engaged the cinema's capacity for recording, transforming, and defamiliarizing the "things" around us (in contrast to story films, in which "things" were generally subordinated to narratives). But Leyda also noted that it was crucial for amateurs to organize and creatively treat their subjects through planning and editing. "The real interest will lie in the treatment," he writes, "and this must come from the mind of the cameraman. The subjects are, of their very nature, commonplace. It is the selection and arrangement of them, originating in the mind of the filmer, that makes them worthwhile."[21]

In a variation on Leyda's advice, Marxist film critic Harry Alan Potamkin wrote articles for amateurs encouraging them to use thoughtful montage and, in particular, to produce works in the style of modernist city symphony films, such as Walter Ruttman's *Berlin, Symphony of a Great City* and Dziga Vertov's *Man with a Movie Camera*.[22] Among the films listed in the ACL's Ten Best lists are a handful of such films, including Leslie Thatcher's 1934 silent film, *Another Day*.[23] Thatcher's film begins with an intertitle that points to the similarity among any "great cities," where "the hustle and bustle which accompanies the demands of commerce . . . means 'just another day.'" The film's opening shots show distant vistas of tall buildings and busy streets, revealing that the setting is not, in fact, "any city" but is specifically Toronto. Like other city symphony films, Thatcher's follows the chronology of a day's activity, and like other similar films it fragments continuous action and emphasizes the quotidian objects (the alarm clock, the toaster, the coffee pot) and the strangers that we encounter. In this, Thatcher appears to be following Leyda's advice to make a film about the things that surround us and to edit these parts together in a way that constructs a new meaning. The film's modernist fragmentation and reconstruction are demonstrated in a sequence about Saturday morning at different kinds of work. In this sequence we see an increasingly abstract depiction of the events of everyday life, with commerce represented as a shower of coins and labor as a swinging hammer (figures 19 and 20). Signs and landmarks, however, specify the setting once again: this is Toronto, not just the anonymous city of the film's opening title. Later, the film will continue to develop this dialectical relationship between specificity and abstraction—we see abstractions of leisure in superimposed, swirling musical notes at a night club, but we also see markers of local specificity in images of Toronto's nighttime streetscape.

Figures 19 and 20. *Another Day* (Leslie Thatcher, 1934) isolates and fragments details of everyday life. Courtesy Toronto Film and Video Club.

Thatcher's film employs modernist techniques to shape his visual record of Toronto. And while it's clear that *Another Day* doesn't present the kind of radical ideological point of view that we expect from avant-garde works, it is definitely engaged in some manner of cultural analysis. In his article about montage films, Potamkin wrote, "Every amateur ought to attempt to film his city or a part of it. It would be interesting to compare the data."[24] Thatcher's film allows us to do just that; on one hand, it raises Toronto to a status that is the aesthetic equivalent of the other great cities (Berlin, New York) chronicled in a similar vein, but on the other hand, it provides specific details about *one* city that can be widely communicated and compared. *Another Day* is one example in a proliferation of cases in which amateurs took up new stylistic vocabularies and techniques in order to present a visual account of their own surroundings. In their recording, transfiguring, and circulation of these images of the world, amateurs opened up a new terrain for pragmatic aesthetic expression. "The function of art," John Dewey writes, "has always been to break through the crust of conventionalized and routine consciousness. Common things, a flower, a gleam of moonlight, the song of a bird, not things rare and remote, are means with which the deeper levels of life are touched so that they spring up as desire and thought."[25] To these traditionally aesthetic things, amateurs added images of urban spaces and routines of everyday life to their visual vocabulary, and in this way they hinted at the potential for transforming the public world into creative and aesthetic modes of communication.

A *Movie Makers* editorial published the same year that *Another Day* was produced emphasized the historical significance of amateur filmmaking to community and even global historiography:

> Amateur filmers, under no "box office" compulsion, are making, from day to day and from year to year, film records of events which commercial movie producers cannot afford to attempt. . . . The fact has been established that history can be written from day to day in an intensely factual medium. Each month adds to the casual documents of humanity thousands of films exposed by noncommercial observers.
>
> It may not be too distant a vision nor too unreal a dream to look forward to a time when, under the leadership of the Amateur Cinema League, there may be prepared a kind of yearly world's history, with the advice of outstanding historians of all countries, and performed by amateurs who alone have the freedom from "box office" compulsion, with its attendant evils of timidity and truckling to those groups that object most vociferously. The movie workers in this historical army are being trained every year in their part of the task; the historical organization and the general staff selection lie far ahead.[26]

This article speaks to amateurs' understanding of their new kind of communication and new kind of history-writing potential. The author's claim seems remarkably prophetic in light of more recent online developments and the idea of webcams, videoblogs, and YouTube. In their recording, transfiguring, and circulation of these recorded images of the world, amateurs hinted at the potential for transforming the public world into creative and aesthetic modes of communication.

TRAVEL CHRONICLE FILMS: *MIGHTY NIAGARA* (LESLIE THATCHER) AND *TOMBS OF THE NOBLES* (JOHN HANSEN)

Mobility was one of the principal characteristic of amateur cinema, and travel films were a key subgenre of its nonfiction film production. Film scholarship has tended to see documentary films in terms of regimes of knowledge; in their presentation of factual materials from the world, it is argued, they are educational works that participate in a discourse of sobriety.[27] It isn't hard to see how this thinking applies to travelogue films, in which distant, and often strange, places are presented for our edification. The ACL's annual Ten Best amateur film lists are full of titles with geographical markers, such as *Moroccan Cities*, *Mexican Fiestas*, and *Canadian Capers*. But while travelogues are certainly implicated in a kind of regime of knowledge—through what they say about the world and therefore our position in it—they are also works that engage us in the dimensions of shared curiosity, the mimetic reproduction of sights both beautiful and strange, and even the affective pleasures of simulated movement through space. This chapter's final section will consider the tension between amateur travelogues that reproduced eroticizing, and sometimes racist, visions of non-American cultures and those that were inflected by a utopian vision of amateur films as a tool for promoting international understanding. In their intertwined aesthetic sophistication and problematic epistemology, amateur travel chronicles constitute a complex and fascinating category of filmmaking.

Leslie Thatcher made a number of polished travel films, including *Mighty Niagara*, which narrates a steamship voyage from Toronto to the Niagara Falls. But Thatcher's film is not just a recorded journey; it also presents a range of different ways that film can capture the visual impressions of travel through light reflections, motion, and temporal change. The film offers a spectacle of churning water and spray and provides brief phantom rides when the camera is placed first at the front of the steamship and later on a radial car. Many aspects of the film recall some of the earliest motion pictures, particularly views of Niagara shot by Edison and Lumière cameramen in the 1890s and early phantom rides produced around the same time. But the film's careful construction is evidence of the more highly developed modes of continuity editing and associational montage. Ultimately, the film provides a kind of microhistory of cinema itself: in its presentation of a spectacle (the falls), in its production of affect and sensation (through motion and phantom rides), and in the shaping of these materials through the sophisticated aesthetic means of continuity and expressive editing.[28]

While Niagara Falls, a world's fair, and similar tourist attractions provided some of the appeal of travel filming, some writers proposed that additional "exotic" subjects could be found within the United States. This attitude pointed toward amateurs' tendency to rely on romantic, and frequently racist, clichés about their subjects when providing shape and narrative structure to their travel films. This is made clear in an account called "Plantation Pictures: The Land of Cotton through a Cine Camera," in which African Americans living in the southern United States were treated as exotic subjects for filming. The author describes the film he made in terms of its travelogue conventions and even supposed ethnological qualities: "The scenario for our movie turned out to be the history of cotton picking; the actors were the negroes engaged on the plantation, with an occasional view of ourselves, and the 'set' was real, this fascinating plantation, probably the nearest thing left to a plantation of the old South." Though the film is couched in terms of its historical interest, the author remained complicit with the starkly racist vision of the South under Jim Crow. He writes, "Near the cabin we 'took' a bunch of pickaninnies rolling hoops. Their costumes were ludicrous. No shoes, and a straw hat on one, while another had carefully buttoned shoes with the toes completely cut out."[29] Though rare in *Movie Makers* articles, this kind of explicit racism shows that the ACL's humanist vision of the cinema as a tool for intercommunication and understanding was not a universally embraced doctrine among amateur filmmakers.

In their tendency to rely on romantic clichés about their subjects, however, amateurs followed in the tradition of travel lecturers such as Burton Holmes and later filmmakers such as Robert Flaherty. As indicated in chapter 1, *Movie Makers* published frequent articles about quasi-ethnographic travel filming and some of the more famous commercial travel films to come out of this tradition. In particular, Merriam Cooper and Ernest Schoedsack were profiled in *Movie Makers* for the "showmanship" of their commercial travel films. Their film *Chang* was particularly notable because it was understood both to be successful artistically and to have educational value. The article praises the filmmakers for defining film in a new way, one distinct from other art forms: "We saw no reason why the movies should follow the same fundamental dramatic structure of the other arts, drama, literature, music. They were too artificial, too far away from the soil and genuine vulgarity, which is the basis of all drama."[30] Nevertheless, the authors make a significant argument about the artistic bases of nonfiction filming; as they point out, there is still a great deal of story construction (planning, selection of material), but the film obeys a dramatic logic drawn from the real world.

The drama of the real world was inevitably subjected to certain manipulations, as commercial filmmaker André La Varre outlined in a pair of *Movie Makers* articles. In one, about his trip to Bali with Burton Holmes to make a travel film, La Varre is remarkably forthright when describing how he directed the subjects of his films; he makes no pretense of filming an unstaged reality. He writes that he and Holmes employed a guide who could communicate their directions to the locals: "We called him our official 'de-shirter,' for he was kept busy getting the men and boys to take off their gaudy western undershirts (worn outside) when they appeared before the camera. Unfortunately, Bali, like the rest of the Orient, is degenerating to the wrong use of Western clothing and will, in time, be spoiled as far as picturesque costumes are concerned."[31] La Varre's comments reflect a clearly orientalist approach to travel filming, as well as one engaged in a kind of quasi-"salvage-ethnography."[32] What was interesting to La Varre and Holmes is not how the locals *actually* were but how they could be made to cohere or to reenact an authentic oriental appearance. Despite this obvious direction, however, one of the photographs accompanying the article shows a Balinese musician (in traditional garb) filming fellow members of a traditional gamelan orchestra. He appears to be holding a 16mm Bell and Howell Filmo amateur camera, which presumably belonged to La Varre and Holmes. Another picture on the same page shows Burton Holmes, dressed in full white safari gear, filming a Balinese dancer with what appears to be the same camera. So a certain amount of collaboration and exchange were also going on between the filmmakers and their subjects. For the Balinese dancers and orchestra who appeared in these images, the reification of traditional images of their culture over more contemporaneous ones may have provided welcome promotion for their tourist industry. Providing a less-intrusive model for amateurs, a 1934 article about Robert Flaherty's *Man of Aran* explores issues of technology—particularly the use of telephoto lenses—in relation to a quasi-ethnographic impulse to capture images of people with any traces of their self-consciousness eliminated.[33] Flaherty's film was praised for the "straightforward and unaffected" presentation of the Aran islanders, which "could serve as a guide as to the best manner of treating similar, natural native life." Some amateurs appear to have followed this advice and used films like *Man of Aran* as a model for their own travel films, even similar films of remote fishing villages. Leslie Thatcher's *Fishers of Grande Anse,* in particular, recalls Flaherty's approach and appears quasi-ethnographic in approach.

Some amateur filmmakers took measures to ensure the interest of their film for a wider audience, as in the family chronicle film; in travel films, this meant removing traces of the filmmaker's friends and travel companions from their movies. La Varre noted that the "universal interest" of travelogue films might be spoiled by unstructured or unstaged images of family and friends in the film: "The inclusion of many shots of Brother Bill or Sister Jane wandering aimlessly through the scenes or posing affectedly against whatever is being filmed will be disastrous to the film's appeal."[34] Though he acknowledges that amateurs were interested in making records of their family and friends, La Varre suggests that the amateur "use family, relatives and friends as part of his 'set' and never to leave them to their own devices unless he wishes to use such scenes privately." The most important rule to keep in mind when making a film appear impersonal and professional was to sustain the diegetic separation between the filmed subjects and the position of the camera/audience: "When a subject looks at the lens the illusion of accompanying him which the audience should experience is lost. The magic of the silver screen is broken and the audience, as well as the subject, at once become conscious of the camera and nine tenths of the charm of the movie has vanished into thin air."[35] Many amateur travelogue filmmakers adopted this attitude, as evidenced by extant award-winning amateur travelogues. The degree of friendly interaction with the camera varied somewhat among filmmakers: Budge Crawley's early travel films include many friends and family, who generally perform actions rather than just looking at the camera; both Vincent Bollinger's and Leo Heffernan's award-winning travel films include groups of people doing actions, but their relationship to the filmmaker isn't clear. Films by Thatcher, John Hansen, and later Crawley don't include any indication at all of personal relationships; if any friends or family of the filmmakers are in the movies, they remain unannounced. In theory, the purpose of this was to allow the film's spectators to feel as though they are accompanying the film; the mugging and playacting of strangers indicate a special relationship to the filmer and therefore exclude an impersonal audience. In amateurs' different approaches to the task of producing hybrids of personal record and impersonal travelogue, we can also see evidence of the tension in amateur discourse—between, on one hand, making films like a professional and, on the other, embracing one's position as an amateur.

La Varre also provided specific advice for how amateurs could balance structure with contingency to make travel films of their voyages that would appeal to large audiences. While he noted the significance of travel films as personal documents of a journey, La Varre emphasized the importance of carefully selecting and shaping films of travel according to fairly generic principles in order to provide a long-lasting aid to memory. His suggestions offer a glimpse of the qualities of the travel film genre that many amateurs worked within, producing variations based on their own creativity and contingent conditions of filming. La Varre's suggestions range from those relating to specific shots and continuity plans ("A good opening shot for a European travel film is a long shot of the boat made from a position far enough away to include the whole thing without 'panoraming'") to those relating more generally to the kinds of materials (guide book or postcards) that amateurs could draw upon for structure and inspiration. "Do not scorn the guide book as a filming chart," he writes, "for the excellence of the finished film will depend more upon treatment of the important points of interest than upon inclusion of out of the way subjects." Far from limiting the potential interest of a travel film, "surprising cinematic beauty" might still be included, La Varre suggests, even if its inclusion involves structures and subjects suggested by fairly typical guides or postcards. "Since the motion picture camera possesses so much greater potentialities than the still," he writes, "surprising cinematic beauty may often be achieved if an exact angle in one of these postcards is followed in making the movie. The postcards should be preserved, for the descriptive wordings on the back may be useful in writing titles." While La Varre's advice suggests a lack of imagination, for him it is the surprising or contingent aspects of filming that counterbalance the structure of typical travel continuities and subjects. Despite La Varre's propensity for structuring films according to generic conventions (not to mention his employment of a "de-shirter"), which might seem completely antithetical to the inclusion of any surprise or contingency in his film, he also suggests ways of unobtrusively filming people unawares in their everyday activities. In particular, he advises setting up a camera to catch people off guard, such as when the chronicler is sitting at a boulevard café. La Varre's instructions are designed to balance travel film structures with unpredictable elements in order to produce works that are "bound to be universally interesting." As he points out, "All of these national or local characteristics and customs in work, play, dress and traffic offer an inexhaustible dramatic store for the amateur movie camera."[36]

Amateur travelogue films may have employed generic structures, but these works were still understood to emerge from the amateur filmmaker's curiosity about the world and to appeal to the viewer's shared curiosity.

Certainly the filmmaker possessed a privileged curiosity—when compared with both the subjects who were filmed in poor countries and the less affluent North Americans who couldn't afford to travel so widely. But significantly, this curiosity was understood by amateur discourse as a kind that could only lead to more enlightened communications between people from different places. "Amateur movies are spread over enough of the world," one ACL editor writes, "to insure a wide interchange of recreatable memories.... Amateur movies can never be predominantly nationalistic. They must always trend towards cosmopolitanism and must progress toward that tolerance and that understanding of other peoples and of other viewpoints which mark the true citizens of the world."[37] This liberal and pluralist point of view came under attack in the 1930s and then again after World War II for its unwillingness to "take sides" with either right or left.[38] And while it seems today to blithely overlook the ways in which North American culture was complicit with harmful economic structures, we should note that at the time of its founding the ACL belonged to a broader social movement that saw thoughtful communication as the best means of counteracting the alienating effects of modern life. The ACL's humanistic faith in cinema as a means of spreading international understanding emerged from this impulse, as did its efforts to form alternatives to commercial and impersonal film culture. Here, we find echoes of Maxim's founding manifesto as well as Dewey's plea for intercommunication.

Perhaps most emblematic of the ACL's utopian social vision for the cinema is its selection of award-winning travel films that also meditated on relationships between cinema and other art forms. These films approached the task of chronicle filming in terms of the cinema's place in a history of recording technologies, modern modes of perception, and utopian possibilities of universal intercommunication. One amateur who was three times rewarded by the ACL for his reflexive travel films was the Danish American engineer John Hansen. As discussed previously, Hansen was particularly respected during the 1930s for his experiments with Kodacolor film, and in 1932 his reel *Studies in Blue and Chartres Cathedral* was named to the ACL's Ten Best list. Described in its award citation as a "cerulean cinema achievement," the film was evidently both a travel film and a meditation on the use of color in amateur filmmaking. While Hansen's *Studies in Blue* appears to be a lost film, his sequences of the Chartres Cathedral survive and are stunning meditations on one era's medium of light and color as seen through another's. The film provides a faithful approximation of the glass's shifting light effects and their play on the eye. This is a travel film that transports an aesthetic experience for us and simultaneously reflects on the cinema's own mimetic capacities. The film appears to ask us if cinema is any different from a mobile version of stained glass.

Like his film of Chartres Cathedral, Hansen's black-and-white travel film *Tombs of the Nobles* uses motion pictures to consider an earlier art form. After a series of introductory titles and images that situate the viewer on the west bank of the Nile near Luxor, an intertitle introduces the principal subject of the film: the Tombs of the Nobles. It announces: "Gruesome and depressing? No, on the contrary, lively and human documents, absorbing and interesting. Important sources of information about the daily life in ancient Egypt." The Amateur Cinema League's award citation for this film praised its technical accomplishment in producing enough illumination to film these dark (and nearly inaccessible) spaces. But what is most striking in this film is Hansen's careful framing and patient reframing of the drawings. Cutting in from an establishing long shot of a wall of the Tomb of Nahkt, full of drawings, Hansen moves into closer shots of the particular actions depicted in the drawings, sometimes panning or tilting the camera across the figures to clarify the actions they are engaged in. To be sure, the beauty of the artwork rests in its original craftsmanship, but Hansen's film makes some significant contributions, providing these ancient images with a new vitality through motion and editing. Hansen articulates these images, sometimes even narrating the figures' actions, as in his movement from images of vineyard to the people treading grapes (figure 21). In this, ancient and static images are given the dimensions of motion and even a strange kind of temporality. Here, Hansen brings a modern technology for creative expression into contact with an ancient one, identifying for us a continuity in these two methods of recording information about everyday life and suggesting the ever-changing dimensions of how knowledge is communicated. Despite the novelty of amateur cinema as a medium, some amateur filmmakers had a keen awareness of their position in a historical tradition; John Hansen's *Tombs of the Nobles* demonstrates this kind of awareness. Seen in this historical trajectory, we can begin to recognize amateur cinema's production of something we might think of as a pragmatic imagination: a domain of modern and technologically mediated creativity that is situated in everyday experience and practice.

. . .

Though it is difficult to measure exactly how prominent chronicle filmmaking was among serious amateurs, a discussion on the subject emerged in the early 1950s. Here, a debate arose concerning the sentiment among

Figure 21. Hansen's film provides these ancient images with a new vitality through motion and editing. *Tombs of the Nobles* (John V. Hansen, 1931). Human Studies Film Archives, Smithsonian Institution HSFA 99.10.14–15.

Movie Makers readers that record films were overrepresented in Ten Best lists compared with story films. A letter to the ACL head office noted:

> After some discussion with different fellows in the club, I feel that somewhere along the line you guys are "missing the boat" on what constitutes a movie. I'm afraid you're putting emphasis on record filming and overlooking creative efforts entirely.
>
> What convinces me of this are some of the past winners you have chosen for honors, such as a masterful job of recording a volcano, a slow motion recording gem, a single frame recording effort and now a beautiful job of extreme closeups of birds.... Recording efforts, all of them!
>
> Maybe you're right and I am wrong. But to me *creative* filming—in which I can be made to feel sorrow, happiness, fear or laughter—is the true medium for the future of amateur movies. As far as you honestly can, the ACL should *encourage* such creative filming—instead of record films—with its Ten Best awards.[39]

Even among amateurs there was a wide range of different views about what constituted a "record" in contrast to what this chapter has described as a more creative "chronicle" film. I have argued that films such as *Duck Soup, Another Day,* and *Tombs of the Nobles* do, indeed, qualify as "creative" films, even while also recording factual materials.

Ratio of record to story films, 1946–1950

	All films seen		Films honored	
Year	Record	Story	Record	Story
1946	75%	25%	68%	32%
1947	91	9	71	29
1948	84	16	56	44
1949	85	15	40	60
1950	82	18	73	27
Average	83	17	62	38

SOURCE: *Movie Makers*, April 1951, 125.

According to the ACL many more record films than story films were submitted to the competition. The ACL managing director James Moore responded to this inquiry by providing statistics for the previous five years' entries in the Ten Best competitions (see table). According to Moore, these statistics lead to the following conclusions: most amateurs made record films; among those who made story films, the quality was relatively high (or higher than the record films, thus accounting for the higher proportion honored). Therefore, he suggested, it was possible that if the ACL favored any kind of filmmaking, it was story filmmaking. But what this discussion reveals is the tensions between the different kinds of filmmaking—and even within certain kinds of filmmaking—and the range of attitudes about the role of chronicling and creativity in amateur filmmaking.

Amateurs often pushed beyond the movie camera's capacity for simple recording and employed it as a tool for transfiguring the everyday and reflecting on their place in it. These films highlighted—in their technical proficiency, their playful appropriation of styles, and their thoughtful reflection on the medium of motion pictures—the *novelty* of amateur cinema as a means of personal, visual communication and the *promise* of intercommunication as a means of bringing about new technologically mediated social relationships. For amateur moviemakers in the mid-twentieth century, the cinema provided a powerful new tool for both recording and reflecting upon everyday life. These amateurs saw themselves as the latest in a long tradition of artists devoted to this kind of reflection—from Egyptian drawings to medieval chronicles, from Chartres Cathedral to photography and early cinema. Such art forms were simply prologue for a new technology and practice that would distribute the power to reflect on the everyday, in motion and far more widely than ever before. With these tools, amateurs engaged in a kind of intercommunication that they hoped would transform modern life into a great community. Of course new technologies always invite such utopian visions—with all the appeal and peril that accompany them—but in their chronicles, films amateurs saw a new aesthetic tool for reflecting upon and communicating their private domestic and public experiences. The question of how such a tool could be developed further through aesthetic experimentation is the subject of the next chapter.

7 **"The Amateur Takes Leadership"**
Amateur Film, Experimentation, and
the Aesthetic Vanguard

In 1928, *Photoplay* magazine held the first major amateur movie contest in North America. Writing in *Movie Makers*, ACL managing director Roy Winton pointed to the contest winner's films as evidence of the importance of amateur work in the development of "cinematics," or a unique film aesthetic: "This is a direct appeal to League members to undertake filming that will be artistically significant. The *Photoplay* contest films point the way to a very rich development. We, as League members, must be the leaders in it."[1] The next year, *Photoplay* held a second competition that resulted in a surprisingly noncommercial prizewinner: receiving top award in the nondramatic category was Ralph Steiner's experimental and abstract work H_2O. In the conflation of the popular magazine *Photoplay* and the abstract film H_2O, we find a fascinating nexus linking the amateur with mass culture, as well as with popular and experimental cinema. *Movie Makers* and other publications paid significant attention to amateur experimental efforts and promoted the idea that aesthetic experimentalism was one of the most important opportunities—even missions—that faced amateurs, as self-taught artists unhindered by commercial demands.[2]

During the late 1920s and early '30s, amateurs saw themselves as the inheritors of silent film aesthetics and argued that continuing the advancement of this nascent art form was their responsibility. Seeing amateur film culture—with its affluent class composition and interest in family and travel filmmaking—as constituting an "avant-garde" may be difficult, but the ACL did, in certain ways, present itself as an aesthetic vanguard and principal locus for film experimentation.[3] Amateur discourse echoed a view of pragmatic experimentation that was espoused by John Dewey's philosophy. Dewey promoted a kind of experimentation that was directed toward the solution of particular problems, not the kind that was guided by a manifesto or theoretical dogma. In his book *Democracy and Education* (1916) Dewey contrasts a reliance on dogma, or mere opinion, with hypotheses or theories that are tested by the scientific method. Dewey returned to this kind of pragmatic experimentation as a means of promoting social and civic engagement in his important work *The Public and Its Problems* (1927). Here he writes, "When we say that thinking and beliefs should be experimental, not absolutistic, we have then in mind a certain logic of method, not, primarily, the carrying on of experimentation like that of laboratories."[4] Dewey explains that the kind of experimentation he favored relies on using knowledge as a tool of inquiry and for the testing of hypotheses in a range of social and creative situations. But if Dewey's kind of practical experimentation resonated with a liberal-democratic social outlook, the ACL's adaptation of it became increasingly problematic by the mid-1930s, when concepts of social experimentation, political affiliation, and aesthetic expression became increasingly polarized. After World War II, experimentation was no longer at the center of the ACL's mission or activities, but many amateurs continued to work in film forms that had been innovated during the ACL's first years (fantasy, city film, abstract, and poetic nature films) but no longer stood on the aesthetic vanguard in film.

This chapter examines the strong vein of experimentalism in amateur film discourse and production during the late 1920s and early '30s, followed by its gradual decline during the mid-1930s and its reevaluation after World War II. Crucial to this discussion is a consideration of how amateur cinema situated itself within and differentiated itself from concurrent experimental and popular film discourses and championed the amateur as the new central figure in the vanguard of silent film aesthetics. J. S. Watson and Melville Webber were the original celebrities of amateur experimental filmmaking, producing such touted and visually complex films as *The Fall of the House of Usher* (1928) and *Lot in Sodom* (1932). But some amateurs also experimented with the limits of photographic representation by transfiguring visual recordings of water and other natural elements as well as machines into abstract shapes and symbolic reflections. Finally, in the early 1930s amateurs experimented with narrative forms that reconfigured familiar social coordinates and urban milieus. Over the course of the 1930s and '40s, experimentalism would fall in and out of favor among amateurs. This chapter will trace the crossing paths of experimental and amateur film during this period, extending to Maya Deren's involvement with amateur groups and the emergence of a distinct field of experimental exhibition and production contexts in the 1940s.

IN SEARCH OF THE "TRULY CINEMATIC": *THE FALL OF THE HOUSE OF USHER* (J.S. WATSON AND MELVILLE WEBBER)

Even before the success of Ralph Steiner's *H₂O* in the 1929 *Photoplay* amateur movie contest, the ACL had already been actively promoting the importance of amateur experimentation for almost two years. Numerous articles in *Movie Makers* linked experimentation with the development of cinema as an artistic, and not just commercial, medium. In these writings, amateurs were encouraged to take advantage of their independence from market demands and produce works that would help film to reach a new level of artistry and aesthetic sophistication. Though the precise nature of this artistry was difficult for these early writers to articulate, they often promoted an essentialist film aesthetic in which filmmakers would gradually come to know and develop those aspects of the filmic medium that differentiated it from other art forms. But as new experimental films were produced, circulated, and discussed among amateurs in the late 1920s, a more precise definition of amateur "cinematics" began to take form, and the amateur's claim to a place on the aesthetic vanguard solidified. But while we can understand that the expansion of film as an aesthetic language played an important role among amateurs, we can have little doubt that Winton, and many others, understood this to be a controlled experiment rather than a foray into the anarchistic world of the modernist avant-garde. As a social body that was striving to achieve and maintain some manner of coherence among its disparate members—affluent hobbyists, students, middle-class club members, experimental artists—the ACL could hardly espouse the radical position of the antagonistic avant-garde, with all of its nihilism and political radicalism. Consequently, the ACL had to negotiate carefully its commitment to new aesthetic developments and clearly distinguish its project from more extreme positions.

The earliest issues of *Movie Makers* urged amateurs to capitalize on their independence and perform aesthetic experiments that commercial producers couldn't risk. One editorial published in 1927 encouraged amateur film production similar to what painters called "waste work" or "painting done not to order, not to sell, not even to exhibit, but attempted and concluded for experiment, for practice, or for the pure joy of doing it."[5] For the anonymous author of this article, this kind of playful production stood at the apex of enjoyable and creative work that might lead to new artistic insights, even if the immediate products were not appropriate for public consumption. But such waste work was particularly necessary in the medium of film, because its history as a commercial entertainment had prevented such unprofitable experimentation. "So far the art of the cinema," the author observes, "has lacked the element of freedom from practicality that would appear to be essential to the more complex and subtle development of any medium for expressing beauty." Into this void, amateurs were invited to move and pursue, in particular, "experiments in camera work, in subject placement, in title writing, in lighting, and in choice of esthetic material."

Roy Winton used an editorial touting the importance of the first *Photoplay* movie contest to explore the question of amateur cinematics. Noting the amateur's freedom from market forces and his important role in the development of film art, he discussed "the importance of making film experiments that are artistically significant." Winton writes, "Filming for purposes of record constitutes a large part of amateur activity. But that record need not be devoid of artistic quality. A straightforward tale may be told in sprightly and racy fashion and a practical film record may be made in a truly 'cinematic' manner—that is, in a manner no other medium except a movie camera could use." Winton begins here to develop a concept of the cinematic, which he goes on to explain in more detail: "If our members would resolve never to shoot a foot of film to catch a picture that would be better caught with a still camera; if they would determine that their filming would all be done with foreknowledge of the essentials of cinematography, as different from still photography or spoken drama (if a photoplay is attempted) and if they would study what professionals call 'continuity,' 'cutting' and 'editing,' we would have more amateur film of the kind that would carry the art of motion picture making forward by leaps and bounds."[6] Though Winton makes many proclamations about the place of amateurs in motion picture art over the years, this is perhaps the closest he ever comes to presenting a manifesto for amateur film as an aesthetic vanguard. Here, he pleads with amateurs to blend the interests of amateurs—recording and storytelling—with the technique of professionals: continuity, cutting, editing. Together, with an awareness of that which is cinematic, these elements could allow the amateur to advance the art of motion pictures.

The question of what constitutes motion picture art, however, was itself much debated in the late 1920s, as talking movies were widely adopted by Hollywood. Amateur filmmakers would obtain widespread access to synchronized sound technology only following World War II, so Winton, like other classical film theorists, argued not surprisingly that film art was to be found in the advances of the silent screen. He argued that talking pictures had little in common with cinematics, or "camera work and direction based on the element of motion and other special functions of the motion picture as an art."[7] But in a surprising move, Winton argued that the advent of the talkies was actually a good thing for film art, because it provided entertainment for the crowd and liberated amateurs from competing with professional works, allowing them to focus on the motion picture's artistic development. Perhaps prophetically, Winton wrote, "With the wedding of the crowd and the 'talkies,' the silent screen can go forward to a free artistic development. Motion pictures without speech will become the unusual thing within another ten years; they will be produced as exotics and not as hardy perennials from the studios. Such as are made will be for an admittedly limited audience composed of people honestly interested in movies as movies—mostly the little picture house groups." Here, Winton pulls the thoughtful amateur out of the flow of mass cultural taste and stakes the amateur's claim not only to the cinema's future but also to its past. "A great part of amateur filming will always be done for silent projection," he writes. "Into amateur hands, then, will come the heritage of the silent movie. Rejected by the professional industry as an old story, amateurs will make of it an art." Winton concludes by inviting "the Vidors, the Borsages [sic], the Flahertys, the Murnaus, the von Sternbergs, the Pudowkins and the rest of the directors who have been discovering the real meaning of the motion picture as an art form" to join the amateurs in their continued appreciation of silent film aesthetics. Winton's remarks placed amateur film aesthetics in a strange temporal position: on one hand it was conservative and backward-looking toward the history of a now-obsolete silent form; on the other hand, the amateur was at the vanguard of motion picture art, picking up where the commercial film industry had abandoned the art form.[8]

J.S. Watson and Melville Webber's modernist adaptation of Edgar Allan Poe's *The Fall of the House of Usher* provided North American amateurs with the first example of successful film experimentation from among their own ranks. The development of this film production was chronicled in *Movie Makers* reports, beginning in January 1928 with the formation of a new movie club in Rochester to produce work exploring the limits of cinematics.[9] A few months later, an article announced the group's plan more specifically: "An amateur group in Rochester, N.Y., seeking true cinematic values, is producing a film version of Edgar Allen Poe's *Fall of the House of Usher*. The story, retold in a highly stylized form in order to interfere as little as possible with cinematic expression, is divided into three episodes, the first covering the arrival of the visitor and the death of Lady Madeline, the second, the mental conflict of the brother and the resurrection of Madeline, and the third the visitor's flight and the destruction of the house."[10] The article explained the filmmakers' clever use of special effects and lighting and provided practical technical advice for amateurs wishing to try something similar. After the film had been completed, *Movie Makers* published a feature article by J.S. Watson called "The Amateur Takes Leadership: How Experimenters, in Circumventing Production Difficulties, Have Achieved the Greatest Cinematic Advance since *The Cabinet of Dr. Caligari.*" In this article, Watson described many of the techniques used in the film in detail and particularly emphasized the potential for amateur film as a nonrealistic artistic medium.

The completed *Fall of the House of Usher* presents less an adaptation of the Poe story than an experiment with the visual evocation of moods and symbols, which built upon the available modernist film styles of the moment. The film has often been compared with *The Cabinet of Dr. Caligari* (Robert Weine, 1920), and it is not hard to see why, with its similar use of angular cardboard sets and its stylized face makeup and costumes (figure 22). The film employs a vivid and dramatic montage, as in a sequence showing Usher hammering his sister's coffin closed. In terms of its cinematography, *Usher* appears at times to be influenced by cubist aesthetics, as it employs special lenses to fragment and multiply images; in one of these prismatic scenes, the frame is filled with moving stairs, creating patterns that move diagonally, horizontally, and vertically all at once. The film's fascination with images of death and reanimation and its cyclical visual style also recall important symbolist works, such as Edward Burne-Jones's painting *The Golden Stairs* (1880).[11]

Beyond these modernist influences, *The Fall of the House of Usher*'s emphatic use of images that are fragmented through prisms provides an experimental and fictional interpretation of the ACL's aspiration to use the cinema as a self-reflective medium for exploring different kinds of subjectivity. One writer in *Movie Makers* even hinted at such a connection in an article about the film:

> *The Fall of the House of Usher* not only represents a new cinema technique but it is also unique in that it does not attempt to tell Poe's story in detail, rather to evoke in its audiences the esthetic impressions and moods which the tale creates in its readers. This revolutionary approach to the cinema opens a fascinating field for further pioneering. Fortified with new scientific instruments which have recently been devised for the detection and recording of emotional reactions, the amateur producer may now truly be said to face a new world for cinematic experimentation in translating such reactions into film.[12]

These remarks simultaneously linked amateur aesthetic and scientific experiments with a new interpretation of the cinema's use as a tool for

Figure 22. *Usher* built upon the available modernist film styles of the moment. *The Fall of the House of Usher* (James Sibley Watson and Melville Webber, 1928). Courtesy George Eastman House.

inscribing and reflecting upon emotional and subjective states. Widely screened and acclaimed both inside amateur circles and more widely in little cinemas, *The Fall of the House of Usher* presented an example of how amateurs could produce work that was small in scope but important in its experiments with visual style and psychological reflection.

The Amateur Cinema League distributed *The Fall of the House of Usher* as part of its film library for affiliated amateur movie clubs and in so doing provided many other amateurs with an important exemplar and inspiration for their own experiments in cinematics. In a similar vein *Movie Makers* reported on numerous other experimental works during the late 1920s, such as the significant successes of Robert Florey, a professional film director who also produced important avant-garde works, such as *Life and Death of 9413—a Hollywood Extra* (1927), in the 1920s. *Movie Makers* claimed Florey as an amateur in the truest sense: "a lover of cinema." Another important filmmaker was Charles Klein, whose experimental adaptation of *The Telltale Heart* (1928) was distributed and screened among amateur movie clubs. The effect of these successful experiments could be found in the production of new experimental projects by individual amateurs or clubs. Some of these efforts employed close-ups to produce experiments in restricted narration, as this report describes:

A photoplay completely cinematic—that is, telling its story in a way that nothing but motion pictures could achieve—is under way at Colgate University.... "A Day in College" presents twenty-four hours—not of the James Joyce type, however—out of the life of a Colgate student, without giving pictures of any faces. The whole film will consist of close-ups of hands and feet and it will follow the hero, in this way, through his entire collegiate day.... The purpose of this film, aside from its being a distinct cinematic experiment, is to enable the spectator to identify himself completely with the hero and live, in imagination, the collegiate routine, without disturbing this identification by seeing on the screen a face, not his own.[13]

Once again, amateur experiments were used to explore the medium's capacity as a surface for subjective reflection. A later article about this same film announced some of the effect of the completed work: "Each spectator, seeing a picture of this nature, finds it contains a personal appeal. No tangible characters make him think of the story as the experience of someone else, but everyone sees himself reflected more or less, and his attention is thus held fast."[14] For amateurs, experimental photoplays could develop new ways of using the cinema as a medium for reflecting on self and subjectivity.

THE DOCUMENT TRANSFIGURED: H_2O (RALPH STEINER) AND *PORTRAIT OF A YOUNG MAN* (HENWAR RODAKIEWICZ)

I have long urged the film makers to begin with the simple documentary.... The document is a basis, and the document transfigured is the ultimate work of art in the cinema.

Harry Alan Potamkin[15]

While experimental photoplays, such as *The Fall of the House of Usher*, occupied a prominent space in amateur experimental aesthetics, films that transfigure documentary material into abstract forms, such as Ralph Steiner's H_2O, soon appeared as an alternative approach. Emerging from the cinema's basic representational capacity, as well as the amateur's penchant for nonfiction scenic and family filming, experimental documentaries responded to the ACL's goal of developing a specifically cinematic art form.[16] To guide amateurs in these filmmaking experiments, *Movie Makers* published articles offering practical advice, and the ACL rewarded and distributed exemplary instances of this form. One such film was Henwar Rodakiewicz's *Portrait of the Artist*, which was named one of the ACL's Ten Best films of 1932. These films and activities reflect the ACL's effort to expand the language of personal filmmaking art and to further the goal of an amateur avant-garde.

H_2O is a film that traversed the space between documentary representation and abstract experimentation, winning Ralph Steiner a prize in the 1929 *Photoplay* amateur film competition. Steiner is best known in film history as a documentary filmmaker; an early member of the New York Film and Photo League, Steiner later photographed Pare Lorenz's film *The Plow That Broke the Plains* (1936) and codirected *The City* (1939). But before this Steiner was a still photographer who worked in both commercial and artistic settings and an amateur filmmaker. As an artistic photographer, Steiner produced starkly realistic and dramatically framed images of everyday objects, such as typewriters and cars, which defamiliarized them through manipulations of scale or unusual context. Steiner participated in the activities of the Camera Club of New York and exhibited his artistic photography in the 1928 International Exposition of Art and Design. A 1929 article in *Movie Makers* indicates that he had also become a member of the Metropolitan Motion Picture Club of New York, where "H_2O, an experimental film showing the movement and reflections of water under varying conditions, produced by Ralph Steiner, a club member, was shown. Over 150 members attended the meeting."[17] So Steiner, like other artists experimenting with film and photography in this period, found himself positioned in a triangulation of commercial advertising work, high art experiments, and amateur club contexts.

Steiner's dramatic combination of straight photography and abstracting composition brought his film to the attention of *Photoplay* even before the amateur movie competition was complete. "H_2O is a study of water and its moods," reported the magazine's amateur film editor: "Mr. Steiner started making it last summer, beginning with an Eyemo and completing the abstract part of the film with a DeBrie. Mr. Steiner used a six and twelve inch lens on both cameras to get his water reflections enlarged and to get pure abstract patterns of shadows on water surfaces. 'No tricks of any kind were used,' said Mr. Steiner, 'as I was interested in seeing how much material could be gotten by trying to see water in a new way, rather than by doing things to it with the camera.'"[18] *Photoplay*'s interest in an abstract and experimental film, such as Steiner's, is perhaps difficult to account for. But Steiner's own remarks on the film set his approach to cinematics apart from that of the Watson and Webber school of experimental filming. In contrast to their anti-realism, Steiner emphasized that he wanted to use the camera to see water in a new way but without resorting to optical manipulations, such as prisms or artificial animations. The resulting film is a fascinating meditation on light reflections and fluid motion as well as on the line between realism and abstraction.

Figure 23. The film's depiction of water gradually shifts from documentary to purely abstract. H_2O (Ralph Steiner, 1929). Courtesy George Eastman House.

Described in *Photoplay* as "a study of water in the new manner," H_2O organizes its imagery through an assemblage of short shots, rarely lasting longer than a second or two, edited together according to graphic contrasts and complementary visual qualities. At first, the film primarily shows water in a specific context: coming down in drops, in a waterfall, or gushing out of a pipe or hole. In the middle section of the film, the images appear more concerned with the reflective properties of moving pools of water, but we almost always see the edges of these pools or some foliage or floating matter that anchor these images in terms of shot scale and angle. In its third section, the film moves increasingly toward abstraction through close-up, high-contrast images of light flickering and reflecting on water (figure 23). Part of the film's playfulness is the game of "figure and ground" that it invites us to join in, offering us both shimmering reflections and drops or dust on the water's surface, forcing us to constantly reorient our viewing of the water itself. In the film's last moments these images become increasingly abstract, and the water appears to be reduced to waving lines, like animated drawings. Even though we've been tutored by the film to see these images as rooted in the world, the last moments of the film strain this belief with their presentation of images that appear sped up or slowed down, and shot scale becomes nearly impossible to determine.

H_2O is fascinating both for its defamiliarization of quotidian materials and its problematization of the basic categories of representational and abstract cinema. On one hand it is a strictly observational film that, in its thirteen-minute duration, gives structure and order to motions and phenomena that continue in nature at every moment. The film's materials are both universally appealing and quintessentially cinematic; who hasn't stood staring, transfixed by the patterns created by a flow of water, or a fountain, or the dappled reflections of light on water? Like light on photographic emulsion and the continual flow of a ribbon of film, the movement of water is both a time- and a light-based fascination. In some sense, this experimental film has its roots in the indexical and representational function of the cinema, both as light registering on celluloid and more generally as a medium that can place our world in a frame and re-present it to us for our consideration. But we can also see it as a film that revels in formal and conceptual play; just as its title suggests a more molecular understanding of the materials and properties that make up something as commonplace as water, so does this film, at its most essential level, offer a consideration of the materials and properties that make up moving pictures—light, time, and motion. Steiner's two subsequent abstract films were well received among New York artists but received little attention in amateur circles. *Surf and Seaweed* (1929–30) is less visually surprising and original than H_2O, in part because it exploits some of the same effects of light shimmering on water as the earlier film. The third in Steiner's trilogy of abstract films, *Mechanical Principles* (1930), is fascinating and more striking than *Surf and Seaweed*. It is composed of close-up shots of mechanical gears of different kinds in motion; rather than an examination of a single machine, it is an examination of the different kinds of motion produced by machines. *Mechanical Principles* emphasizes the tension in such machinery between the constancy of force and repetition on the one hand and the irregularity of shapes, sizes, and motions on the other.

Steiner's motion pictures marked an important development in amateur experimental film, both in their award-winning status and their use of straight-representational methods to produce abstraction. A *Movie Makers* article called "The Magic of Machine Films—the World of Moving Metal Invites Your Camera," by Harry Alan Potamkin, explores a similar affinity between movie cameras and machines. Here, Potamkin proposed an aesthetic of machine movies that specifically exclude showing people and machines in relation to each other, much as Steiner's film would.[19] Rather than producing a work about the social meaning of machines, Potamkin suggested filming a machine according to the principles of "absolute composition." In a similar vein, in the article "Modernistic Movie Making: New Trails That Beckon the Amateur Experimenter," C.W. Gibbs outlined some practical ways amateurs could develop film aesthetics. Gibbs itemized some of the key modernist film techniques: "odd angles," moving lights; ultra-close-ups; multiple images created by multifaceted glass; prisms, distorting lenses, and distorting mirrors; trick fades and dissolves; moving viewpoint; flashbacks to unlikely objects to draw a juxtaposition. Although, by 1929, these were somewhat familiar techniques, Gibbs also suggested the potential for a new, more abstract direction that film might take: "I hope someday to see a purely abstract motion picture. . . . A pure abstraction is a picture made without any subject matter."[20] In articles such as these, amateurs were given specific instructions in how to think about film experiments as well as a sense of their role in the advancement of film art.

The specific instructions provided by *Movie Makers* were intended to spark amateur filmmakers' creativity but not lead them to produce identical and unthinking copies of works like Steiner's. Roy Winton stressed the pragmatic nature of film experimentation rather than its position in a larger artistic movement: "We do not want to build up the body of motion picture esthetics by any less common sense method than experiment and reflection on the results of experiment. What motion picture art becomes will be decided by continued effort and product and not by a forced and manufactured scheme of cinematic theory."[21] Winton's remarks here suggest a definition of experimentation in the most pragmatic sense of that term. John Dewey promoted an understanding of experimentation that had been adapted from its scientific origins and directed toward social scientific and even artistic problems. In ACL writers' and amateur filmmakers' rejection of absolutist aesthetic theories, we can find a similarly pragmatic view of experimentation. Motion pictures, Winton argued, should let the amateur express his own personality freely: "Let him be sincere and film only that which really interests him, with a sportsmanlike determination to make it interesting to others."[22]

Though it is difficult to see how a film could be both abstract in nature and an expression of an individual personality, Henwar Rodakiewicz's *Portrait of a Young Man* explores both of these avenues. Named one of the ACL's Ten Best films of 1932, *Portrait* is an abstract work that, like H_2O, employs montage to organize documentary shots of water, surf, nature, smoke, and occasionally machines. But unlike Steiner's film, Rodakiewicz's draws a direct relationship between abstract composition and symbolic and subjective meaning.[23] Divided into three "movements," *Portrait of a Young Man* presents a fifty-four-minute montage study of several visual elements, presented without any additional narrative, intertitles, or human characters. The film's principal guide to its symbolic register is an opening intertitle: "As our understanding and sympathy for the things about us must reveal our character, so is this an endeavor to portray a certain young man in the terms of the things he likes and his manner of liking them: the sea, leaves, clouds, smoke, machinery, sunlight, the interplay of forms and rythms [sic], but above all—the sea." And so, without any further elaboration, the film's first movement begins with shots of surf crashing and tumultuous water, along with patterns of light reflecting off its surface. The camera in this film is generally static, but our position is constantly shifting as the film cuts between different subjects and points of view in shot scale or angle. Initial swirling liquid abstractions are later juxtaposed with shots of machine gears and wheels spinning and eventually with the third element of this opening movement: white smoke curling, shifting, rising against a dark background, like delicate ribbons of abstract light patterns. Unlike Steiner's films, which employed "no tricks," this film appears to make use of slow-motion photography in some of these shots.

If the film's first movement is concerned with different kinds of fluid motions—in water, in cyclical machinery, and in smoke—the second gradually turns its gaze upward to consider qualities of light, foliage, and clouds. This movement alternates between familiar shots of flowing water, patterns of refracted light, and interludes of leaves and branches against the sky; the film works into progressively closer shots of leaves and branches until eventually we see a leaf in extreme close-up, revealing its veins. Finally, this movement presents a series of shots of cloud formations, clouds moving across the sky, and vapors forming and reconfiguring. *Portrait*'s third movement reaffirms the centrality of water as a motif in the film but emphasizes its pulsing rhythm by showing waves crashing onshore. This final movement reprises the images of branches and machine gears spinning, but just for a shot at a time, until we return to shots of crashing surf. As the film nears its conclusion, waves roll across the frame more dramatically, sometimes in slow motion. These actions are *naturally* repetitive—unlike the machines we see in the film, which are technological and precise in their repetition. The film's last shots are of these big waves, slowed down and presented in long shot but still filling the screen with their surging force as they rise up and then crash back down.

Portrait of a Young Man is similar to Steiner's films—in a sense it is a combination of his three works dealing with water, surf, and machines—but it is more explicit in its interest in producing a symbolic interpretation of these elements. Rodakiewicz wrote about this symbolism in *Movie*

Makers, where he distinguished between the usual scenic films, which present images as facts about the world, and his own effort to present an individual and symbolic relationship to the documentary material: "In creating a film of nature that represents the cameraman's individuality, the importance of selection cannot be overestimated.... So, as we use our eyes, we should use the camera, gathering and selecting the significant parts in order to build a vivid impression of the whole."[24] Even though his article suggests how specific symbolic meanings might be produced in a film (the feeling or mood of dawn, for example), the overall effect of *Portrait* is less easy to grasp. Certainly, it reflects the filmmaker's fascination with movement, in its cyclical and natural, as well as mechanically repetitive, forms, and it meditates on light, both at its source in the skies and at its reflection on different kinds of surfaces and membranes.[25] It is tempting to find in these elements—repetitive motion and the registration of light on and through different media—a metaphor for the cinema. But even if this interpretation may be part of the film's symbolic language, we are not permitted such a direct or clear conclusion, because these elements are also reflective of more general kinds of lived experience: the repetition of our pulse and biological cycles as well as our dealings with the world as filtered through vision and consciousness. *Portrait of a Young Man* offers a meditation on these as both distinct and interrelated phenomena: it presents us with a representation of lived experiences as well as a phenomenological counterpart to this experience in the cinema.

As if inspired by Rodakiewicz's film, *Movie Makers* published an editorial in May 1932, which promoted and explained experimental filmmaking in unusually direct terms: "The habit that so many good words have of narrowing down to limited concepts of their real meaning is the reason why many amateur filmers shy at the word experiment," the author explains. "In the school days of many of us whose childish teaching came from small communities, to experiment was to engage in a more or less mysterious operation in chemistry or physics, an operation that called for special equipment that was often a perplexing assembly of strangely shaped and peculiarly acting apparatus. We approached an experiment with caution and mental tension, because we knew, from experience or observation, that sometimes one blew up."[26] In contrast to a technical, gadget-oriented brand of experimentation, however, the author promotes a kind that does without complicated equipment and theories and seems almost directly inspired by Steiner's and Rodakiewicz's films: "Every photographic requirement can be met with the simplest mechanism that will produce a motion picture. Mental energy, inventiveness and the capacity of seeing old things in a new way must come from the experimenter and he cannot borrow them or buy them." For this author, an experimental film does not produce technical tricks so much as it reflects "originality and pungency and on any subject that you may choose."

This article concludes by encouraging amateurs to submit their experiments for consideration as the year's Ten Best films. And indeed the Ten Best of 1932 included a surprising number of experimental films, most notably Rodakiewicz's *Portrait of a Young Man* and Watson and Webber's *Lot in Sodom*. Also included, among the year's honorable mentions, were an experimental travel film called *Water* (B.H. Blood), which compiled "sequences of water, waterways, wells and ice in a variety of places in the world," and *I'd Be Delighted To!* (S. Winston Childs), which narrates a dinner between a man and a woman told entirely in close-ups. The *Movie Makers* review notes that this latter film is "a splendid example of what, with skill and care, can be done in this distinctly advanced amateur filming method."[27] In praise of *Portrait*, the reviewer writes:

> Abstract in treatment, and speaking through the delicately rhythmed [sic] scenes of smoke, leaves, grasses, the sea, machinery and the heavens, this film is an attempt to portray in graphic terms a young man's reactions to the beauty, force and mystery of the natural world. . . . Although using material to be found in nature, he [Rodakiewicz] has so transmuted it, by the creative artistry of his selection and control, as to get from each selected scene, not a mere reproduced likeness, but a trenchant and symbolic image. *Portrait of a Young Man* is beautiful, exciting, workmanlike and distinguished.[28]

In this, *Movie Makers* both confirms the kind of cinematic alchemy that Potamkin promoted—the "document transfigured"—and juxtaposes the film's subjective and more workmanlike qualities. Much as the early motto of the ACL reflected an urge to use cinema as a self-reflective technology to "see ourselves as other see us," Henwar Rodakiewicz's film expands on Steiner's experimental aesthetic by joining it with themes of symbolic self-reflection.

THE GREAT DEPRESSION AND AMATEUR EXPERIMENTATION: *MR. MOTORBOAT'S LAST STAND* (JOHN FLORY)

Despite their interest in advancing film aesthetics through experimentation, amateurs and writers working within the ACL found themselves increasingly at odds with social and politicized art during the early 1930s.

The reasons for this are not hard to locate, as the dire social conditions of the Great Depression brought ideology and politics to the center of a public debate about the function of art in society.[29] But the ways in which these debates played out in amateur writing and filmmaking are more difficult to identify. Many amateurs who had happily aligned their artistic work with the ACL during the late 1920s found themselves occupied with more politicized documentary work in the 1930s. This was the case with Ralph Steiner, who set aside his abstract experiments in favor of work with the Workers' Film and Photo League. Lewis Jacobs, whose comments on abstract filmmaking had appeared in *Movie Makers* in the late 1920s, also turned in a new direction, making important social commentary films and launching the politically radical magazine *Experimental Cinema*.[30] However, despite a seemingly clear rift between the ACL and the more radical activities of Potamkin and Jacobs, *Movie Makers* still carried intermittent news of these individuals, such as an announcement that Potamkin was to present a course on motion pictures at the New School for Social Research in New York, in the fall of 1932.[31]

Even if the ACL shared John Dewey's rejection of absolutism and support of liberal-democratic ideology, this position proved increasingly incommensurate with the social and political crises of the 1930s. The emerging tension between art and politics in the ACL is vividly illustrated by film experiments that depicted urban milieus. By the late 1920s, the urban montage film had become a familiar experimental form among amateurs. In 1930 Harry Alan Potamkin wrote, "Every amateur ought to attempt to film his city or a part of it. It would be interesting to compare the data."[32] Many amateurs seemed to take up this invitation, producing works set against an urban social backdrop. But as more politicized experimental films showed, such as Jay Leyda's *Bronx Morning* (1931) and Lewis Jacobs's *A Footnote to Fact* (1933), these works also invited a much wider consideration of social problems than earlier abstract or symbolic experiments had. The tension between aesthetic experimentation and social realism in amateur discourse became increasingly problematic over the early 1930s; it reached a crisis for the ACL in 1934 around its response to John Flory's film *Mr. Motorboat's Last Stand*, whose reception marked an important turning point for the amateur's role at the aesthetic vanguard.

During the early 1930s, articles in *Movie Makers* discussed the nature of film art in a largely apolitical tone. At the same time, their promotion of aesthetic issues became increasingly defensive. In 1930, Roy Winton delivered an address about "movie art" to the Hartford Amateur Movie Club. The presentation included examples from both conventional works and modernist experiments, such as H_2O, "representing the abstract film," and *The Fall of the House of Usher*.[33] But according to reports in *Movie Makers*, what was most distinctive about the meeting was its practical and unpretentious nature:

> It is significant that an entire amateur movie club should be thinking in these terms and that it should be inquiring in a practical and thoroughly un-arty way concerning them. It is a healthy sign that so large a group of amateur filmers can approach the question of art without awkwardness and without pretentious punditry. It holds out more than a hope that the eighth art, unlike its earlier brothers, will come to adult powers without the long-haired bluffers and wordy ineffectuals who have clouded the issue with the others. Art may be long but real art is never long-winded.[34]

This editorial points to a definite interest in keeping discussions about the artistry of filmmaking at a practical level while also reaffirming the amateur's position as patron and arbiter of cinematic taste. In a similar vein, an editorial in 1931 praised amateurs for their inherently sensible nature: "The practitioners of amateur movies represent, we believe, a very creditable slice of present day life. They are not 'arty' nor are they faddists. They are not, on the other hand, vulgar and cheap minded. They represent the good middle average of their countries. Their filming can rightly be of them and by them and can present them as they are."[35] Such articles reaffirmed the amateur's middlebrow position in relation to society in contrast to a vanguard or radical position. This is the middle path that the amateur increasingly occupied: not arty but not the vulgar and cheap-minded mass public either.

As the economic climate worsened, editorials in *Movie Makers* continued to hold an optimistic view about both the Depression and the advances in amateur movie production and culture. One editorial from 1932 seemed to echo Herbert Hoover's promise that "prosperity is just around the corner" and cautioned against any kind of extreme solution to economic depression, either in a return to the excesses of the 1920s or in new radical political directions.[36] Eschewing both radical aesthetic experimentation and radical politics, *Movie Makers* increasingly called for a more moderate path.[37] But nothing exemplified the growing tension between amateur experimentation and politicized art better than the reception of John Flory's 1933 film *Mr. Motorboat's Last Stand: A Comedy of the Depression*. Hailed as the best amateur experimental film of 1933, Flory's film received extensive attention in *Movie Makers* for its ingenious narration and the winning performance of its lead actor. The film is a comic-fantasy about the destitute

Figure 24. Mr. Motorboat displays poise and deliberation in the face of poverty and ridicule. *Mr. Motorboat's Last Stand* (John Flory, 1933). Courtesy George Eastman House.

protagonist's efforts to imagine himself as dignified, distinguished, and even affluent, despite living in a junkyard and selling apples for a living. Played by the African American vaudeville performer Leonard "Motorboat" Sturrup, Mr. Motorboat is reminiscent of Chaplin's Tramp; he displays a similar poise and deliberation in the face of poverty and ridicule. Waking up in a junkyard, Motorboat performs his morning calisthenics, puts on a carefully pressed suit and top hat, and feeds his pet bunny, all before playing a quick round of golf with an umbrella as a club (figure 24). In contrast to Chaplin's films, however, close-ups, stop-motion animation, and surprising eye-line matches are intercut with more typical visual narration, thus presenting us with a sense of Motorboat's interior and far-fetched view of the world.

The film's narrative concerns a conflict between Motorboat and a rival apple seller. When Motorboat wins a customer from this nemesis, his vision of personal prosperity is quickly inflated, and he imagines himself on Wall Street as a pre-Depression investor. The film then presents a series of visual transformations: Motorboat takes his nickel and goes "fishing" for new investments; his rod becomes a spool of stock-market ticker tape; and gradually inflating balloons, with the years 1928, 1929, and 1930 written on them, fill the screen. Finally we see a stack of investment certificates catch fire, followed by a series of bubbles and balloons popping and tires deflating as Motorboat's apple cart is simultaneously destroyed by his competitor. Though Mr. Motorboat, destitute once again, briefly considers suicide, the last shot of the film shows him entertaining working folks on the side of the street by pulling a rabbit out of his hat. Once again, he is rich (in spirit), happy, and adored.

Though *Mr. Motorboat's Last Stand* was named one of the ACL's Ten Best films of the year, it also prompted a critical reaction from *Movie Makers*. Commenting about the film's award citation, an anonymous author notes that it "is filled with remarkable directorial touches and cinematic symbolism and, although it suffers to some extent from the admixture of fantasy and realism, it is decidedly the best experimental film of the year."[38] But in its combination of aesthetic experimentation and urban social themes, *Motorboat* seems to have sparked some controversy among amateurs. In February 1934, some two months after the film was lauded in the Ten Best list, an editorial cautioned against experimenting too broadly in amateur work. In an article called "Keep It Simple" an anonymous writer praised the emergence of "a definitely experimental trend in personal filming" that is "of the greatest possible benefit to the future of amateur movies [as] it places the amateur in the front rank of cinematographic pioneers of new trials."[39] But the author cautioned against too much experimentation: "There is an obligation upon everybody who would essay the unusual to see to it that this unusual does not become that which is merely obscure. Granted that cine amateurs are not given to that childish exhibitionism which induces too many modern artists to present puzzling creations for the sole purpose of getting themselves talked about and written about as prophets of the incredibly novel, it is all too easy for these modest and serious experimentalists to fail, through the lack of clear thinking, in making themselves intelligible." Once again we find in *Movie Makers* an admonition of more radical and puzzling kinds of artists. As the editorial continues, however, even though it never refers by name to the film that provoked this reaction, it becomes increasingly clear that it must have been none other than *Mr. Motorboat's Last Stand*. The author refers to "a recent film, to which exceeding praise is due," although it "presents an example of a lack of that clear thinking which must restrain and govern all cinematic experiment." The author explains further: "This film dealt with situations that were presented deliberately as fantastic but its fault lay in the fact that fantasy was sandwiched in between realism and that the realism was weakened by including the fantastic. The mood of the film was, like Mohammed's coffin, suspended between a heaven of make believe and a hell of the baldly factual, with no definite anchorage up or down." Ultimately, the author suggests that greater care and analysis of the film were required by its filmmaker in order to make it more coherent. Even if "a satirical opposition of fantasy and realism" was intended, it needed to be presented more clearly. "To the 1934 experimentalists," the author concludes, "no better advice could be given than the old fashioned admonition to 'keep it simple.'"

Though frank criticism was a regular feature of *Movie Makers*, this editorial seems a particularly striking reversal of the previous praise of the film. Why did the magazine's position on *Mr. Motorboat*, and indeed on film experimentation in general, require this reevaluation or clarification? This editorial suggests that the intermingling, or even contamination, of realism with fantasy posed too great a threat to the ACL's increasingly fragile distinction between experimentation in the aesthetic realm and that in the social realm. Even as writers for *Movie Makers* continued to promote experiments in film form during the early 1930s, they were explicit in their rejection of social and political experiments. These two kinds of experimentation were related in John Dewey's pragmatic philosophy, which saw experimentation on the individual level—testing hypotheses, trial and error, searching for new results—as a necessary component of good liberal-democratic citizenship. By the 1930s, however, experimentation at the mass political level must have seemed to middle-class and affluent amateurs to be increasingly threatening, in the forms of both the fascist and the communist movements. If the ACL's leaders were already feeling this threat, then the experimental and playful critique of the American socioeconomic order found in *Mr. Motorboat's Last Stand*—and presented by a black performer no less—may have required a direct response.

The mid-1930s saw the ACL becoming increasingly cautious in its promotion of amateur experimentation. Though the 1934 list of the Ten Best amateur films did bring a citation for an experimental work, it was for a somewhat conventional city symphony film. Leslie Thatcher's well-executed, but socially benign, film *Another Day* marked significant new territory neither in film aesthetics nor in its treatment of urban social reality. The award citation for Thatcher's film seems to acknowledge this, calling it "a splendid example of the relatively simple avant-garde film, so popular among European amateurs but so seldom attempted by even the advanced workers of the American continent."[40] No longer urging filmmakers to pursue "waste work" or new kinds of "cinematics," *Movie Makers* now promoted avant-garde forms as available for mastery to all amateurs. The city film would become a standard form for amateurs in North America, but it was no longer a sign of the amateur's place in the aesthetic vanguard (or the desire to be there).[41]

As if to clarify *Movie Makers'* withdrawal from the experimental vanguard in both art and politics, a 1934 editorial there referred to amateur filmmaking as necessarily a "free art." In what was perhaps an oblique criticism of radical experimentation of both the aesthetic and the political kinds, such as those promoted in *Experimental Cinema*, the anonymous author writes, "It is a relief to turn from the harsh, negative and forbidding picture of experiments in social regimentation to a field of human activity in which there is either expression or nothing."[42] Although pragmatic experimentation had once been an important terrain for amateur artistic activities, this editorial appears to cede that definition of *experiment* to its affiliation with radical positions, both political *and* aesthetic. In the late 1920s, Roy Winton and others had urged amateurs to stand at the vanguard of cinematic artistry, but now *Movie Makers* asked them to defend a rearguard position of the "gospel of expression." When Hiram Percy Maxim reflected on the first ten years of the ACL in 1936, his comments echoed some of the earlier ideals for amateur experimentation:

> Everywhere in the world, men are experimenting with new methods and are following new trails. Those of us who have faith in the common sense of the common people believe that from these experiments will come a new technique of living. . . . The movie makers of the earth have, for more than a decade, been trail blazers, because they have been dealing with a new technique of human expression. They should be exceptionally well fitted to take part in the larger task of working out new ways of life. They have caught the tempo of the pioneer.
> . . . In the world that is so clearly being made into something different to what it used to be, our Amateur Cinema League can face the future confidently, because it has learned how to experiment, without forgetting how to criticize its own attempts, to move forward, without abandoning its road maps, and consolidate its gains, as it goes along.[43]

But most amateurs had evidently lost their appetite for experimentation; the heady times of the ACL's birth and its encouragement of experimentation and artistic exploration had come to end, stopped by the bleak realities of the Great Depression and the turn among those committed to artistic and political change to more radical alternatives.

AMATEURS AND THE NEW AVANT-GARDE

The remaining years of the Great Depression and World War II saw little evidence of experimentation among amateur filmmakers. It was no longer promoted as a central aspect of their work or featured prominently among the winners of the Ten Best competitions.[44] Though it might be argued that the latter half of the 1930s marked a low-water mark for experimental film worldwide, the few Americans who were engaged in this activity, such as Joseph Cornell, Mary Ellen Bute, and Douglas Crockwell, do not appear to have been involved with the ACL. Experimental aesthetics made a brief resurgence in the ACL after World War II, particularly through the films and writing of Maya Deren. Though Deren was probably not a member of the league—her name appeared without the initials "ACL," which typically designated membership—she wrote two important articles about creative filmmaking for *Movie Makers*. And her film *Meshes of the Afternoon*, produced with Alexander Hamid, received an "Honorable Mention—Special Class" in the 1945 Ten Best competition. In the award citation for this film, an anonymous *Movie Makers* writer notes, "*Meshes of the Afternoon* is experimental in nature and exciting in its cinematic development."[45] The author, describing the film as a depiction of the subjective and interior states of an individual, writes that Deren's "creative use of her camera to suggest these emotions blazes new and stimulating trails in pure cinematography."[46]

The late 1940s saw a handful of significant amateur experiments in film form, including abstract color films and clay animation works. In 1947, the Cuban doctor Roberto Machado received a Ten Best award for his abstract film *Kaleidoscopio*. In an article he penned for *Movie Makers*, Machado emphasized the important role of music in motivating his film work: "The intimate relationship between music and movies has long been recognized, and filmers who also have musical knowledge very frequently undertake experiments in combining the two art forms."[47] Citing his interest in opening a new area of "cine adventure," Machado notes the important relationship among color, optics, and music that occurred to him after seeing his son's kaleidoscope: "Immediately the inspiration rose in my mind to capture these colored images with my camera and later to synchronize them with phonograph records, obtaining in this way an abstract and rhythmic film which would represent to a certain point, the visualization of the music." In addition to Machado's experiments, Leonard Tregillus was awarded in consecutive years for his experimental claymation works, *No Credit* (1948) and *Proem* (1949).[48]

But even when the late 1940s saw a slight resurgence in experimentation among amateurs, it continued to play a very minor role in amateur discourse. The postwar years saw an enormous increase in new amateur filmmakers whose primary interest lay in producing films to chronicle their families and travels and who were much less concerned with filmmaking in the aesthetic vanguard. For the growing number of filmmakers and onlookers who were interested in avant-garde films, *Movie Makers* noted the emergence of new venues and societies for this purpose. These included the founding of Cinema 16 in New York and the Art in Cinema programs at San Francisco's Museum of Fine Art.[49] Established in 1947, Cinema 16 exhibited some films that had been made or awarded as ACL films, including works by Watson and Webber, Tregillus, and Flory. Though it is tempting to see the emergence of Cinema 16 as a new and distinct alternative that allowed experimental film to escape from its amateur limbo, this film society included amateurs among its constituency of filmmakers and spectators. As its Statement of Purposes indicated: "Cinema 16 will encourage the production of new amateur and professional documentary and experimental films. First it will provide an audience for new releases of special interest by both exhibition and distribution. Secondly, by sponsoring film contests, it will provide recognition to individual film producers. Thirdly, by purchases and rentals of prints, by establishing regular booking circuits in various cities for films of this type, it will provide funds for amateur and professional producers to help them carry on their work."[50] So even though amateurs were less involved in avant-garde production than they had been in the late 1920s and early '30s, new film societies specifically engaged in that field still welcomed their participation.

Avant-garde-inspired films and topics occasionally reappeared in *Movie Makers* and its Ten Best lists, right up to the ACL's demise in 1954. But after the Depression and political rifts of the 1930s, amateurs never truly regained their position—or at least their claim to it—in the aesthetic vanguard of cinema. In the years following the Amateur Cinema League's demise, genuinely fascinating and experimental works would still sometimes emerge from amateur ranks. The Photographic Society of America expressed some support for experimental filmmaking in its journal and invited Maya Deren as a speaker at its 1955 annual conference. And some later avant-garde filmmakers, such as Stan Brakhage, revisited the concept of amateurism as a metaphor for their own liberation of art from commercial restrictions and conventions. But increasingly, members of the American avant-garde came to see amateurs as little more than bourgeois hobbyists with little interest in or capacity for artistic expression. George and Mike Kuchar, who made their first films just as the ACL passed out of existence, tell of their visits to the New York 8mm Club:

> "It was run by the fuddy-duddies," George recalls. "Everybody got dressed up and they showed their vacation footage. There'd be old ladies, and the old ladies would be sitting next to the old men, and their stomachs would be acting up and making noises. And the old ladies

would get offended at my movies because they were 'irrelevant' I guess. I was looking for . . . **subject matter** . . . and I'd pick anything out of the newspaper. That was after the Thalidomide scare came out and ladies were giving birth to deformed babies, and I made a comedy out of that (A WOMAN DISTRESSED, 1962)—that was the last time I was at the 8mm Motion Picture Club, and it was the only time they ever gave a bad review to a movie." [boldface in original][51]

The Kuchar brothers' films would, no doubt, have shocked and offended amateurs even during the late 1920s, when the amateur was "taking leadership." While amateurs may have tried to elevate themselves above mass taste and popular consumption, occupying a vanguard position during the Great Depression ultimately became untenable for this "sensible" group. Never interested in occupying the radical political spaces opened up by Potamkin, Jacobs, or the Kuchar brothers, the ACL gradually withdrew from aesthetic experimentation. Although amateurs were indeed interested in the fate of film aesthetics, the amateur vanguard was always a qualified and pragmatic one.

8 Mechanical Craftsmanship
Amateurs Making Practical Films

> As yet we are very self-conscious about expressing the industrial and economic forces that surround us. . . . Our minds have found the new world, but our deeper life of feeling and emotion lags behind. Is it too much to hope that with the wealth of new techniques with which we have been experimenting, the human spirit, once its vision of life has grown spontaneous and unlabored, will quicken again with imagination? . . . If we ever succeed in making an adequate adjustment to the city and the laboratory, if we ever turn our dread and dislike into an active faith, we shall not need a host of reasoned artistic theories. We shall find creative insight spontaneous and natural, and who knows but imagination will raise mechanical craftsmanship to the level of fine art?
>
> **John Herman Randall,** *Our Changing Civilization*[1]

Though written over two decades after Bliss Perry's essay "The Amateur Spirit," Randall's remarks suggest that in 1929 critics, artists, and philosophers were still struggling with the question of how to balance the "deeper life of feeling" with a modern industrial world. Though Randall, like many thinkers of the moment, believed that industrial design was one place where modern craftsmanship might be found, scholars since the 1930s have also identified motion pictures as a quintessential locus for such a joining together of modern technology, culture, and "creative insight." But while film scholarship has tended to see moviegoing as an experience of mass entertainment that plays important roles in representing and negotiating social discourses on a large scale, Randall's comments suggest a creative collaboration between modern life and an individual's imagination.[2] And although recent scholarly accounts have emphasized the instrumental use of motion pictures in nontheatrical contexts, Randall's interest in balancing modern life with a deeper life of feeling represents a different kind of encounter with technology.[3] From the 1920s through the '50s, many amateurs were keenly interested in bringing creativity into dialogue with questions of modern industry, education, and spirituality. Amateur filmmakers called this broad category of moviemaking "practical films," and here is where we find a particularly direct intersection between modern work and individual creativity.

The need for a balance between imagination and technical skill has been a central ingredient in amateur movie production but nowhere more so than in practical films. We see evidence of this practical impulse in the very first announcements in the "SWAPS" column, the Amateur Cinema League's first movie exchange, which advertised amateur films on medical subjects in 1927. By the early 1930s, "practical films" was an established category of work—they were the only genre to receive their own regular column in *Movie Makers*—and even otherwise experimental filmmakers, such as J.S. Watson and Melville Webber, ventured into this territory. Echoing the pragmatic tradition of Randall's mentor, John Dewey, amateur discourse eschewed theoretical approaches to filmmaking and instead promoted practical, experimental, and individual engagements among motion picture technology, creativity, and everyday life. Even though we might think of amateur filmmaking as an activity in which people make films primarily for recreation, during the 1930s amateurs also became involved in other kinds of nontheatrical film production, including industrial and educational moviemaking. The ACL even included sponsored and commercial nontheatrical films in a special category of its annual competitions from 1936 to 1947, a provision that might seem to contradict a basic tenet of amateurism: not receiving compensation.

This chapter explores the overlap between the worlds of amateur and practical film production. In particular, it considers how amateurs responded to Randall's aspiration for an individual and creative engagement with modern life and technology. In contrast to both popular cinema, which addressed spectators as part of a mass audience, and documentary film, which quickly came to designate a specific kind of government or institutional propaganda, amateur films generally reflected a personal and independent attitude toward practical filmmaking.[4] In fact, rather than presenting an anomaly in amateur filmmaking, this creative engagement with the practical conditions and activities of modern life stood at the center of the Amateur Cinema League's mission. During the 1930s, amateur activities expressed a utopian aspiration to move cinema beyond its theatrical settings and into nontheatrical contexts, in order to explore, in imaginative ways, the motion picture's pragmatic relationship to work and social problems. This chapter develops the relationship between amateurs and "practical films" by considering how the ACL defined and encouraged the production of four different subcategories of the genre: educational, industrial, social problem, and religious.⁵ While these are all categories of filmmaking that predate the founding of the ACL in 1926, they occupied an important place in amateur film publications and contests. This chapter by no means allows for a complete taxonomy of all the different variations or developments of the amateur practical film. But in offering a brief survey, as well as discussing specific notable cases for each subgenre, I will show the range of possible interpretations that amateurs brought to these practical films.

AMATEUR EDUCATIONAL FILMMAKING: *CERAMICS* (KENNETH BLOOMER AND ELIZABETH SANSOM)

> To itemize the applications of amateur or semi-professional cinematography, means to go on indefinitely. With each thought and each possibility other avenues of usage appear until one actually wonders how civilization has progressed without the cine-camera.
>
> J.H. McNabb, "The Amateur Turns a Penny"⁶

Movies were touted as an educational tool almost immediately after their invention; indeed, early film pioneers such as Thomas Edison and Charles Urban promised a future in which motion pictures would quickly replace textbooks. But not until the late 1910s and the introduction of nonflammable safety film, which could safely be shown in classrooms, did the widespread use of films for educational purposes seem likely to become a reality. By the early 1920s, a number of national organizations and publications had been established to address the burgeoning topic of visual education.⁷ But even with the introduction of 16mm film in 1923, the supply of reliable educational films lagged far behind the demand suggested by this discourse. When the Amateur Cinema League was established in 1926, educators saw a way of resolving the problem of unreliable supply: they could make their own films. Articles in the *Movie Makers* magazine often addressed how amateurs might use their new 16mm equipment for educational and scientific purposes. "The motion picture field," wrote one contributor, "hitherto confined to the realm of professionalism, is now being invaded by an insistent and ever increasing demand of amateur desire, made possible through amateur genius."⁸ By May 1927, *Movie Makers* had a regular column that addressed educational and applied uses of amateur film. This meant that amateurs were kept appraised of developments in educational, scientific, social, and industrial filmmaking, much as readers of visual education magazines were becoming aware of amateur filmmaking. In 1928 Roy Winton cemented this relationship: "Amateur cameras and projectors have released the potency of motion pictures into an immensely larger field than existed four years ago. As film entertainment spread from theatres into homes, so film education has spread from school into homes.... We believe that schools and homes can better carry on their educational processes by using this great force of personalized movies, and we feel we have a clear mission to foster this use as far as we can."[9]

For Winton the amateur field offered two ways of expanding educational film: the first was by using amateur equipment to allow educational films into the home (though they also spread to many other locations); the second was to promote the production of "personalized movies," which meant instilling practical films with something of the personal, or amateur, "desire and genius." One frequent justification for amateur practical films was that by "join[ing] their filming experience to the exact knowledge of the field" amateurs could infuse a film related to their professional work with a personalized quality, thus amplifying its subject matter with a kind of personal authority.[10] Articles in *Educational Screen* from the 1930s made a similar claim; one educator wrote that his amateur educational films are "a happy union of my vocational and avocational interests."[11]

Movie Makers reported on a wide range of amateur educational films about biology, math, geography, and other subjects, which were made for use in both classrooms and other nontheatrical venues. Beyond these fairly conventional films, there were also educational works that exceeded the informational requirements of the genre and appeared interested in developing creative and aesthetic expressions of their subject matter. John Grierson's first film, *Drifters* (1929), is an excellent example of this combination. His "solid adventure of the herring fishery" is in one sense a process film that illustrates the herring's journey from the depths of the sea to the family dinner table. But it is also a poetic interpretation of this process and, according to Grierson, a film with all the "crescendo in energies, images, atmospherics and all that make up the substance of the cinema."[12] In its annual Ten Best competitions, the ACL awarded works that displayed a similar interest in aesthetically shaping their educational material. *Ceramics*, a silent film made by Kenneth Bloomer and Elizabeth Sansom of the Mount Kisco Cinemat Club, was named one of the "Ten Best Amateur Films of 1933" for this reason.

Stylistically, *Ceramics* has a familiar actuality-film structure that shows the process by which the potter Leon Volkmar produced his ceramic works. But like *Drifters*, *Ceramics* is also a visually complex work that explores the aesthetic dimensions of an educational topic. Industrial processes are common among silent educational films, both because they are visually striking and because they share with cinema a kind of temporal and mechanical linearity.¹³ The most interesting process films are those that recognize moments of particular visual affinity between process and camera. In *Ceramics*, such an affinity is evident in the extended sequences of Volkmar working his clay at the potter's wheel. Shown in medium long shots from several different angles, the clay's shifting shapes, height, and depth take on a dance-like quality (not unlike the undulating waves in *Drifters*) that is representable only with motion pictures. The idea of a dance is further suggested by an intertitle at the beginning of this sequence that announces: "The Potter's Wheel—coordinating the brain, the hands, and the feet." Occasional shots of Volkmar's feet turning the wheel reinforce the dance motif even further, as they provide a counterpoint to the undulations of the clay itself. Finally, the spinning action of the wheel offers a visual synecdoche of a film spool turning in the camera. So even as the film presents an informational record of the potter at work, it also traces a kind of creative and visual movement across three different media: dance, pottery, and film.

While these aesthetic qualities might seem to be secondary in importance to the film's presentation of practical information—it shows how a clay pot is made—writers in *Movie Makers* suggest an important link between aesthetics and practicality: "The makers of the film were fortunate in having the cooperation of a famous ceramic artist, Leon Volkmar, who maintains his atelier at Bedford Village, N.Y. It was here that the entire film was produced, its makers having imbibed the spirit of the artist craftsmen so thoroughly that every deft touch, every careful step in the process of making a lovely vase are recorded. . . . Such a film might be described as a 'glorified industrial' but, more than that, it is an educational film in the best sense of the word."¹⁴ What is an "educational film in the best sense of the word"? I think it is best defined by the sense suggested by Roy Winton, who saw amateurs "placing at the disposition of all those who have to do with the complex problems of human relations in industry, in education, in recreation, in religion, and in daily life as a whole, a new factor which they can use with all the variations suitable to their personal desires."¹⁵ In *Ceramics*, we can see the amateur's attempt to work out these human relations in industry aesthetically, and in doing so the film compares an old kind of craftsman (Volkmar) with a new one (the filmmakers). What we find here is not just the recording of a process for educational purposes but also a situation in which the amateur filmmakers' sensitivity to creativity and imagination primed them to imbibe the spirit of the artist craftsman and reinterpret it in light of the cinema's mechanical visual craft.¹⁶

Ceramics also evokes the idea of the "practical artist," a figure that appeared a number of times in amateur publications and was perhaps best exemplified by the advertising and artistic photographer Edward Steichen: "an artist and a dreamer ... a hard worker, a shrewd craftsman, and a firm believer that there is nothing on earth without interest if you are attracted to it."[17] A similar interest in mixing creativity and hard work informed amateur discourse around the practical use of amateur films. This is particularly evident in articles about the use of films to create a broader understanding of classroom learning; although some saw educational films as effective instruments for conveying the practical substance of lessons, others focused more fundamentally on the experimentation of the films' production itself. Some made their own films so they could unite "vocational and avocational" interests, while others experimented with film production as a classroom activity in which students could gain firsthand experience of both the subject being filmed and the craft required to film it.[18] In these ways, film became a pragmatic way of reinforcing the union between artistic and practical work.

In the late 1930s, amateurs were active in New York's Metropolitan Motion Picture Council, a film-betterment organization affiliated with the National Board of Review and spearheaded by the New York University education professor Frederic Thrasher.[19] Some award-winning amateurs, such as Charles Carbonaro and Kenneth Space, also acted as filmmaking instructors at NYU's School of Education, providing a practical counterpoint to the more theoretical examinations of film that Thrasher offered in his courses.[20] Amateurs shared with early film educators an interest in advancing film appreciation, developing the pedagogy of film production, and expanding alternative approaches to film as a cultural object in classrooms or little theatres. Following World War II, many of these activities would become formalized as the production of educational film increasingly became big business and film schools expanded the professionalization of filmmaking. By the 1950s, some amateurs and semiprofessionals were engaged in the production of educational films, but often this pursuit was distinct from their own filmmaking as a hobby. Budge and Judith Crawley, who began as amateurs in the 1930s, left the nonprofessional world behind altogether when their Crawley Films grew to become a major producer of educational films during the postwar era.

AMATEUR INDUSTRIAL FILMMAKING: "BUILDING A BAKERY 1930" (DENT HARRISON) AND *THE EYES OF SCIENCE* (WATSON AND WEBBER)

Early industrial films, such as *A Visit to Peek Frean & Co.'s Biscuit Works* (Cricks and Martin, 1906), exploited the cinema's ability to record and display the fascinating complexity of modern factories for purposes of both advertising and visual spectacle. Thus it is not surprising that the industrial application of amateur movies and movie technology was also evident from the early years of the amateur film movement. In 1930, *Movie Makers* reported that amateurs were "generally awakening to the fact that the universal applicability of the motion picture extends to business and industry as well as fields of recreation." While acknowledging that professional publicity firms were necessary for more extensive production and use of industrial film, the author pointed to the personal appeal of such films to amateurs: "Every movie maker wants the personal satisfaction of himself recording one of the most important of his interests—his business or vocation."[21] While it might be tempting to dismiss this editorializing as merely an effort to expand amateur filmmaking into new areas of activity, practical films made by amateurs were discussed with increasing regularity in the 1930s. These works approached industrial topics in a variety of different ways, and, like the amateur educational films, they often explored aesthetic or personal dimensions of the subject matter that pushed industrial filmmaking beyond its familiar coordinates.

To promote its relationship to industrial works, the Amateur Cinema League offered a consultation service to help amateurs make practical films. As a result, it was able to offer specific statistics on amateur industrial filmmaking. In 1931 "more than one hundred and twenty seven first rate industrial films [had] been made by amateur movie makers. Almost an equal number are now in the process of production."[22] The author of the article that reported these statistics, Arthur Gale, goes on to categorize three different kinds of amateur industrial film projects as follows:

> First, there is the industrial film made by an amateur for his own satisfaction and pleasure, in much the same spirit that he would make a film record of a vacation. Such films are more entertaining than one might realize and they offer a great deal of satisfaction in the making. Second, there is the industrial film record, the purpose of which is to analyze the operation of machines, scientific apparatus or perhaps the movements of a workman. Such films are most often made in order to secure increased efficiency.... Third, there are films made for the purpose of publicizing or advertising products or for direct sales appeal.[23]

This delineation of categories shows that what was productive about amateur industrial filming was that it might serve as a satisfying personal chronicle, an analytic tool that produced a commercial advantage, or a relatively inexpensive form of publicity. Writers also commented on the ability of amateur industrial film to reveal overlooked aspects of a business as well as on the value of the amateur's "personal touch" in these films; some writers even suggested that the amateur industrial film's quality of personal sincerity more than made up for its technical shortcomings.[24]

Dent Harrison's incomplete film about his own Pride of Montreal (POM) bakery illustrates some of the personal and aesthetic qualities that characterize amateur industrial work.[25] Though missing its head titles and out of sequence at certain moments, the silent footage on the film's two reels, titled "Building a Bakery 1930" and "Harvesting and Baking," nevertheless features moments of surprising complexity and departs from our usual expectations of industrial films in its creative playfulness. The film shows the construction of the filmmaker's new bakery and, later, the process of bread making more broadly, from harvesting grain to the delivery of the freshly baked bread. The first reel's footage of the bakery's construction appears at first very rough in technique, employing unsteady panning shots and choppy in-camera editing. But if Harrison's film initially seems like little more than a point-and-shoot, personal chronicle of the construction project, it soon becomes clear that the film has some logic in its own right as a construction project. Beginning with roughly taken images of mechanical shovels and men pouring a foundation, the footage gradually assumes greater technical proficiency as it shows bricklayers working on a nearly completed exterior and other, more advanced stages, of the bakery's construction. Intertitles narrate the footage throughout this process, and one title in particular seems to confirm the relationship between style and content in the film, announcing, "Order comes out of the chaos," at just the moment when both building and film style are beginning to assume a coherent form. Evidently, Harrison crafted the earlier footage to mimic in style the rough and embryonic stage of the building's construction; in doing so he gave aesthetic shape to personal-chronicle footage. The film's second reel shows the bakery at work and advertises its products. Much as in the *Peak Frean* film, made over two decades earlier, we see bakers and machinery at work as well as shots of cakes and loaves. Finally, an intertitle foregrounds the publicizing function of this film: "When you want the best say POM."

Harrison's two reels about his bakery mark the intersection of both his personal interests (in cinema *and* in business) and the commercial application of amateur work. Harrison's film has a number of elements in common with Gale's itemization of amateur industrial works, functioning as both a chronicle and a personalized advertisement. But distinguishing between these amateur films and professional advertising work is also important. As Jackson Lears argues in his history of advertising, *Fables of Abundance*, professional advertisers address themselves to the masses: they have a managerial project that sees the masses as impersonal markets to be managed.[26] Amateurs in the 1930s, on the other hand, were interested in resisting this kind of assimilation into mass society. Even in films that advertised a business, amateur industrials were a kind of personal advertising, earnestly seeking a bond with the viewers rather than trying to dupe them. These films depart from our expectations of industrial impersonality by proudly showing off images related to the filmmaker's own business or profession, much as one would show off images of his or her children in more typical home movies. The intimacy of this kind of film was reinforced at the realm of exhibition: Harrison likely showed his film of the POM bakery in person at amateur cinema club meetings and to other small groups but probably didn't intend it to be distributed widely and impersonally.

The Eyes of Science (J.S. Watson and Melville Webber), on the other hand, is an industrial film that pushes the conventional model toward a radical visual experiment. Produced in 1931 and named to the ACL's Ten Best list for that year, *The Eyes of Science* was commissioned to explain how lenses and optical instruments were made at the Bausch and Lomb factory. Though in certain respects a polished industrial film, *Eyes* is perhaps better characterized as a hybrid work that reveals the aesthetic interests of Watson and Webber and recalls aspects of their experimental amateur films *Fall of the House of Usher* (1928) and *Lot in Sodom* (1932). These aspects of experimentation are particularly evident in the filmmakers' efforts to complement content with aesthetic style in *The Eyes of Science*, which they do by foregrounding experiences of self-conscious and distorted vision.

The Eyes of Science begins with a shot of scientists working in a laboratory, accompanied by voice-over narration that announces man as a "scientific animal." But the conventionality of this introduction is quickly, and literally, dissolved when a distorting lens intervenes, obstructing our clear view of the scientists. As this distortion gives way to an extreme close-up of a human eye, the narrator tells us that man "has constructed new eyes with which to extend the range and acuity of his vision." The enormous eye fills the screen and looks straight out, confronting us with a gaze that is both human and mechanically mediated, mirroring our own spectatorship through the visual prosthesis of the cinema. *The Eyes of Science* later presents images of a movie camera and projector, each upside down with spinning shutters, at once revealing and estranging our own encounter with moving pictures. Tracing vision to its constituent elements, the film presents a study of prisms, in which the camera follows rays of light as they travel down from the heavens, through clouds, a cathedral, and a glass prism, as if

Figure 25. *The Eyes of Science* (James Sibley Watson and Melville Webber, 1931) reveals the aesthetic interests of Watson and Webber even as it functions as an industrial film. Courtesy George Eastman House.

to offer a short journey of light from divine origin to scientific instrument (figure 25). Notably, this stylized sequence of clouds and refracted light foreshadows the relationship developed among light, prisms, and divinity in Watson and Webber's *Lot in Sodom* the following year. Elsewhere, the film proceeds more conventionally by depicting the process of making glass and lenses, but again, lessons in tempering glass are made visually stunning through slow-motion photography and repetition.

Even though *The Eyes of Science* is an industrial film, it reveals the insistent influence of amateur experimentation. Since Watson and Webber's own amateur experimental films made extensive use of prisms like those manufactured by Bausch and Lomb, there is something appropriate about such aesthetic flourishes in their industrial film.[27] For amateurs such as Harrison or Watson and Webber, machinery and industry were like the movie camera itself, presenting new modern tools and landscapes with which—and *through* which—individuals could produce creative interpretations of the world. *Movie Makers* praised both the aesthetic and the industrial aspects of *The Eyes of Science*, noting, "The combination of cinematic art and skill with which this film is composed places it well in the front rank of all existing industrials regardless of the source of their production."[28] During the 1930s, the ACL further promoted this blending of art and industry, renaming its annual competition the "Ten Best Non-Theatrical [not just amateur] Films" in 1935 and creating a new category of awards for sponsored or commissioned films in 1936. A retrospective account of these changes provides a fascinating overview of the shifting terrain of amateur filmmaking during this period, starting with developments in the early 1930s, when "it soon became apparent ... that experienced amateurs could, on occasion, produce films on specialized subjects for gain."[29] This was particularly the case for doctors, dentists, and various other professionals, but according to the editorial, "not one of these filmers, in *Movie Makers* judgment, could reasonably be classed as a professional cameraman." Because these "amateurs" didn't make the majority of their income from filmmaking, *Movie Makers* included their films in the Ten Best competitions starting in 1932. By 1935, in recognition of the "increasing numbers of un-amateur yet still non-professional pictures" submitted to the contest, it was renamed with the "Non-Theatrical" designation. Though amateurs responded to industrial filmmaking with varying degrees of personalization and aesthetic experimentation, the ACL consistently rewarded these aspects of practical filmmaking. The postwar era saw a reversal of some of these developments, and in 1948 the contest name reverted to the "Ten Best Amateur Films."

AMATEUR SOCIAL PROBLEM FILMMAKING: *THE FORGOTTEN FRONTIER* (MARVIN BRECKINRIDGE)

Nonprofessional uses of the cinema for social causes long predate the history of organized amateur film activities, first becoming prominent as a tool of progressive causes in the 1910s and '20s. From Jane Adams's exhibition of films in Hull House, to the production of independent films about child labor, white slavery, and temperance, to the adoption of film in schools and other practical training contexts, Progressive Era reformers were quick to take up film for their causes.[30] For these reformers, however, film was a double-edged sword. The popularity of commercial films, they argued, posed a danger to the supposedly impressionable minds of the young, the working class, and recent immigrants, but if the popularity of film could be harnessed to productive ends, film stood to become a powerful instrument for behavioral and social change. Consequently, blending entertainment with instruction became a hallmark of progressive appropriations of the cinema. This could take place in the realm of the program, in which Chaplin comedies brought in the crowds and then didactic reform films drove the message home. Or entertainment and instruction could be blended in the film text itself, such as in *Traffic in Souls* (IMP/Universal, 1913), in which a dramatic narrative animates the reformer's lesson. These examples shared with later amateur films a desire to recontextualize the subject matter and exhibition spaces of motion pictures. But at the same time, distinguishing between these two modes is important; while reformers saw movies as an instrument that could be put to work on impressionable minds, amateurs were more likely to see the medium as a tool for personalized expressions of their commitments and causes.

In 1930, the very first year of the ACL's Ten Best list, social problem films were already represented among the notables. Listed among the year's special mentions was Marvin Breckinridge's epic amateur film *The Forgotten Frontier*. In its commendation of this film, *Movie Makers* observed, "*The Forgotten Frontier*, filmed by Miss Marvin Breckinridge, is the most ambitious amateur made welfare film yet recorded. To show the operation of the Kentucky Nursing Service, Miss Breckinridge spent several months filming in the mountain districts reached by that organization. With the cooperation of the mountain folk, she staged several short dramas, each demonstrating the usefulness of one of the centers or some phase of their work. The completed picture runs 6000 ft., 35mm., and in spite of the numerous technical difficulties, it is excellently photographed."[31] This brief comment notes the film's extraordinary ambition as an amateur production, including its length and use of 35mm film, as well as its blend of fictional and factual elements. And although the article does not mention it, the ACL deserved some credit for the structure and execution of this film; Marvin Breckinridge's diaries reveal that after deciding to make a film about the nursing service, she sought out training from the Amateur Cinema League and received several lessons in cinematography and editing from the *Movie Makers* technical consultant Russell Holslag.[32] Also unacknowledged here is Breckinridge's personal connection to the film's subject: the Frontier Nursing Service had been founded just a few years before, by her cousin Mary Breckinridge, who appears in the film. As a rare silent film that is directed by a woman and has since been named to the United States Film Registry list (in 1996), *The Forgotten Frontier* has been seen and discussed surprisingly little.

The Forgotten Frontier pays careful attention to the rules of continuity editing and makes extensive use of both "working in" and shot/reverse-shot structures.[33] But the film also contains a number of elements that seem to exceed any social or narrative motivation. On one hand, it has a clearly established narrative structure, made up of a series of five docudrama episodes and framed by a conversation with some visitors to

Kentucky. On the other hand, *The Forgotten Frontier* employs a set of recurring images and visual motifs that mark it as a more complex aesthetic object than its structure and social purpose might suggest. The images that stand out most memorably in *The Forgotten Frontier* are recurring long shots of nurses and doctors fording rivers on horseback: these occur five different times over the course of the film, appearing in four of the episodes and at the film's conclusion. In a film that otherwise makes consistent, if sometimes clumsy, use of continuity editing, these long takes of medical personnel battling their way across strong river currents seem particularly strange; their lengthy duration—the longest one clocks in at slightly more than a minute—marks these shots as important, yet they are not necessarily informational. These images are carefully composed, placing small figures on horseback against a background of rough riverside terrain as they cut the water's reflective surface, moving slowly through its swift-moving current. In other words, these shots are emblematic of the Frontier Nursing Service practitioners' heroic struggles to reach their patients in remote Appalachia under any circumstances. But they do not simply foreground the nurses' heroism; they are also emblematic of the aesthetic possibilities of the cinema, its ability to capture such dramas and to reframe the grueling work of social hygiene as a heroic, and even an epic, struggle.

Indeed, *The Forgotten Frontier* produces a number of similar aesthetic emblems that both augment and exceed the film's narrative and practical dimensions, revealing the potential for practical films to give amateurs a momentary glimpse of their lives reframed as aesthetic and dramatic experiences. For example, in several sequences that follow closely from the fording scenes, the nurses are shown transforming their identities through changes in clothing and uniform. From western-hero stars that have just braved the Kentucky wilderness, the women become modern and professional as they remove outer coats to reveal their crisp white shirts, trousers, and black neckties. Though practically concerned with depicting different aspects of the nursing service, such as midwifery, home visits, inoculations, and emergency medical treatment, the film also serves as a visual expression of the shifting—but always professional—identities that these women have taken on. The film's dramatization of scientific hygiene in a "forgotten frontier" is what marks it most clearly as a progressive-influenced film. But even though it presents a staging of this struggle for good health, *The Forgotten Frontier*'s intent doesn't seem solely to serve as an instrument of social propaganda; rather, the film appears to address spectators in Breckinridge's own affluent peer group, presenting to them a creative and personal engagement with practical social problems.[34] Ultimately, *The Forgotten Frontier* embodies a range of both aesthetic and historical tensions. It blends fact with fictional elements; it interrupts narrative episodes with these emblematic sequences of shifting identity and costume; and it offers an epic portrayal of life on the forgotten frontier—a historical contradiction, some three decades after the American frontier was declared closed. And, notably, it does all of this through the contradictory medium of 35mm amateur cinema, a mode that is neither professional in quality nor a rough home movie. As a modern application of motion picture technology, with an already outmoded form of silent cinema, *The Forgotten Frontier* offers a potent symbol of the aesthetic and historical contradictions of practical amateur cinema itself.

Amateurs continued to address progressive causes in their practical filmmaking, and amateur publications reported on many films about social causes and local charities, particularly as social conditions during the Depression worsened.[35] Over the course of the 1930s, however, the meaning of social filmmaking shifted and became the principal terrain of the documentary film. Some (primarily nonamateur) organizations, like the Workers' Film and Photo League, redefined their filmmakers as artist-workers so as to narrow the gap between themselves and the subjects they filmed. But there were other key distinctions between amateur and progressive or documentary works: whereas the progressive tradition hoped to harness the cinema's powers to indoctrinate, even as it transmuted into "documentary film," practical amateurs more often claimed a fair-minded, rational communication with their spectator. In contrast to Grierson, who, following Walter Lippmann, saw the cinema as a means of conveying mass propaganda that could reduce the complexity of modern social issues, amateurs were more likely to echo John Dewey's call for "free and enriching communication" as a way of negotiating social problems in a modern democracy.[36] The amateur's goal was not to indoctrinate others using the medium's instrumentality so much as to inform them about a particular, personally held value. In many cases, amateurs understood themselves to be using motion pictures as a tool for just the kind of informed and personalized—not mass, not propagandistic—intercommunication that Dewey had promoted.

AMATEUR RELIGIOUS FILMMAKING: *IN THE BEGINNING* (FRED C. ELLS) AND *HELL BOUND TRAIN* (JAMES AND ELOYCE GIST)

Religious filmmaking is a subgenre of amateur work that marks a more challenging negotiation of the instrumental and artistic—as well as the personal and practical—poles of moviemaking in this history. Religious films had appeared in nontheatrical contexts since at least the 1910s, when

Passion play films were distributed among churches and Chautauqua meetings. But churches, like schools, often had difficulty finding suitable materials to exhibit well into the 1920s and '30s. One writer suggests that amateur religious works were prompted by exactly this shortage of professionally made religious films: "Into this 'problem situation,'" he writes, "came the amateur movie photographer with his intense 'mother love' for every picture he took, whether it was good or bad."[37] Amateur publications commented on such productions from time to time, observing the efforts of a number of different churches in their use of amateur films as a way of "raising funds, stimulating membership, holding attention of the congregation, widening its educational interests and providing palatable and, at the same time, suitable entertainment."[38] Thus, amateur film equipment allowed for the possibility of even more numerous and smaller-scale productions about specialized topics, questions of quality notwithstanding.

One of the most acclaimed amateur religious films of the 1930s was also a film that drew on experimental montage techniques in order to present an aesthetic interpretation of Christianity. *In the Beginning* (Fred C. Ells, 1935) was named one of the *Movie Makers* "Ten Best Nontheatrical Films for 1935" but was also praised much higher than this—as one of the best films (amateur or professional) ever made: "*In the Beginning*, although far from being a perfect picture, is nevertheless one of the few truly great films thus far to come from a motion picture camera—either theatrical or amateur. Here, the magnificent beauty and awesome strangeness of the natural world have been seen in their fundamental and ultimate meanings. As an interpretation of the epic story of creation, *In the Beginning* follows directly in the noble tradition of Homer, Dante and Milton."[39] This is clearly very high praise and sheds some light on the critical assumptions of the Amateur Cinema League at this moment. Though the aesthetic tradition evoked here—of transcendental beauty and of Homer, Dante, and Milton—long predates the movies, Ells's accomplishment lay in joining this tradition with the mechanical craftsmanship of amateur moviemaking.

Composed almost exclusively of noncontinuous shots placed in graphic and associational montage sequences, *In the Beginning* illustrates the first verses of the book of Genesis. The film's structure is carefully controlled, alternating between intertitles that narrate the biblical creation story and montage sequences of increasing duration and cutting rate. Ells's film begins with slow, contemplative images, suggesting "the face of the deep"; it reaches its most complex point when it visualizes the diversity of the animal kingdom through montage, in a sequence that combines twenty-eight shots over two and a half minutes. The film's rapid cutting tempo subsequently drops off and presents human figures for just a single shot, drawing in fishing nets on a beach. Many of the film's individual images are visually striking in their own right: shots of dramatic skies that open and close the film recall paintings by the old masters; shots of the complex patterns formed by droplets of water are reminiscent of abstract films by Joris Ivens and Ralph Steiner; and plants and animals take on strange shapes when presented in extreme close-up, recalling the abstraction of science films. Ells composes his shots to emphasize lighted objects, details, and backlit silhouettes against otherwise dark backgrounds; in this way, the images sustain a great deal of their graphic and estranging qualities rather than functioning merely as representations.

This kind of religious film evidently differs from the practical amateur movies that recorded histories of local churches or the story of the Catholic mass.[40] Nevertheless, writers in *Movie Makers* praised *In the Beginning* for its creative evocation of religious materials:

> One is left stilled and humble before the simple purity of imagination which conceived it. To this superb document of nature F. C. Ells, ACL, the producer, has brought a technical skill and sensitive craftsmanship more than equal to the demands of his subject.... Somber and stunning scenes of the heaving waters, the new born earth and bursting streams in the first reel are followed in the second, by flawlessly executed telephoto and macroscopic studies of the earth's myriad creatures. Integrating the entire production is a musical accompaniment of stately church music, recorded on disc by the Sistine Choir. Mr. Ells, who has looked upon the earth and found it is good, has produced a sincere and beautiful film, great even as it falls short of perfection.

While praising the sensitive craftsmanship and technical skill evinced in Ells's film, these remarks again allude to some slight, though unspecified, shortcoming. The glowing review suggests that any discernable imperfection is less a measure of the film's inadequacy than a mark of the filmmaker's broad imaginative scope and his willingness to experiment with film form and technique in new innovative ways. But if this inclines us to see this film as a primarily artistic work, archival papers and program notes related to its exhibition emphasize the ways in which it could also be seen as practical. An exhibitor's guide contains detailed suggestions for the film's use in religious and educational programming in different venues, such as college or high school classes in English literature; book clubs, in connection with Bible study; at YMCA, YWCA, and Young Men's (and Women's) Hebrew Association gatherings; in Sunday school classes; and at outdoor showings at youth conferences, to name just a few. The guide also includes discussion notes, "observation tests," and a cue sheet for music to be played live or with specified Victor Phonograph records.⁴¹ Though these materials suggest an extensive educational apparatus, one letter from the film's production file suggests a limit to the educational practicality of this film. In a note from the Library Bureau, a correspondent indicates: "I feel that as it stands, IN THE BEGINNING is beautiful but not educational. Public school authorities, I think properly, generally shy away from presenting religion in any form, and for that reason, the present treatment would be taboo." Even though there were clear restrictions on its practical application, the film presents a union of practical, spiritual, and aesthetic qualities.

Although *In the Beginning* lacks the general practicality of public school use, it clearly had specialized value for religious or church screenings. In this sense, it is reminiscent of other specialized amateur religious films, such as those made by the African American husband and wife team James and Eloyce Gist. The Gists collaborated on at least three films in the early 1930s, *Hell Bound Train; Verdict: Not Guilty at the Judgment Day;* and *Heaven Bound Travelers*, which were primarily exhibited at Baptist churches.⁴² Although the Gists appear to have worked outside organized amateur circles, their work shows some similarity to that of Ells in terms of both motivation (the personal and creative animation of religious themes) and nontheatrical exhibition contexts (showings at churches and limited other uses). But perhaps more telling are the differences between these filmmakers in both styles and production milieus. Although there is evidence that some African Americans held memberships to the Amateur Cinema League, African Americans were not prominent members of the organization.⁴³ Consequently, films made by African Americans—either amateur or professional—were rare and remarkable during the 1930s. Probably for this reason the NAACP decided to sponsor some of the Gists' film screenings, despite some reservations the association had about the films' content. Echoing the Library Bureau's critique of *In the Beginning*, one NAACP officer wrote of *Verdict: Not Guilty:* "The picture is a very good religious picture, but I do not see how in its present form it could be used for NAACP propaganda." The NAACP still hoped that the presentation of the film could be used for fundraising and general outreach to the African American community.⁴⁴

Like *In the Beginning*, the Gists' films present creative treatments of religious themes. But unlike Ells's impressionistic interpretation of Genesis, the Gists' films were dramatized religious parables that featured all-black casts. *Hell Bound Train*, for example, depicts the devil as a train's engineer, both driving his locomotive toward hell and tempting the sinner-passengers that occupy various cars on the train. The film is divided into episodes, each one representing a different kind of sin or sinner and set in a corresponding car of the train. Stylistically, *Hell Bound Train* is both rough and playfully rapid, almost mimicking the rapid transit of the train itself in the film's movement from car to car, narrative to narrative. The film is reminiscent of professionally made race films, such as Oscar Micheaux's *Body and Soul* (1925), which, though more skeptical about the role of preachers in African American life, has similar sequences in which the rhythm of the film's cutting and camera movement takes on the rollicking tempo of the religious service. Spencer Williams's later film *The Blood of Jesus* (1941) also shares aspects of *Hell Bound Train*'s narrative structure as well as the film's blending of mystical folk parable with popular-culture showmanship. But unlike professional race films, which featured well-known actors, raised production capital, and were exhibited in commercial theatres, the Gists' films reflect an amateur production mode, which relied on friends and family for actors, used local neighborhood settings, and made use of artisanal postproduction methods. The Gists made films to complement their existing activities as entrepreneurs and traveling evangelists, but like Ells's film work, the creativity of their work exceeded the stylistic norms of the religious film.

Though there is a great distance between the practical uses of amateur films for church history and the more creative works made by Fred Ells or by James and Eloyce Gist, the films represent a broad terrain of amateur works concerned with religious themes. These works have different degrees of creative experimentation and artistry—and therefore somewhat different interpretations of the relationship between religion and film—but all of these films were produced by amateurs so that they could have a practical effect on religious education and experience. This encounter could take the form of conveying a religious lesson, or use aesthetic means to elicit spiritual wonder, as *In the Beginning* does, or employ a narrative parable framework to engage spectators in a drama of religious conversion, as *Hell Bound Train* does. In all of these cases, however, amateurs were able to respond to a personal perception of the relationship between film and religion and to produce films that could be understood to have some practical, religious value.

THE HARMON FOUNDATION'S SPONSORED AMATEUR FILMS: *THE STORY OF BAMBA* (RAY GARNER) AND *WE ARE ALL ARTISTS* (ALON BEMENT)

> In themselves, amateur movies are deeply satisfying because they offer just the right combination of creative quality and manual dexterity with a mixture of technical skill that fits the temper of a mechanically served world.
>
> "Play—1932," *Movie Makers*[45]

In addition to being practical films awarded by the ACL, *In the Beginning* and *Ceramics* were also distributed by the Harmon Foundation. The Harmon Foundation was a philanthropic organization that supported a range of activities, from school playgrounds to awards for African American artists, and entered the world of motion pictures by establishing the Religious Motion Picture Foundation in 1925. By the mid-1930s, the Harmon Foundation's film activity had developed into its Division of Visual Experiment, which distributed and sometimes produced films on religion, social progress, education, and artistic instruction. Many of these films were made by amateurs but were sponsored and distributed by the Harmon Foundation, and about a dozen were named to the ACL Ten Best lists during the 1930s and early '40s. The Harmon Foundation's film work provided both a support and a challenge to amateur activities: on one hand, the foundation espoused a policy that was directly supportive of independent and amateur film producers, but on the other hand, its financial support of amateur work vexed the definition of amateurs' activities. At a time when documentary film production—as sponsored by Britain's General Post Office and the U.S. government—was becoming increasingly institutionalized, the Harmon Foundation supported practical filmmaking without compromising its creative independence. In order to negotiate the conflict between sponsorship and amateurism, the Harmon Foundation often commissioned or partly funded amateur filmmakers working with a specialist to produce a film in their field of expertise.

Two consequences of the Harmon Foundation's support of individual film projects are a somewhat idiosyncratic body of films in the foundation's distribution library and a seemingly incoherent ideological stance. At one end of the ideological spectrum, we find amateur-produced works such as *The Story of Bamba* (Ray Garner, 1939), a religious docudrama shot in the Belgian Congo as part of a Christian missionary tour.[46] The plot centers on an African boy who is saved by Western medicine after being left to die by his "witch doctor" uncle (figure 26); converted to Christianity, he then studies to become a doctor and eventually converts his tribe (and uncle) to both Western scientific ways and Christianity. The Harmon Foundation promoted this film as a work that "may be used in study of African customs, consideration of youth around the world, character training, mission study, modern history, geography, economic geography, and in discussion groups. Some groups may want to consider it as an example of social history and customs, interpreted with a dramatic theme." More accurately, it is a work that both perpetuates and reveals the sleight of hand required for Western religious propaganda. By dramatized analogy, the film suggests

Figure 26. The Harmon Foundation distributed an eclectic mix of films, including amateur-made Christian missionary films. *The Story of Bamba* (Ray Garner, 1939). National Archives and Records Administration, DM-H-HFF-10a-4313.

that to accept Western medicine is to accept Western religion. The dubious logic of this colonial proposition is camouflaged by the film's own dual reliance on both geographical credibility (the film was shot in Africa and features a cast of African actors) and dramatic narrative (the story of the protagonist). Medical and hygiene propaganda films, such as *The Story of Bamba*, were common throughout the 1930s and '40s.[47]

The Harmon Foundation produced a variety of films with both religious and African or African American themes during the 1930s and '40s and with a range of political and ideological coordinates. Most laudable of the foundation's activities was its annual awards for African American artists, a project in which it worked closely with the African American philosopher and writer Alain Locke. The Harmon Foundation filmed the winners and artworks of these awards every year in the mid-1930s. There is also evidence that one of these award winners, the Harlem photographer James L.

Allen, was briefly a member of the Amateur Cinema League and was commissioned by the Harmon Foundation to produce a film called "The City of Harlem." However, poor health prevented Allen from completing the project.[48] The Harmon Foundation also collaborated with the NAACP in the mid-1930s to produce a film about educational inequalities in the American South. And in 1941, Ray and Virginia Garner, the amateurs who had shot *The Story of Bamba*, were commissioned to make *Education for Life*, a film about African American vocational training at the Hampton Institute. This film received an honorable mention from the ACL for its solutions to a variety of technical challenges, such as "recording, in color, a wide variety of skin tones" and "well-balanced" subject matter.[49] So rather than producing a consistent kind of propaganda about African and African American culture and religion, the Harmon Foundation supported a range of different projects and viewpoints in its films.

What seems to unite both the reprehensible and the laudable efforts among the Harmon Foundation films is an attitude of Christian humanism. Even though *The Story of Bamba* conflates medical progress with Christianity, the film praises in particular Bamba's *individual decision* to pursue Western medicine and to convert to Christianity. This kind of humanistic philosophy is closely related to the popular pragmatism espoused by Dewey and even the cultural pluralism promoted by Locke, himself a student of pragmatism.[50] Such an emphasis on individual actions—an individual's education, a photographer's award-winning work, an amateur's impressive technique—overlooks the broad systemic problems of cultural imperialism and of racial and social inequality that inform and constrain individual actions. But precisely the personal, individual experience of creative or aesthetic work and that work's contrast with the individual's absorption into the crowd and his or her subsumption by mass commercial culture are what characterize these amateur practical works and amateur film more generally. At the level of the institution, the Harmon Foundation seems to have been less interested in producing a singular propagandistic message than in producing and distributing a plurality of messages on related topics.

The Harmon Foundation also produced several films that directly addressed the issue of aesthetic experience in the modern world. Its collaboration with Alon Bement, an arts educator and the director of the National Alliance of Art and Industry, resulted in *We Are All Artists*, produced by the Harmon Foundation in 1936. *We Are All Artists* traces our experience of the aesthetic in the everyday; it begins by considering the related categories of beauty, art, and craftwork before moving on to suggest some of the many ways that modern art and design have made our world more beautiful. Offering a broad definition of art as any "skillful or purposeful endeavor," the film suggests that we are all artists to the extent that we exercise aesthetic judgment through a range of quotidian activities. The film presents a montage sequence showing a woman cleaning, men painting a wall, a letter being typed, and activities in gardening and pottery and then concludes by proposing that even "exercising the powers of selection"—as in purchasing a hat—makes use of some attributes of the artist. The impulse to broaden a definition of artistic activity that is presented in the film has important relevance for a discussion of amateurs. As a cultural discourse, it reflects a liberal-democratic desire to integrate art and life, and as this chapter's discussion of practical filmmaking illustrates, amateurs often took seriously this kind of invitation to individual aesthetic experience. But for them, this was a two-way process; not only did they take up the tools of creative expression, but they also hoped to transform practical subjects such as industry, education, religion, and social issues into material for such artistry (figure 27). The Harmon Foundation was particularly interested in promoting this kind of art education in the broader sense.[51] More than simply a theoretical lesson in arts appreciation, the film program encouraged a pragmatic and applied understanding of craftsmanship and the use of machines as personal instruments.

John Dewey expressed a similar interest in expanding the relationship between everyday work and artistic experience. In his writings about art, understood distinctly as a kind of purposeful and reflective *experience*, Dewey explored the necessary balance between "instrumental" (useful) and "consummatory" (delightful) aspects in artworks. "For arts that are merely useful," he wrote, "are not arts but routines; and arts that are merely final are not arts but passive amusements and distractions, different from other indulgent dissipations only in dependence upon a certain acquired refinement or 'civilization.'"[52] Ultimately, Dewey argued that art (and artful experience) occurs when useful and pleasurable activities are brought into dialogue and "when activity is productive of an object that affords continuously renewed delight." It is hard to think of a more precise distillation of the amateur filmmaker's ethos than this formulation of the practical and pleasurable working together to produce continuously renewed delight.

Completing the circle of the Harmon Foundation's interest in using movies to promote individual aesthetic experience, the organization produced a series of six films called *You Can Make Good Movies!* at the end of the 1930s. The series was shot by Harmon's staff photographer, Kenneth Space,

Figure 27. *We Are All Artists* (Alon Bement, 1935) features photographer Margaret Bourke-White and appears to have been filmed by the prominent amateur filmmaker Charles Carbonaro (both pictured here). National Archives and Records Administration, DM-H-HFF-88–8.

who was also an ACL member and a regular contributor to *Movie Makers*. Produced by an active amateur-turned-professional, these films present lessons in moviemaking for amateurs; three of the films in the series were recognized by the ACL in its Ten Best lists. As the films of the Harmon Foundation suggest, amateur practical films were profoundly concerned with the relationship between "productive arts" and aesthetic experience in everyday life. The foundation's films return to these questions over and over again, as they both emerge out of amateur filmmaking aesthetics and speak to the importance of an amateur spirit in a time of mass culture.

World War II offered an opportunity for amateurs to bring the practical aspects of their filmmaking to the forefront of their activities (as was discussed in chapter 3), but it also shifted the terms of this practical engagement away from its pleasurable associations. Following the war, in 1948, the ACL eliminated the special categories for sponsored films. An editorial called "All Amateur" explained the change: "Few, if any, amateur filmers are now interested in making pictures for gain—even non-professionally. The production of such films is now big business, carried on by elaborately equipped, highly trained and well paid professionals. Their product, for better or for worse, has lost the amateur touch. As such, it no longer belongs in competition with true amateur movies."[53] The editorial speaks to the emergence of a professional industry of practical moviemakers that had displaced the role of amateurs in that genre. And given the experience of World War II, when all aspects of life became practical, it is perhaps not surprising that the postwar years would bring with them a swing in the opposite direction, to amateur filmmaking as a strictly leisure activity. The shift away from practical films among amateurs was also prompted by the increasing number of postwar moviemakers who saw the 16mm format as a "film of fact" or a professional medium; they understood 8mm film, first introduced in 1932, as the "true" amateur format. For these reasons, the ACL moved away from "practical films" as an amateur genre after World War II. Practical filmmaking, like experimental amateur work, had been central to the first two decades of amateur moviemaking but found itself displaced in the 1940s and '50s by more family-oriented production.

9 Photoplaying Themselves
Amateur Fiction Films

> Individuals will refind themselves only as their ideas and ideals are brought into harmony with the realities of the age in which they act.
>
> **John Dewey**, *Individualism Old and New*[1]

King Vidor's silent film *The Crowd* (1928) presents a cautionary tale for those who wish to rise above the ranks of mass society. At the center of this film is Johnny, both a member of the crowd and someone who aspires to be different. Johnny's ambition, as well as the price he pays for it, is vividly depicted in the film with his participation in an advertising slogan contest. After searching for years for a way to express his unique talents, Johnny is finally rewarded when he wins the contest with a slogan for Sleight of Hand soap. At the very moment of his greatest personal success, however, disaster strikes: With gifts purchased from the prize money in hand, Johnny calls his young daughter into the apartment; crossing the street after leaving her place of play on the sidewalk, she is hit by a car and dies soon after. The film's only other reference to Johnny's contest "success" comes years later in his life, in the movie's final shot; Johnny is sitting in a packed theatre when he notices the advertising slogan that he wrote in a playbill. Nudging the stranger sitting next to him, Johnny points at the ad and says, "I wrote that." But this moment of differentiation from the crowd is brief, and he soon rejoins the mass audience laughing at the show; his position among them is reaffirmed by the scene's visual style, as the camera cranes out from a medium shot to an extreme long shot showing Johnny in his appropriate place—surrounded by the ranks of mass society.

What are we to make of this film's depiction of media production—as opposed to consumption—as a dangerous, and ultimately futile, activity? *The Crowd* poses Johnny's aspiration for fame and fortune as the most natural and American trait imaginable, but the film brings punishment on the scale of a Greek tragedy when this aspiration approaches fulfillment. Did the minimal creativity involved in dreaming up an ad slogan pose such a significant threat to the social order? How, then, should we think about the activities of amateur filmmakers, whose works and social attitudes were often influenced by mass culture even while they strove to differentiate themselves and their films from the products intended for the crowd? *The Crowd* suggests that in the late 1920s media production was a privileged and (literally) contested activity that intertwined aspects of creativity and social existence in modern life. At the same moment that *The Crowd* was released into theatres, in February 1928, *Photoplay Magazine* was promoting the first major contest for amateur filmmakers. *Photoplay*'s second amateur movie contest was organized the following year, and among the contest judges was none other than King Vidor, director of *The Crowd*. Vidor's participation, alongside two directors of the ACL, suggests an almost a personified confrontation of some of the key tensions in amateur film production: between individual and collective film production and between personal expression and standardized, commercial entertainment.[2] If *The Crowd* presented a narrative about the pleasures of mass media, articles published in *Movie Makers* and fiction films produced by ACL members frequently championed a kind of creative individualism. Amateur fiction films, production contexts, and discourse reveal that amateurs were constantly negotiating these seemingly opposed forces.

This chapter examines the amateur "photoplay," or fiction film, that emerged with the appearance of amateur filmmaking and remained central to amateur activities throughout the amateur cinema era. While works within this mode of amateur production are sometimes referred to as fiction films or "story films," I use the term *photoplay* for them, because it was frequently used in amateur publications and also because its slightly anachronistic use resonates with the amateur's privileged relationship to silent film history. From the moment of its origin, the ACL believed that the photoplay film would be one of the central categories of amateur movie production.[3] The league encouraged the production of this category of films by publishing frequent newsletters and articles and establishing the Continuity Department, which provided constructive criticism for amateurs who submitted their scenarios or finished films. Although the ACL's vision for the centrality of the amateur photoplay films faded somewhat over the organization's nearly three-decade lifespan, amateurs continued to produce fictional works that both explored new stylistic territories and revitalized older ones.

Amateur photoplays represent the category of amateur work that existed in closest relationship to commercial film and mass culture, sometimes providing an homage to Hollywood, sometimes a send-up or critique. But photoplays also developed their own themes and subject matter that emerged from small-scale production values or local topics. Amateur photoplays could take the form of adaptations of existing literary or theatrical texts; stories that had topical relationships to the makers' own lives; or tributes, experimental reworkings, or historical revivals of commercial film styles. In making these films, amateurs displayed a pragmatic approach to the problem of creative expression, adapting different kinds of stylistic and thematic qualities to their own personal or club-produced films. And even though they employed commercial technologies and drew upon formal strategies innovated by the impersonal film industry, their films were the product of unalienated creative work that carried the traces of their own specific ingenuity and preoccupations. Consequently, amateur photoplays constitute a mode of vernacular film production that traces a relationship between institutional styles and practices—for example, Hollywood or art cinemas—and informal, local, and unofficial practices in works by amateurs.[4] What might, in individual films, look like an idiosyncratic approach to filmmaking can actually be tied to a larger tendency to see commercial film spectatorship as providing a kind of energy and visual language for amateur film production. In considering the relationship between Hollywood and amateur production, this chapter also returns once again to the amateur's use of motion pictures as a "self-reflective" surface for trying on different versions of identity and modern individuality. Through their use of modern motion picture technology and their relationship to both popular and literary culture, amateurs were able "try out" different visions of themselves. And in their links to both mass culture and local filmmaking clubs, amateurs also developed dynamic and dialectical relationships between collective experience and individual creativity.

AMATEUR ADAPTATIONS: *THE HIGHWAYMAN* (ALAN MOORHOUSE) AND *PEER GYNT* (DAVID BRADLEY)

The Amateur Cinema League published many articles and bulletins that advised its members on the most practical and productive ways of going about producing their own photoplays. One of these bulletins, *Making a Simple Film Story: A Guide to the Amateur in Filming Short Photoplays*, by the ACL photoplay consultant Arthur Gale, noted the modest and pragmatic goals of most amateur filmmakers: "We produce simple film stories for the amusement of filming them and of screening them after they're filmed. We do not aim at serious dramatic work or at artistic cinematography. However, though we do it for the fun of it entirely and, often, on the spur of the moment, there is no reason why we should not do a workmanlike job of the sort that we can screen for our friends with a little pride."⁵ Although Gale emphasizes workmanlike rather than artistic qualities, many amateurs did draw on established literary or theatrical texts for their film subjects. In this, they sought to blend aspects of the artistic with the workmanlike, borrowing from the genius and status of their source material in order to elevate their final amateur motion picture. *Movie Makers* closely tracked many of the group activities and aesthetic forms that adapted preexisting literary or theatrical works. As early as 1927, for example, the magazine touted a Yale University student group adaptation of *Tom Jones*, a film that later found its way into the ACL library.⁶ Literary texts could provide dramatic materials that appeared particularly appropriate to filmic representation. Of course adapting literary texts to film was a common strategy from the earliest days of the commercial cinema, but these professional productions, such as the French Film d'Art films, were noteworthy for their "staginess." In contrast, amateur techniques allowed for a greater attention to scenic and location shooting.

One example of amateur adaptation was the Toronto Amateur Movie Club's 1938 group production of *The Highwayman*, based on the poem of the same title, by Alfred Noyes. Reminiscent of works by Edgar Allan Poe, this ballad of love and murder emphasizes atmosphere and explores the sympathetic relationship between natural and dramatic elements. The opening stanza reads:

> The wind was a torrent of darkness among the gusty trees,
> The moon was a ghostly galleon tossed upon cloudy seas,
> The road was a ribbon of moonlight over the purple moor,
> And the highwayman came riding—
>   Riding—riding—
> The highwayman came riding, up to the old inn-door.⁷

The poem then narrates the highwayman's secret meeting with his lover Bess, a landlord's daughter, their discovery by a group of soldiers who hold Bess as bait for the highwayman, and her grisly death by musket. The poem concludes with a return to a natural atmosphere in a repetition of the opening stanza, which provides the setting for a ghostly reunion of the lovers. A closing verse recounts the meeting of the highwayman and Bess, now dead but still returning for their clandestine meetings. Throughout the poem, the natural settings play an important role in amplifying its *super*natural dramatic content.

Given the amateur filmmaker's propensity for filming expressive natural settings (in travelogues, for example), *The Highwayman*'s evocation of both natural and dramatic atmosphere seems particularly well suited to a film adaptation. The Toronto Amateur Movie Club's film version of the poem begins with shots of the cloudy skies and barren tree branches blowing in the wind, evoking the gusty trees and cloudy seas of the poem's opening verse. With the appearance of the characters, however, the film takes on a more theatrical quality, reminiscent in its staging of D.W. Griffith's Civil War one-reel films or even the French Film d'Art adaptations. But in *The Highwayman*, which was shot on location at an old eighteenth-century house near Toronto (known as the Old Mill), the period quality of the film as a costume drama is therefore mitigated somewhat by the vividness of its natural settings. Furthermore, *The Highwayman* is presented without intertitles; it was originally presented with a recorded recitation of the poem accompanied by music.[8] In an article about the film, its producer, Alan Moorhouse, notes, "The film will be half a talkie.... We were lucky enough to find a complete score for the poem set to music, and by having a record made with hoof-beats, and so forth, with the music as a background, we'll have first-class sound effects." So the film itself would serve as a visual supplement to the poem, presenting for the human eye what the poem merely provides to the mind's eye. One of the challenges in this visualization, Moorhouse notes, was to make sure that the players acted for film, not as they would onstage: "You have to under-act for the camera, not over-act, as you do on stage. That's the trouble. Most stage people grimace." Like its use of natural settings, a natural acting style was employed to set this film adaptation apart from its source materials and its rival media. Finally, the film's use of double exposure in order to create the impression of ghostliness in the tragic couple's final reunion marks a particularly cinematic solution to the problem of visual representation.

The production of a film like *The Highwayman* was an important way for movie clubs to extend their activities beyond the exhibition of personal travelogues or chronicle films. The Toronto Amateur Movie Club had recently started leasing permanent clubrooms, published a regular newsletter, and charged dues of approximately ten dollars per year to support these activities. Producing *The Highwayman* brought helpful publicity to the club. Reporting on the club's production, the *Toronto Star* ran an article called "Highwayman's Romance before Camera Near End—May Finish All-Canadian, All-Color, All-Amateur 'Quickie' To-morrow."[9] The article pointed to the familiarity of the film's source material, noting, "The story which many Canadians learned or are learning in grade school is about a brave highwayman who promised to come back either by night or day to the beautiful Bess." Although its title uses the lingo of Hollywood ballyhoo, the article was also certain to point out the distinction between amateur and commercial films: "There is no commercial value to the 16mm film, Mr. Moorhouse added, because it cannot be shown on the standard projection machines, hence only clubs and possibly schools will see the finished product." *The Highwayman* was subsequently circulated among amateur movie clubs and exhibited in these nontheatrical venues across Canada.[10] In 1938, following the production of this film and its resulting publicity, the Toronto Amateur Movie Club saw a boost in its membership, growing to eighty-six members, from only around fifty just two years earlier.[11]

Despite the collective dimensions of producing an amateur photoplay, according to Moorhouse, who was also the president of the Toronto club, the main appeal of amateur moviemaking was still its capacity for individual expression:

> It is indeed one of the strongest lures of our hobby that a man can stamp his personality on his film so definitely and vitally that it is, in effect, a picture of his own mind—his own thoughts—and his own reactions to the place and circumstances he sets out to depict. It is a chapter from his own autobiography "where all who look may read"!
>
> So when we make a film, and call upon our friends to sit down and watch it through, surely we owe it to both ourselves and them to make it worth watching. For it is not a few hundred feet of film that we are showing, but a cross-section of our own mentality.[12]

While this may have been a widely held view, it was necessarily tempered when amateurs joined together to produce club films like *The Highwayman*. There were also, however, instances in which a single filmmaker brought together a wide number of collaborators but still presented their productions as the product of his strong personal vision. This was certainly the case for the Chicago-area amateur David Bradley's films, all of which were adaptations of literary or theatrical texts but were produced and exhibited as film adaptations that revealed Bradley's own creative imprint.

David Bradley's amateur films provide an excellent case of the amateur's aesthetic and pragmatic adaptation of literary works to local circumstances and cinematic techniques. While still in his late teens and early twenties, Bradley produced several films that are striking for their evocation of cinematic fantasy atmosphere as well as for their clever use of available images and locations (figure 28). He adapted these films from either literary or theatrical sources and reconceptualized them for screen treatment. But even before Bradley turned his hand to producing films, he was evidently already something of a cinephile. As early as 1936, when he was only sixteen years old, Bradley operated a small movie theatre out of the basement

Figure 28. David Bradley (pictured with camera, c. 1941) produced several ambitious films in his teens and early twenties. Courtesy Lilly Library, Indiana University, Bloomington, Indiana.

in his affluent family home in Winnetka, Illinois. One announcement published in the local paper, *Wilmette Life*, notes, "*The Hunchback of Notre Dame*, magnificent film version of Victor Hugo's masterpiece, acclaimed several years ago as one of the greatest, most spectacular offerings in screen history, will be shown at the Bradley theatre, 808 Willow Road, Winnetka, at three matinee performances, Thursday, Friday and Saturday of this week at 2:30 o'clock.... David Bradley, who conducts the theatre, is offering a 'Popeye' comedy as an extra."[13] This article, perhaps penned by Bradley himself, displays his fascination with the spectacular cinematic adaptations of literary texts. How often and how long Bradley ran his small home cinematheque is unclear, but it was still in operation in 1938, when he exhibited the silent film adaptation of Arthur Conan Doyle's *The Lost World* (1925).[14] A lifelong cinephile and film collector, Bradley's early screenings show that he also sought out a community of other viewers to share these films with.

The community that participated in his own film productions included family, schoolmates, teachers, and members of the local amateur theatre community. While a student at Lake Forest Academy, Bradley made film productions of *Treasure Island* (1937), *Doctor X*, *Emperor Jones* (both

1938), *Marley's Ghost* (1939), and *Oliver Twist* (1940); he also produced a chronicle of life at school, called *Preps in Action*, during these years. Bradley's earliest extant film, a 1941 adaptation of *Peer Gynt*, follows in the tradition of these ambitious literary adaptations. But in addition to being a loose adaptation of Henrik Ibsen's play Bradley's film also employed Edvard Grieg's *Peer Gynt Suite*, originally composed as incidental music for the play. So the film version draws on the intertwined dramatic resources of both Ibsen's text and Grieg's music. Shot in black and white, the film has three tinted sections and employs only one sound sequence aside from Grieg's music played on disc. The completed film was full feature length (one hundred minutes) and presented local acting student Charlton Heston in his screen debut.

Bradley's *Peer Gynt* is notable both for its haphazard stylization and its imaginatively pragmatic staging of Ibsen's and Grieg's original works. The film, like the play, is difficult to summarize: it follows Peer's romantic entanglements, encounters with trolls and other supernatural characters, his long travels around the world while trying to discover his true "Gyntian self," and his eventual return to Norway and his one true love. The film begins with stock-shot images of Norway drawn from library travel films. After these specific geographical markers, Bradley's use of the carefully framed locations in northern Illinois, Indiana, and Wisconsin are surprisingly convincing. In an article that he wrote for *Movie Makers*, Bradley describes the opening sequence:

> *Peer Gynt* opens with the strains of *Morning Moods* [a prelude to act 4 in Grieg's suite] as the musical background for the main title, which is superimposed over beautiful cloud pictures. The production gets under way with stock shots of Norway, the locale of the story, which were carefully edited and synchronized to the rest of the mood music. For example, the gurgling motif in the music is represented by a bubbling brook on the screen, and the forceful passages by a majestic waterfall, and so forth. (The stock shots came from library travel films).
>
> As the concluding bars of *Morning Moods* are being played, Peer Gynt [Heston] is seen lying on the bank of a mountain stream to drink from it. A Norwegian stock travelog, showing reindeer, is intercut. The next scene is an upward shot of Peer rising from the stream; he wipes his dripping mouth and sees the reindeer. Another stock shot of the reindeer is inserted. A distant shot of Peer running in the direction of the reindeer, with hunting knife in hand, follows.[15]

The sophisticated visual language employed in the opening sequence is remarkable. By using available 16mm travel footage, expressive and narrative editing techniques, and a musical sound track, Bradley is able to

Figure 29. Charlton Heston's screen debut in *Peer Gynt* (David Bradley, 1941); the film seamlessly blends stock footage of Norway with scenes shot in northern Illinois. Courtesy Lilly Library, Indiana University, Bloomington, Indiana.

construct an opening sequence that almost seamlessly connects Norway with Illinois, as well as connecting amateur with professional filmmaking.[16] The staging of Peer's introduction to the film is deft and effective, and the sequence as a whole establishes this fantasy setting—in truth neither Norway nor Illinois but somewhere in between—as the appropriate place for the beginning of Peer's physical and existential journey (figure 29). Later in the film, at the beginning of its second part, Bradley again makes extensive use of stock shots; this time he establishes the setting as Morocco and cuts between nonfictional footage of that country and his own photoplay's action, which was filmed at the Indiana Dunes State Park.

Some of the most striking sequences in Bradley's adaptation are those that depart from natural settings in dramatic ways. Most notable in this respect is the "Hall of the Mountain King" sequence, which moves from natural exterior settings to increasingly indeterminate spaces. From initial shots of bright, green-tinted foliage where Peer meets the Green-Clad Woman, the mise-en-scène shifts to more dense foliage, which is darker and blue tinted. The Green-Clad Woman takes Peer inside the mountain, where little is visible beyond the characters themselves; there, Peer meets

Figure 30. "The great Boyg!—go 'round about, Peer." *Peer Gynt* (David Bradley, 1941). Courtesy Lilly Library, Indiana University, Bloomington, Indiana.

her father, the fearful and grotesque-looking king of the trolls. A shot of red-tinted flames marks the beginning of the next sequence, in which trolls, witches, imps, and other beasts dance in rhythm to Greig's music around Peer, who is bound to a stake. As the music intensifies in volume and tempo, the trolls become more numerous and grotesque and dance more rapidly around Peer; they are shown in increasingly close shots and sometimes even in fast motion in order to intensify their fearsomeness. Finally, the beasts attack Peer, and as the music concludes the screen goes black.

The next scene, scene 7 of act 2 in Ibsen's play, is famous for its unusual stage direction: "pitch darkness." While Bradley's version of this scene is not presented in pitch darkness, it still achieves a dramatic effect as the only scene in the film that employs lines of speech on the sound track. The scene begins in darkness but quickly cuts to Peer in a low-angle medium shot, recoiling backward into an inky black setting. The next shot shows a grotesque mask, suspended in air and presented in close-up so that it fills the entire frame (figure 30). Peer draws back a little farther, staring up at the face, before asking—via intertitle—"Who are you?" The face, shown floating, tinted blood-red against the black background, replies in a slow deep voice: "Myself." When Peer demands, again via intertitle, "Let me pass!" the face grows larger and the voice replies: "Go 'round about, Peer." When

Peer asks again, "Who are you?" the face grows still larger and this time replies, "The great Boyg!—go 'round about, Peer." As the screen goes completely dark, a different voice narrates that Peer has escaped.

Though shortened and simplified considerably from the original text, the scene nevertheless carries some of the horror and existential weight of Peer's encounter with "the Boyg," his instruction to "go around," and his flight from death. Stylistically, Bradley makes the decision to only suggest the pitch darkness of the setting, instead emphasizing the scene's formal incongruity with the rest of the film by presenting its only instance of recorded speech for the Boyg's voice.[17] This moment is also noteworthy because it revisits the amateur preoccupation with problems of selfhood and individuality. Ibsen's play is rich with existential problems, and although the film is a loose adaptation of Ibsen's play that develops its existential themes only in passing, Peer nevertheless spends the rest of the film "going around." A later sequence, set on the Moroccan beach, touches again on the theme of selfhood. At the height of his immoral profiteering, Peer announces to three other capitalists his wish to become rich enough to be emperor but notes: "The Gyntian Self would need a lot of gold to be Emperor." While the film leaves it at that, in the play, the significance of the Gyntian (or in this translation "Gyntish") Self is explored more extensively:

> The Gyntish Self—it is the host
> of wishes, appetites, desires,—
> the Gyntish Self, it is the sea
> of fancies, exigencies, claims,
> all that, in short, makes my breast heave,
> and whereby I, as I, exist.
> But as our Lord requires the clay
> to constitute him God o' the world,
> so I, too, stand in need of gold,
> if I as Emperor would figure.[18]

In this search for an outward expression or satiation of one's inner desires, it is tempting to find a metaphor for both Bradley and the amateur filmmaker more generally. Early in his career, Bradley referred to himself as "the Orson Welles of 16mm film," alluding to both their similar creative ambitions and their proximate origins north of Chicago.[19] While the Orson Welles of 16mm is a far cry from an emperor, amateurs like Bradley employed pragmatic approaches in adapting literary texts to local circumstances, and in doing so these amateurs inserted themselves into an imaginary creative community that satisfied their desires by placing amateurs alongside literary greats like Ibsen as well as contemporaneous movie stars and directors like Welles.

Peer Gynt was widely shown in the Chicago area and in nontheatrical contexts around the United States. *Movie Makers* gave the film an honorable mention in their listing of 1941's Ten Best. Surprisingly, though, it was the film's adaptation of Ibsen's play that the *Movie Makers* writer was most critical of: "The chief fault in this tremendous undertaking is that Ibsen's gigantic play has been transliterated to the screen rather than translated. That is, Mr. Bradley, by his own admission, modeled his scenario as closely as possible on a work written expressly for the theatre. Had he taken more liberties with the dramatic form in favor of a more peculiarly cinematic treatment—as exemplified so strikingly in the fine Hall of the Mountain King sequence—there would have been no structural weaknesses in his film."[20] Bradley's subsequent reediting of the film in 1965 possibly corrected some of the problems noted here, because the extant version of the film seems to me the most cinematic of any of Bradley's adaptations. Compared with his next three amateur works, *Peer Gynt* is highly selective in its use of the source material and utilizes the text of the play sparingly and effectively.

Bradley made three more amateur films, with the increasingly specific goal of using them to break into the Hollywood industry. In these, he used sound with growing frequency but perhaps to diminishing effect. Bradley's adaptation of Saki's short story "Sredni Vashtar" (1943) presents a visual narrative accompanied by an unsynchronized spoken narration of the story and occasional rough-synch lines of dialogue in the storyteller's modulated voice. Here, the disjunction between sound and image is emblematic of the limitations of amateur equipment; Bradley used this limitation effectively, to produce a ghostly distance between image and sound that heightens the film's macabre narrative. Bradley's final two amateur (though increasingly quasi-professional) productions, adaptations of *Macbeth* (1946) and *Julius Caesar* (1951), employ some striking formal strategies, such as dramatic camera angles and compositions, but they also rely heavily on the spoken lines of the plays, which, recorded and postsynchronized, make the films—*Macbeth* in particular—seem especially stagy. Nevertheless, *Macbeth* was named one of the ACL's Ten Best films of 1946, in the "special" category for sponsored or semiprofessional productions. *Julius Caesar* was produced with amateur actors and makes impressive use of available, neoclassical Chicago locations, including the steps of the Art Institute and the pillars of Soldier Field. But the film, which cost at least fifteen thousand dollars to produce, was seen by both the ACL and the local Chicago press as a quasi-professional—if independent—production; indeed, it was on the merits of this film that Bradley won his much-sought-after contract with MGM. The success of Bradley's film adaptations, like the Toronto Amateur Movie Club's *The Highwayman*, rested with his ability to transfigure the dramatic or literary material via the available settings, resources, and ingenuity of his group of amateur collaborators. Many amateurs, however, not only employed available spaces more extensively but also drew directly from their milieu and experiences in producing their photoplay scenarios.

PHOTOPLAYING THEMSELVES: *A RACE FOR TIES* (DOROTHEA MITCHELL) AND *A STUDY IN REDS* (MIRIAM BENNETT)

Although literary and theatrical texts remained an important source of scenarios for amateur photoplay producers, many amateurs, individually and in groups, looked to local circumstances and topics for their narrative materials. The Rochester Community Players' production of *Fly Low Jack and the Game* (Marion Gleason, 1927) was an early example of how a community theatre group transformed itself into a filmmaking unit and how they created a scenario that was specifically tailored to the milieu and available resources of the company. Gleason explains, "The scenario was written locally for the occasion. That fact gave the director and the two assisting cameramen a very great deal of latitude to improve on it as they went along. This is a liberty that amateurs might scruple to take with a scenario based on a story from current fiction or from the classics and near-classics of the language, which might entirely possibly be considered amateur photoplay material."[21] As we have seen, amateurs did not necessarily scruple to take liberties when adapting literary or theatrical texts to their amateur productions, but the creation of scenarios and narratives derived more specifically from the milieu of the amateur moviemakers is a crucial aspect of the amateur's pragmatic imagination. Indeed, the production of photoplay scenarios and scripts, by amateurs, was an activity that predated the widespread production of amateur movies themselves. As early as 1915, publications such as C.G. Winkopp's *How to Write a Photoplay* coached readers in the necessary turn of mind (and formatting requirements) for writing photoplays. And while the goal of this particular publication was to provide members of the general public with enough information to sell their photoplays to commercial producers (even including a three-page listing of potential buyers), some aspects of its suggested approach would continue in the creation of scripts and scenarios for amateur production. Most notable in this respect was the use of familiar, even quotidian, events as potential source materials for a photoplay: "Plot material is to be found everywhere; the requisites to discover it are a keen perception to find the plot germ, a vivid imagination to develop and elaborate it with dramatic incidents. Daily happenings in the newspapers, unique stories in magazines, novel experiences in the lives of your acquaintances, visiting the films, are all excellent sources from which to draw the main idea. The creative faculty is the most wonderful part of the mind, and the more you develop it by trying to create plots from simple incidents the more it will grow."[22] Amateur photoplays show extensive evidence of this mode of thinking, looking to examples from newspapers or local circumstances as a spark from which to develop an amateur photoplay scenario.

Drawing inspiration from local happenings seems to have been particularly appealing to amateurs who lived far away from large, urban entertainment centers. The Amateur Cinema Society of Thunder Bay's feature-length photoplay, *A Race for Ties* (1929), for example, presents a locally specific and community-based narrative. Like Bradley's productions, *A Race for Ties* also evinces the central role of a specific individual's creative contribution. This film's author, the so-called lady lumberjack Dorothea Mitchell, was a British-born entrepreneur, homesteader, and writer who consistently challenged, over the course of her colorful life, expectations about the different roles that an unmarried woman could play in business and backwoods life. In an oral history recorded in 1964, Mitchell tells how the plans came about to produce an amateur movie in the northern Ontario city of Port Arthur (later, Thunder Bay): "Fred Cooper, a business friend of mine, purchased a 16mm amateur movie-camera . . . to accompany him and his wife on a trip to England. After their return, they naturally threw a big party and showed the results to friends and employees. From this came requests to give a public showing in aid of charity. However, feeling that his pictures were too personal, Cooper asked me, a bit of a camera fiend myself, (but of the still variety) if we could not make a picture."[23] Mitchell agreed and was put in charge of writing the scenario for the film. The film's script drew directly on her personal experiences in the timber business, as later recounted in her memoir, *The Lady Lumberjack*. Here she tells about an effort to secure a contract from a remote timber camp for railroad ties before a corporate buyer could beat her to it; in the end, the corporate agent reaches the camp first and goads its owner into signing an unfavorable deal. Ultimately, however, Mitchell and her partner get the contract after the raw deal is recognized as invalid because it was signed on a Sunday and without any witnesses.[24]

The film version of *A Race for Ties* adapts this story into an adventure-chase comedy. Silent, black and white, and running approximately fifty-six minutes in duration, the film employs a rudimentary narrative film structure and techniques in order to present its uniquely localized narrative. The film begins with a series of intertitles that introduce the film's protagonist, Attwood, his son and daughter, and their aunt (who is played by Mitchell). In the film adaptation, Attwood has fallen on hard times and needs a new timber contract in order to keep sending his fashionable teenage daughter to college. The characters are introduced in an establishing interior scene that uses rudimentary continuity editing (cutting in from long shot to closer details) as well some characteristic amateur features, such as slow, jerky pans. Noting that railroad construction was producing new demand for railroad ties, Attwood determines to produce a deal selling a neighbor's surplus timber to the Fir Deal Timber Company. The film follows Attwood as he visits the exterior space of his neighbor, Barlow, and the backwoods before going to town and the offices of the timber company. When the company's agents "U. Cheetum" and "Watnot" determine to cut Attwood out of the deal, the race is on to reach Barlow first. The hapless and urban Watnot is sent into the wilderness to secure the contract. First Aunt Sarah (Mitchell) and then daughter, Marion, are sent out across the snowy wilderness to reach Barlow, but both arrive too late. As in Mitchell's memoir, however, the corporate contract is invalidated, and the protagonist's livelihood is saved. In the film version, this favorable outcome is amplified by the flourishing of a romance between Marion and a sympathetic camp superintendent named Larkin.

While the plot is clearly derived from highly local issues, the film's drama and humor focus on the more easily generalized themes of mobility and manners. The distance between the city and the backwoods, in terms of both geography and sympathetic relations, provides the film's thematic tension. The film's objectives (timber for railway ties) and its plot (the journey to Barlow's remote cabin) are emphasized and thematized around problems of mobility. For Larkin, who travels on horseback, and Aunt Sarah, who easily dons snowshoes, travel through the hinterland is habitual and easy (figure 31). But for those who are associated with urban culture, like Watnot and Marion, travel in the backwoods is turned into a comic spectacle. Watnot travels at first by car, but when the snow becomes too deep to drive through he turns to the range of backup modes of transportation that he has brought with him: snowshoes, skis, and ice skates. Eventually, he borrows a horse from Larkin but again is the source of numerous pratfalls as he shows his inexperience with unmechanized transportation and remote

Figure 31. *Left:* For Aunt Sarah, who easily dons snowshoes, travel through the hinterland is habitual and easy. *A Race for Ties* (Dorothea Mitchell, 1929). Frame capture. **Figure 32.** "For crying out loud! Me wearing those things? Supposing I should meet a Sheik?—I sure would look some Sheba!!" *A Race for Ties* (Dorothea Mitchell, 1929). Frame capture.

spaces. Despite his ease with backwoods manners, young Jack Attwater is prevented from traveling because of a lame leg; so, his older and more stylish sister, Marion, is forced into the wilderness after Aunt Sarah leaves behind some important papers. Wearing high heels and a knee-length dress, Marion complains about compromising fashion for function as she stands at the doorway of the Attwood cabin and considers putting on heavy boots: "For crying out loud! Me wearing those things? Supposing I should meet a Sheik?—I sure would look some Sheba!!" (figure 32). Though she dons the boots and later snowshoes (backward), her romance with Larkin flourishes only when she has returned to her urban dress.

What is perhaps most suggestive about Marion's remarks is their obvious reference to popular culture and the movie star Valentino and thus to the cinema's mediating place in this negotiation of geography and manners. The only creature that is able to efficiently traverse the spaces between city and backwoods in the film is the dog, Laddie, who carries a message from Attwater in the city to Aunt Sarah back home. But facilitating this animal's heroic journey, by stitching these distant spaces together, is the cinema, which switches from urban to hinterland space via montage. Like many commercial films, *A Race for Ties* capitalizes on the medium's ability to cross-cut between spatially remote locations and to develop drama and suspense in the process. The comedy of this film is heightened because the difficulty with which Watnot and Marion move across spaces is turned into a joke when compared with the cinema's ease in doing the same thing. Moreover, as Marion's

Figure 33. *A Race for Ties* (Dorothea Mitchell, 1929) begins with the ACL logo and leader that was sent to new members when they joined the organization. Frame capture.

comments suggest, the film seems aware of the comic potential of comparing the remote setting of this amateur production with the urban and fashionable culture of commercial films. Like the film's brother and sister (Jack and Marion), amateur and professional films exist here as close relations, even if they seem to have little in common with each other. Finally, the film's ability to establish a connection with the larger world of filmmaking is at least in part thanks to the Amateur Cinema League. Although *A Race for Ties* was not awarded any ACL prizes, references to this film in *Movie Makers* suggest that Mitchell and her club were aware of the organization and perhaps even students of its magazine's instructive articles. Furthermore, the extant version of *A Race for Ties* begins with the ACL logo and leader that was sent to new members when they joined the organization. The leader shows an ACL insignia and then an image of a turning globe with text superimposed over it: "Member—Amateur Cinema League—The World-Wide Organization of Amateur Movie Makers" (figure 33). In this, the ACL's aspirations of connecting the world—both urban and backwoods—through motion picture production is reinforced and amplifies once more these thematic and formal concerns in Mitchell's film.

A similar production that cinematically juxtaposes local and imaginary circumstances is Miriam Bennett's 1932 film, *A Study in Reds*. This silent, black-and-white film (eighteen minutes in length) playfully considers how the town of Kilbourn, Wisconsin, might look if it were placed under Soviet administration. On first appearance, this scenario is characterized by an obvious Soviet phobia, but the film is also a playful parody of how a small-town women's club meeting works and how women's "society" is regimented and comical in its own right. The film's title might refer to both of these meanings: it suggests the Soviet communist red, but it also alludes to lady's rouge or other red makeup. The film's opening titles give us a hint at this second meaning, as the letters of the credits are seen emerging from a rouge pot. Additionally, some of the first scenes in the film show a woman putting on her makeup, and, at the film's climax, a woman about to be executed refuses a blindfold and instead pulls out a cosmetics compact and begins powdering her nose.

A Study in Reds borrows from commercial films in some of its formal techniques, but its narrative is highly localized in the small-town "club" milieu. The film begins with the ironic intertitle: "Tuesday night—club night—and all is in readiness for a feast of reason." As the club meeting is called to order, the camera pans jerkily around the room, showing the ladies seated in a large semicircle (figure 34). The speaker for the evening then invites the ladies to take an imaginary journey: "Tonight, ladies, let us travel in fancy to reddest Russia and see the famous Soviets." The camera provides a shot of the presenter with her books and a close-up of the title page of one gloomy-sounding tome: *Black Bread and Red Coffins*.[25] The reaction of the ladies listening to the report, however, seems very far from a travel in fancy. The film presents a choppy passing of time with a jump-cut, time-lapse close-up of a clock; shots of one lady doodling on a pad turn into a brief but surprising animated drawing of two faces—one surprised, one scowling—that flashes across the screen but in a few seconds is gone, replaced again by the ladies reading, yawning, tapping their feet, and eventually nodding off. It is tempting to find the inspiration for the film's events in a lecture about Russia's five-year plans that was given to the Kilbourn Kiwanis Club some six months before the film was produced. That lecture, by a Miss Mary Conway, drew on books and other written materials to talk about the current Soviet economic, social, and political conditions.[26] Perhaps the feast of reason that was provided by the Kiwanis Club meeting is what is gently parodied in *A Study of Reds*.

When the lecturer suggests, "And now let us pause to consider how we would like to be governed by a Soviet," one audience member falls asleep, and the film really begins to travel in fancy. The room of club members is shown in an out-of-focus long-shot that gradually pulls into focus to reveal the same women in Soviet-style clothing, wearing big hats, kerchiefs, and frumpy coats. What follows is evidently the dream of the woman who has fallen asleep: a

Figure 34. *Left:* The Tuesday Club is assembled for a "feast of reason." *A Study in Reds* (Miriam Bennett, 1932). Frame capture. **Figure 35.** The club members transformed into a Soviet firing squad. *A Study in Reds* (Miriam Bennett, 1932). Frame capture.

series of episodes shows the ladies of the Tuesday Club transformed into workers and party leaders, suggesting comical interpretations of Soviet life. This begins with the handing out of ration cards ("The comrades will eat cabbage and soup and like it!") but soon travels beyond the sitting room to present a scene of mothers "freed from domestic shackles." After one woman is sent to prison for being "too affectionate" with her child, she is shown in a dramatic pictorialist composition, her head and face illuminated in the dark cell by only a single shaft of light coming in through an opening above. After a moment, this painterly composition is replaced with a more evenly lit shot of the woman in the cell, as though moving from an experiment in composition and artistic expression to the safety and reassurance of narrative intelligibility. A final episode in this part of the film shows a woman (perhaps the one who has fallen asleep) sneaking an egg from her basket before being accosted by a party official: "But the five-year plan calls for ten eggs! You have nine only!" After her theft is discovered, the woman smashes her egg and throws the entire basket—via trick montage—to the ground. An intertitle notes, "In the Soviet it is a short step from eggs to eggsecution," and the woman is taken before a firing squad (figure 35). There, she refuses a blindfold and instead powders her nose (figure 36); in this *A Study in Reds* perhaps pays self-conscious homage to Marlene Dietrich's similar gesture in *Dishonored* (Joseph von Sternberg, 1931), released the year before.[27] But just as the party official gives the order to fire, the shot dissolves to a close-up of hands clapping, and we are back in the Tuesday Club meeting. As the lecture ends, there is more clapping, and the woman wakes in time for the club to adjourn.

Figure 36. The egg thief refuses a blindfold. *A Study in Reds* (Miriam Bennett, 1932). Frame capture.

A Study in Reds is interesting at both narrative and formal dimensions. Though it shows a certain amount of amateur clumsiness, it is nevertheless a coherent, clever, and sometimes striking film. The film's jerky panning shots remind us of its amateurish production values, as do its combination of in-camera editing (jump cuts) and smoother, postproduction continuity editing. Despite these rough qualities, the film nevertheless presents its narrative using clear, well-lit interior settings, mainly in long and medium shots. Articles in the local Kilbourn weekly newspaper attribute the film to Miriam Bennett in particular and indicate that this was not her first film. "Miss Bennett," one article notes, "has been interested in motion pictures for several years past, and during that time had made numerous sketches of considerable interest to those who have seen the pictures, which display her ability in selecting beautiful settings, but the latest production eclipses anything that has gone before."[28] Bennett's eye for beautiful settings should come as little surprise given her still photography training in the studio that her father, the prominent landscape photographer H. H. Bennett, had established in Kilbourn. So even though the credits of *A Study in Reds* announce the film as a production made collectively by the Tuesday Club, local press and context suggest that the film should also be understood as the creative product of a single individual: Miriam Bennett.

The tone and social significance of *A Study in Reds* are more difficult to pin down. Though it pokes fun at both ladies clubs and Soviet Russia (as distant from one another as these groups might seem), its ultimate ideological point of view remains elusive. Perhaps one clue to the film's social philosophy rests with an article in *Movie Makers* that described the production as a "reversal of the customary Sovkino drama."[29] The article suggests that the film can be seen as a photoplay that engages in a mental experiment—rather than a social or stylistic one—about a different kind of American political system. Whether or not the film's characters ultimately return to the "reassuring banalities of private ownership," it is worth noting that the filmmakers occupy neither of the parodied positions. Rather, Bennett and her coproducers express through the film's humor a moderate dissatisfaction with both of these alternatives. And, in taking up filmmaking as a means of exploring two unsatisfactory positions (radicalism and complacency), these women provided a means of communicating their local responses to these general social problems. Like *A Race for Ties*, *A Study in Reds* not only stages a narrative that has local significance but also, through generalized stylistic and thematic concerns, stages an encounter between local and national or even international points of view. In their production of photoplays that were grounded in local specificity, amateurs once again pointed to the value of cinema as a tool for both *intra-* and *inter*communication.

THE MIRROR OF BURLESQUE: *HER HEART'S DESIRE* (OTHON GOETZ), *TARZAN AND THE ROCKY GORGE* (ROBBINS BARSTOW), AND *HEARTS OF THE WEST* AND *LITTLE GEEZER* (THEODORE HUFF)

> The amateur should not feel that he is dealing in a lowly form of art in which it is fruitless to exert himself fully. It is a field in which he can outdo the professional.
>
> Theodore Huff, "The Mirror of Burlesque"[30]

Not all amateur photoplays sought to reimagine a local milieu or an ideological alternative in light of motion picture technology. Some amateurs produced narratives in available, local spaces but sought, in one way or another, to tap into a vernacular version of the fantasy worlds produced by Hollywood. One striking example of this kind of work is Othon Goetz's 1949 film, *Her Heart's Desire*. *Movie Makers* named *Her Heart's Desire* as an honorable mention in its 1949 competition, citing the following reasons: "A blonde model and the sights of New York divide the honors in Othon Goetz's *Her Heart's Desire*, a pleasant story of the girl who came to the big city to model and got married instead. Good city footage is quite rare; Mr. Goetz has succeeded in achieving some startling shots of New York's splendors as he follows the thin thread of his story."[31] This film is noteworthy because it employs the urban milieu of New York, using what might otherwise be considered scenic city footage as a backdrop for the narrative (figure 37). The narrative itself, however, seems to be drawn more from popular mythology and films than from specific and personal experience. It draws—both stylistically and thematically—on a popular genre of aspiring model

Figure 37. *Her Heart's Desire* (Othon Goetz, 1949) draws on urban scenery and popular mythology and re-presents these materials in a distinctly amateur world. Courtesy Chicago Film Archives, Margaret Conneely Collection.

films and is particularly reminiscent (in much simplified form) of Max Ophuls's *Caught*, which was released in February of the same year. Patricia R. Zimmermann argues that Hollywood's influence among amateurs was no more than "discursive colonization" and that amateur films and organizations, like the ACL, merely acted as Hollywood's "adjunct and promoter."[32] But what is striking about *Her Heart's Desire* is that it situates the fictional characters and actions in a Kodachrome and silent, amateur milieu; here Hollywood's thematic conventions are appropriated, adapted, and re-presented in a distinctly amateur world.

Many amateurs made films that reflected their position as fans of the popular cinema. An example of this kind of work is *Tarzan and the Rocky Gorge*, made in 1936 by a sixteen-year-old amateur (and ACL member) named Robbins Barstow. Produced silent, with a voice-over narration, Barstow's film makes playful reference to the popular MGM films *Tarzan the Ape Man* (1932) and *Tarzan and His Mate* (1934). Barstow confesses to having been a huge Johnny Weissmuller fan, and in his amateur film he casts himself as the heroic Tarzan, with his brothers and friends in supporting roles (figure 38). In one sense, we can see his film *Tarzan and the Rocky Gorge* as a fan's tribute film, produced with friends for a lark. But such tributes were also efforts to engage and play with Hollywood's products

Figure 38. Robbins Barstow cast himself as Tarzan, with his brothers and friends in supporting roles. *Tarzan and the Rocky Gorge* (Robbins Barstow, 1936). Frame capture from the Internet Archive (https://archive.org).

and conventions and, for that reason, shouldn't be seen as simply parasitic or derivative. Instead, they mark an effort to be both part of "the mass" of moviegoers and also engaged in a negotiation about this participation. As John Dewey noted, "The particular interactions that compose a human society include the give and take of participation, of a sharing that increases, that expands and deepens the capacity and significance of the interacting factors. Conformity is the name for the absence of vital interplay; the arrest and benumbing of communication."[33] In contrast to the passive viewer, amateurs like Barstow made films as a way of initiating a conversation—a give and take of participation—with commercial films, in this way staving off the conformity of mass culture.

Films like *Her Heart's Desire* and *Tarzan and the Rocky Gorge* suggest a more playful relationship between amateur and Hollywood productions than has generally been acknowledged by scholars. This is a relationship in which amateurs *responded* to Hollywood. Throughout the ACL's lifespan, *Movie Makers* frequently discussed the amateur film's relationship to professional works. Generally speaking, the magazine developed a relationship of helpful difference, in which amateurs were urged to study professional films for technical advice but not to try to duplicate professional works in terms of content or form. Even as amateurs were encouraged to look to the commercial film as a model for certain kinds stylistic proficiency, writers like Roy Winton were quick to reinforce the amateur's difference from professional filmmakers, particularly after the arrival of sound film: "[It] might appear as if we amateurs regretted the advent of 'talkies.' Far from it. We should welcome them because they will liberate the cinema from the necessity of pleasing the great crowd. With the wedding of the crowd and the 'talkies,' the silent screen can go forward to a free artistic development."[34] Winton believed that the commercial cinema's move away from the style and aesthetic achievements of the silent era created a special opportunity for the amateur, whom he called "the inheritor of the silent films."[35] On one hand Winton suggested that the amateur should continue to pursue, in experimental forms, the development of the aesthetic possibilities of the photoplay. But on the other hand, Winton's program was also backward looking, working with what was already a commercially obsolete medium: the silent film. This paradoxical position—at once experimental and backward looking—allowed amateurs to produce some fascinating films about films. Far from being strictly derivative, many amateurs looked to the commercial cinema for stylistic and narrative inspiration, which could then be transformed through amateur means. Reviews in the *Movie Makers* "Critical Focusing" column pointed out how amateurs could learn specific skills from professionals, as was discussed in chapter 1. Through its discussion of stylistic devices distilled from their filmic context, this column identified the vocabulary of a vernacular film language, in effect refashioning a mode of film spectatorship into an alternative filmmaking practice.

Theodore Huff produced films in this referential vein and consequently occupies an awkward position between amateur and avant-garde filmmaking of the 1930s. Between 1930 and 1933, Huff directed two amateur photoplays *(Hearts of the West* and *Little Geezer)*, codirected an industrial film *(The Russell Sage Foundation)*, and assisted with an experimental film (Flory's *Mr. Motorboat's Last Stand*). All of these films received some kind of recognition from the Amateur Cinema League (either chosen as Ten Best or given honorable mentions). While Huff's films have received more scholarly attention than most amateur works, there has been some recent controversy about how best to understand his 1930s productions. Jan-Christopher Horak and Chuck Kleinhans have argued that Huff is an important protoexperimental filmmaker. Andrew Lampert, on the other hand, suggests that little is experimental about Huff's own photoplays, which he compares to Hal Roach productions. More recently, Tom Gunning has traced links between the campiness of Huff's photoplay films and the queer, experimental camp of Kenneth Anger's and Jack Smith's films.[36] Huff's photoplays demonstrate a playful and dynamic relationship to popular culture, film forms, and genres but were not typically received by the ACL as avant-garde works.

Certainly Huff's photoplays are unusual films. Both *Hearts of the West* and *Little Geezer* feature all-boy casts, even in romantic parts, with actors ranging in age from approximately nine to fourteen. Kleinhans suggests that Huff was a closeted homosexual, and it may indeed be helpful to think of his films retrospectively in relation to queer cinema, as Gunning does. But this was probably not how the ACL, a generally conservative organization, would have understood them. Rather, Huff's works fit within at least two strands of familiar amateur activities: the first was the tradition of boys school theatricals and their nascent movie clubs, and the second, that of cinephelia and movie fan culture more generally. The son of a physician, Huff grew up near Fort Lee, New Jersey, an important center of American film production during the 1910s. At Fort Lee, Huff might have seen films, like those he lampoons in *Hearts*, being produced when he was himself between ages nine and fourteen (c. 1914–19).[37] Huff wrote a first draft of the script for *Hearts of the West* in 1926, while still a student at Princeton University, which was then a college for men only. But it wasn't until the summer of 1929 that he began shooting the film. *Hearts* was edited during the summer of 1930, and by August, Huff was screening it privately for the film's young actors and their families. Huff's meticulous record keeping allows us to see that *Hearts* was exhibited, perhaps as many as a hundred times between 1930 and 1934, at a range of different venues, including private parties, movie clubs, schools, church groups, boy scout troops, and other venues that were arranged through the ACL.[38] Although Huff helped to organize an amateur movie club in Bergen, New Jersey, in 1932 and was an active member of the ACL, *Hearts* appears to have been a project that he developed on his own, with neighborhood kids.

The film itself pokes fun at the narrative conventions of silent westerns. While technically clumsy at times, it demonstrates a keen awareness of scene dissection, makes effective use of close-ups for emphasis, and even employs moments of dramatic rapid montage. The cast of boys play their roles earnestly, and the romantic leads are strangely convincing, if certainly campy, even queer. The children's unaffected acting style (even when imitating clichés) makes the film at times seem compelling, if in a very different way from the kind of movie it is imitating. An author in *Movie Makers* notes, "Under his direction, the children act their parts with complete seriousness and, in some cases, with mimetic ability that would have given their prototypes pause."³⁹ Huff made a similar comment in an article he penned for *Movie Makers*, noting, "All children are natural mimics; it is part of their makeup as much as the instinct to play, and it is lost as they mature even as the other childish instincts disappear."⁴⁰ *Hearts* is imbued with nostalgia for an earlier moment in film history and poignantly uses children to re-create a sense of the ephemeral past, but these comments also suggest nostalgia of a different, more personal kind. *Movie Makers* praised *Hearts* as one of the Ten Best amateur films of 1931, calling it "a delightful and whimsical burlesque of the Griffith melodrama days when titles were long and plots of villainy and intrigue laid in the great open places swept grandly to a moral conclusion in which 'true hearts were united.'" But the article also notes that not only had Huff revisited these old narratives, but he had also used old production techniques: "In those days, producers did not hesitate to use a cyclorama or to place painted canvas scenery on an outdoor location. Mr. Huff revives all of the old technique, even to the dance hall set, with its inevitable balcony, and the flight to the finish at the edge of the cliff."⁴¹ In this way Huff not only produced a new and strange homage to a past era of filmmaking but also recuperated its practices and reanimated them for future amateurs.

In a similar way, *Little Geezer* (1932) employs elements of rapid film editing and montage (perhaps inspired by Eisenstein) in order to lampoon the generic structure and characters of the more contemporaneous Hollywood gangster film. Recalling one of the "Critical Focusing" columns, Huff called this style of photoplay a "movie burlesque." In an article called "The Mirror of Burlesque," Huff argued that satire, or "burlesque," films were an appropriate genre for amateurs to work in because of their entertainment value, playfulness, and relationship to Hollywood popular films. He suggested, "A burlesque is the easiest type of photoplay for the amateur to produce for, while it is difficult to compete with Hollywood producers on their own ground in a straight story since amateur actors are apt to suffer by comparison, in a burlesque, errors and crudities only add to the fun."⁴² In this approach we can see that amateur limitations of technique and skill are actually transformed into virtues, similar to the appeal of a vernacular slang or shorthand. Huff's films point toward an alternative film aesthetic in which imperfections were acceptable parts of the form. And it is easy to see why—in *Little Geezer*'s rapid montage and surreal casting of a young boy as "Greta Garbage"—the film might be thought of as avant-garde (figure 39). This is perhaps a natural conclusion to draw from a film that is composed of an equal fascination with Eisenstein, Griffith, and Hal Roach.

But some of what is strange about Huff's films might also be illuminated by what the French surrealists noted in their fascination with "the recently

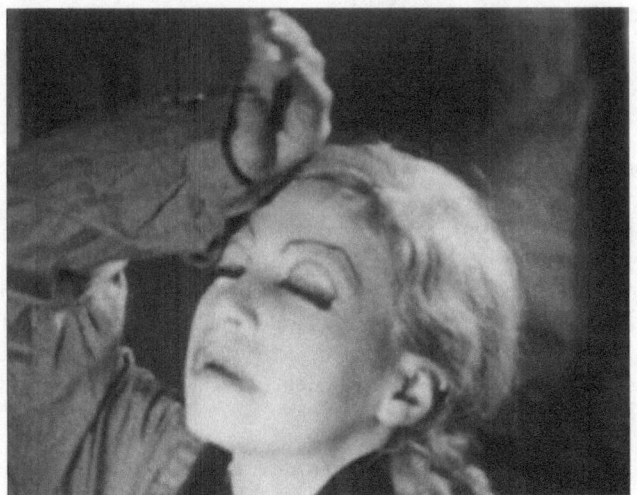

Figure 39. Greta Garbage: "I'm sick—tired—fed up with Life." *Little Geezer* (Theodore Huff, 1932). Frame capture.

obsolete." In Huff's case, this fascination was with the silent cinema, and his surprising move in *Little Geezer* is to have transposed a tribute to the sound-era gangster film into silent film idioms. In another article for *Movie Makers*, Huff explains how to write a scenario, revealing along the way how much of his technique relied upon silent film methods and indeed was (by 1934) a kind of resurrection of an earlier period in film history.[43] Huff recounts the emergence of silent film narration in Griffith and explains the conventional formal structure of silent films that he developed, including the practice "working in" from establishing to closer shots. But Huff also adapts this silent movie technique to amateur technology, noting that even though close-ups were conventionally to be reserved for emphasis, amateurs faced a challenge when it came to longer shots, since, as he points out, "when working with substandard [that is to say 16mm] film, it is very difficult to register facial expressions when the camera is much more than fifteen feet away." In a similar vein, Huff published an article in *Movie Makers* that describes how best to position intertitles in amateur films, some five years after the arrival of sound films.[44] So again we see how at the very level of film language, a translation from popular to amateur, from sound to silent, and from commercial to vernacular was taking place.

Amateurs continued to use silent film techniques throughout the 1930s and '40s. This was demonstrated by the need for what would otherwise be obsolete film knowledge, such as James Moore's 1947 article on spoken titles.[45] But *Movie Makers* also compared amateur filmmakers to early cameramen because of their limited means of production and their need to be "cine craftsmen" who could make the best of the available materials:

> In the early days of theatrical motion pictures, before great studios were equipped with complex machinery to perform cinematic tasks with exquisite and satisfying results on the screen, the technicians of pre Hollywood days were contrivers and inventors of simple ways of getting novel effects. They were cine craftsmen and not cine mechanics. From them came novelties piled upon novelties. They had little to do with and did much with it. It seems entirely probable that this same craftsman's spirit will push cine amateurs forward to new developments in their own special range of endeavor.[46]

On the other hand, their relationship to silent film techniques also seems to have perpetuated a privileged relationship between amateurs and the history of the cinema.

No doubt, not all amateurs approached their filming with anything close to Huff's degree of pre- and postproduction sophistication. But in placing his film alongside Barstow's *Tarzan and the Rocky Gorge* and other amateur works (rather than just in a corpus of avant-garde works), we can see that they share a playful fascination with film styles and conventions. Ultimately, such amateur films can provide us with evidence of a vernacular film aesthetic emerging between the wars and persisting even in the 1940s and '50s.[47] This was an aesthetic that oriented itself in relation to dominant paradigms of expression and then adapted these forms to local conditions or less-established approaches. Rather than providing evidence of ideological complicity or a parasitic relationship to Hollywood, amateur film culture constituted an alternative sphere of film spectatorship and production. Amateur filmmaking was a vernacular film aesthetic through which amateurs playfully situated themselves among commercial film practices while also taking film in aesthetic and expressively productive new directions.

The production of photoplay films engaged the amateur's capacity for visual narrative production as well as creative problem solving. As we have seen, the question of what "experimentation" meant to both amateur film style and its relation to social movements is complex, but for the production of photoplays it meant the expansion of the amateur's filmic language. In 1946, many years after the formation of the ACL, Roy Winton looked back at some of its original goals and observed that the role of the photoplay was one that had developed in a different direction from the role anticipated. Noting that the Photoplay Department had been one of the founding elements of the league's constitution, Winton points out, "The League was to bring about an increase in pleasure to amateur cinematographers, by aiding them to originate and produce motion pictures. . . . It soon became clear that personal films were not, for the most part, to be photoplays."[48] No longer anticipating the photoplay's central position in the amateur Little Cinema movement, Winton points to the eminently practical directions in which amateur work had developed, especially during World War II. Though he emphasizes the possibility of amateur photoplays emerging from a single creative vision, we have seen that many also emerged from club productions, though perhaps on a more modest scale than envisaged by the ACL's founding members. As indicated by the statistics in *Movie Makers* about the ratio of photoplay to chronicle films (chapter 6), amateurs produced many more films that documented some aspect of their world than films that were strictly fictional.

But as we have seen, amateur photoplays were not the products of mere fancy; they carried with them—in their adaptation, locations, and reworking of commercial film techniques—evidence of the same thread of pragmatic imagination that we find running through so many of the films produced in association with the Amateur Cinema League. Writing in 1931, John Dewey pointed to the need for just such a new art form that blended together social, technological, and individual influences: "The art which our times need in order to create a new type of individuality is the art which, being sensitive to the technology and science that are the moving forces of our time, will envisage the expansive, the social, culture which they may be made to serve."[49] In this kind of art, individuality was produced out of a creative interaction with the material, technological, and emotional conditions of everyday life. Peering into Dewey's prediction for a new kind of art, we can clearly see the activities of amateur filmmakers reflected back at us.

Conclusion

He could not paint a picture to save his life. He does not know the names of the great artists. He is an ignoramus in art matters. But he has the artistic sense. He loves the beautiful, and gets a profound pleasure out of creating something that is beautiful.

Dr. Kinema, *"Movies as Mirrors"*[1]

Human beings are generally pragmatists. If anything works, it can be understood and condoned, if not accepted.

Movie Makers[2]

This book has presented some of the range and richness of North American amateur movie culture between 1923 and 1960, suggesting a history of amateur motion pictures that was a complex and varied alternative to the history of commercial motion pictures. Amateur filmmaking was engaged in a practical negotiation of personal creativity, everyday life, and modern technology, and it produced a combination of responses to art, mass culture, and motion pictures. It also occupied a middle ground between participation in the crowd of mass-media audiences and more individual or local experiences. Amateurs also developed a vernacular visual language, putting everyday elements and locations into a dialogue with commercial film styles and formal strategies.

Amateur film culture was a form of middlebrow leisure with both ideals and limitations. Despite the tendency in scholarship to reduce middlebrow culture to its function as commodity consumption, amateur moviemakers presented a more complex ideological terrain. The ACL, in particular, promoted a liberal, pragmatic view that allowed for the possibility of the free exchange of ideas and experimental developments. Additionally, this study has uncovered a significant area of creative work by women and shows how amateur film *could* provide a visual language for experimenting with or negotiating social issues. However, most amateur groups did not actively work to address widespread social problems or inequalities; the cross-section of amateur films discussed in this book suggests that amateurs did not often choose to address specific social ills. Aside from amateurs' freedom from commercial requirements and production codes, one editorial suggests that their advantage was precisely this: "their right to say whatever they may wish to say on film, without the obligation to say it to advance a particular social or political idea." The author then elaborates: "They need neither be socially constructive, to please those who would remodel the existing state of things, nor seek that adroit blend of the commonplace and the spicy which has been so dependably certain a prescription for below the average Hollywood productions."[3] For writers in *Movie Makers*, amateur filmmaking could be seen as a context for expression as well as refuge—for reassurance but also aesthetic experience and experimentation in an otherwise mass-media-saturated and commodified society. Amateurs largely viewed their film activities as personal, creative, and even social *without* being necessarily political in any way. But the amateur's middlebrow form of expression was neither simplistic nor one-dimensional; while it does not fit into contemporary ideas of politicized filmmaking, amateur cinema was nevertheless a complex mode of alternative film practice.

In particular, amateur films and activities provide us with an important historical examination of the complex interrelationships between film reception and production and between communal and private participation. The amateur filmmaking experiences chronicled in this study reveal how people consumed commercial motion pictures and refashioned characteristics of mass culture in a range of personal ways. But we can identify at least two broad impulses in this cycle of film reception and ensuing production, each with its own interpretation of the cinema's social function. On one hand are the amateurs who saw their filmmaking and participation in a network of other filmmakers as producing a coherent alternative film public that stood in contradistinction to the mass, popular film public. In this category we might find a film experimenter, such as Ralph Steiner, whose participation in amateur activities foreshadowed the development of an American film avant-garde. But in a related, if surprising, way, we might also find ACL leaders and theorists like Maxim and Winton, whose writings expressed a similar—if differently organized—interest in connecting amateurs and communities of amateurs in order to facilitate their social and aesthetic intercommunication.

On the other hand—and in contrast to these amateurs who hoped to actively shape an alternative film public—we find filmmakers whose participation in amateur culture provided a continuation of middle-class parlor culture. Like those members of the middle class who, in the late nineteenth and early twentieth centuries, performed music and participated in amateur theatricals as part of their regular leisure activities, some amateurs understood filmmaking as a continuation of this kind of activity and a logical alternative to the more passive recreations provided by the phonograph and commercial radio, movies, and eventually television. We find this mode suggested by amateurs who were principally engaged in chronicle filming as well as in photoplay productions like *A Study in Reds*, which drew on genteel club culture. In these instances, amateurs understood filmmaking as a happy and active pastime and understood the ACL and PSA as organizations that could help identify fellow hobbyists and therefore expand the walls of their parlor almost infinitely. By emphasizing the parlor-like, or domestic, aspects of amateur film activity over the more public versions, some amateurs were able to insulate themselves from mass popular culture, in effect wrapping a new technology in a domestic context and a "culture of reassurance."[4] These two poles of amateur film practice—the alternative film public and the expanded domestic parlor—provide us with a broad spectrum within which we can locate the activities of particular films or filmmakers.

But even as this study of amateur cinema provides a number of ways for analyzing the social terrain of middlebrow culture in the mid-twentieth century, this book has argued that a consideration of the films themselves needs to play a central role in this historical account. Nearly all of the movies discussed in this study draw from commercial film style and are therefore in some way "vernacular" in their relationship to both institutional practices (Hollywood or art cinemas) and informal, local, and unofficial practices (in works by amateurs). But we can specify three principal relationships to dominant practices: first were the amateur works that drew on commercial film as a model of technical competency and stylistic clarity; second were amateur movies that engaged commercial film as homage to or parody of its genre, content, and narrative conventions; third, and finally, were amateur works that presented an explicit alternative to dominant practices through their use of modernist visual styles and narrative fragmentation. Amateurs also engaged film as a self-reflective surface that allowed them to see themselves in different ways and imagine themselves according to different situations, social conditions, and narrative scenarios. Amateur film competitions were populated by works reflecting these different relations to dominant commercial production—but if technical proficiency (not perfection) provided a crucial component of award-winning films, so too did sincerity of purpose and expression.

In contrast to accounts of middlebrow culture that dismiss the significance of aesthetic objects and experiences, this book has argued that amateur films are complex and meaningful objects: these are texts that reveal, with varying degrees of success, a striving for aesthetic experience in everyday life. From the creative shapings of personal material, to meditations on fleeting but quotidian—and even practical—phenomena, to the playful rearticulations of established or popular narrative modes, amateurs outlined an aesthetics that engaged a technological means of representation in order to imbue everyday materials with compositional sophistication, wonder, and sincerity. In this belief in the creative potential of the everyday, we find an affinity between amateur work and John Dewey's aesthetic philosophy. "The task," Dewey writes, "is to restore continuity between the refined and intensified forms of experience that are works of art and the everyday events, doings, and sufferings that are universally recognized to constitute experience."[5] In this quotation, we can see how Dewey's pragmatic theory attempts to narrow the gap between aesthetic experience and everyday experience. Correspondingly, amateur filmmaking may be understood as a creative attempt to make everyday life more meaningful and thus to ameliorate the alienation associated with a modern and mass-media-oriented world.

Amateur film culture in the mid-twentieth century was a mode of participatory leisure and creative art making that brought technological craftsmanship into contact with everyday experience. This middle-class and middlebrow form was defined, therefore, by its pragmatic application of creative sensibility and technical proficiency to everyday experiences and diverse viewpoints. The recent development of amateur digital media equipment, which makes individual responses and expressions more numerous and widely circulated than ever before, testifies to the widespread desire for this kind of participatory media engagement. Indeed, the amateur film culture discussed in this book constitutes an important prehistory of examinations of our contemporary intermedial reception and digital convergence culture.[6] The gradual emergence, in recent decades, of home theatres, DVDs, and the Internet has allowed for a return of the more active spectator-participant. And if recent digital technologies facilitate new and more widely disseminated personal motion pictures, tribute works, and multimedia "mash-ups," surely the cases discussed in this book suggest that the impulse—and indeed some of the technical capability—to produce such works has a much longer history. My point here is not to suggest a direct lineage between the ACL and YouTube; important distinctions should be made between the social and aesthetic operations of these two media cultures, separated by many decades.[7] Rather, I want to emphasize that these groups share certain qualities of the pragmatic imagination, including the complex set of relationships between mass media and private production, commercial and vernacular styles, and consumer technology and personal creativity.

Finally, this study of amateur cinema also provides some methodological insights. Tracking down individual amateur films and researching them allows us to connect local (and localized) materials, documents, and artworks to larger cultural and aesthetic issues. Taken individually, many of these films are fascinating and idiosyncratic works; when looked at as a group they evidence a significant cultural and aesthetic phenomenon that we are just beginning to understand. Works that existed sometimes in only a single copy, amateur films are singular and ephemeral artifacts belonging to an era of mass reproducibility and at risk of disappearing from our record of twentieth-century visual culture. What these films represent is equally singular: they are individual traces of experience, recorded in motion pictures and shaped by pragmatic imagination.

APPENDIX 1

Amateur Filmography

This filmography presents a list of extant amateur films consulted during the research for this book. A complete list of the annual ACL Ten Best films can be found in Alan Kattelle, "The Amateur Cinema League and Its Films," *Film History*, 15, no. 2 (2003). The list here is more restricted in the sense that it includes only extant films. But it also includes other significant amateur works that won honorable mention or prizes in other competitions as well as works that are noteworthy for other reasons.

KEY TO ABBREVIATIONS

Amateur Award or Reference

AC	American Cinematographer
AMM	Amateur Movie Makers
HM	honorable mention, ACL
MM	Movie Makers
PSA	Photographic Society of America
SC	Special Class, ACL

Location

CFA	Chicago Film Archives
EAFA	East Anglian Film Archive (Norwich, UK)
GEH	George Eastman House (Rochester, NY)
HSFA	Human Studies Film Archive (Washington DC)
IU	Indiana University, Lilly Library
LAC	Library and Archives Canada (Ottawa)
LOC	Library of Congress (Washington DC)

NARA	National Archives and Records Administration (Washington DC)
NHF	Northeast Historic Film (Bucksport, ME)
NLM	National Library of Medicine (Bethesda, MD)
PA	Prelinger Archives (San Francisco, CA)
SUNY	State University of New York, Binghamton
TFVC	Toronto Film and Video Club
WCFTR	Wisconsin Center for Film and Theater Research (Madison)

Title	Producer	Year released	Amateur reference	Location/online video
Annapolis	Edward Bollinger	1934	ACL member	LAC
Another Day	Leslie Thatcher	1934	Ten Best 1934	TFVC
				www.nyu.edu/orphanfilm/amateurfilms/
An Apple a Day	F. R. Crawley	1939	HM 1939	LAC
At the Sandpits	F. R. Crawley	1933	ACL member	LAC
Autumn Glory	John Kibar	1946	HM 1946	CFA
				www.chicagofilmarchives.org/collections/index.php/Detail/Object/Show/object_id/3522
A Bronx Morning	Jay Leyda	1931	MM contributor	Unseen Cinema[1]
"Building a Bakery 1930: Harvesting and Baking"	Dent Harrison	1930	ACL member	LAC
Camera Clippings	Narcisse Pelletier	1940s	ACL member	LAC
Ceramics	Kenneth Bloomer, Elizabeth Sansom	1933	Ten Best 1933	NARA
Duck Soup	Delores and Timothy Lawler Harmon Foundation	1952	Ten Best 1952	Filmmaker's private collection
Education for Life	(Mr. and Mrs. Ray Garner)	1941	HM (SC) 1941	NARA
Eyes of Science	James Sibley Watson and Melville Webber	1931	Ten Best 1931	GEH

(continued)

(continued)

Title	Producer	Year released	Amateur reference	Location/online video
Fairy Princess	Margaret Conneely	1956	PSA Ten Best	CFA
				www.chicagofilmarchives.org/collections/index.php/Detail/Object/Show/object_id/4797
The Fall of the House of Usher	James Sibley Watson and Melville Webber	1928	MM, Jan. 1929	Unseen Cinema
The Farmer's Daughter	Long Beach Cinema Club	1947	MM, Nov. 1947	CFA
Film Editing	Harmon Foundation (Kenneth Space)	1939	HM (SC) 1939	NARA
Filmorama Travels	Ron Doerring and George Ives	c. 1955	Movie club member	CFA
Fishers of Grande Anse	Leslie Thatcher	1935	Ten Best 1935	TFVC
Fluffy, the Kitten	Kenneth Space	1940	Ten Best 1940	SUNY[2]
Fly Low Jack and the Game	Marion Gleason	1927	AMM, October 1927	GEH[2]
A Footnote to Fact	Lewis Jacobs	1933	MM contributor	Unseen Cinema
The Forgotten Frontier	Marvin Breckinridge	1930	HM 1930	NLM
				www.youtube.com/watch?v=OWu5IuzOt9c
Glimpses of a Canoe Trip	F.R. Crawley	1937	HM 1937	LAC
Hail British Columbia	Leo Heffernan	1941	Ten Best 1941	LAC
Happy Day	T. Lawrenson	1934	AC 1935 contest	EAFA
			1937 Japan Intl. Contest	www.eafa.org.uk/catalogue/3397

Hearts of the West	Theodore Huff	1931	Ten Best 1931	GEH
Hell Bound Train	James and Eloyce Gist	c. 1933	None	LOC www.youtube.com /watch?v=V2gCY2P8qR8
Her Heart's Desire	Othon Goetz	1949	HM 1949	CFA www.chicagofilmarchives.org /collections/index.php/Detail /Object/Show/object_id/2619
The Highwayman	Toronto Amateur Movie Club	1938	MM, May 1938	TFVC
The Highway of Tomorrow or How One Makes Two	Dent Harrison	1930	Member (ACL logo)	LAC
How to Use Filters	Harmon Foundation (Kenneth Space)	1940	HM (SC) 1940	NARA
How to Use Your Camera	Harmon Foundation (Kenneth Space)	1938	Ten Best (SC) 1938	NARA
H₂O	Ralph Steiner	1929	MM, June 1929	*Unseen Cinema*
I'd Be Delighted To!	S. Winston Childs	1932	AC Contest 1932	EAFA www.eafa.org.uk/catalogue/3436
In the Beginning	Fred C. Ells	1935	Ten Best 1935	NARA
Julius Caesar	David Bradley	1950	MM, Mar. 1950	IU
Life and Death of 9413— a Hollywood Extra	Robert Florey	1927	MM, Jan. 1929	*Unseen Cinema*
L'Isle d'Orléans	F. R. and Judith Crawley	1939	Ten Best 1939	LAC
Little Geezer	Theodore Huff	1932	HM 1932	*Unseen Cinema*
Lot in Sodom	Watson and Webber	1932	Ten Best 1932	*Unseen Cinema*

(continued)

(continued)

Title	Producer	Year released	Amateur reference	Location/online video
The Love of Zero	Robert Florey	1928	MM, Jan. 1929	Unseen Cinema
Lullaby	Tatsuichi Okamoto	1932	AC Contest 1932	EAFA
Macbeth	David Bradley	1947	Ten Best (SC) 1947	IU
Mag the Hag	Hiram Percy Maxim	1925	Maxim	NHF http://oldfilm.org/content/mag-hag
Manhatta	Charles Sheeler and Paul Strand	1921	None	Unseen Cinema
Man of Aran	Robert Flaherty	1934	MM, Dec. 1934	DVD
Mechanical Principles	Ralph Steiner	1930	None	Unseen Cinema
Meshes of the Afternoon	Maya Deren	1943	HM (SC) 1945	DVD
Mighty Niagara	Leslie Thatcher	c.1933	ACL member	TFVC
Mr. Motorboat's Last Stand	John Flory (with Theodore Huff)	1933	Ten Best 1933	GEH
Nanook of the North	Robert Flaherty	1922	AMM, May 1927	DVD
Old Vic at Kronborg: Hamlet	John Hansen	1937	ACL member	HSFA
On the Farm	Harmon Foundation (Mr. and Mrs. Ray Garner)	1940	Ten Best (SC) 1940	NARA
Peer Gynt	David Bradley	1941	HM 1941	IU www.unseen-cinema.com/PeerGynt.mov

Title	Filmmaker	Year	Recognition	Source
Portrait of a Young Man	Henwar Rodakiewicz	1932	Ten Best 1932	*Unseen Cinema*
A Race for Ties	Dorothea Mitchell	1929	MM, Sept. 1929	DVD
				http://vimeo.com/19344084
Safari	Margaret Conneely	1950	MM, Dec. 1950	CFA
San Francisco	Tullio Pellegrini	1955	PSA member	PA
				https://archive.org/details/SanFrancisco1955CinemascopeFilm
The Sea	H.P. Maxim	c. 1928	*Photoplay* 1929	NHF
Seaside Holiday	F.R. Crawley	1934	ACL member	LAC
Skyscraper Symphony	Robert Florey	1929	MM, Jan. 1929	*Unseen Cinema*
Snow White	F.B. Richards	c.1916	None	NHF
So Long Ago	Margaret Conneely	1950s	ACL member	CFA
Sredni Vashtar	David Bradley	1943	ACL member	*Unseen Cinema*
The Story of Bamba	Harmon Foundation (Ray Garner)	1939	HM (SC) 1939	NARA
Studies in Blue and Chartres Cathedral	John V. Hansen	1932	Ten Best 1932	HSFA
				www.youtube.com/watch?v=QRNlHILGZQ4
Study in Reds	Miriam Bennett	1932	MM, Feb. 1932	WCFTR
				www.youtube.com/watch?v=6Vqt7-HK-YA
Surf and Seaweed	Ralph Steiner	1930	None	*Unseen Cinema*
Susie Steps Out	George Ives and Ron Doerring	1955	Movie club member	CFA
				www.chicagofilmarchives.org/collections/index.php/Detail/Object/Show/object_id/3573

(continued)

(continued)

Title	Producer	Year released	Amateur reference	Location/online video
Tarzan and the Rocky Gorge	Robbins Barstow	1936	Member (ACL logo)	LOC https://archive.org/details/homemovie_tarzan_and_rocky_gorge
Tarzan Jr.	William Palmer and Ernest Page	1932	AC contest 1932	EAFA
Telltale Heart	Charles Klein	1928	MM	Unseen Cinema
Then Came the King	Earl Clark	1939	Ten Best 1939	LAC
The Tie That Binds	Ottawa Ciné Club	1942	ACL members	LAC
Tombs of the Nobles	John Hansen	1931	Ten Best 1931	HSFA
Toronto's Royal Day	Toronto Amateur Movie Club	1939	ACL members	www.youtube.com/watch?v=w6RE7l5jt7g TFVC
Toy Town Fantasy	Henry Sedziak	1941	Ciné club member	LAC
24 Dollar Island	Robert Flaherty	c. 1926	AMM, May 1927	Unseen Cinema
Ultima Thule and Peggy's Cove	Mr. and Mrs Edward Bollinger [sic]	1935	Ten Best 1935	LAC
We Are All Artists	Harmon Foundation Alon Bement (Charles Carbonaro, filmer)	1936	ACL affiliated	NARA www.youtube.com/watch?v=bcsIm6m6DBk

[1] *Unseen Cinema* refers to a multidisc DVD collection titled *Unseen Cinema: Early American Avant Garde Film 1894–1941*, seven discs, curated by Bruce Posner (Image Entertainment, 2005). Some additional clips of amateur and related films can be found here: www.unseen-cinema.com.
[2] Located but not viewed.

APPENDIX 2

A Preliminary Directory of Movie Clubs (by location)

While not an exhaustive listing, this directory is based on references to movie clubs in *Movie Makers, American Cinematographer,* and other amateur ephemera (c. 1926–60, earliest citation listed). Reflecting the American focus of these sources, the directory is most detailed as a listing of clubs in the United States; its listing of clubs in other countries is only fragmentary but is included here for additional context.

AUSTRALIA

Australian Amateur Cine Society (1938)

Australian Amateur Film Club (Sydney) (1928)

Cinematographers of Melbourne (1941)

Mosman Cine Club of Sydney (1927)

AUSTRIA

Club der Kino-Amateure Oesterreichs (Austrian Cine-Amateurs' Club, Vienna) (1928)

ARGENTINA

Cine Club Argentino of Buenos Aires (1938)

CANADA

Amateur Cinema Club of Montreal (1930)

Hamilton Movie Makers (1940)

Movie Makers Club of Ottawa (1940)

Toronto Amateur Movie Club (1934)

CHINA

Amateur Cinema League of Shanghai (1930)

GERMANY

Bund der Film-Amateure Deutschlands (German Alliance of Film Amateurs, Berlin) (1928)

INDIA

Amateur Cine Society of India (1941)

Motion Picture Society of India (1937)

JAPAN

Baby Kinema Club (1928)

Cherry Amateur Movie Society (Sakura Kogata Eiga Kyokai) of Tokyo (1938)

NETHERLANDS

Smalfilmliga Amsterdam (1933)

NEW ZEALAND

Auckland Amateur Motion Picture Club (1928)

UNITED KINGDOM

Amateur Movie Makers Club of Sheffield (1928)

Bradford (UK) Amateur Kinematograph Society (1930)

Grasshopper Group (1956)

Thames Valley Photoplayers (Reading) (1928)

UNITED STATES

California

Amateur Movie Makers Club of San Francisco (1928)

Amateur Movie Makers of California (San Francisco) (1927)
Cinema Club of San Francisco (1933)
Cine-Section of the California Camera Club (1927)
Columbia Cub Productions (Columbia Studios) (1938)
Columbia's Camera Club (CBS Radio, Hollywood) (1939)
8–16 Movie Makers Club of Santa Ana (1944)
Greater Oakland Motion Picture Club (1933)
La Casa Movie Club of Alhambra (1944)
La Jolla Cinema League (1928)
Long Beach Cinema Club (1941)
Los Angeles Amateur Cine Club (1932)
Los Angeles 8mm Club (1934)
Oakland Motion Picture Club (1942)
Paramount Movie Club (AC, April 1937)
Playcrafters Club of Stockton High School (1928)
San Diego Motion Picture Club (1927)
Sierra Cinema League of Fresno (1933)
Southern California Projectionists' Amateur Camera Club (1940)
Southern Cinema Club (Los Angeles) (1942)
Stanford Studios (Stanford University) (1928)
Valley 8mm Club (Los Angeles) (1950)
Westwood Movie Club of San Francisco (1942)

Colorado

Colorado Springs Cinema Club (1941)

Connecticut

Hartford Amateur Picture Players (1928)
Moving Picture Club of New Haven (1927)
Purity Players (Yale University) (1927)
Stamford Cinema Club (1950)

District of Columbia
- Washington Cinema Club (1928)
- Washington Society of Amateur Cinematographers (1941)

Georgia
- Amateur Movie Makers of Atlanta (1950)

Hawaii
- Honolulu 8mm Club (1937)

Idaho
- Pocatello Idaho Camera Club (1944)

Illinois
- Aurora Cine Club (1944)
- Avondale Methodist Camera Club (1952)
- Blue Island Movie & Slide Club (1952)
- Chicago Cinema Club (1933)
- Edison Camera Club (Chicago) (1952)
- Metro Movie Club of River Park (1937)
- Movie Makers Club of Chicago (1927)
- Palmer Park Movie & Slide Club (1952)
- Rockford Movie Makers (1942)
- South Side Cinema Club (Chicago) (1939)
- Suburban Movie Club (Cicero) (1944)
- Triangle Cinema League of Chicago (formerly the Jewish Peoples' Institute [JPI] Cinema League) (1933)
- Waukegan Camera Club (1952)

Indiana
- Calumet Movie & Slide Club (1952)
- Indianapolis Amateur Movie Club (1937)

Iowa
- Amateur Movie Club of Waterloo (1929)
- Cinema Club of Sioux City, Iowa (1941)

Players' Club (Roosevelt High School, Des Moines) (1927)

Tri-City Cinema Club (Davenport, IA, and Rock Island and Moline, IL) (1937)

Maryland

Parkville Cinema Club (1941)

Massachusetts

Boston Camera Club (1950)

Boston Cinema Club (1933)

Little Screen Players of Boston (1927)

Movie Club of Western Massachusetts (Springfield) (1927)

Michigan

Blue Bell Camera Club (Detroit) (1937)

Grand Rapids Amateur Movie Club (1944)

Minnesota

Metropolitan Cine Club of St. Paul (1940)

Minneapolis Cine Club (1936)

Minneapolis Octo-Cine Guild (1941)

St. Paul Amateur Movie Makers' Club (1940)

Missouri

Amateur Motion Picture Club of St. Louis (1943)

8–16 Movie Club of Kansas City (1950)

Kansas City Cinema League (1933)

New Jersey

Amateur Motion Picture Club Siegfried (Jersey City) (1927)

Bergen County Cine Club (1932)

Cumberland Amateur Motion Picture Club of Vineland (1928)

Millville Society of Cinematographers (1942)

Motion Picture Club of the Oranges (1926)

Patterson Cinema Club (1941)

Undergraduate Motion Picture Club of Princeton (1928)

New York
- Amateur Movie Makers of Flushing (1928)
- Brooklyn Amateur Cine Club (1943)
- Colgate University Amateur Motion Picture Club (1927)
- Flower City Amateur Movie Club (Rochester) (1928)
- Metropolitan Motion Picture Club (1933)
- Mount Kisco Cinemat Club (1933)
- Mount Vernon Movie Makers (1941)
- New York 8mm Club (1939)
- Photo Engravers Camera Club (1950)
- Rochester Cinema Club (1928)
- Rochester Community Players (1927)
- Staten Island Cinema Club (1937)
- Syracuse Movie Club (1927)
- Syracuse Movie Makers (1941)
- Taft Cinema Club (Bronx) (1950)

Ohio
- Canton Movie Club (1950)
- Cincinnati Movie Club (1950)
- Cine-Section of the Cleveland Photographic Society (1927)
- Cleveland Amateur Cinematographers (1940)
- Petite Movie Makers Club (Toledo) (1927)

Oklahoma
- Movie Makers of Oklahoma City (1950)

Oregon
- Portland Cine Club (1927)

Pennsylvania
- Cinema Crafters of Philadelphia (1927)
- Cinema League of Philadelphia (1933)
- Little Film Guild of Philadelphia (1927)
- Paramount Motion Picture Club (Manheim) (1927)

Philadelphia Amateur Moving Picture Club (1927)
Philadelphia Cinema Club (1937)
Philadelphia 8–16 Movie Club (1941)
Philadelphia Motion Picture Club (1927)
Pittsburgh Amateur Movie Club (1933)
Zutto Players of Philadelphia (1928)

Tennessee
Memphis Motion Picture Club (1927)

Texas
San Antonio Camera YMCA Camera Club (Cine Section) (1928)

Utah
Utah Amateur Movie Club (1941)
Utah Cine Arts Club (1946)

Washington
Seattle Amateur Movie Club (1946)
Seattle 8mm Club (1938)

West Virginia
Greenbrier Movie Club (White Sulphur Springs) (1932)

Wisconsin
Amateur Movie Society of Milwaukee (1946)
Cinema Guild of Milwaukee (1927)
Kenosha Movie Club (1952)
Milwaukee Movie Makers (1932)

Notes

INTRODUCTION

1. Stan Brakhage, "In Defense of Amateur," in Stan Brakhage, *Essential Brakhage: Selected Writings on Film-Making,* ed. Bruce R. McPherson (1971; New York: Documentext, 2001), 144.
2. "Amateur Cinema League: A Close-Up," *Amateur Movie Makers,* December 1926, 7. The magazine title was shortened in 1928 to simply *Movie Makers;* hereafter referred to as *AMM* or *MM*.
3. Abraham Rees, *The Cyclopedia: Or, Universal Dictionary of Arts, Sciences, and Literature* (London: Longman, Hurst, Rees, Orme, and Browne, 1820), c. 1803; from *Oxford English Dictionary Online* definition of *amateur*.
4. Robert A. Stebbins, *Amateurs, Professionals, and Serious Leisure* (Montreal: McGill-Queen's University Press, 1992).
5. See, for example, Neil Harris, *Humbug: The Art of P. T. Barnum* (Chicago: University of Chicago Press, 1973); especially chapter 3, "The Operational Aesthetic," 61–89.
6. Bliss Perry, "The Amateur Spirit," in *The Amateur Spirit* (Boston: Houghton, Mifflin, and Company, 1904), 20.
7. Ibid., 31.
8. Ibid., 30, 31.
9. Walter Benjamin, "The Work of Art in the Age of Its Technological Reproducibility," in *Walter Benjamin: Selected Writings,* vol. 3: *1935–1938,* ed. Howard Eiland and Michael W. Jennings (Cambridge, MA: Harvard University Press, 2002), 114.
10. Paul Spencer Sternberger, *Between Amateur and Aesthete: The Legitimization of Photography as Art in America, 1880–1890* (Albuquerque: University of New Mexico Press, 2001), 110–11. See also Grace Seiberling, *Amateurs, Photography, and the Mid-Victorian Imagination* (Chicago: University of California Press, 1986).
11. Pierre Bourdieu, *Photography: A Middle-Brow Art,* trans. Shaun Whiteside (Stanford, CA: Stanford University Press, 1990), 64–65. In a similar

vein, studies of the American Book-of-the-Month Club (which, like the ACL, emerged in the late 1920s) have traced the social terrain of middlebrow culture, but tended to undervalue the aesthetic experiences such organizations facilitated; see Joan Rubin, "Self, Culture, and Self-Culture in Modern America: The Early History of the Book-of-the-Month Club," *Journal of American History* 71, no. 4 (March 1985); and Janice Radway, "The Scandal of the Middlebrow," *South Atlantic Quarterly* 89, no. 4 (Fall 1990). See also Dwight Macdonald, "Masscult and Midcult," in *Against the American Grain* (New York: Random House, 1960); and Lawrence Levine, *Highbrow/Lowbrow: The Emergence of Cultural Hierarchy in America* (Cambridge, MA: Harvard University Press, 1988).

12. Roger Cardinal, "The Self in Self-Taught Art," in *Self-Taught Art: The Culture and Aesthetics of American Vernacular Art*, ed. Charles Russell (Jackson: University of Mississippi Press, 2001), 70. Certainly, most amateur films—travelogues, informational films, and goofy theatricals—don't look like "folk art," which is more brazenly fantastic, tending to deface clear images and surfaces. In a more recent context, the term *folk art* is already being used to describe media phenomena such as the digital camera self-portraiture ("selfies") on networking websites like Facebook; see Alex Williams, "Here I Am Taking My Own Picture," *New York Times*, February 19, 2006, section 9, 1.

13. Michael Owen Jones, "The Aesthetics of Everyday Life," in *Self-Taught Art*, ed. Russell, 60. Jones's comments chime with the title of the amateur sponsored film *We Are All Artists* (Harmon Foundation, 1936), which will be discussed in more detail in chapter 8.

14. Richard Chalfen, *Snapshot Versions of Life* (Bowling Green, OH: Bowling Green State University Popular Press, 1987); and Richard Chalfen, "Media Myopia and Genre Centrism: The Case of Home Movies," *Journal of Film and Video* 38, nos. 3–4 (Summer/Fall 1986): 58–62.

15. See, for example, Karen L. Ishizuka and Patricia R. Zimmermann, eds., *Mining the Home Movie: Excavations in Histories and Memories* (Berkeley: University of California Press, 2008); and Frances Guerin, *Through Amateur Eyes: Film and Photography in Nazi Germany* (Minneapolis: University of Minnesota Press, 2011).

16. Patricia R. Zimmermann, "Startling Angles: Amateur Film and the Early Avant-Garde," in *Lovers of Cinema: The First American Film Avant-Garde, 1919–1945*, ed. Jan-Christopher Horak (Madison: University of Wisconsin Press, 1995), 142–43; see also Zimmermann's *Reel Families: A Social History of Amateur Film* (Bloomington: Indiana University Press, 1995); and "Morphing History into Histories," *Moving Image* 1, no. 1 (2001): 109–30.

17. Ryan Shand productively suggests that we consider a "community mode" alongside the "home mode" of amateur cinema in his essay "Theorizing Amateur Cinema: Limitations and Possibilities," *Moving Image* 8, no. 2 (Fall 2008): 36–60.

18. See, for example, Melinda Stone and Dan Streible, eds., *Small-Gauge and Amateur Film*, special issue of *Film History* 15, no. 2 (2003). Amateur

filmmaking has also received more attention in Europe: for amateur film culture in the United Kingdom see Ian Craven, ed., *Movies on Home Ground* (Newcastle upon Tyne: Cambridge Scholars Publishing, 2009); and Heather Norris Nicholson, *Amateur Film: Meaning and Practice, 1927–77* (Manchester: Manchester University Press, 2012); on Polish amateur film culture, see Neil Cummings and Marysia Lewandowska's *Enthusiasts: From Amateur Film Clubs* (Warsaw: Centre for Contemporary Art, 2004); and *Enthusiasm: Films of Love, Longing and Labour* (London: Whitechapel Art Gallery, 2005); for France, *Le cinema en amateur*, special issue of *Communications* 68 (1999), edited by Roger Odin; for Germany, see Michael Kuball's two-volume study *Familienkino: Geschichte des Amateurfilms in Deutschland* (Hamburg: Rowohlt, 1980).

19. Melinda Stone, "'If It Moves, We'll Shoot It': The San Diego Amateur Movie Club," *Film History* 15, no. 2 (2003); and her dissertation of the same title, University of California, San Diego, 2003.

20. Jan-Christopher Horak, ed., *Lovers of the Cinema: The First American Avant-Garde, 1919–1945* (Madison: University of Wisconsin Press, 1995). See also Bruce Posner's multipart *Unseen Cinema* retrospective and DVD compilation.

21. Alan Kattelle, *Home Movies: A History of the American Industry, 1897–1979* (Nashua, NH: Transition Publishing, 2000).

22. Alan D. Kattelle, "The Amateur Cinema League and Its Films," *Film History* 15, no. 2 (2003).

23. Tom Gunning, "The Cinema of Attractions: Early Film, Its Spectator and the Avant-Farde," in *Early Cinema: Space, Frame, Narrative*, ed. Thomas Elsaesser (London: BFI, 1990), 57.

24. Miriam Hansen, "The Mass Production of the Senses: Classical Cinema as Vernacular Modernism," *Modernism/Modernity* 6, no. 2 (1999).

25. Pragmatism offers a productive, but generally overlooked, context for considering not only the history of amateur film but also a range of issues in cinema and media studies. American pragmatism has undergone a minor resurgence in the past decade, thanks in part to Louis Menand's anthology of texts, *Pragmatism: A Reader* (New York: Vintage, 1997), and his intellectual history of the movement, *The Metaphysical Club* (New York: Farrar, Straus and Giroux, 2001). John Durham Peters's *Speaking into the Air: A History of the Idea of Communication* (Chicago: University of Chicago Press, 1999) begins a similar recuperation of Dewey's work in the area of communication studies.

CHAPTER 1. CINÉ-PROPHECY

1. For example, there is something queer about this film's final shot. Though it may not be deliberately subversive (women often played male roles at boarding schools), the drawn-out quality of the kiss is at very least meant to draw our attention to this comical aspect of the casting. The talisman's powers—and indeed the film's narrative—might reflect a wish to transform an inappropriate

couple into an appropriate match, but this is ultimately a wish that is only partly fulfilled. Mark Neumann follows a similar—if more explicitly Freudian—line of interpretation of this aspect of the film in his "Home Movies on Freud's Couch," *Moving Image* 2, no. 1 (Spring 2002).

2. "The Newest Magic of Motion Pictures," *Kodakery* 13, no. 9 (May 1926): 3.

3. In the context of the original poem, the poet begs for the power of supplementary vision in hopes of avoiding personal humiliation (of having visible lice in church, for example), suggesting not so much narcissism as a good-humored modesty: that we would all benefit from seeing our social performances and foolishness. Of course the quote also points to the strong Anglo-Scottish demeanor of Maxim and to the cultural homogeneity of the founding members of the league, almost all of them affluent New Englanders.

4. William James, "The Self," excerpt from *The Principles of Psychology* (1891), reprinted in *The Philosophy of William James* (New York: Random House, 1925), 128.

5. "Amateur Cinema League: A Close Up," *AMM*, December 1926, 7.

6. Maxim's declarations recall claims for cinema as a universal language that had circulated since the medium's earliest days; see Miriam Hansen's *Babel and Babylon: Spectatorship in American Silent Film* (Cambridge, MA: Harvard University Press, 1991).

7. For an authoritative account of Alexander Black's career see Kaveh Askari's "Moving Pictures before Motion Pictures: The Pictorial Tradition and American Media Aesthetics, 1890–1920," PhD dissertation, University of Chicago, 2005; and "Early 16mm Color by a Career Amateur," *Film History* 21, no. 2 (2009): 150–63.

8. Black also penned a guide to photography for amateurs. C. L. Gregory, "Amateurs Organize," *The Camera,* October 1926: 247; Charles Musser, *The Emergence of Cinema* (Berkeley: University of California Press, 1994), 40–42.

9. Quoted in Noël Burch, *Life to Those Shadows,* trans. Ben Brewster (Berkeley: University of California Press, 1990), 26.

10. Tom Gunning, "New Thresholds of Vision," in *Impossible Presence: Surface and Screen in the Photogenic Era,* ed. Terry Smith (Chicago: University of Chicago Press, 2001), 79.

11. Historian Deac Rossell suggests that during the earliest period of film history, before 1910, there was a somewhat blurry line between amateurs and professionals and that "amateur" and "professional" film productions in the 1890s looked very similar. "Amateur Film," in the *Encyclopedia of Early Cinema,* ed. Richard Abel (New York: Routledge, 2005), 17–18.

12. The EHK format was introduced in 1912, but only five hundred projectors were sold, and no camera was made available; see Ben Singer, "Early Home Cinema and the Edison Home Projecting Kinetoscope," *Film History* 2 (1988). Pathéscope was introduced the same year and had a longer and more successful lifespan; see Anke Mebold and Charles Tepperman, "Resurrecting the Lost History of 28mm Film in North America," *Film History* 15, no. 3 (2003). For

the history of amateur film technology more generally, see Alan Kattelle, *Home Movies: A History of the American Industry, 1897–1979* (Nashua, NH: Transition Publishing, 2000).

13. "Cinematography, a New Art of Amateurs," *Arts and Decoration*, September 1919, 230.

14. The few amateur 28mm productions that survive demonstrate this while also foreshadowing the kinds of films made by later amateurs, including home movies, travelogues, and even amateur dramatics. An interesting example of this final category is a theatrical-dance version of *Snow White* (Colonel F. B. Richards, c. 1916–17) performed at a Maine country club, which foreshadows the later links between theatrical production and amateur cinema. Though little evidence suggests that the 28mm format became a medium for widespread amateur film production, some amateurs continued to shoot on 28mm stock late into the 1920s.

15. Robert Allerton Parker, "The Art of the Camera, an Experimental Movie," *Arts and Decoration*, October 1921, 414, reprinted in *Spellbound in Darkness*, ed. George C. Pratt (Greenwich, CT: New York Graphic Society, 1973).

16. "Those Millimeters," *AMM*, March 1927, 5.

17. The quoted phrase comes from Tom Gunning, "'Animated Pictures': Tales of Cinema's Forgotten Future," *Michigan Quarterly Review* 34 (Fall 1995).

18. On the relationship between guns and cameras, see Paul Virilio, *War and Cinema*, trans. Patrick Camiller (London: Verso, 1989); and Patricia R. Zimmermann, "Cameras and Guns: 1941–1949," in her *Reel Families: A Social History of Amateur Film* (Bloomington: Indiana University Press, 1995). There was also a direct link between hunting and filmmaking in *Amateur Movie Makers* as hunting films became a common subgenre for amateur moviemakers.

19. Dorothy Rowden, "Colored Home Movies by Radio?," *AMM*, December 1926, 25.

20. Katherine M. Comstock, "Hiram Percy Maxim—Inventor and Fan; First of a Series of Portraits of Leaders of the Amateur Cinema League," *MM*, June 1928, 396.

21. Clinton DeSoto, *Two Hundred Meters and Down: The Story of Amateur Radio* (West Hartford, CT: American Radio Relay League, 1936), 38–43; Alice C. Schumacher, *Hiram Percy Maxim* (Electric Radio Press, 1998).

22. Rowden, "Colored Home Movies by Radio?," 24–25.

23. Television would also, within a couple of years, start to emerge as a theme in both articles and films by amateurs.

24. Roy W. Winton, "The Amateur Cinema Camera Man—before the 1927 Meeting of the National Board of Review of Motion Pictures," *AMM*, March 1927, 28.

25. Ralph Block, "The Movies versus the Motion Pictures," *Century Magazine*, vol. 102, October 1921, 890. In 1921, Block proposed the founding of

a little movie movement and prophetically suggested that "a nation-wide amateur organization growing out of such a movement might find at once a potential audience which the professional movie-producer and distributor has never touched."

26. Roy Walter Winton, "A Maecenas for the Movies," *AMM*, December 1926, 32.

27. Block, "The Movies versus the Motion Pictures," 892.

28. No less than Eugene O'Neill, a central figure of the Little Theatre movement, supported Ralph Block's call for a little movie movement, writing him in 1921 to say, "I am interested in what you say of planning for a new latitude in screen expression. I saw *Caligari* and it sure opened my eyes to wonderful possibilities I had never dreamed of before. So, count me in by all means. Why not a picture Little Theatre movement—at least for one theatre in New York?" Quoted in Richard Hayes, "'The Scope of the Movies': Three Films and Their Influence on Eugene O'Neill," *Eugene O'Neill Review* 25, nos. 1–2 (Spring/Fall 2001). Another, related phenomenon is the relationship between amateur cinema and the so-called Little Magazines, which were small-circulation journals for new poetry, literature, and criticism. One of the most significant of these Little Magazines was *The Dial*, whose publisher, James Sibley Watson Jr., was also one of the most important experimental amateur filmmakers of the late 1920s and early '30s.

29. The author continues, "Consider the Abbey Theatre, and how the two Fay brothers began it with only ambitious amateurs for artists. Consider the Moscow Art Company, and Stanislavsky's story of the family theatricals. It is possible for any family with a cinematographic taste to buy a little camera and projector, and for any theatrical group of screen aspirants to do likewise." "The Little Movie in England," *AMM*, December 1926, 18.

30. Dorothy Chansky, *Composing Ourselves: The Little Theatre Movement and the American Audience* (Carbondale: University of Southern Illinois Press, 2004), 3.

31. Winton, "The Amateur Cinema Camera Man," 37.

32. Marguerite Tazelaar, "Portrait of a Pioneer," *AMM*, July 1927, 18–19.

33. Ibid., 19. See also Roland Marchand, *Advertising the American Dream* (Berkeley: University of California Press, 1985), for a discussion of how advertising filtered high art styles into American mass culture during this period.

34. Winton, "The Amateur Cinema Camera Man," 37.

35. Haidee Wasson, *Museum Movies* (Berkeley: University of California, 2005), 39.

36. Mina Brownstein, "Filming with Flaherty," *AMM*, May 1927, 7. Block advocated a refinement of film taste; Seldes, on the other hand, praised popular genres like the slapstick and advocated an intellectual cinema that tapped into these "lively" energies. Gilbert Seldes, *The Seven Lively Arts* (New York: Harper, 1924).

37. Brownstein, "Filming with Flaherty," 44.

38. Ibid., 7.

39. Ibid., 44.
40. "Critical Focusing," *AMM*, May 1927, 45.
41. Ibid.
42. Miriam Hansen, "The Mass Production of the Senses: Classical Cinema as Vernacular Modernism," *Modernism/Modernity* 6, no. 2 (1999).
43. On *Sunrise*, see "Critical Focusing," *AMM*, November 1927, 20; on *Seventh Heaven*, "Critical Focusing," *AMM*, July 1927, 22; on *Secrets of a Soul*, "Critical Focusing," *AMM*, June 1927, 22; and on *Metropolis* and *Potemkin*, see "Critical Focusing," *AMM*, May 1927, 45.
44. "Critical Focusing," *AMM*, July 1927, 23.
45. "Critical Focusing," *AMM*, June 1927, 22.
46. "Critical Focusing," *AMM*, August 1927, 26.
47. Ibid., 27.
48. Ibid. The reviews also present a kind of protoauteurism, often noting continuities among the previous work of important directors (like Browning), actors (such as Jannings), and cinematographers (Hal Mohr, John Arnold, and Dudley Murphy).
49. "Critical Focusing," *AMM*, September 1927, 23. This description also recalls French film criticism from the 1910s and '20s that explored the cinema's power to transform (through close-ups, framing, and the mysterious properties of *photogénie*) banal objects into fantastic or sinister ones; see Louis Aragon, "On Décor," and Jean Epstein, "Magnification," both in *French Film Theory and Criticism*, vol. 1: *1907–1929*, ed. Richard Abel (Princeton, NJ: Princeton University Press, 1988).
50. "Critical Focusing," *AMM*, October 1927, 28.
51. "Critical Focusing," *AMM*, November 1927, 20.
52. "Animating Insects," *AMM*, November 1927, 31.
53. At least one black photographer, James Lattimer Allen, was an ACL member in 1935; correspondence between Mary Brady and Alain Locke, c. 1934–35, box 1, Harmon Foundation Records (MSS51615), Library of Congress.
54. Eloyce and James Gist are best known for their amateur religious film, *Hell Bound Train* (c. 1933), which is discussed in more detail in chapter 8.
55. Dr. Kinema, "The Clinic—Amateur Movie Clubs," *AMM*, January 1927, 30.
56. Arthur L. Gale, "Amateur Clubs," *AMM*, October 1927, 35.
57. The Movie Makers Club of Chicago, for example, listed a number of prominent or affluent members, including a member of the Wrigley family, the president of a coal company, the president of the Zenith Radio Corporation, and Albert Howell, of the Bell and Howell Company. According to the article, charter memberships cost ten dollars per year; "Closeups and Swaps," *AMM*, August 1927, 30.
58. "Hollywood At Harkness," *AMM*, August 1927, 28; "Scenario Contest Winner," *AMM*, September 1927, 2; *New York Herald Tribune* quoted in "They Tell the Story," *AMM*, January 1927, 21.
59. Mina Brownstein, "Cinema Democracy," *AMM*, July 1927, 20–21.

60. Ibid., 21.

61. Dwight Swanson, "Inventing Amateur Film: Marion Norris Gleason, Eastman Kodak and the Rochester Scene, 1921–1932," *Film History* 15, no. 2 (2003). Gleason's films are held at the George Eastman House film archive.

62. "Actors as Amateurs: The Rochester Community Players Produce a Photoplay," *AMM*, October 1927, 26.

63. "Home Movie Exhibition," *AMM*, December 1927, 52.

64. Though sometimes with the fascinating addition of specialized medical or specifically surgical films: "Medical Films—Karyokenesis (Indirect Cell Inversion), Ehrlich Slide Chain Theory and Inflammation," "SWAPS" column, *AMM*, December 1926, 25; January 1927.

65. "Amateur Contests," *AMM*, December 1927, 24.

66. Books advertised include Herbert McKay's *Motion Picture Photography for the Amateur*, Carl L. Gregory's *Motion Picture Photography*, T. O'Connor Sloanne's *Motion Picture Projection*, *Screen Acting*, by Inez and Helen Klumph, *Photoplay Writing*, by William Lord Wright, and *Motion Picture Directing*, by Peter Milne; advertisement, "Why Not Study Your Hobby?," *AMM*, January 1927, 32. Books reviewed included Iris Barry's *Let's Go to the Movies: Motion Pictures for Instruction*, by A. P. Hollis; and James R. Cameron's *The Taking and Showing of Motion Pictures for the Amateur*; "Book Reviews," *AMM*, June 1927, 48.

67. Dr. Kinema, "Perils of Panoraming," *AMM*, May 1927, 32.

68. Marion D. Kerr, "What Makes a Film Interesting?," *AMM*, December 1926, 26.

69. The idea of appeal does recall the equally nebulous quality of *photogénie*—"any aspect of things, beings, or souls whose moral character is enhanced by filmic production"—which was discussed by French film critics of the same era; Jean Epstein, "On Certain Characteristics of Photogénie," trans. Tom Milne, in *French Film Theory and Criticism*, vol. 1, ed. Abel, 314.

70. "The Significance of the Club Movement," *AMM*, November 1927, 36.

CHAPTER 2. CINÉ-COMMUNITY

1. William J. Shannon, "Amateur Clubs—What They Offer," *MM*, November 1930, 694, 717–18.

2. "Through the Editor's Finder—21st Birthday of *American Cinematographer*," *American Cinematographer* (hereafter abbreviated as *AC*), November 1941, 520.

3. Hal Hall, "Introducing the Amateur Dept.," *AC*, May 1929, 6.

4. David Bordwell, Janet Staiger, and Kristin Thompson, *The Classical Hollywood Cinema* (New York: Columbia University Press, 1985), 254–55. The new amateur department coincided with a structural overhaul of the ASC that eliminated the different classes of members but simultaneously limited the number of active, resident members of the society to 150. "A.S.C. Plans Announced," *AC*, June 1929, 6. Later, there were still different classes of ASC

members, but membership was stipulated as "by invitation only." *AC*, August 1934, 148.

5. "Outside of subscriptions, *AC* found its widest circulation in consumer camera stores." Bob Birchard, writing in an eighty-fifth anniversary issue of *American Cinematographer* in August 2004: www.theasc.com/magazine/aug04/record/index.html.

6. Advertisement, *AC*, October 1929, 32.

7. See, for example, Frank B. Good, "Ten Common Mistakes of the Amateur," *AC*, October 1933, 226: "1. Over exposure; 2. Poor focus; 3. Too fast panning; 4. Unsteady camera; 5. Walking while shooting; 6. Too much footage on no action pictures; 7. Poor composition; 8. Lack of continuity; 9. Not enough close-ups; 10. Do not change exposure for close-ups."

8. Hall, "Introducing the Amateur Dept.," 6.

9. "Here's How," *AC*, April 1936, 169.

10. *AC*, November 1933, 274.

11. "Home Movie Previews," *AC*, April 1941, 180.

12. J. Belmar Hall, "Definitions of Elements in Composition," *AC*, December 1935, 536; "Using Light to Help Composition," *AC*, February 1936, 71; "Editing Is Really an Art," *AC*, April 1936, 167.

13. Max Liszt, "Just What Is 'Montage' Anyway?," *AC*, January 1936, 31; "Montage and Symbolism Are Entirely Different," *AC*, March 1936, 117; "Explaining the Laws of 'Symbolism,'" *AC*, April 1936, 165; "If Story Is Not the Thing What Is?," *AC*, July 1936, 303. Max Liszt is described in the magazine as "Guest-instructor in 'direction and story-construction' at the 'New Film Group' and also Director of 'Lives Wasted,' a 'New Film Group' Studio Picture."

14. For example, Joseph August, "Cinematographers Have Language All Their Own," *AC*, March 1937, 122.

15. Gregg Toland, "Realism for 'Citizen Kane,'" *AC*, February 1941, 54–55, 80; see also Toland's editorial in the May 1941 issue about *Citizen Kane*'s landmark significance (221) and a review of the film in the "Photography of the Month" column of that same issue (222).

16. These were usually published in April of the year; see 1935.

17. William Stull, "Amateurs and Novices," *AC*, August 1929, 27.

18. William Stull, "Professional Amateurs: Fred Niblo Gets His Fun with an Eyemo," *AC*, October 1929, 34.

19. William Stull, "Professional Amateurs," *AC*, June 1930.

20. William Stull, "Professional Amateurs," *AC*, July 1930, 31; see also Conrad Nagel, *AC*, August 1930.

21. Quoted in William Stull, "Professional Amateurs," *AC*, October 1930, 36.

22. Ibid., 42.

23. Throughout the 1930s *American Cinematographer* continued to publish articles about Hollywood professionals—including Henry Fonda and Marlene Dietrich—that highlighted their amateur filmmaking experiences. "Adventuring on the Kodachrome Trail," *AC*, January 1936, 26; William Stull, "Marlene Dietrich—Kodachrome Moviemaker," *AC*, May 1941, 229, 247–48.

24. "You Are Not an Amateur," *AC*, May 1933, 31.

25. Ibid.

26. A full-page announcement provided the tally of votes and presented a sample of comments received from supportive amateurs: "Long live CINEPHOTOGRAPHER. Deep down in my heart I always hated to admit that I was an amateur. The name Cinephotographer is going to make us a bit more proud of our hobby." *AC*, June 1933, 66.

27. Clark Gable, "I Like to Hunt—with a Camera," *AC*, June 1933, 59. Similarly, an article called "Studying the Professional" used both *amateur* and *cinephotographer*. *AC*, June 1933, 61.

28. W.H. McCullough, amateur, "When an Amateur Turns Professional," *AC*, May 1933, 34.

29. Harry Burdick, "Oh, Ho! For the Life of a Cameraman," *AC*, September 1936, 394, 403. The framing here is of an amateur cameraman becoming a cinematographer rather than a director, which is natural for the publication but perhaps not for all aspiring amateurs.

30. *AC*, April 1936, 181. One can't help but see the relationship between the West Coast *American Cinematographer* and the East Coast ACL/*Movie Makers* as competitive, if not adversarial. Conversely, George Blaisdell wrote of his visit to New York: "One of the pleasures of the visit was the meeting, at the convention and at the offices of *Movie Makers*, of the men who make that magazine." George Blaisdell, "Stranger in New York," *AC*, June 1939, 247.

31. "Amateur Filmers Throng to Junior Society," *AC*, August 1936, 352. Also clarified was that semiprofessional filmmakers were indeed welcome to join, provided they did not qualify for admission to the ASC.

32. The main noticeable evidence of SAC's existence during 1938 was on the contents page of the Amateur Movie Section of *American Cinematographer*, which presented a "SAC" insignia and "Society of Amateur Cinematographers" printed in large letters. *AC*, February 1938. In April 1938, a half-page ad appeared announcing, "Society of Amateur Cinematographers—Charter Membership Closed—There will be only 1000 regular memberships available—then the membership will be closed"; opposite page 176, inside back cover.

33. Leonard Smith, "25 Years of Service," *AC*, November 1945, 367.

34. Eileen Bowser, *The Transformation of Cinema, 1907–1915* (Berkeley: University of California Press, 1990), 136; see also Dana Polan, *Scenes of Instruction: The Beginnings of the U.S. Study of Film* (Berkeley: University of California Press, 2007), on screenplay contests.

35. "Scenario Contest Winner," *AMM*, September 1927, 2. The winning scenario appeared in a later issue of *AMM*. Carl Kahn, "Doubling in Wyoming," March 1928, 170.

36. "Want to Win a Contest Prize? Then Read This," *Photoplay*, May 1927, 49.

37. Frederick James Smith, "Amateur Movies," *Photoplay*, April 1928, 72.

38. Relatively little information is available about Russell T. Ervin's experience in Hollywood. *Photoplay* reported his work as an assistant in various

divisions the following year, and he evidently worked for many years as a cinematographer and an associate director of Hollywood short subjects (i.e., Paramount's "Sportlight" series: *Better Bowling*).

39. "Amateur Movies," *Photoplay*, December 1927, 64.

40. Roy Winton, "The Significance of the First Amateur Film Contest," *AMM*, June 1928, 373.

41. "New Amateur Movie Contest," *Photoplay*, September 1928, 69.

42. "Amateur Movies," *Photoplay*, April 1929, 66.

43. "Amateur Movies," *Photoplay*, November 1928, 74. The rules indicated that "officers and directors of the ACL—other than judges—may enter the contest," thus clearing the way for Maxim's participation.

44. Editorial, *AMM*, November 1928, 697.

45. The film was produced by a club based in Stockton, California: Foto-Cine Productions. Frederick James Smith, "The Amateur Movie Contest Prizes," *Photoplay*, November 1929, 67. The description recalls Paul Fejos's short experimental film, *The Last Moment*, which was released in early 1928, employed a similar flashback structure, and was well-received among amateur and experimental film enthusiasts. Placing third in the dramatic category was a film by the Princeton Undergraduate Motion Pictures club, starring the future film and communications scholar Erik Barnouw: *Photoplay*, March 1929, 68.

46. Steiner's and Maxim's films appear to be the only extant works from either of the *Photoplay* contests.

47. For a list of the annual Ten Best winners, see Alan D. Kattelle "The Amateur Cinema League and Its Films," *Film History* 15, no. 2 (2003): 238–51; detailed descriptions appeared annually in the December issue of *Movie Makers*.

48. "The Ten Best Amateur Films of 1930," *MM*, December 1930, 758.

49. Ibid.

50. Ibid., 788.

51. "The Ten Best," *MM*, December 1931, 657.

52. "Try This," *MM*, May 1932, 195.

53. "The Ten Best," *MM*, December 1932, 537.

54. "The Ten Best," *MM*, December 1934, 547–48.

55. "The Ten Best for 1935," *MM*, December 1935, 515.

56. "New Ten Best," *MM*, June 1936, 240. In addition to the creation of these two categories, the New Ten Best would consider 35mm films in the General Class, but not in the Special Class, where it was seen as too much of an advantage and a mark of industrial, rather than amateur or artisanal, production.

57. "All Amateur," *MM*, August 1948, 338.

58. "The Ten Best and the Maxim Memorial Award," *MM*, December 1937, 601.

59. Roy W. Winton, "Choosing the Ten Best," *MM*, September 1945, 347.

60. Ibid., 361.

61. The categories were: Photography; Kodacolor; Home Movie; Production; Scenic; Animated Cartoon; News Reel; Nature Study; Medical; Technical Process; Educational; Travel Film; Aerial Photography. Top prize in the contest was five hundred dollars, with the awards totaling one thousand dollars; these awards were subsequently complemented with sponsor awards of products and services. The contest rules initially stipulated that the films had to be produced on 16mm or 9.5mm film—no 35mm films allowed—and that "only Bona Fide Subscribers to the *American Cinematographer* Can Compete," but this last requirement was dropped in subsequent years.

62. William Stull, "Highlights of the Amateur Contest," *AC*, December 1932, 20. Stull also comments on the surprising number of 9.5mm films submitted; half of the films from Japan were on 9.5mm but only one from the United States was.

63. Ibid., 20, 48.

64. Though experimental filmmaker J. S. Watson was a member of the ASC and an occasional contributor to *AC*, he does not appear to have been present in the judging of these amateur/experimental films (nor does his influence).

65. "More Than 200 Compete for Amateur Prizes," *AC*, December 1932, 7.

66. The top three films are now held at the East Anglian Film Archive.

67. "900 View Prize Pictures in Kansas City," *AC*, May 1933, 29.

68. *AC*, July 1933, 108. Subsequent articles announced the circulation of the 1932 prize-winning films further: five hundred people saw the films in Indianapolis, and the films also visited Pendleton (Oregon) Club; Movie Makers of Grand Rapids (MI); Amateur Cinema Club of the Oranges (Orange, NJ); Club at Ossining (NY); Greater Oakland Motion Picture Club and Cinema Club of San Francisco; the Camera Club of Philadelphia; Amateur Movie Club (Austin, MN); Hudson City Cine Club (Jersey City, NJ), the Amateur Cinema League (Newark, NJ). "500 See Prize Pictures," *AC*, September 1933, 186.

69. "France Invites Cinematographer Prize Winners," *AC*, May 1933, 28.

70. The article noted the rules of the contest and a few features of 1934's winning films, including the information that both were made on 8mm film. *AC*, February 1935, 79; the original article was from *Time*, January 7, 1935.

71. William Stull, "Musical Scores for the Prize Pictures," *AC*, February 1936, 68.

72. *AC*, October 1936, 448.

73. "Honorable Mention Extended to Amateurs," *AC*, February 1937, 73.

74. "Sherlock of Australia Winner of Cinematographer's Contest," *AC*, January 1938, 26.

75. William Stull, "Highlights of the Amateur Contest," *AC*, December 1932, 20.

76. "8mm Picture Ranks High in 1933 Competition," *AC*, December 1933, 321; "Ruth Stuart Wins Triple Recognition in 1936 Contest," *AC*, January 1937, 25.

77. "Sherlock's 'Nation Builders' Winner," *AC*, January 1939, 16–17.

78. "Well Received," *MM*, September 1930, 570, describes *The Ghetto*, a production of the Jewish Amateur Film Society of London (UK). In 1934, the Cinema League of the Jewish Peoples Institute of Chicago planned the production of a film; "Amateur Clubs—Plans Production," *MM*, April 1934, 67.

79. The ACL "has avoided two evils that may readily wreck any organization, national or international, by not becoming embroiled in questions of relationship and control with local and regional bodies and by not permitting subservience to commercial interest"; "A Recipe," *MM*, September 1932, 377.

80. Arthur Gale, "A Seven Year Record," *MM*, August 1933, 329.

81. "Among the Movie Clubs—Calling All Secretaries!," *AC*, January 1941, 28.

82. "Amateur Clubs—New York Elects," *MM*, January 1932, 18.

83. "Amateur Clubs," *MM*, December 1934, 525.

84. *AC*, July 1933, 108; February 1934, 416.

85. "Club's Monthly Contest," *AC*, October 1932, 37.

86. *AC*, September 1933, 186. Members of the *AC* staff and ASC acted as judges for the Los Angeles Amateur Cine Club contest; *AC*, November 1933, 282. *AC* also sponsored the club's contest.

87. A.L. Gram, "Amateur Cinematographers Seek to Make Better Motion Pictures," *AC*, January 1938, 30.

88. Ibid.

89. Betty Peterson, *The Toronto Movie Club: Its First Fifty Years, 1934–1984*, pamphlet (Toronto, n.d. [1984]), 1.

90. Cliff Shorney, "Club Rooms—Pro and Con," *Shots and Angles* 2, no. 8 (November 1936): 2.

91. "An Editorial by the Club President," *Shots and Angles* 3, no. 6 (November 1, 1937): 1.

92. *AC*, December 1934, 381. Meetings were held at the Bell and Howell and Eastman Auditoriums. The yearly membership fee was established at three dollars.

93. M.R. Armstrong, "Going Places Is This 8mm Club of Los Angeles," *AC*, August 1937, 336; *AC*, December 1937, 526.

94. *AC*, February 1938, 86.

95. "Paramount Club Discusses Color," *AC*, April 1937, 164.

96. Canadian amateur Jack Carey recalls joining a movie club at a steel company (Stelco) in Hamilton when he started working there, which was part of the organized hobby activities for employees. Conversation with author.

97. The article "Columbia Studio Professionals Are Barred by Cubs from Own Work," *AC*, February 1938, 72–73, shows production stills for *Lucky Piece*, "the first and probably the last amateur picture to be made in major studio with major 35mm. equipment."

98. Ibid. According to the article, the Columbia Cub Productions membership of about fifty was "pretty evenly divided as to sex."

99. "Keeping Up with the Amateur," *AC*, October 1932, 28. Collective filming of a city was a common project for amateur movie clubs and was, for instance, pursued in New York.

100. Later, the Portland Cine Club compiled a "library of 16mm film which that organization maintains for its members" and compiled an "'Oregon Film,' made up from the best shots of its members of scenes and activities in the State of Oregon"; *AC*, February 1934, 416. See also "How Movie Clubs May Profit by Maintaining a Stock Shot Library," *AC*, May 1938, 212.

101. R. Fawn Mitchell, "Filming the Fair," *MM*, July 1933, 284.

102. Bill Seineke Jr., "Forming Cooperative Amateur Production Units," *AC*, October 1939, 441, 477; "Closeups," *MM*, June 1940, 160.

103. Harry E. Ward Jr., "Scenario Films—Unlimited! The Story of the Long Beach Cinema Club," *AC*, March 1941, 118–19, 147–49. The practice continued after the war; Ralph Lawton, "Amateurs Make Movies the Hollywood Way," *AC*, August 1948, 276–78.

104. "Amateur Clubs," *MM*, March 1938, 139.

105. Ibid., 129.

106. "Amateur Clubs—Los Angeles Ladies," *MM*, October 1939, 510.

107. "Amateur Clubs," *MM*, June 1936, 249.

108. Alexander B. Lewis and John A. Deady, "The Camera in School," *MM*, September 1936, 381.

109. Polan, *Scenes of Instruction*, 341–42.

110. Donald A. Eldridge, "High School Films without Subsidy," *MM*, November 1937, 541.

111. "Amateur Clubs—Anti War," *MM*, October 1936, 447. Max Liszt would later become a regular contributor to *American Cinematographer* on amateur and independent film.

112. Ibid.

113. *AC*, October 1933, 230.

114. *AC*, April 1941, 181.

115. "Columbia Tells of Camera by Broadcast," *AC*, August 1939, 378–79.

116. "British Cine Organization Issues Monthly Bulletin," *AC*, September 1933, 186. *American Cinematographer* also covered the expansion of this organization, praising its development again in a 1936 article, by which time the group had expanded to include professional filmmakers. "British Institute Expands," *AC*, April 1936, 172.

117. K. Knegt, "Amateur Movie Making in Europe," *AC*, October 1933, 223.

118. Arthur Campbell, "Survey of Foreign Cinephotography," *AC*, September 1934, 226. The survey sketched national stereotypes of amateurism as well, suggesting that while amateurs were much alike all over the world, the French and German amateurs were very serious, the French in artistic ways, and the Germans in technical ways. Acted play films dominated in France, while travel films dominated in Germany.

119. "Amateur Clubs—All Australian," *MM*, October 1939, 510. Reports of moviemaking in the United States and other countries also reflected colonial

and racist attitudes at times; this was especially the case in relation to Sherlock's 1938 award-winning film *Nation Builders*. See George Blaisdell, "Here's Camera Club in Real Home," *AC*, August 1938, 311.

120. *MM*, March 1937, 125. Winning the top prize was *Happy Day*, a 16mm film by Scottish amateur T. Lawrenson. According to reports, a Tokyo screening of the winning films was attended by more than seven hundred people. "Amateur Clubs," *MM*, March 1938, 129.

121. "Lawrenson's 'Happy Day' Takes Honors in Japan," *AC*, January 1938, 35–36. A copy of *Happy Day* is held at the East Anglian Film Archive.

122. "Amateur Clubs," *MM*, August 1937, 392.

123. Ben Davis, "Beginnings of the Film Society Movement in the U.S.," *Film and History* 24, nos. 3–4 (1994): 6–26. See also Haidee Wasson's *Museum Movies* (Berkeley: University of California, 2005); and Douglas Gomery's *Shared Pleasures* (Madison: University of Wisconsin Press, 1992). While there's no specific evidence that these film societies screened amateur works, they presented a similar interest in artistic filmmaking and alternatives to commercial Hollywood fare.

124. "Amateur Clubs," *MM*, April 1937, 179.

125. "Amateur Clubs," *MM*, June 1936, 249.

126. "Amateur Clubs," *MM*, July 1940, 337.

127. Ormal Sprungman, "Why Not Stage Real Movie Party," *AC*, June 1939, 249–52.

128. *AC*, October 1933, 230.

129. "Recent Accessions," *MM*, September 1930, 569. The films added in September 1930 (there were four) include *The California Raisin Festival* (400 feet, 16mm, Sierra Cinema League); *Tom Jones* (5,000 feet, 16mm, Purity Players of Yale University); *The Horsemen of Death* (2,000 feet, 16mm, Winston Childs—who also directed *Tom Jones*); *Galleon Gold* (1,600 feet, 16mm, San Jose Players).

130. "Amateur Clubs," *MM*, March 1933, 124.

131. "Featured Releases," *MM*, October 1936, 449. Producers listed include Bell and Howell, Eastman Kodak, Garrison Film Distributors, Inc. ("offers 16mm. silent comedies starring Louise Fazenda, Al. St. John, Clyde Cook, Larry Semon, Lee Mran, Ned Sparks and others"); Walter O. Gutlohn, Inc., New York; Guv D. Haselton Travelettes, Hollywood; Kodascope Libraries (includes Mickey Mouse); Lewis Film Service, Wichita, Kansas; Nu-Art Filmco, New York (Flip the Frog cartoons and William J. Burns detective stories); Ernest M. Reynolds, Cleveland, Ohio (scenic films); World Pictures Corporation, New York (*Nanook of the North* for sale or rent).

132. "Long Beach Shows Documentaries," *AC*, October 1941, 483.

133. Wasson, *Museum Movies*, especially chapter 5.

134. Polan, *Scenes of Instruction*, especially chapters 1 and 7.

135. "International Salon Is Planned by Little," *AC*, May 1937, 205.

136. "Eleventh Annual International Show of Amateur Motion Pictures, 1940," program, "Amateur Films," Subject Files, Margaret Herrick Library, n.p.

CHAPTER 3. CINÉ-ENGAGEMENT

1. "A Free Art," *MM*, May 1934, 185.

2. Similarly, one reason that amateur cinema has not received more attention in film historical accounts of this period—compared with the rise of documentary filmmaking, for example—is perhaps its perceived detachment from political and ideological conflicts. See, for example, Charles Wolfe, "The Poetics and Politics of Nonfiction: Documentary Film," in *Grand Design: Hollywood as a Modern Business Enterprise, 1930–1939*, ed. Tino Balio (Berkeley: University of California Press, 1995).

3. Patricia R. Zimmermann offers the most trenchant critique of amateur filmmakers for their retreat into domesticity, disengagement from politics, and general failure to fulfill the oppositional promises of amateur movie equipment. See her *Reel Families*.

4. Neil Harris, "John Philip Sousa and the Culture of Reassurance," in Neil Harris, *Cultural Excursions: Marketing Appetites and Cultural Tastes in Modern America* (Chicago: University of Chicago Press, 1990).

5. See also Michael Parish, *Anxious Decades: America in Prosperity and Depression, 1920–1941* (New York: W.W. Norton, 1994); and Ann Douglas, *Terrible Honesty: Mongrel Manhattan in the 1920s* (New York: Farrar, Straus and Giroux, 1995).

6. "$2000 for Best Amateur Films," *Photoplay*, September 1927, 69.

7. "Without Any Loss," *MM*, March 1932, 97.

8. Arthur L. Gale, "How to Plan a Social Welfare Film," *MM*, April 1932, 162.

9. "Double Duty," *MM*, June 1932, 245.

10. "Back Yards," *MM*, July 1932, 289.

11. "Play—1932", *MM*, October 1932, 423.

12. "Responsibility," *MM*, November 1932, 475.

13. Ibid.

14. The final comment on this election season came in the December issue of *Movie Makers*, which offered its own "new deal" in the form of *Making Better Movies*, a book available only to ACL members, free with their membership. Ad for ACL *MM*, December 1932, 518.

15. "Equipment and film are available at greatly reduced prices over anything known before 1932.... There is no real barrier to everyone's filming and filming with full satisfaction." "Let's Go!," *MM*, January 1933, 9. However, it seems that equipment prices fluctuated considerably during this period; subsequent articles commented on the inflation in prices—a result of the Industry Recovery Bill—and urged amateurs to see this in a reasonable, constructive way. "Reflective personal filmers will realize the obvious truth that an industry that is being forced below the fair margin of return in its manufacturing and selling must be rescued before it perishes." "Cooperation," *MM*, July 1933, 273.

16. "A New Crusade," *MM*, June 1933, 229.

17. Ibid.

18. "A Free Art," *MM*, May 1934, 185.
19. "The Free Screen," *MM*, February 1935, 61.
20. "From the President," *MM*, December 1937, 599.
21. Barry Staley, "The Election Provides Fine Filming," *AC*, October 1936, 437.
22. "Home Movie Previews," *AC*, September 1941, 435.
23. "Practical Films," *MM*, March 1937, 128.
24. Untitled editorial, *MM*, April 1937, 159.
25. "Amateur Clubs," *MM*, October 1936, 447.
26. "Featured Releases," *MM*, March 1937, 143.
27. Roy Winton, "Can We Hate?," *MM*, November 1938, 533.
28. Stephen F. Voorhees, "From the President," *MM*, December 1938, 593.
29. "A Fruitful Year," *MM*, January 1939, 11.
30. "While There Is Time," *MM*, May 1939, 211.
31. Ibid.
32. Fred C. Ells, "An American Films in Japan," *MM*, November 1936, 486.
33. Fred C. Ells, "Dodging Japan's Camera-Censorship," *AC*, January 1942, 20–21, 36.
34. "War's Effect," *MM*, November 1939, 547.
35. Stephen Voorhees, "From the President," *MM*, December 1939, 605.
36. "Closeups," *MM*, June 1940, 160.
37. "Closeups," *MM*, July 1940, 314.
38. "Through the Editor's Finder," *AC*, February 1941, 62, 82.
39. "Through the Editor's Finder," *AC*, December 1941, 569.
40. Ibid. According to *American Cinematographer*, in 1941 there were over two million amateur photographers in the United States alone; this included still and motion picture photographers.
41. "What We Can Do," *MM*, June 1940, 319; James W. Moore "These We Defend," *MM*, June 1940, 329.
42. "Dreams Live," *MM*, September 1940, 415.
43. "British Amateurs Make Defense Films," *AC*, November 1941, 532.
44. "Amateur Clubs," *MM*, June 1940, 297. The same club would later produce films for more didactic purposes, such as one that promoted the Red Cross blood transfusion operations.
45. "Amateur Clubs," *MM*, November 1940, 549: "One recent member film shown at the club was 'Shots from a Bomber' by Cam Warren."
46. "Movies for National Defense," *AC*, March 1941, 109; "Through the Editor's Finder," *AC*, May 1941, 221; July 1941.
47. "Through the Editor's Finder," *AC*, June 1941, 271. The Long Beach (CA) Cinema Club initiated this effort, which was soon supported by *American Cinematographer*.
48. "Home Movie Previews," *AC*, August 1941, 383.
49. "Home Movie Previews—Our Hero," *AC*, January 1942, 29. *American Cinematographer* also commented on the possibility of amateurs serving in the Signal Corps so that their camera experience could help the war effort. "Through the Editor's Finder," *AC*, June 1942, 257.

50. "Through the Editor's Finder," *AC*, January 1942, 17.
51. Stephen Voorhees, "To Members of the Amateur Cinema League," *MM*, January 1942, 10; "ACL Volunteer Registration," *MM*, February 1942, 51.
52. "War Work for Clubs," *AC*, December 1941, 595; "Among the Movie Clubs," *AC*, January 1942, 28.
53. The amateurs were released after police checks. "Wartime Filming Restrictions," *MM*, January 1942, 11.
54. "Statement from Director of Censorship," *MM*, April 1942, 174.
55. "URGENT, WHERE HAVE YOU FILMED?," *MM*, April, 1942, 150–51; "Where Have You Made Pictures," *AC*, May 1942, 218.
56. William Stull, "Amateurs Make Defense Films!," *AC*, February 1942, 68; "Scenario of America's First Amateur-Made Civil Defense Film," *AC*, April 1942, 159; La Nelle Fosholdt, "Diary of a Defense Film" and "Scenario of America's First Amateur-Made Civil Defense Film," *AC*, April 1942, 162–63.
57. Phil Tannura, "Short-Cuts for Defense Filmers," *AC*, April, 1942, 168; "The Bulletin Board," *AC*, April 1942, 171.
58. "A New Call to Service," *MM*, June 1942, 233. See also article by Roy Winton in same issue (235) and template treatment for Red Cross films (238, 256–58); also Roy Winton, "OCD Calls Movie Makers," *MM*, July 1942, 277.
59. "War Time Ten Best," *MM*, September 1942, 359.
60. Stephen F. Voorhees, "From the President," *MM*, December 1942, 485.
61. "Among the Movie Clubs," *AC*, January 1944, 24.
62. "Congratulations Syracuse," *AC*, June 1944, 204.
63. "Among the Movie Clubs: Blackouts," *AC*, January 1942, 28; "Shelter Shows," *AC*, April 1942, 169.
64. "Among the Movie Clubs: Editor's Note," *AC*, December 1941, 580.
65. "16mm. Films for Army Camps," *AC*, September 1942, 413.
66. "Among the Movie Clubs: Films to Show to Service-Men," *AC*, May 1943, 183.
67. "Among the Movie Clubs: Inter-Club Cooperation," *AC*, February 1942, 74.
68. "Among the Movies Clubs: Club Cooperation," *AC*, April 1942, 169; "National Association of Movie Clubs Gets Action!," *AC*, May 1942, 218–19; "Film for Exchange," *AC*, June 1942, 268 (films listed are from Syracuse and the 8–16 Movie Club of Philadelphia).
69. "Through the Editor's Finder," *AC*, September 1942 399.
70. "Among the Movie Clubs: Editor's Note," *AC*, December 1942, 527.
71. "Among the Movie Clubs: Share the Films!," *AC*, January 1943, 23.
72. "Free Films for Movie Club Programs," *AC*, February 1943, 65: The *American Cinematographer* library consisted of thirty-five titles divided into categories and gauge.
73. "Among the Movie Clubs: Films for Exchange," *AC*, August 1942, 361.
74. "Among the Movie Clubs," *AC*, March 1945, 92.

75. Claude W. Cadarette, "Formation and Progress of Amateur Movie Clubs," *AC*, November 1945, 382.

76. Roy Winton, "Twenty Years of the ACL—How an Assignment Has Been Carried Out," *MM*, August 1946, 300.

CHAPTER 4. CINÉ-TECHNOLOGY

1. Dorothy Rowden, "Colored Home Movies by Radio?" *AMM*, December 1926, 24.

2. C. F. Nicholson, "Tinting Motion Picture Film" *MM*, May 1928, 314; C. F. Nicholson, "Coloring Film with Brushes," *MM*, July 1928, 466.

3. "Color Unlimited," *MM*, May 1935, 193.

4. Other natural color formats, such as Vitacolor and Dufaycolor, were also marketed to amateurs during this period. Kodacolor and Kodachrome were the two most widespread natural color film processes in North America, and so are the focus of my discussion here. For alternatives see Max B. Du Pont, "Color or the Amateur," *AC*, May, 1929, 33; "Capturing Autumn's Tints" *AC*, October 1929, 2; and W.T. Crespinel, "Cinecolor Makes Contribution to Color," *AC*, October 1939, 443.

5. Editorial, *MM*, September 1928, 567.

6. Roy Winton, "A Defense Inherited," *MM*, February 1930, 85.

7. John Boyle, "Kodacolor Gives Life to Travel Films," *AC*, June 1934, 86.

8. John V. Hansen, "Color Counsel," *MM*, August 1933, 320; John V. Hansen, "Joseph's Coat Indoors," *MM*, February 1934, 61. "Kodacolor lighting, you will find, approaches professional lighting-practice more closely than does the usual run of amateur lighting for black-and-white pictures." A.L. Gilks, "Kodacolor Comes Indoors," *AC*, May 1933, 23.

9. Casual filmmakers' avoidance of Kodacolor perhaps had less to do with its quality than with its ease of use. Boyle, "Kodacolor Gives Life to Travel Films," 86.

10. Kaveh Askari has also written recently about Kodacolor films made by early cinema pioneer and Amateur Cinema League member Alexander Black. Askari links Black's Kodacolor filmmaking with his protocinematic illustrated lectures and his editing of the *Sunday World*'s color supplement. Kaveh Askari, "Early 16mm Color by a Career Amateur," *Film History* 21, no. 2 (2009): 150–63.

11. "The Ten Best," *MM*, December 1932, 538. The footage of *Chartres Cathedral* survives and is discussed in chapter 6; the *Studies in Blue* section appears to be lost.

12. "The Ten Best," *MM*, December 1934, 534, 545. No copies of Hansen's *Venice* are known to survive.

13. John V. Hansen, "Kodacolor, Unlimited," *MM*, July 1932, 295.

14. Ibid.

15. Ibid., 308.

16. Hansen, "Color Counsel," 320.

17. "Eastman's New 16mm Color Film Sensational," *AC*, May 1935, 208–9. Some also viewed Hollywood as aesthetically inferior in its use of color film: a writer in *American Cinematographer* presented *Becky Sharp* as an example of clashing color composition that amateurs should avoid; K. Hale, "Learn about Shooting Color from 'Becky Sharp,'" *AC*, July 1935, 312.

18. "8mm Kodachrome," *AC*, June 1936, 264.

19. "Color Unlimited," *MM*, May 1935, 193.

20. Ibid.

21. "Closeups," *MM*, March 1937, 136; George Blaisdell, "Cinema Club Sees Elton Walker's Remarkable 'Yellowstone' Scenic," June 1938, *AC*, 254.

22. Advertisement, "Color Adventure Drama!!," *MM*, May 1940, 235.

23. Hiram Percy Maxim, "Chromatic Aberration," *MM*, February 1936, 73.

24. "New Ten Best," *MM*, June 1936, 240, 258.

25. "*Denmark in Color* is a six reel cine document, largely in Kodachrome, which, in addition to the exquisite color compositions for which Mr. Hansen is famous, includes light, genre studies of Danish life." A New York screening of this film was sponsored by World Peaceways, an organization that presented media images to counteract the glorification of war and promote international understanding. "Practical Films," *MM*, March, 1937, 128.

26. "Closeups," *MM*, July 1938, 332.

27. Hale, "Learn about Shooting Color from 'Becky Sharp,'" 312.

28. Neil Harris, "Color and Media: Some Comparisons and Speculations," reprinted in Neil Harris, *Cultural Excursions* (Chicago: University of Chicago Press, 1990), 327.

29. Hiram Percy Maxim, "From Our President," *MM*, December 1935, 513.

30. Though sometimes these developments occurred in directions that don't correspond to our traditional expectations for experimental cinema, *Keratoplasty*, for example, was "a beautifully perfect" "experimental and demonstrative operation on the eye of an anesthetized rabbit." Here, scientific and aesthetic experimentation are conflated; "The Ten Best for 1935," *MM*, December 1935, 515, 550.

31. "The Ten Best for 1936," *MM*, December 1936, 542, 551.

32. "The Ten Best and the Maxim Memorial Award," *MM*, December 1939, 634.

33. Russell C. Holslag, "News of the Industry," *MM*, May 1940, 232.

34. "Well Done!," *MM*, October 1940, 461.

35. Nadine Pizzo, "The Drama of Color," *AC*, December 1955, 720.

36. William Stull, "Tinting and Toning 16mm. Films," *AC*, May 1933, 18.

37. Charles Clarke, "Color in Black and White Films," *AC*, February 1937, 72; an adaptation of the same article was reprinted in the column "Tips to Amateurs from the Pros," *AC*, July 1949, 252. Both articles provide advice for color tinting black-and-white film.

38. Olin Downes, "Music and Film," *New York Times*, March 8, 1931, 114. Cavalcanti's *P'tite Lillie* was also shown, with music by Darius Milhaud.

39. Ibid. Scores for McPhee's composition are lost; it was the last work he composed before going to Bali. The Blitzstein score for *Surf and Seaweed* is reproduced on the *Unseen Cinema* DVD. Carol Oja, *Colin McPhee: Composer in Two Worlds* (Champaign: University of Illinois Press, 2004), 51–53.

40. H.G. Tasker and A.W. Carpenter, "Motion Pictures with Sound on Standard 16mm Film," *AC*, October 1932, 32.

41. The year 1931 was described as "the first real year of development in home talkies." John Beardslee Carrigan and Russell C. Holslag, "Sound Ahoy!," *MM*, February 1931, 73.

42. Russell C. Holslag, "Sound on Film—16mm," *MM*, February 1933, 63.

43. Ibid.

44. "Club Makes Sound Picture," *AC*, October 1933, 230.

45. See Alan D. Kattelle, *Home Movies: A History of the American Industry, 1897–1979* (Nashua, NH: Transition Publishing, 2000). Later, 1949 saw the release of the Auricon Cine-Voice, a camera that also recorded optical sound. The cost of this camera was $695, and although it was marketed to amateurs it was primarily used by semiprofessional newsreel and documentary filmmakers. Glenn B. Lewis, "A 16mm. Sound Camera for the Home Movie Maker," *AC*, December 1949, 444.

46. Advertisement for the Berndt-Maurer Corporation, *MM*, January 1940, 35.

47. William Stull, "Sound for Home Movies," *AC*, March 1934, 450.

48. Ibid. On the commercial use of this turntable system see Emily Thompson, "Remix Redux," *Cabinet*, issue 35 (Fall 2009), http://cabinetmagazine.org/issues/35/thompson.php.

49. William Stull, "Show It with Music," *AC*, April 1934, 507; Arthur H. Smith, "Non-Sync Setup for Silent Pictures," *AC*, January 1935, 25.

50. William Stull, "Musical Scores for the Prize Pictures," *AC*, February 1936, 68.

51. "A Record List for Film Scores," *MM*, January 1940, 15.

52. Advertisement, *MM*, February 1940, 81.

53. Hamilton Jones, "Sound It Yourself," *MM*, July 1934 275; see also Frederick G. Beach, "The Clinic," *MM*, July, 1937, 336.

54. Ormal I. Sprungman, "Home Movies Need Sound," *AC*, October 1939, 449–51, 476.

55. Duncan MacD. Little, "Overcoming Difficulties in Putting on Amateur Shows," *AC*, June 1940, 257–58, 286.

56. William Stull, "Randolph Clardy Makes First 8mm Talker," *AC*, April 1939, 164.

57. Carl Brisson, "Making Silent Movies Talk," *AC*, October 1934, 272; J. Lloyd Thompson, "Putting Sound on Silent 16mm Film," *AC*, July 1935, 308.

58. "Amateur Clubs," *MM*, June 1940, 297.

59. Don W. Loomer, "Sound and the Amateur," *AC*, September 1945, 304.

60. Edward Pyle, "Film Review," *AC*, December 1943, 448.

61. Bernarr Wixon, "Synchronized Sound for Home Movies," *AC*, March 1949, 91.

62. James W. Moore, ACL, "Titles That Talk," *MM*, February 1947, 108.

63. Lisle Conway, "Cine-Chronized Sound on Wire for Amateurs," *AC*, September 1945, 300.

64. "Magnetic Tape Sound Recording," *AC*, June 1947, 199; "Progress on 8mm. Synchronized Sound," *AC*, April 1948, 135; "ACL Annual Meeting," *MM*, June 1953, 152. James Moore called 1952 "the year which truly opened the era of magnetic sound on film." "Do-It-Yourself Sound Recording Adds Class to 16mm Films," *AC*, November 1954, 554–55.

65. John Forbes, "Magnetic Sound for Home Movies," *AC*, April 1952, 162.

66. "Summing Up for Sound," *MM*, January 1954, 26.

67. George W. Cushman, "Judging Amateur Sound Films," *AC*, May 1954, 242–43.

68. Though the French Pathé 9.5-mm format was another significant amateur gauge globally, it was much less widely used in North America, where Kodak's dominance of the film stock and processing fields was nearly complete.

69. The cost of the full Ciné-Kodak outfit was the equivalent of approximately $4,510, and the camera alone $1,680, in 2012 dollars. All equipment prices from Kattelle, *Home Movies*, whose encyclopedic appendixes list the cost of different brands and models of 16mm and 8mm film equipment. Historical price calculation made using the Consumer Price Index metric, www.measuringworth.com/uscompare/. A Model-T Ford was priced at $290 in 1925. See Samuel H. Williamson, "Seven Ways to Compute the Relative Value of a U.S. Dollar Amount, 1774 to Present," MeasuringWorth, April 2013.

70. "A Wider Field," *MM*, August 1932, 333; "Enter the Eight!," *MM*, August 1932, 335.

71. Advertisement for 8mm Ciné-Kodak, *MM*, August 1932, 346–47. Kodak's 8mm projector was offered at twenty-four dollars; more expensive models of both 8mm camera and projector were also available.

72. William Grace, "How about the Eight?" *AC*, March 1934, 452.

73. Arthur C. Miller, "A Professional Looks at 8-mm," *AC*, May 1934, 33; and in a similar vein, Ray Fernstrom, "The Professional Learns from the Eight," *AC*, June 1934, 81.

74. William Stull, "8 mm. vs. 16 mm," *AC*, September 1932, 30.

75. Guido Seeber, "Forerunners of the Amateur film," translated by Hatto Tappenbeck, *AC*, November 1932, 27: EDITOR'S NOTE: "It is the belief of the editor of 'Filmtechnik' that the 8 mm. will be the final standard of the amateur and that the 16mm will be adopted by industrial concerns, making it semi-professional. This is the first of a series of articles which delves into the history of the narrower width films."

76. Russell C. Holslag, "News of the Industry," *MM*, May 1933, 200.

77. Karl Hale, "A 'Professional' 16mm. Camera from Eastman," *AC*, May 1933, 20–21.

78. Ibid.

79. "No Limit," *MM*, May 1933, 185; see also Frederick Beach, "Now You Can Film Anything!," *MM*, May 1933, 187, about the features of the Ciné-Kodak special.
80. Ibid.
81. A. Shapiro "Trend in 16mm Projection, with Special Reference to Sound," *AC*, February 1936, 70.
82. "16mm Sound Displacing 35mm in Business Way," *AC*, June 1937, 262.
83. William Stull, "16mm Goes Professional," *AC*, January 1941, 12, 34.
84. William Stull, "Bell & Howell's First Professional Sixteen," *AC*, April 1941, 170.
85. "16mm Business Movies," *AC*, April 1941, 184.
86. James A. Larsen, "Professional Production in 16mm," *AC*, March 1942, 111.
87. See, for example, Reed N. Haythorne, "Sixteen Millimeter Teaches Airmen to Shoot," *AC*, June 1941, 266; "Through the Editor's Finder," *AC*, July 1942, 307.
88. "Through the Editor's Finder," *AC*, May 1942, 207.
89. "Through the Editor's Finder," *AC*, November 1942, 479. William Stull also published a historical survey of small-gauge film equipment in 1943: "Forty-Eight Years of Home Movies," *AC*, February 1943, 58–60; see also Alexander Victor, "The History and Origin of 16 Millimeter," *AC*, November 1945, 376.
90. Alvin Wyckoff, "Are You Ready for Industrial and Educational Filming?" *AC*, December 1944, 409; see also Russell Holslag, "Planning for 16mm Production," *AC*, March 1944, 84.
91. A related by-product of filmmaking during the war was a greater public appreciation for documentary film; see John Grierson's address to the 1942 Academy Awards about documentary films in wartime, and Joris Ivens's more practical advice about making documentary films. John Grierson, "Documentary Films in Wartime" (from address at Academy Awards), *AC*, March 1942, 101; Joris Ivens, "Making Documentary Films to Meet Today's Needs," *AC*, July 1942, 298.
92. Terry Ramsaye, "Sixteen—the Film of Facts: A Look into the Future of Motion Pictures," *MM*, September 1944, 349.
93. "Through the Editor's Finder," *AC*, July 1943, 255. At the same time, Bell and Howell sent an open letter to American amateur movie clubs asking amateurs what they wanted to see in new equipment, and DeVry solicited similar input. James R. Oswald, "Post-War 'Dream Camera,'" *AC*, September 1943, 332; "DeVry Asks Amateur Aid for New Camera Design," *AC*, September 1943, 345.
94. "Review of the Film News," *AC*, December 1945, 414.
95. Ray Fernstrom, "Sixteen Goes Hollywood," *AC*, January 1946, 12.
96. "No Miracles," *MM*, January 1947, 13.
97. "For the Fun of It," *MM*, November 1947, 463.
98. "The Big Switch," *MM*, July 1953, 194.

99. Also discussed is the Eumig electric-powered camera; Canon, which was the first Japanese-made 8mm camera on the U.S. market and included many of these features as well as additional ones; and auto-exposure 8mm cameras (Bell and Howell). John Forbes, "8mm Comes of Age," *AC*, September 1957, 590–91.

100. John Belton, *Widescreen Cinema* (Cambridge, MA: Harvard University Press, 1992); see also Ariel Rogers, "'Smothered in Baked Alaska': The Anxious Appeal of Widescreen Cinema," *Cinema Journal* 51, no. 3 (Spring 2012): 74–96.

101. Herbert O. Johansen, "Widescreen Movies Come to the Home," *Popular Science*, February 1955, 225–28.

102. John Forbes, "Widescreen for 16mm Movies," *AC*, September 1953, 436.

103. Johansen, "Widescreen Movies Come to the Home."

104. Forbes, "Widescreen for 16mm Movies," 458.

105. Bart Brooks, "Cinemascope for 16mm—the Vidoscope 16 Lens," *PSA Journal*, November 1955, 28: "As an integral part of widescreen, you must provide a larger screen, 3 × 8 ; 4 × 10½ ; 5 × 13½ etc." See also O.W. Schneider, "An Amateur Tries Wide Screen," *PSA Journal*, February 1956, 33–36. The *PSA Journal* is the publication of the Photographic Society of America.

106. Doerring interview with author. For more about the British history of amateur widescreen, see Guy Edmonds, "Amateur Widescreen; or, Some Forgotten Skirmishes in the Battle of the Gauges," *Film History* 19, no. 4 (2007).

107. "Kinney Moore Is Making Third Dimensional 16mm," *AC*, September 1937, 388.

108. Jack V. Wood, "Making Stereoscopic 8mm. Pictures in Color," *AC*, May 1939, 210.

109. Philip Tannura, "Cine Amateur Can Make 3-D Movies, Too," *AC*, March 1953; John Forbes, "Elgeet Stereo Attachments Fit Most 16mm Cameras and Projectors," *AC*, August 1953, 384; advertisement, "3-D with Bolex," *AC*, September 1953, 441.

110. "Eight 16mm 3-D Films Presented Filming Awards in *American Cinematographer*'s 3-D Film Festival," *AC*, March 1954, 140–41.

111. Thomas Elsaesser, "The 'Return' of 3-D: On Some of the Logics and Genealogies of the Image in the Twenty-First Century," *Critical Inquiry* 39 (Winter 2013): 231.

112. The Photographic Society of America's "Stereo [Photography] Division" was established in 1951 and continues today as the "3D Division"; see www.psa-photo.org/index.php?divisions-3d-historian. One of the most famous amateur stereographic photographers was Harold Lloyd, who was an avid 3-D photographer from 1947 until his death in 1971.

113. Ed Ludes, "These Things Called 'Tricks,'" *AC*, August 1935, 355.

114. "Closeups," *MM*, July 1940, 314.

115. Jerry Fairbanks, "Films for Television," *MM*, May 1949, 186.

116. Frederick Foster, "The Big Switch Is to TV!," *AC*, January 1955, 27.

117. Clifford Harrington, "Our Movie on TV," *AC*, April 1955, 227: "It started out simply as a planned documentary of a day in the life of a rural Mexican boy."

118. "Amateur Film Festival," *AC*, November 1956, 675, 690.

119. George Merz, "You Can Film Television—an Inquisitive Amateur Reports His Successful Methods for Shooting the Air-Borne Programs," *MM*, December 1947, 528.

120. "Television Broadcasts—a New Field for Amateur Movie Makers," *AC*, May 1948, 172.

121. Leo Caloia, "Home Movies from Television," *AC*, April 1952, 168: "Focus your camera on your home TV screen for a new sources of movie making pleasure." Also see George Cushman, "Cinema Clinic—T.V. Helps," *PSA Journal*, February 1955. Cushman notes that because of TV use of 16mm film, costs for film went down, processing got faster, home processing became possible, and better quality film stock was also developed (Tri-X); "And last but not least, T.V. has brought the movie projection screen right into our living rooms. Now, any hour of the day or night, we can sit at home and study filming techniques. We can study composition, lighting, unusual angles, different treatments, titling tricks by thousands, and thereby increase our knowledge."

122. Robert J. Berry, "Video Tape Recording and Home Movies," *AC*, March 1954, 142.

CHAPTER 5. CINÉ-SINCERITY

1. James W. Moore, ACL, "The Amateur: 1923–1950," *MM*, December 1950, 475.

2. Many magazines, companies, and organizations outside film, such as the American Humane Society, also organized numerous small amateur contests. "Bergman Wins Humane Society Film Contest" *AC*, June 1947, 222; "16mm Amateur Contest Announced by American Humane Society," *AC*, September 1947, 336.

3. "Among the Movie Clubs," *AC*, July 1946, 252; see also Roger Hawkins, "The Man Who Shot MacArthur: Gaetano Faillace Military Photographer," *Captions*, 2008: 1–5.

4. "Among the Movie Clubs," *AC*, September 1946, 328; "Among the Movie Clubs," *AC*, July 1947, 250, 252.

5. "Through the Editor's Finder," *AC*, May 1946, 166.

6. "Among the Movie Clubs: New York Metropolitan," *AC*, April 1948, 130.

7. Fred Evans, "Why Join a Movie Club? Some of the Advantages Offered by Cine Groups," *MM*, November 1946, p. 431.

8. "Organizing an Amateur Movie Club," *AC*, June 1948, 212.

9. Marcella Schield, "A Movie Picnic: Where Filming Was the Chief Lure," *MM*, July 1946, 267.

10. "L.A. Cinema Club Amateur Exposition Huge Success," *AC*, September 1947, 330.

11. AACC programs, Margaret Conneely Collection, Chicago Film Archives (hereafter referred to as CFA).
12. "Amateur Clubs," *MM*, July 1946, 270.
13. "Clubs," *MM*, March 1949, 114.
14. Helen E. King, "Run a Nickelodeon Night!," *MM*, November 1949, 423.
15. Walter F. Chappelle Jr., "Aids for the Ailing Movie Club," *MM*, January 1949, 23.
16. Sidney Moritz, "Break It Up!," *MM*, October 1949, 381.
17. Alvin D. Roe "The Cine Amateur Today," *AC*, July 1951, 271, 285, 287, 290.
18. The writer also noted that film circulation and government support were essential elements present in Europe but not the United States; Alvin D. Roe, "Is Organization the Answer?," *AC*, September 1951, 364.
19. Editorial, *Metro News*, January 1953, 2, Margaret Conneely Collection, CFA.
20. Quoted in *Metro News*, November 1954, 3, Margaret Conneely Collection, CFA.
21. Gordon Malthouse, "Good Films Deserve an Audience," *AC*, November 1951, 458, 464–66.
22. "Amateur Film Festival," *AC*, November 1956, 675, 690.
23. Curriculum vitae files, Margaret Conneely Collection, CFA.
24. *MM*, December 1947, 553: announcement of Cinema 16 opening. In this, Cinema 16 followed on the specialized film exhibitions that the Museum of Modern Art had begun some years earlier. See Haidee Wasson, *Museum Movies* (Berkeley: University of California, 2005).
25. "Are You 'One in a Million?,'" *AC*, July 1948, 240.
26. Don Mohler, "Start with Triangle Lighting," *AC*, December 1947, 444.
27. Ralph Lawton, "Making Movies for Money," *AC*, July 1948, 237.
28. Arthur E. Gavin, "The American Cinematographer Award," *AC*, September 1949, 326, 343–44.
29. *AC*, November 1949, 411.
30. "*American Cinematographer* Annual Amateur Film Awards," *AC*, April 1950, 132–35.
31. Announcement of the 1951 *AC* Amateur Motion Picture Competition, *AC*, August 1950, 276.
32. "*American Cinematographer* Award Winners," *AC*, May 1951, 188–90, 192.
33. Ibid.
34. Announcement of the 1952 *AC* Amateur Motion Picture Competition, *AC*, October 1951, 410, 424.
35. The contest also excluded international entries because of customs issues. "*American Cinematographer* Award Winners," *AC*, May 1952, 210–11, 221.
36. Arthur Rowan, "Filming a Winner," *AC*, July 1952, 302; John Forbes, "The Making of a Prize-Winning Film," *AC*, December 1951, 504; Leo

Heffernan, "The 'Once in a Lifetime' Thrills," *AC*, October 1952, 441; John Forbes, "Rugged Individualism in Amateur Movie Making," *AC*, August 1952, 346.

37. Charles Loring, "The Cinema Workshop: 1. The Cinematic Idea," *AC*, July 1946, 244.

38. "The Cinema Workshop: 20. (Conclusion) Distributing Your Film," *AC*, February 1948, 58: 20.

39. Over the course of the 1950s, *AC* presented a variety of articles about film aesthetics that were relevant to amateur activities. Articles about Norman McLaren focused on his experiments with the camera and noted his roots as an amateur. (A clipping of this article appears in Margaret Conneely's papers.) Nadine Pizzo, a California-based painter and amateur filmmaker (with her husband, Sal), wrote several articles for *American Cinematographer*: "The Drama of Color," December 1955, 720; "Our Goals Were Too Ambitious for 8mm," January 1956, 36; "The Drama of Color in Cinematography," February 1956, 100; and "Pictorial Significance of Light," September 1956, 550. Profiles of other successful amateurs also appear, such as a story titled "The Grasshopper Group," about "Britain's best-known cine club," which included future film historian Kevin Brownlow. Harold Benson, "The Grasshopper Group—a Cine Amateur Cooperative," *AC*, December 1956, 736–37, 750–52.

40. William Goetz, ". . . The Future of Cinematography," *AC*, October 1948, contents page.

41. Charles Loring, "The 'Pro' Touches in Amateur Movies," *AC*, July 1949, 250–51; Arthur Rowan, "An Amateur with Professional Ideas," *AC*, March 1949, 92.

42. Jay Devon, "Cinematography's Changing Pace," *AC*, August 1949, 280.

43. Leigh Allen, "Ralph Gray, Number One Movie Amateur," *AC*, August 1949, 290, 304.

44. Herb A. Lightman, "'Caesar's' Hollywood Triumph," *AC*, May 1951, 180–81.

45. A.D. Roe, "Amateurs Who Became 'Pros,'" *AC*, August 1952, 348–49.

46. Arthur Rowan, "So, You Want to Be a Hollywood Cameraman," *AC*, November 1955, 657, 679.

47. Charles Loring, "New Horizons for 16mm News Filmers," *AC*, April 1950, 131.

48. Earl L. Clark, "Cameramen Are a Breed Apart," *AC*, October 1954, 503.

49. Charles W. Herbert, "Travelogues Offer Filming Challenge!," *AC*, January 1955, 36.

50. Roy Creveling, "Cashing in on 16mm Filming," *AC*, April 1956, 240.

51. Frank Daugherty, "The Cinematographer and the Independent," *AC*, June 1955, 344.

52. Ibid.

53. Ray E. Long, "Cinematography in Small Studio Production," *AC*, June 1956, 364; Clarence Duncan and Robert Basset, "Religious Films—a Major Industry," *AC*, February 1957, 96.

54. Earle Memory, "Cannes Festival—Incentive for Amateur Movie Makers," *AC*, September 1958, 568, 570, 572.

55. Jay Devon, "Collegiate Movie Makers," *AC*, July 1951, 220–21.

56. Herbert Skoble and Roger Andrew Caras, "'Let Me See'—Top Intercollegiate Film Award Winner," *AC*, October 1953, 482–83. (Notably, this article appears outside the amateur section of the magazine.)

57. "Anniversary" (editorial), *MM*, August 1946, 299.

58. "A Path to Peace" (editorial), *MM*, May 1947, 189.

59. See, for example, "Great Britain Reporting! International Contacts," *MM*, December 1950, 479; "Clubs," *MM*, June 1949, 234–35. The "Clubs" section included a very international selection of clubs and their reports, including news of amateur movie clubs from Costa Rica, the United States, South Africa (Durban), Canada (Winnipeg), France, the United Kingdom, and Australia. The Institute of Amateur Cinematography, UNICA, and numerous other international organizations still survive today, hold annual conventions, and preserve libraries of amateur movies.

60. "Craftsmanship," *MM*, February 1947, 57.

61. Untitled editorial, *MM*, July 1947, 287.

62. "A New President," *MM*, August 1947, 331.

63. "The New Movie Makers," *MM*, December 1947, 554.

64. "More Than Labeled," *MM*, March 1948, 86.

65. Lawrence B. Foster, "The Reader Writes," *MM*, February 1948, 50.

66. Responding to a letter by amateur filmmaker Frank Gunnell, several other amateurs commented on the creative versus realist approaches to filmmaking. "The Reader Writes," *MM*, February 1948, 50.

67. George F. Hartshorn, "How Amateur Is Amateur?," *MM*, March 1948, 94.

68. In the same issue: "Scenic long shots, with maximum crispness of detail, are better in the larger image of Sixteen, experts agree." "Eight or Sixteen?," *MM*, March 1948, 102–3.

69. "The Reader Writes," *MM*, April 1948, 140.

70. Ibid.

71. "The Reader Writes," *MM*, May 1948, 182.

72. Ibid.

73. Ibid. After initially claiming that his own camera had cost only $10, Hartshorn provides more details about his 8mm equipment here, which *MM* calculated as worth $205.15; the magazine proposes that he could outfit himself similarly in 16mm film for $194.00, though this wouldn't account for the difference in film costs.

74. "Splinters," *MM*, April 1948, 174.

75. "The Feeling of Sincerity," *MM*, July 1951, 242.

76. "Hints from Hollywood," *MM*, May 1948, 200; "Busman's Holiday—How Spare Time and a Couple of Spare Cameras Led Red Skelton, ACL, into Filming for Fun," *MM*, February 1949, 59. According to the article, the actor was an avid amateur and a member of the ACL, but this could be studio publicity at work.

77. Paul R. Stout, "Films for the Few?," *MM*, June 1948, 226–27.
78. "Closeups—What Filmers Are Doing," *MM*, September 1948, 346: "From San Francisco came Frank Stauffacher, ACL, on a talent hunt for his Art in Cinema programs of the city's Museum of Fine Art. We suggested seeing Maya Deren, just back from Haiti with new footage, and Amos Vogel, of New York's burgeoning Cinema 16."
79. "Closeups—What Filmers Are Doing," *MM*, January 1949, 33.
80. "Closeups—What Filmers Are Doing," *MM*, August 1949, 285.
81. "League Loses Pioneer Leader—Roy W. Winton, ACL, Managing Director since the League's Founding, Passes at Sixty-Five," *MM*, February 1949, 55.
82. Ibid., 78.
83. "Roy W. Winton, ACL," *MM*, February 1949, 78.
84. "ACL Annual Meeting," *MM*, June 1949, 218, 230. About James W. Moore, the article says, "His hobbies are still photography, travel, cats, American jazz music and the collection of books on maritime subjects. Mr. Moore is forty five years of age, married and lives in the Greenwich Village section of New York City."
85. "The Second Generation," *MM*, June 1949, 238.
86. William L. Lucas, "Got Any Ideas?," *MM*, October 1949, 370.
87. "Renascence," *MM*, December 1949, 478.
88. "Which Do *You* Choose," *MM*, March 1951, 102.
89. Don Bennett, "The Diffuser," *PSA Journal* (*PSAJ* hereafter), April 1955, 3; Harris Tuttle, "A Note to All Former A.C.L. Members," *PSAJ*, June 1955, 33. Tuttle writes, "First I would like to say that the A.C.L. has been in financial difficulty for quite a few years. Colonel Roy W. Winton, managing director of the League up until his death in 1949, told me in 1945 that for several years he had been using his personal fortune to keep the League out of the red. . . . But it was impossible to rent a suite of offices in New York City, pay a staff of capable technical experts and an editor and put out 12 issues of a magazine without going in the hole, particularly in view of the general rising costs of publishing and other services, plus inflation. Since Colonel Winton's death other friends of the League have contributed money from their own pockets, the staff was cut, and those that did remain, continued on greatly reduced salaries. . . . Knowing the situation at League headquarters it is a mystery to know how they kept going as long as they did." Discussions to combine ACL with the Motion Picture Division of PSA had taken place as early as 1947.
90. "Aims and Accomplishments of the PSA," *PSAJ*, June 1947, 352.
91. Harris B. Tuttle, "The First Years of the Motion Picture Division," *PSAJ*, January 1955, 36.
92. Ibid.
93. Ernst Wildi, "What Can the Movie Maker Learn from Still Photography?," *PSAJ*, February 1955, 34.
94. "Beginners Page," *PSAJ*, February 1958, 48. The article notes a "definite relationship between good movie making and good slide lectures."

95. Harris Tuttle, "Today's Amateur Movie Maker," *PSAJ*, April 1947, 219.

96. Prior to the merger, there had been around seven hundred Motion Picture Division members of the PSA. Norris Harkness, "Welcome to PSA," *PSAJ*, January 1955, 21; Norris Harkness, "The President Reports," *PSAJ*, March 1955, 2. Not all ACL members were aware of the change; apparently ACL members were notified of the merger and then were automatically sent *PSAJ* starting in January. Earlier they had been asked to vote on the merger, though some evidently didn't read "letter from ACL asking you to vote for or against the move. The vote of your fellow members was about 900 in favor and 2 against." Don Bennett, "The Diffuser," *PSAJ*, April 1955, 3.

97. Norris Harkness, "Welcome to PSA," *PSAJ*, January 1955, 21. PSA was described as "a true membership organization" in which members contributed to the general welfare of the whole, much as in small camera clubs, but here on a larger scale.

98. "MPD Starts Club Film Exchange," *PSAJ*, November 1955, 52.

99. Calls for this separate section for moviemakers had come as soon as the ACL merger took place in 1955. "The Diffuser," *PSAJ*, May 1955, 3.

100. Cushman was also the chairman of the MPD in the late 1950s and author of books for amateurs.

101. George Cushman, "Cinema Clinic," *PSAJ*, January 1955, 14.

102. George Cushman, "Cinema Clinic," *PSAJ*, April 1955, 52.

103. George Cushman, "Movie Clubs," *PSAJ*, August 1955, 52; George Cushman, "Cinema Clinic," *PSAJ*, October 1955, 54.

104. George Cushman, "Professional Technique," *PSAJ*, November 1955, 52.

105. George Cushman, "Why Criticism," *PSAJ*, May 1956, 38; George Cushman, "Movie Programs for a Year," *PSAJ*, August 1956, 26.

106. George Cushman, "When They Get What They Want," *PSAJ*, March 1958, 52.

107. The authors of these regular articles were George Cushman, Harris Tuttle, Herbert McKay, Tullio Pellegrini, Nadine and Sal Pizzo, Esther Cook, Ed Kentera, and Dick Bird. Margaret Conneely was also a presence but more behind the scenes, not an author of articles here. Also Herbert McKay, "What's Wrong with Home Movies?," *PSAJ*, April 1957, 36.

108. George Cushman, "Interests," *PSAJ*, April 1956, 44.

109. Dennis Pett, "How to Produce a Documentary Film," *PSAJ*, October 1956, 36.

110. "The Ten Best," *PSAJ*, November 1956, 44.

111. Ed Kentera, "On Judging the Motion Picture," *PSAJ*, August 1957, 42.

112. Ernest F. Humphrey, "Judging the Amateur Film," *PSAJ*, February 1958, 44; George Cushman, "'Still' Technique," *PSAJ*, March 1959, 42.

113. Al Morton, "Are Contests Necessary?," *PSAJ*, June 1959, 47.

114. "The Cine Section," *PSAJ*, August 1958, 44.

115. George Cushman, "PSA-MPD Course in Motion Pictures: Lesson One," *PSAJ*, August 1959, 40–43. Information about "how to use these lessons" was also included.

116. George Cushman, "All Time Best," *PSAJ*, February 1959, 45.
117. George Cushman, "The Motion Picture," *PSAJ*, June 1959, 50.
118. The Cine Section also published debates on the creative use of sound in amateur film: George Cushman, "Does a Motion Picture Need Sound?," *PSAJ*, July 1959, 44–45; Peter Gibbons, "The Film as Art," *PSAJ*, September 1959, 47–49; George Cushman, "The Close Up," *PSAJ*, September 1959, 50–51.
119. Ed Kentera, "Cobwebs and Cameras," *PSAJ*, December 1959, 51–52: "Experimental films may include all films related to any subject in which a previously established pattern has not been set."
120. Harris Tuttle suggested that the initial impetus for forming the MPD was the PSA's need for evening programming (i.e., film screenings) at the annual convention. Harris B. Tuttle, "The First Years of the Motion Picture Division," *PSAJ*, January 1955, 36. At the 1955 Boston convention, Maya Deren appeared as a speaker on an MPD panel.
121. "The 1955 PSA International Cinema Competition," *PSAJ*, May 1955, 20; *PSAJ*, June 1955, 47.
122. "The Ten Best," *PSAJ*, November 1956, 44; see also *PSAJ*, November 1959, 46–49; and "The Ten Best Films," *PSAJ*, November 1960, 39.
123. George Cushman, "8 and 16," *PSAJ*, February 1957, 54.
124. "The 1958 PSA International Cinema Competition," *PSAJ*, June 1958, 53.
125. George Cushman, "British Ten Best," *PSAJ*, July 1959, 50.
126. *Fairy Princess* and other Margaret Conneely films are part of the Conneely Collection at the Chicago Film Archives.
127. Biographical information from the Margaret Conneely files (CFA) and conversations with the author. See also "AACL, 1954," *MM*, August 1954, 205, 214–16.
128. Margaret Conneely, "Making a Movie," *New York Times*, May 16, 1954, X15.

CHAPTER 6. "COMMUNICATING A NEW FORM OF KNOWLEDGE"

1. "'Why I Film' Contest Letters," *MM*, March 1933, 108.
2. Roy W. Winton, "Why They Film," *MM*, July 1933, 292.
3. See also Carl Becker, "Everyman His Own Historian," *American Historical Review* 37, no. 2 (January 1932): 221–36. This is the published version of Becker's presidential address to the American Historical Association, December 29, 1931.
4. Hiram Percy Maxim, "Amateur Cinema League—a Close Up," *AMM*, December 1926, 7.
5. Marion Norris Gleason, "Movie Portraiture," *MM*, March 1932, 102.
6. Sue Rice, "The Child and the Cinema—the Secrets of Successful Juvenile Cinematography," *MM*, March 1928, 153. These remarks on the psychological value of motion pictures also recall Arthur Gale's comments on Watson and Webber's *The Fall of the House of Usher*.

7. Harris B. Tuttle, "New Facts on the New Film," *MM*, October 1931, 533; see also Frank R. Knight Jr., "Scenarios for Superspeed," *MM*, November 1931, 596. As this suggests, amateurs had some understanding of the concept of "documentary film"—though it was often adapted to amateur contexts; see "Real Popular Interest in these Documentaries," *AC*, March 1939, 104; Edward H. Schustack, "Documentary Filming in America," *AC*, March 1939, 130–31; James A. Sherlock, "Documentaries for the Amateur," *AC*, Sept. 1939, 414–15; "John Grierson: Maker of Documentaries," *AC*, October 1939, 442–43; Irving Browning, "The Documentary Film," *AC*, February 1945, 44; and Herb A. Lightman, "The Technique of the Documentary Film," *AC*, November 1945, 371.

8. S. Richard Solomonick, "Montage Uses," *MM*, February 1933, 57.

9. "A Solid Base," *MM*, July 1934, 273.

10. William L. Lucas, "Got Any Ideas?," *MM*, October 1949, 370: "Even the simplest theme, says this family filmer, will change your cine snapshots into a real motion picture." See also "Let's Say Something," *MM*, October 1949, 394.

11. Patricia R. Zimmermann, *Reel Families: A Social History of Amateur Film* (Bloomington: Indiana University Press, 1995), 122.

12. "Let's Say Something," 394.

13. Hiram Percy Maxim, "Amateur Cinema League—a Close Up," *AMM*, December 1926, 7.

14. John Dewey, *The Public and Its Problems* (1927; Athens, OH: Swallow Press, 1991), 184. Dewey's comments were in large part a response to Walter Lippman's writings in *The Phantom Public* (1927), which challenged the idea that a North American "public" could be identified and relied upon to intelligently participate in civil and democratic society.

15. Timothy Lawler, "From Review to Reward," *MM*, January 1953, 14.

16. Paul D. Hugon, "Getting the Games," *MM*, April 1933, 143.

17. See also collaborative club city films, discussed in previous chapters, *AC*, October 1947, 366. Among the movie clubs, the Oakland Camera Club has plans for "compiling a complete 'movization' of the city of Oakland. Every member is expected to participate by filming 10 to 15 foot clips of what the individual considers an outstanding feature of the city or its environment. Later, all film clips will be edited according to classifications (transportation, industry, scenic, civic buildings, recreation, etc.) and spliced in continuity to provide a complete picturization of the community."

18. R. Fawn Mitchell, "Filming the Fair," *MM*, July 1933, 284.

19. Ibid., 293.

20. "From the President," *MM*, June 1939, 267.

21. Jay Leyda, "Tips on Topicals," *MM*, January 1931, 13.

22. Harry Alan Potamkin, "The Montage Film: Europe's Contribution to the Art of Editing," *MM*, February 1930, 89; see also Louis M. Bailey, "City Cinematics: How to Make Significant Movie Portraits of American Towns," *MM*, August 1928, 501.

23. For a more detailed discussion about Leslie Thatcher's work see my essay "Uncovering Canada's Amateur Film Tradition: Leslie Thatcher's Films

and Contexts," in *Cinephemera: Archives, Ephemeral Cinema and New Screen Histories in Canada*, ed. Zoë Druick and Gerda Cammaer (Montreal: McGill-Queen's University Press, forthcoming).

24. Potamkin, "The Montage Film," 89.

25. Dewey, *The Public and Its Problems*, 183–84.

26. "The Free Amateur," *MM*, September 1934, 361. This vision of cinematic history writing also recalls Albert Kahn's utopian project, the Archives de la Planète; see Paula Amad, "Cinema's 'Sanctuary': From Pre-Documentary to Documentary Film in Albert Kahn's Archives de la Planète (1908–1931)," *Film History* 13, no. 2 (2001).

27. Bill Nichols, *Representing Reality* (Bloomington: Indiana University Press, 1991); and Bill Nichols, "Documentary Film and the Modernist Avant-Garde," *Critical Inquiry* 27 (Summer 2001). An alternate view of nonfiction film has recently emerged in writing about travel films (particularly during the early and silent eras); see Jeffrey Ruoff, ed., *Virtual Voyages: Cinema and Travel* (Durham, NC: Duke University Press, 2006).

28. Tom Gunning argues that many early travel films appealed to a "sensational" approach to filmmaking, provoking the sensation of physical movement through space (on a train, for example, as in Hale's Tours and the *Georgetown Loop [Colorado]*, Biograph 1903). As Gunning points out, these panoramic and sensational films—perhaps like moments in Thatcher's film of a trip to Niagara—"promote a truly modern perception of landscape, one mediated by technology and speed." Tom Gunning, "'The Whole World within Reach': Travel Images without Borders," in *Virtual Voyages*, ed. Jeffrey Ruoff (Durham, NC: Duke University Press, 2006), 37.

29. Paul Pridham, "Plantation Pictures: The Land of Cotton through a Cine Camera," *AMM*, July 1927, 10.

30. Eve St. John, "Are Elephants Art? The Story of Chang—Surprise Success of the Cinema Season," *AMM*, July 1927, 8.

31. André La Varre, "Bali Adventure," *MM*, April 1933, 148.

32. Edward Said, *Orientalism* (New York: Pantheon, 1978). As Jennifer Peterson argues, "Travelogues offer up a dreamlike cinematic geography [and] are more about desire than pedagogy, with all the perilous implications of fantasy and fetishism that implies.... Travelogues presented images of the real world that allowed the spectator to experience a flight from out of the real, a flight towards exotic fantasy." Jennifer Peterson, "Travelogues and Early Nonfiction Film: Education in the School of Dreams," in *American Cinema's Transitional Era: Audiences, Institutions, Practices*, ed. Charlie Keil and Shelley Stamp (Berkeley: University of California Press, 2004), 208.

33. Robert Flaherty, "Filming Real People: The Dean of Amateurs Tells How He Made His *Man of Aran*," *MM*, December 1934, 516.

34. Andre La Varre, "Guides for Globe Trotters: In Which a Travel Movie Expert Tells How He Makes Them," *MM*, June 1931, 312.

35. Ibid.

36. Ibid.

37. Untitled editorial, *MM*, June 1931, 309.

38. For accounts of this conflict in American cultural and intellectual history, see Michael Denning, *The Cultural Front* (London: Verso, 1997); and Andrew Ross, *No Respect: Intellectuals and Popular Culture* (New York: Routledge, 1989).

39. This letter from an unnamed Kansas amateur is quoted in James Moore, "Talking of the Ten Best," *MM*, April 1951, 125.

CHAPTER 7. "THE AMATEUR TAKES LEADERSHIP"

1. Roy W. Winton, "The Significance of the First Amateur Film Contest," *MM*, June 1928, 373.

2. Histories of American avant-garde filmmaking have typically begun with Maya Deren's work in the 1940s, but a number of recent studies have reexamined earlier experimental filmmaking and even noted important intersections between amateur and avant-garde activities. See, for example, P. Adams Sitney's influential text *Visionary Film: The American Avant-Garde, 1943–1978*, 2nd ed. (Oxford: Oxford University Press, 1979). Jan-Christopher Horak's volume *Lovers of Cinema: The First American Film Avant-Garde, 1919–1945* (Madison: University of Wisconsin Press, 1995) provides the most comprehensive collection of work reevaluating early experimental film. David James's recent study of experimental film culture in Los Angeles also examines the figure of the amateur: *The Most Typical Avant-Garde: History and Geography of Minor Cinemas in Los Angeles* (Berkeley: University of California Press, 2005).

3. As a socially mainstream, and at times even conservative, organization, the ACL rejected some crucial aspects of more typical avant-gardes, such as their nihilism, radical politics, and agonistic rejection of establishment social values. Renato Poggioli, *The Theory of the Avant-Garde*, trans. Gerald Fitzgerald (Cambridge, MA: Harvard University Press, 1968).

4. John Dewey, *The Public and Its Problems* (1927; Athens, OH: Swallow Press, 1991), 203.

5. "Waste Work," *AMM*, January 1927, 5.

6. Roy Winton, "The Significance of the First Amateur Film Contest," *MM*, June 1928, 373. Similar arguments appeared elsewhere in *Movie Makers*: Hastings White, "Professional Standards?—in Which an Amateur Scans Far Horizons," *MM*, May 1929, 295.

7. Roy W. Winton, "Talking Movies and Cinematic Art," *MM*, August 1928, 513–14.

8. But amateurs were not strictly opposed to new technological developments. In a later article, Winton noted that some amateurs might wish to experiment with "talkies" much as they had experimented with radio technology in the past. But, he noted, it was important not to confuse that activity with the goal of advancing motion picture art; for Winton, talkies had no place in the latter. Roy Winton, editorial, *MM*, June 1929, 361; editorials, *MM*, September 1928, 567.

9. The initial announcement of the club noted a number of Rochester arts community leaders and Kodak personnel among its members; in addition to James Sibley Watson, this original group included C. E. Mees, a Kodak scientist instrumental in the invention of 16mm reversal film, and Marion Gleason, who had already established a name for herself as director of an early amateur photoplay, *Fly Low Jack*. An interesting shift is evident in this article, from doing the kind of chemical/technical experiments that led to a new amateur film format (16mm) to the kind of experiments that explored the new art form's aesthetic dimensions. "Rochester Pundits," *MM*, January 1928, 58.

10. "Amateur Clubs—Advanced Cinematics," *MM*, March 1928, 164.

11. Lisa Cartwright has persuasively argued that Watson and Webber saw their work as distinct from outmoded modernist formalism and instead were guided by the critical writings of e. e. cummings and Ezra Pound, creating an example of how amateurs could employ film "tricks" to develop a new visual language of poetic meaning. Cartwright sees Watson's role as coeditor of the small literary magazine *The Dial* as crucial to understanding how poetry and literary criticism influenced his filmmaking work. Lisa Cartwright, "The Right Wing of Film Art," in *Lovers of Cinema: The First American Film Avant-Garde, 1919–1945*, ed. Jan-Christopher Horak (Madison: University of Wisconsin Press, 1995), 164–75.

12. "The Amateur Takes Leadership," *MM*, January 1929, 847.

13. "Hamlet Left Out," *MM*, January 1928, 58.

14. *MM*, October 1928, 648–49.

15. First published in *Close Up*, October 1930; reprinted in Harry Alan Potamkin, *The Compound Cinema: The Film Writings of Harry Alan Potamkin*, ed. Lewis Jacobs (New York: Teachers College Press), 397.

16. Though the relationship between early documentary filming and the avant-garde has traditionally been overlooked, Bill Nichols considers some dimensions of this relationship in his "Documentary Film and the Modernist Avant-Garde," *Critical Inquiry* 27 (Summer 2001). Nichols's article focuses primarily on John Grierson's writings, which shift over the course of the 1920s and '30s from an interest in experimental aesthetics to an increasingly propagandistic rhetoric. Though tracing similar themes, my discussion attempts to outline shifts that occurred in the relationship between politics and aesthetics among amateurs in the late 1920s in greater detail and in this way provides further nuance to the discussion of documentary film and experimentation during this period.

17. "Amateur Movies," *Photoplay*, July 1929, 106; a similar report appeared in the "Amateur Clubs" column, *Movie Makers*, June 1929, 372.

18. "Amateur Movies," *Photoplay*, August 1929, 71.

19. Harry Alan Potamkin, "The Magic of Machine Films—the World of Moving Metal Invites Your Camera," *MM*, November 1929, 723.

20. By C.W. Gibbs, "Modernistic Movie Making: New Trails That Beckon the Amateur Experimenter," *MM*, August 1929, 505, 533.

21. Roy Winton, "Why Films Go Wrong: Some Important 'Don'ts' for the Amateur," *MM*, May 1929, 287.

22. Ibid.

23. By April 1932, *Move Makers* had announced that *Portrait* had been screened in New York in exhibitions organized by Alfred Stieglitz and Julien Levy. Rodakiewicz was a member of the ACL. James W. Moore, "Closeups—What Amateurs Are Doing," *MM*, April 1932, 179.

24. Henwar Rodakiewicz, "Something More Than Scenic," *MM*, June 1932, 249.

25. My reading of the film assumes that the "young man" whose portrait the film presents is Rodakiewicz, but this is by no means certain; it could just as easily be the portrait of an imaginary character. The film's title also recalls James Joyce's novel *A Portrait of the Artist as a Young Man* (1916), and although the film's stream-of-consciousness form is more reminiscent of Joyce's later works, it is interesting to consider how it might draw inspiration from any of these writings.

26. "Try This," *MM*, May 1932, 195.

27. "The Ten Best," *MM*, December 1932, 562. A copy of *I'd Be Delighted To!* is held by the East Anglia Film Archive.

28. Ibid., 538.

29. These debates in American intellectual and aesthetic history are presented particularly well in *No Respect: Intellectuals and Popular Culture*, by Andrew Ross (New York: Routledge, 1989); and *The Cultural Front*, by Michael Denning (London: Verso, 1997).

30. Founded in 1930, this magazine was published by the Cinema Crafters of America (an interesting variation on *moviemakers*) and appeared irregularly between 1930 and 1935. There are virtually no references to amateur work or amateurism in the magazine. Instead, it focuses extensively on Soviet and political filmmaking. Formalist and ideological concerns take center stage as the magazine espouses an increasingly radical and revolutionary tone. See also Hans Richter's book *Struggle for the Film: Towards a Socially Responsible Cinema*, trans. Ben Brewster (1939; New York: St. Martin's Press, 1986).

31. "Closeups," *MM*, September 1932, 398.

32. Harry Alan Potamkin, "The Montage Film: Europe's Contribution to the Art of Editing," *MM*, February 1930, 89.

33. Arthur Gale, "Amateur Clubs: What Is Art?," *MM*, March 1930, 153.

34. Editorial, *MM*, March 1930, 141.

35. Editorial, *MM*, January 1931, 11.

36. "Play—1932," *MM*, October 1932, 423.

37. "Responsibility," *MM*, November 1932, 475.

38. "The Ten Best," *MM*, December 1933, 522.

39. "Keep It Simple," *MM*, February 1934, 51.

40. "The Ten Best," *MM*, December 1934, 513, 534,

41. John Flory received a second *Movie Makers* citation for his 1941 city symphony film about Cleveland, after a short contract in Hollywood as an assistant director—won on the strength of *Mr. Motorboat*—expired and left him an amateur/independent filmmaker once again. A few articles referencing

"experimentation" continued to appear in *Movie Makers* during the mid- to late 1930s, but they tended to promote experimentation as ways of revitalizing existing amateur forms and genres, such as travelogue, scenic, and family films.

42. "A Free Art," *MM*, May 1934, 185.

43. Hiram Percy Maxim, "From Our President," *MM*, December 1936, 521.

44. Though John Flory's 1941 city symphony film about Cleveland, *Song of a City*, appears to have had some imaginative, perhaps even experimental, elements, these were not noted in *Movie Makers*. A 1942 film called *Cine Whimsy* (Robert Fels) received an honorable mention in that year's ACL competition and was described as "surrealist." But from the description, it appears to be a kind of domesticated surrealism that produced literal visualizations of figures of speech—for example, the characters "lose their heads"—through trick photography. "The Ten Best and the Maxim Award Winner," *MM*, December 1941, 568; "The Ten Best and the Maxim Memorial Award," *MM*, December 1942, 507.

45. "The Ten Best and Maxim Memorial Award," *MM*, December 1945, 497. *Meshes* was in a "special category" for films that received some manner of compensation or financial support.

46. Deren's writings in *Movie Makers* are less concerned with "pure cinematography" than with suggesting how amateurs might unlock creative approaches to their familiar subject matter. Deren's activities and successes also received fairly consistent attention in *Movie Makers*, which noted her award of a Guggenheim Foundation fellowship in 1946 and her production of *Ritual in Transfigured Time*.

47. Roberto Machado, "Adventures in Abstraction," *MM*, May 1947, 195.

48. See Michael Frierson, *Clay Animation* (New York: Twayne Publishers, 1994), 107–15.

49. *MM*, December 1947; "Closeups—What Filmers Are Doing," *MM*, September 1948, 346. The Museum of Modern Art was also instrumental in the emergence of a film art culture; see Haidee Wasson, *Museum Movies* (Berkeley: University of California, 2005).

50. Scott MacDonald, *Cinema 16: Documents toward a History of the Film Society* (Philadelphia: Temple University Press, 2002), 7.

51. Jack Stevenson, *Desperate Visions 1: Camp America—the Films of John Waters and the Kuchar Brothers* (London: Creation Books, 1996), 166.

CHAPTER 8. MECHANICAL CRAFTSMANSHIP

1. John Herman Randall, *Our Changing Civilization: How Science and the Machine Age Are Reconstructing Modern Life* (New York: Frederic A. Stokes Company, 1929), 306–7.

2. For general versions of this historical approach see Warren Sussman, *Culture as History* (New York: Pantheon, 1984); Robert Sklar, *Movie Made America*, rev. ed. (New York: Vintage, 1994); and Larry May, *Screening Out the Past* (Chicago: University of Chicago Press, 1983). More recently, Miriam

Hansen has provided an important reconsideration of these ideas in her essay "The Mass Production of the Senses: Classical Cinema as Vernacular Modernism," *Modernism/Modernity* 6, no. 2 (1999): 59–77.

3. See Charles Acland and Haidee Wasson, eds., *Useful Cinema* (Durham, NC: Duke University Press, 2011); Gregory Waller, ed., *Moviegoing in America* (Malden, MA: Blackwell, 2002); and Melvyn Stokes and Richard Maltby, eds., *American Movie Audiences* (London: BFI, 1999).

4. In both Britain (with John Grierson) and the United States (with Pare Lorenz), most significant work in documentary film during the 1930s was government-sponsored or politically motivated.

5. These are categories that recur in *Movie Makers* through the 1930s; to these we might add the subcategory of surgical films, which were like educational films in some ways but also had their own specific production and exhibition contexts and, starting in 1934, their own separate ACL film exchange.

6. J. H. McNabb, "The Amateur Turns a Penny," *AMM*, December 1926, 19.

7. Most prominent among the organizations were the National Education Association's Department of Visual Education and the Society for Visual Education; important publications included *Moving Picture Age*, *Educational Screen*, and *Visual Education*. For the early history of educational film, see Devin Orgeron, Marsha Orgeron, and Dan Streible, eds., *Learning with the Lights Off* (New York: Oxford University Press, 2012); Anthony Slide, *Before Video* (Westport, CT: Greenwood Press, 1992); Arthur Edwin Krows, "Motion Pictures—Not for Theatres," serial publication in *Educational Screen*, 1938–44; Anke Mebold and Charles Tepperman, "Resurrecting the Lost History of 28mm Film in North America," *Film History* 15, no. 2 (Fall 2003): 137–51; and Elizabeth Wiatr, "Between Word, Image, and the Machine: Visual Education and Films of Industrial Process," *Historical Journal of Film, Radio and Television* 22, no. 3 (2002): 333–51.

8. McNabb, "The Amateur Turns a Penny," 19.

9. Roy W. Winton, "A Clear Mission," *MM*, April 1928, 219.

10. Louis M. Bailey, "Educational Films: Film Progress in School, Medical, Civic, Welfare and Related Fields," *MM*, November 1929, 728.

11. "Making an Educational Movie," *Educational Screen*, February 1934, 41.

12. John Grierson, "Drifters," in *Grierson on Documentary*, ed. Forsyth Hardy (New York: Praeger, 1971), 135. The question of whether we should consider Grierson an amateur filmmaker is an interesting one; his lack of technical film training and his interest in exploring the relationships between practical life and experimental film aesthetics suggest some commonalities with amateurs. But Grierson's writings reflect an interest in his being understood as a professional propagandist, and his ideas about institutional filmmaking might be seen as the result of many years of studying the field of mass communication.

13. These process films also recall the appeal of what Neil Harris describes as "the operational aesthetic," a common feature in nineteenth-century

American popular science literature and display. Neil Harris, *Humbug: The Art of P.T. Barnum* (Chicago: University of Chicago Press, 1973), 61–89.

14. "The Ten Best," *MM*, December 1933, 499–500. It is also worth noting that most amateur practical films during the 1930s were silent works, due to the expense and unreliability of early amateur sound technologies. It was not until the arrival of magnetic sound equipment after World War Two that amateur sound films became a widespread reality.

15. Roy W. Winton, "The Amateur Cinema Camera Man—before the 1927 Meeting of the National Board of Review of Motion Pictures," *AMM*, March 1927, 37.

16. This consideration of a craftsman spirit suggests certain affinities between the ACL and the American Arts and Crafts movement; see T. J. Jackson Lears, *No Place of Grace: Antimodernism and the Transformation of American Culture, 1880–1920* (Chicago: University of Chicago Press, 1981).

17. Marguerite Tazelaar, "Portrait of a Pioneer," *AMM*, July 1927, 18–19.

18. See, for example, Ann M. Filut, "Fractions—How One School Has Dramatized Them on Substandard Film," *MM*, February 1936, 70; Donald A. Eldridge, "High School Films without Subsidy," *MM*, November 1937, 541; and "Practical Films," *MM*, June 1938, 296.

19. Laurence S. Critchell Jr., "Practical Films," *MM*, July 1940, 336. On Thrasher's involvement in early film education, see Dana Polan, *Scenes of Instruction: The Beginnings of the U.S. Study of Film* (Berkeley: University of California Press, 2007), 299–300.

20. "Practical Films," *MM*, August 1936, 351; "Cine Course at N.Y.U.," *MM*, October 1940, 482: "For the second successive year, the School of Education, Washington Square Branch of New York University, in New York City, will present Elementary Film Making for Educational Purposes, a two term course in practical film production. Kenneth F. Space, ACL, cinematographer with the Harmon Foundation, will again be the instructor."

21. Arthur Gale, "Note—Tabloid Industrial Scenarios," *MM*, September 1930, 540.

22. Arthur Gale, "Continuity of Amateur Industrials," *MM*, May 1931, 256. *Movie Makers* also published occasional articles specifically about distributing practical films, such as Ross Parmenter, "Distributing Industrial Films," *MM*, September 1938, 436.

23. Gale, "Continuity of Amateur Industrials," 256–57.

24. Kenneth Space wrote, "The most common fault of all is the lack of personal touch which is necessary to arouse and keep the interest of spectators who are not familiar with the plant itself." Kenneth Space, "Amateur Industrial Films: Suggestions for Making Them Interesting," *MM*, November 1929, 706; see also Paul D. Hugon, "Dramatizing Industrials: Suggestions on How to Film Your Business Effectively," *MM*, December 1929, 793.

25. Harrison was an active member of the ACL and Montreal amateur movie clubs; his better-known completed film, *The Highway of Tomorrow, or How One Makes Two* (1930), marks him as a technically sophisticated and

gifted amateur filmmaker. His films are now held by the National Archives of Canada, in Ottawa.

26. T. J. Jackson Lears, *Fables of Abundance* (New York: Basic Books, 1994).

27. Some amateurs delved even further into modernist abstractions of machinery and industrial processes and displayed a fascination that was at times closely related to avant-garde film. See, for example, Harry Alan Potamkin, "The Magic of Machine Films," *MM*, November 1929, 722. The late 1920s and early '30s saw growing interest in both photography (Charles Sheeler and Margaret Bourke-White) and films (such as Ralph Steiner's *Mechanical Principles*) that focused on machinery and industrial processes as objects of aesthetic fascination in their own right.

28. "The Ten Best," *MM*, December 1931, 657.

29. "All Amateur," *MM*, August 1948, 338.

30. For comprehensive and detailed histories of Progressive reformers and the movies, see Lee Grieveson, *Policing Cinema* (Berkeley: University of California Press, 2001); Melvyn Stokes and Richard Maltby, eds., *American Movie Audiences* (London: BFI, 1999); and Garth Jowett, Ian Jarvie, and Kathryn Fuller, eds., *Children and the Movies* (New York: Cambridge University Press, 1996).

31. "The Ten Best Amateur Films of 1930," *MM*, December 1930, 788.

32. Travel diary, October to December 1929, Patterson (Mrs. Jefferson) Collection File, Motion Picture and Television Reading Room, Library of Congress.

33. *Working in* is a term that appeared in *Movie Makers* articles to signal the conventions of analytical editing, which involve beginning scenes with an establishing (long) shot, before cutting to closer (medium long) shots of figures in the space, and then, finally, beginning a (medium close-up) shot/reverse-shot alternation. Theodore Huff, "Writing the Scenario," *MM*, April 1934, 143. This system is described in detail in David Bordwell, Janet Staiger, and Kristin Thompson's *The Classical Hollywood Cinema* (New York: Columbia University Press, 1985), 56–57.

34. According to Mary Breckinridge, the film drew a full house at its fundraiser premier in New York; it was subsequently shown "hundreds of times ... sometimes to drawing room groups (in 16 mm. size) and sometimes (in 35 mm. size) at regular motion picture theatres and in large halls." Mary Breckinridge, *Wide Neighborhoods: A Story of the Frontier Nursing Service* (New York: Harper and Row, 1952), 278–79.

35. For example, a film about "agricultural despotism and destitution" was produced in 1937 by the ACL member Alan S. Hacker, the proceeds of which were to aid southern sharecroppers. "Practical Films," *MM*, March 1937, 128.

36. Dewey wrote, "[Democracy] will have its consummation when free social inquiry is indissolubly wedded to the art of full and moving communication." John Dewey, *The Public and Its Problems* (1927; Athens, OH: Swallow Press, 1991), 184. The imagery Dewey uses here of course brings motion pictures poetically (if coincidentally) to mind. Grierson frequently remarks on his

own debt to Lippman in his writing, most notably in "The Course of Realism," in *Grierson on Documentary*, 207. For a succinct account of documentary film in the United States during the 1930s, see Charles Wolfe, "The Poetics and Politics of Nonfiction: Documentary Film," in *Grand Design: Hollywood as a Modern Business Enterprise, 1930–1930*, ed. Tino Balio (Berkeley: University of California Press, 1995).

37. William Rogers and Paul Veith, *Visual Aids in the Church* (Philadelphia: Christian Education Press, 1946), 14. For a more general history of religious filmmaking during this period, see Slide, *Before Video;* and Krows, "Motion Pictures—Not for Theatres."

38. Louis M. Bailey, "Motion Pictures and the Minister," *MM*, March 1931, 134.

39. "The Ten Best for 1935," *MM*, December 1935, 550. The copy of *In the Beginning* held by NARA doesn't correspond exactly to this description.

40. As reported, for example, in Louis Miller Bailey's article "Church and Film Take a New Step," *MM*, March 1932, 112. "The mass is subject of teaching film for Catholic schools," notes the subtitle of this article, which goes on to report, "Details of the Mass, seldom seen hitherto, are revealed by film."

41. RG 200-HF-138, Harmon Foundation Files, NARA. *In the Beginning, Ceramics,* and about a dozen other winners of ACL Ten Best recognition during the 1930s and early '40s were distributed by the Harmon Foundation, whose collection of films and film documentation is now held at NARA. Materials in the *In the Beginning* file include discussion topics of the following titles: "The Source of the Story; What Creation Means; Steps in Creation; The Purpose of Creation; Does Creation Continue?; Observation Test (and discussion); Project Activity Suggestions: Creation through the Ages; The Variety of Creation; Various Creation Stories."

42. For more about the Gists' films see, Amy Kael Petrine, "Hell Bound, Heaven Bound, the Journey: Black America, 1930s Quest for Personal Advancement Using Motivational Imagery in Dramatic Productions," unpublished manuscript in Eloyce Gist Collection File, Library of Congress; Gloria J. Gibson-Hudson, "Recall and Recollect: Excavating the Life History of Eloyce King Patrick Gist," *Black Film Review* 8, no. 2 (1994): 21–22; and Gloria J. Gibson, "Cinematic Foremothers: Zora Neale Hurston and Eloyse King Patrick Gist," in *Oscar Micheaux and His Circle,* ed. Pear Bowser, Jane Gaines, and Charles Musser (Bloomington: Indiana University Press, 2001).

43. During the 1930s the Harmon Foundation made some efforts, with the guidance of Alain Locke, to join their support of African American artists with their interest in amateur filmmaking. But there is no evidence that the Gists were involved with this activity.

44. Internal correspondence, May-June 1933, NAACP Papers (photocopies in Eloyce Gist Collection File), Library of Congress.

45. "Play—1932," *MM*, October 1932, 423.

46. The film was scripted by the African Missionary Project and distributed by the Harmon Foundation; *Movie Makers* praised the film for its drama and

its skillful handling of native actors, awarding it with an honorable mention in the 1939 annual Ten Best contest.

47. See, for example, a similar film set in Mexico, *The Forgotten Village* (Alexander Hamid and Herbert Kline, 1941).

48. Correspondence during the winter of 1935 between Locke and the director of the Harmon Foundation, Mary Brady, shows that the organization provided Allen with a membership to the ACL and a 16mm camera for him to work on the film. By spring of 1935, however, both correspondents expressed their disappointment at Allen's lack of progress, which they attributed to his ill health. Correspondence between Brady and Locke, 1934–35, box 1, records of the Harmon Foundation, Library of Congress.

49. "The Ten Best and the Maxim Memorial Award," *MM*, December 1941, 568. The Garners' third award-winning film was *On the Farm*, which was named one of the Ten Best of 1940 and shows the story "of child life on a Midwestern farm." "The Ten Best and the Maxim Memorial Award," *MM*, December 1940, 600.

50. Louis Menand, *The Metaphysical Club* (New York: Farrar, Straus and Giroux, 2001), 376–408.

51. The production files for *We Are All Artists* include suggestions for programming an educational meeting around the screening of the film. Among the "suggestions for opening remarks" are further efforts to link art with everyday life, the historical development of art in the machine age, and even "the humanizing qualities of work in the crafts."

52. John Dewey, "Experience, Nature and Art," excerpt from his *Experience and Nature* (1925), reprinted in *Pragmatism: A Reader*, ed. Louis Menand (New York: Vintage, 1997), 238–41.

53. "All Amateur," *MM*, August 1948, 358.

CHAPTER 9. PHOTOPLAYING THEMSELVES

1. John Dewey, *Individualism Old and New* (London: George Allen & Unwin, 1931), 67.

2. In fact Vidor made some "amateur" films during a drip to Europe in 1928: "Amateur Movies," *Photoplay*, July 1928, 107. Vidor noted about his European films: "I did not take a single scenic shot of well known buildings or scenes. . . . I did not go after the usual postcard stuff. I tried only to get the feeling of the country . . . characteristic oddities." "New Amateur Movie Contest," *Photoplay*, September 1928, 68–69.

3. In fact, the league's founding by-laws noted the possibility of establishing specific "divisions" but specified only one: the Amateur Cinema Dramatic Division. This division was proposed "to stimulate the production of community photoplays [and] . . . the creation, in communities, of a greater consciousness of the motion picture and its proper use in community life, the increase of intelligent appraisal and appreciation of motion pictures in general; the provision of an outlet for talent in writing scenarios, motion picture acting and

camera work and the development, through the means of the cinematographic art." "Rules of the Game: Official Constitution and By-Laws of the Amateur Cinema League," *AMM*, December 1926, 35.

4. This idea of a vernacular amateur film style is strongly indebted to Miriam Hansen's idea of "vernacular modernism." But whereas Hansen's formulation is particularly attentive to the circulation and appropriation of modernist aesthetic techniques, vernacular amateur films are not necessarily modernist (sometimes they are specifically anti-modernist) in their style. Miriam Hansen, "The Mass Production of the Senses: Classical Cinema as Vernacular Modernism," *Modernism/Modernity* 6, no. 2 (1999).

5. Arthur Gale, *Making a Simple Film Story: A Guide to the Amateur in Filming Short Photoplays* (New York: Amateur Cinema League, 1929), 3. The ACL published many bulletins like this, including *Scenarized Film Plans* (1934) and *Film Plans and Scripts* (1937), both by James Moore.

6. "Hollywood at Harkness—Yale Students Are First to Film Famous Novel," *MM*, August 1927, 28.

7. Alfred Noyes, *Collected Poems* (New York: Frederick A. Stokes Company, 1913).

8. The version that I have seen is also in black and white, though articles in *Shots and Angles: The Bulletin of the Toronto Amateur Movie Club* suggest that the film was originally shot in color.

9. *Shots and Angles*, May 1937, 3–4.

10. *Shots and Angles*, November 1937, 2, contains a request from the Winnipeg Movie Club to borrow and show *The Highwayman*.

11. *Shots and Angles*, June 1938, 3–4.

12. Alan Moorhouse, "An Editorial by the Club President," *Shots and Angles*, November 1937, 1.

13. "Amusement Seekers," *Wilmette Life*, August 27, 1936, n.p., box 1, folder 1, David Bradley Papers, series 55/16, Northwestern University Archives.

14. *Winnetka Talk*, August 4, 1938, 42, Bradley Papers. Later in his life, Bradley was best known for his enormous collection of 16mm film prints; these cinematheque screenings of literary adaptations accompanied by cartoon shorts may have drawn on the beginnings of this collection. Both of the feature films cited here were included in the David Bradley collection deposited at Indiana University.

15. David Bradley, "Amateurs Film Heroic Saga," *MM*, August 1942, 322, 340. Because Bradley revised and reedited several of his films, including this one, in the 1960s, it is difficult to be certain how it looked when first completed.

16. Bradley's use of commercial film footage in his own production is particularly skillful but not unique among amateurs. For example, Margaret Conneely's film *So Long Ago* (c. 1950s) intercuts footage of children reading about dinosaurs with special-effects shots of dinosaurs, borrowed from a commercial film (perhaps *The Lost World*, 1925).

17. The version rerecorded in 1965 uses the voice of Frances X. Bushman, who, perhaps ironically here, first became famous as a silent-era movie actor.

18. Henrik Ibsen, *Peer Gynt*, trans. R. Farquharson Sharp (New York: Dutton, 1921), act 4, scene 1.

19. Both attended the Todd School for Boys, though at different times—Welles from 1926 to 1931, Bradley from 1935 to 1937.

20. "The Ten Best and the Maxim Memorial Award," *MM*, December 1941, 566.

21. *An Amateur Photoplay in the Making* (Rochester, NY: Eastman Kodak Company, c. 1927), 5. See also "Actors as Amateurs—the Rochester Community Players Produce a Photoplay," *MM*, October 1927, 26.

22. C. G. Winkopp, *How to Write a Photoplay*, 6th ed. (New York: Winkopp, 1915), 21. In a similar vein, the Palmer Photoplay Corporation published a series of lectures in 1920 for subscribers to the Palmer Plan of Photoplay Writing course, presumably designed to train aspiring screenwriters; one of these lectures, "The Point of Attack, or How to Start the Photoplay," was contributed by director Clarence Badger.

23. Dorothea Mitchell, "A Race for Ties (Its Inception)," reprinted in *The Lady Lumberjack: An Annotated Collection of Dorothea Mitchell's Writings*, ed. Michel Beaulieu and Ronald Harpelle (Thunder Bay, Ontario: Center for Northern Studies, 2005), 125.

24. As recounted in chapter 8, "I Buy Timber," of Mitchell's *The Lady Lumberjack*. Of course, the degree of reliability of this "factual" account is hard to know, given Mitchell's flair for the dramatic and also because it was written many years after *A Race for Ties* was completed.

25. Suggesting a link to the travelogue aesthetic, one review of this (real) book noted, "Negley Farson with a photographic eye and a clear reportorial style has observed contemporary Russian life in the closest possible way and, in *Black Bread and Red Coffins*, has written a compelling book about it." *Harvard Crimson*, December 9, 1930.

26. *Wisconsin Dells Events*, December 17, 1931, 1.

27. Miriam Hansen tracks the vernacular circulation of this gesture as far away as Shanghai in her essay "Fallen Women, Rising Stars, New Horizons: Shanghai Silent Film as Vernacular Modernism," *Film Quarterly* 54, no. 1 (Fall 2000): 19.

28. *Wisconsin Dells Events*, May 26, 1932, 1. An earlier article notes that previous Bennett films shown in the town included *A Trip Down the Dells of the Wisconsin* and *The Early Pioneers*, which were described as alive with "professional photographic talent." *Wisconsin Dells Events*, December 10, 1931.

29. "Closeups," *MM*, August 1932, 361; see also James W. Moore, "Closeups," *MM*, February 1932, 72. The August article's offhand allusion to a "Sovkino drama" is also noteworthy as an indication of the circulation and familiarity of this kind of film in amateur circles.

30. Theodore Huff, "The Mirror of Burlesque," *MM*, October 1932, 448.

31. "The Ten Best and the Maxim Memorial Award," *MM*, December 1949, 470.

32. Patricia R. Zimmermann, *Reel Families: A Social History of Amateur Film* (Bloomington: Indiana University Press, 1995), 67–71.

33. Dewey, *Individualism Old and New*, 81.

34. Roy W. Winton, "Talking Movies and Cinematic Art," *MM*, August 1928, 513–14.

35. Roy W. Winton, "A Defense Inherited: What the Amateur Can Learn from Hollywood's Mistakes," *MM*, February 1930, 85.

36. For this position, as well as general information on Huff, see Chuck Kleinhans, "Theodore Huff: Historian and Filmmaker," in *Lovers of Cinema: The First American Film Avant-Garde, 1919–1945*, ed. Jan-Christopher Horak (Madison: University of Wisconsin Press, 1995). Lampert claims that it was only Huff's collaborative works (*Motorboat*, with John Flory, and later collaborations in the 1950s) that contain any experimental elements and that these elements should be primarily attributed to his collaborators; more detailed information on the production of Huff's films, as well as Andrew Lampert's report on categorization, can be found in the papers of the Theodore Huff Collection, George Eastman House (GEH, Rochester, NY). Tom Gunning, "Flaming Images: Burning through the Celluloid Closet," paper presented at the conference Beyond Warhol, Smith, and Anger: The Significance of Postwar Queer Underground Cinema, 1950–1968, University of Chicago, April 7–8, 2006.

37. In 1935 Huff codirected (with Mark Borgotte) what Kleinhans describes as a "short, undistinguished" documentary about the movie studios there, called *Ghost Town: The Story of Fort Lee*.

38. Theodore Huff Papers, GEH.

39. "The Ten Best," *MM*, December 1931, 658.

40. Theodore Huff, "The Mirror of Burlesque," *MM*, October 1932, 429.

41. "The Ten Best," *MM*, December 1931, 658. "This year's listing was chosen from nearly a thousand different amateur subjects."

42. Theodore Huff, "The Mirror of Burlesque," *MM*, October 1932, 429.

43. Theodore Huff, "Writing the Scenario," *MM*, April 1934, 143.

44. Theodore Huff, "Spoken Titles," *MM*, November 1933, 456. Huff was a lifelong cinephile and worked, after his amateur efforts in the early 1930s, as a film historian in a variety of institutions, including MoMA, the Library of Congress, and NYU.

45. James W. Moore, "Titles That Talk—Planning, Preparation and Use of the Spoken Caption," *MM*, February 1947, 108.

46. "Cine Craftsmen," *MM*, April 1935, 149.

47. After a period of several years' absence, the "Critical Focusing" column reappeared in *Movie Makers* in the 1940s and was a regular feature throughout the late 1940s and '50s, commenting on films like *Body and Soul*, *Mr. Blandings Builds His Dream House*, and *Boomerang*.

48. Roy Winton, "Twenty Years of the ACL—How an Assignment Has Been Carried Out," *MM*, August 1946, 314.

49. Dewey, *Individualism Old and New*, 94.

CONCLUSION

1. Dr. Kinema [Maxim], "Movies as Mirrors," *MM*, July 1927, 16.
2. "A Path to Peace," *MM*, May 1947, 189.
3. "The Free Screen," *MM*, February 1934, 61.
4. Neil Harris employs this term to describe the ideological effect accomplished by John Philip Sousa's bridging of the gap between classical and popular music as well as the gap between art and commerce. Neil Harris, "John Philip Sousa and the Culture of Reassurance," in *Cultural Excursions: Marketing Appetites and Cultural Tastes in Modern America* (Chicago: University of Chicago Press, 1990).
5. John Dewey, *Art as Experience* (1934; New York: Perigree, 2005), 2.
6. See Barbara Klinger, *Beyond the Multiplex: Cinema, New Technologies, and the Home* (Berkeley: University of California Press, 2006); and Henry Jenkins, *Convergence Culture: Where Old and New Media Collide* (New York: New York University Press, 2006).
7. Between these points were other utopian calls for amateur action, such as this from Gene Youngblood in 1985: "Behold: armies of amateurs gather even now, preparing for the Image Wars, conspiring to abolish once and for all the ancient dichotomy between art and life, destiny and desire." Gene Youngblood, "The Redemption of the Amateur," *LA Weekly*, December 13, 1985.

Selected Bibliography

PRIMARY AND ARCHIVAL SOURCES

Bennett, H.H. Papers. State Historical Society of Wisconsin.
Bradley, David. Papers. Northwestern University Archives.
Conneely, Margaret. Collection. Chicago Film Archives.
Doerring, Ron. Collection. Chicago Film Archives.
Gist, Eloyce. Collection File. Library of Congress.
Harmon Foundation. Production Files. U.S. National Archives.
Harmon Foundation. Records. Library of Congress.
Huff, Theodore. Papers. George Eastman House.
Institute of Amateur Cinematographers. Collection. East Anglian Film Archive.
Maxim, Hiram Percy. Collection. Northeast Historic Film, Bucksport, Maine.
Maxim, Hiram Percy. Papers. Connecticut State Library, Hartford.
Toronto Film and Video Club.

PERIODICALS

Amateur Movie Makers (just *Movie Makers* after 1928)
American Cinematographer
Educational Screen
Experimental Cinema
Journal of the Photographic Society of America
Photoplay Magazine
Shots and Angles

BOOKS AND ARTICLES

Abel, Richard, ed. *Encyclopedia of Early Cinema*. New York: Routledge, 2005.
———, ed. *French Film Theory and Criticism*, vol. 1: *1907–1929*. Princeton, NJ: Princeton University Press, 1988.

Acland, Charles, and Haidee Wasson, eds. *Useful Cinema*. Durham, NC: Duke University Press, 2011.

Amad, Paula. "Cinema's 'Sanctuary': From Pre-Documentary to Documentary Film in Albert Kahn's Archives de la Planète (1908–1931)." *Film History* 13, no. 2 (2001).

Amateur Cinema League. *The ACL Movie Book: A Guide to Making Better Movies*. New York: Amateur Cinema League, 1940.

An Amateur Photoplay in the Making. Rochester, NY: Eastman Kodak Company, n.d. (c. 1927).

Askari, Kaveh. "Early 16mm Color by a Career Amateur." *Film History* 21, no. 2 (2009): 150–63.

———. "Moving Pictures before Motion Pictures: The Pictorial Tradition and American Media Aesthetics, 1890–1920." PhD dissertation, University of Chicago, 2005.

Becker, Carl. "Everyman His Own Historian." *American Historical Review* 37, no. 2 (January 1932): 221–36.

Belton, John. *Widescreen Cinema*. Cambridge, MA: Harvard University Press, 1992.

Benjamin, Walter. "The Work of Art in the Age of Its Technological Reproducibility." In *Walter Benjamin: Selected Writings*, vol. 3: *1935–1938*. Edited by Howard Eiland and Michael W. Jennings. Cambridge, MA: Harvard University Press, 2002.

Block, Ralph. "The Movies versus the Motion Pictures." *Century Magazine*, vol. 102, October 1921.

Booth, Wayne. *For the Love of It: Amateuring and Its Rivals*. Chicago: University of Chicago Press, 1999.

Bordwell, David, Janet Staiger, and Kristin Thompson. *The Classical Hollywood Cinema*. New York: Columbia University Press, 1985.

Bourdieu, Pierre. *Distinction: A Social Critique of the Judgment of Taste*. Translated by Richard Nice. Cambridge, MA: Harvard University Press, 1984.

———. *The Field of Cultural Production*. New York: Columbia University Press, 1993.

———. *Photography: A Middle-Brow Art*. With Luc Boltanski, Robert Castel, Jean-Claude Chamboredon, and Dominique Schnapper. Translated by Shaun Whiteside. Stanford, CA: Stanford University Press, 1990. First published in French in 1965.

Bowser, Eileen. *The Transformation of Cinema, 1907–1915*. Berkeley: University of California Press, 1990.

Brakhage, Stan. "In Defense of Amateur." In Stan Brakhage, *Essential Brakhage: Selected Writings on Film-Making*. Edited by Bruce R. McPherson. New York: Documentext, 2001. First written in 1971.

Breckinridge, Mary. *Wide Neighborhoods: A Story of the Frontier Nursing Service*. New York: Harper and Row, 1952.

Burch, Noël. *Life to Those Shadows*. Translated by Ben Brewster. Berkeley: University of California Press, 1990.

———. "Primitivism and the Avant-Gardes: A Dialectical Approach." In *Narrative, Apparatus, Ideology*, edited by Philip Rosen. New York: Columbia University Press, 1986.
Cameron, James R. *The Taking and Showing of Motion Pictures for the Amateur*. New York: Cameron Publishing, 1927.
Cardinal, Roger. "The Self in Self-Taught Art." In *Self-Taught Art: The Culture and Aesthetics of American Vernacular Art*, edited by Charles Russell. Jackson: University of Mississippi Press, 2001.
Cartwright, Lisa. "The Right Wing of Film Art." In *Lovers of Cinema: The First American Film Avant-Garde, 1919–1945*, edited by Jan-Christopher Horak. Madison: University of Wisconsin Press, 1995.
Chalfen, Richard. "Media Myopia and Genre Centrism: The Case of Home Movies." *Journal of Film and Video* 38, nos. 3–4 (Summer/Fall 1986).
———. *Snapshot Versions of Life*. Bowling Green, OH: Bowling Green State University Popular Press, 1987.
Chansky, Dorothy. *Composing Ourselves: The Little Theatre Movement and the American Audience*. Carbondale: Southern Illinois University Press, 2004.
"Cinematography, a New Art of Amateurs." *Arts and Decoration*, September 1919.
Craven, Ian, ed. *Movies on Home Ground*. Newcastle upon Tyne: Cambridge Scholars Publishing, 2009.
Cummings, Neil, and Marysia Lewandowska. *Enthusiasm: Films of Love, Longing and Labour*. London: Whitechapel Art Gallery, 2005.
———. *Enthusiasts: From Amateur Film Clubs*. Warsaw: Centre for Contemporary Art, 2004.
Davis, Ben. "Beginnings of the Film Society Movement in the U.S." *Film and History* 24, nos. 3–4 (1994): 6–26.
Denning, Michael. *The Cultural Front*. London: Verso, 1997.
Deren, Maya. "Amateur versus Professional." In *Essential Deren: Collected Writings on Film*, edited by Bruce R. McPherson. New York: Documentext, 2005.
DeSoto, Clinton. *Two Hundred Meters and Down: The Story of Amateur Radio*. West Hartford, CT: American Radio Relay League, 1936.
Dewey, John. *Art as Experience*. New York: Perigree, 2005. First published in 1934.
———. *Democracy and Education*. New York: Macmillan, 1916.
———. "Experience, Nature and Art." Excerpt from *Experience and Nature* (1925), reprinted in *Pragmatism: A Reader*, edited by Louis Menand. New York: Vintage, 1997.
———. *Individualism Old and New*. London: George Allen & Unwin, 1931.
———. *The Public and Its Problems*. Athens, OH: Swallow Press, 1991. First published in 1927.
Douglas, Ann. *Terrible Honesty: Mongrel Manhattan in the 1920s*. New York: Farrar, Straus and Giroux, 1995.

Downes, Olin. "Music and Film." *New York Times*, March 8, 1931, 114.
Edmonds, Guy. "Amateur Widescreen; or, Some Forgotten Skirmishes in the Battle of the Gauges." *Film History* 19, no. 4 (2007).
Elsaesser, Thomas. "The 'Return' of 3-D: On Some of the Logics and Genealogies of the Image in the Twenty-First Century." *Critical Inquiry* 39 (Winter 2013).
Epstein, Jean. "On Certain Characteristics of Photogénie." Translated by Tom Milne. In *French Film Theory and Criticism*, vol. 1: *1907–1929*, edited by Richard Abel. Princeton, NJ: Princeton University Press, 1988.
Erens, Patricia, ed. "Home Movies and Amateur Filmmaking." Special issue of the *Journal of Film and Video* 38, 3–4 (1986).
Fine, Gary Alan. *Everyday Genius: Self-Taught Art and the Culture of Authenticity*. Chicago: University of Chicago Press, 2004.
Frierson, Michael. *Clay Animation*. New York: Twayne Publishers, 1994.
Gale, Arthur. *Making a Simple Film Story: A Guide to the Amateur in Filming Short Photoplays*. New York: Amateur Cinema League, 1929.
Gibson, Gloria J. "Cinematic Foremothers: Zora Neale Hurston and Eloyse King Patrick Gist." In *Oscar Micheaux and His Circle*, edited by Pearl Bowser, Jane Gaines, and Charles Musser. Bloomington: Indiana University Press, 2001.
Gleason, Marion Norris. *Scenario Writing and Producing for the Amateur*. Boston: American Photographic Publishing, 1929.
Gomery, Douglas. *Shared Pleasures*. Madison: University of Wisconsin Press, 1992.
Gregory, C.L. "Amateurs Organize." *The Camera*, October 1926.
Grierson, John. *Grierson on Documentary*. Edited by Forsyth Hardy. New York: Praeger, 1971.
Grieveson, Lee. *Policing Cinema*. Berkeley: University of California Press, 2001.
Guerin, Francis. *Through Amateur Eyes: Film and Photography in Nazi Germany*. Minneapolis: University of Minnesota Press, 2012.
Gunning, Tom. "'Animated Pictures': Tales of Cinema's Forgotten Future." *Michigan Quarterly Review* 34 (Fall 1995).
———. "The Cinema of Attractions: Early Film, Its Spectator and the Avant-Garde." In *Early Cinema: Space, Frame, Narrative*, edited by Thomas Elsaesser. London: BFI, 1990.
———. "Flaming Images: Burning through the Celluloid Closet." Paper presented at the conference Beyond Warhol, Smith, and Anger: The Significance of Postwar Queer Underground Cinema, 1950–1968, University of Chicago, April 7–8, 2006.
———. "New Thresholds of Vision." In *Impossible Presence: Surface and Screen in the Photogenic Era*, edited by Terry Smith. Chicago: University of Chicago Press, 2001.
———. "'The Whole World within Reach': Travel Images without Borders." In *Virtual Voyages*, edited by Jeffrey Ruoff. Durham, NC: Duke University Press, 2006.

Hansen, Miriam. *Babel and Babylon: Spectatorship in American Silent Film.* Cambridge, MA: Harvard University Press, 1991.

———. "Early Cinema, Late Cinema: Transformations of the Public Sphere." In *Viewing Positions,* edited by Linda Williams. New Brunswick, NJ: Rutgers University Press, 1995.

———. "Fallen Women, Rising Stars, New Horizons: Shanghai Silent Film as Vernacular Modernism." *Film Quarterly* 54, no. 1 (Fall 2000).

———. "The Mass Production of the Senses: Classical Cinema as Vernacular Modernism." *Modernism/Modernity* 6, no. 2 (1999): 59–77.

Harris, Neil. *Cultural Excursions: Marketing Appetites and Cultural Tastes in Modern America.* Chicago: University of Chicago Press, 1990.

———. *Humbug: The Art of P.T. Barnum.* Chicago: University of Chicago Press, 1973.

Hayes, Richard. "'The Scope of the Movies': Three Films and Their Influence on Eugene O'Neill." *Eugene O'Neill Review* 25, nos. 1–2 (Spring/Fall 2001).

Horak, Jan-Christopher, ed. *Lovers of the Cinema: The First American Avant-Garde, 1919–1945.* Madison: University of Wisconsin Press, 1995.

Ibsen, Henrik. *Peer Gynt.* Translated by R. Farquharson Sharp. New York: Dutton, 1921.

Ishizuka, Karen L., and Patricia R. Zimmermann, eds. *Mining the Home Movie: Excavations in Histories and Memories.* Berkeley: University of California Press, 2008.

Jacobs, Lewis. "Experimental Cinema in America, 1921–1947." In Lewis Jacobs, *The Rise of the American Film.* New York: Teachers College Press, 1968.

James, David. *The Most Typical Avant-Garde: History and Geography of Minor Cinemas in Los Angeles.* Berkeley: University of California Press, 2005.

James, William. "The Self." Excerpt from *The Principles of Psychology* (1891), reprinted in *The Philosophy of William James,* edited by Horace M. Kallen. New York: Random House, 1925.

Jenkins, Henry. *Convergence Culture: Where Old and New Media Collide.* New York: New York University Press, 2006.

Johansen, Herbert O. "Widescreen Movies Come to the Home." *Popular Science,* February 1955.

Jones, Bernard E., ed. *The Cinematograph Book: A Complete Practical Guide to the Taking and Projecting of Cinematograph Pictures.* London: Cassell and Co., 1915.

Jones, Michael Owen. "The Aesthetics of Everyday Life." In *Self-Taught Art: The Culture and Aesthetics of American Vernacular Art,* edited by Charles Russell. Jackson: University of Mississippi Press, 2001.

Jowett, Garth, Ian Jarvie, and Kathryn Fuller, eds. *Children and the Movies.* New York: Cambridge University Press, 1996.

Kattelle, Alan D. "The Amateur Cinema League and Its Films." *Film History* 15, no. 2 (2003).

———. *Home Movies: A History of the American Industry, 1897–1979.* Nashua, NH: Transition Publishing, 2000.

Kleinhans, Chuck. "Theodore Huff: Historian and Filmmaker." In *Lovers of Cinema: The First American Film Avant-Garde, 1919–1945*, edited by Jan-Christopher Horak. Madison: University of Wisconsin Press, 1995.

Klinger, Barbara. *Beyond the Multiplex: Cinema, New Technologies, and the Home.* Berkeley: University of California Press, 2006.

Krows, Arthur Edwin. "Motion Pictures—Not for Theatres." Serial publication in *Educational Screen Magazine*, 1938–44.

Kuball, Michael. *Familienkino: Geschichte des Amateurfilms in Deutschland.* Hamburg: Rowohlt, 1980.

Lears, T. J. Jackson. *Fables of Abundance.* New York: Basic Books, 1994.

——. *No Place of Grace: Antimodernism and the Transformation of American Culture, 1880–1920.* Chicago: University of Chicago Press, 1981.

Levine, Lawrence. *Highbrow/Lowbrow: The Emergence of Cultural Hierarchy in America.* Cambridge, MA: Harvard University Press, 1988.

Lippman, Walter. *The Phantom Public.* New York: Macmillan, 1927.

Lounsbury, Myron. *The Origins of American Film Criticism, 1909–1939.* New York: Arno, 1973. Publication of 1966 PhD dissertation.

Macdonald, Dwight. "Masscult and Midcult." In Dwight Macdonald, *Against the American Grain.* New York: Random House, 1960.

——. "A Theory of Mass Culture." In *Mass Culture: The Popular Arts in America*, edited by Bernard Rosenberg and David Manning White. Glencoe, IL: Falcon's Wing Press, 1957.

MacDonald, Scott. *Cinema 16: Documents toward a History of the Film Society.* Philadelphia: Temple University Press, 2002.

Marchand, Roland. *Advertising the American Dream.* Berkeley: University of California Press, 1985.

Marvin, Carolyn. *When Old Technologies Were New.* New York: Oxford University Press, 1988.

Maxim, Hiram Percy. "The Amateur in Radio." *Annals of the American Academy of Political and Social Science* 142, supplement: *Radio* issue (March 1929): 32–35.

May, Larry. *Screening Out the Past.* Chicago: University of Chicago Press, 1983.

McKay, Herbert. *Motion Picture Photography for the Amateur.* New York: Falk Publishing, 1924.

Mebold, Anke, and Charles Tepperman. "Resurrecting the Lost History of 28mm Film in North America." *Film History* 15, no. 2 (2003).

Menand, Louis. *The Metaphysical Club.* New York: Farrar, Straus and Giroux, 2001.

——, ed. *Pragmatism: A Reader.* New York: Vintage, 1997.

Mitchell, Dorothea. *The Lady Lumberjack: An Annotated Collection of Dorothea Mitchell's Writings.* Edited by Michel Beaulieu and Ronald Harpelle. Thunder Bay, Ontario: Center for Northern Studies, 2005.

Moran, James M. *There's No Place Like Home Video.* Minneapolis: Minnesota University Press, 2002.

Musser, Charles. *The Emergence of Cinema*. Berkeley: University of California Press, 1994.
———. *High Class Moving Pictures*. Princeton, NJ: Princeton University Press, 1991.
Neumann, Mark. "Home Movies on Freud's Couch." *Moving Image* 2, no. 1 (Spring 2002).
"The Newest Magic of Motion Pictures." *Kodakery* 13, no. 9 (May 1926).
Nichols, Bill. "Documentary Film and the Modernist Avant-Garde." *Critical Inquiry* 27 (Summer 2001).
———. *Representing Reality*. Bloomington: Indiana University Press, 1991.
Nicholson, Heather Norris. *Amateur Film: Meaning and Practice, 1927–77*. Manchester: Manchester University Press, 2012.
Noyes, Alfred. *Collected Poems*. New York: Frederick A. Stokes Company, 1913.
Odin, Roger, ed. "Le cinema en amateur." Special issue of *Communications*, no. 68 (1999).
Oja, Carol. *Colin McPhee: Composer in Two Worlds*. Champaign: University of Illinois Press, 2004.
Orgeron, Devin, Marsha Orgeron, and Dan Streible, eds. *Learning with the Lights Off: Educational Film in the United States*. New York: Oxford University Press, 2012.
Parish, Michael. *Anxious Decades: America in Prosperity and Depression, 1920–1941*. New York: W.W. Norton, 1994.
Parker, Robert Allerton. "The Art of the Camera, an Experimental Movie." *Arts and Decoration*, October 1921. Reprinted in *Spellbound in Darkness*, edited by George C. Pratt. Greenwich, CT: New York Graphic Society, 1973.
Perry, Bliss. *The Amateur Spirit*. Boston: Houghton, Mifflin, and Company, 1904.
Peters, John Durham. *Speaking into the Air: A History of the Idea of Communication*. Chicago: University of Chicago Press, 1999.
Peterson, Betty. *The Toronto Movie Club: Its First Fifty Years, 1934–1984*. Pamphlet. Toronto, n.d. [1984].
Peterson, Jennifer. "Travelogues and Early Nonfiction Film: Education in the School of Dreams." In *American Cinema's Transitional Era: Audiences, Institutions, Practices*, edited by Charlie Keil and Shelley Stamp. Berkeley: University of California Press, 2004.
Poggioli, Renato. *The Theory of the Avant-Garde*. Translated by Gerald Fitzgerald. Cambridge, MA: Harvard University Press, 1968.
Polan, Dana. *Scenes of Instruction: The Beginnings of the U.S. Study of Film*. Berkeley: University of California Press, 2007.
Posner, Bruce, ed. *Unseen Cinema: Early American Avant-Garde Film 1893–1941*. New York: Anthology Film Archives, 2001.
Potamkin, Harry Alan. *The Compound Cinema: The Film Writings of Harry Alan Potamkin*. Edited by Lewis Jacobs. New York: Teachers College Press.

Radway, Janice. "The Scandal of the Middlebrow: The Book-of-the-Month Club, Class Fracture, and Cultural Authority." *South Atlantic Quarterly* 89, no. 4 (Fall 1990).

Randall, John Herman. *Our Changing Civilization: How Science and the Machine Age Are Reconstructing Modern Life*. New York: Frederic A. Stokes Company, 1929.

Richter, Hans. *Struggle for the Film: Towards a Socially Responsible Cinema*. Translated by Ben Brewster. New York: St. Martin's Press, 1986. Written in 1939; first published in German in 1976.

Rogers, Ariel. "'Smothered in Baked Alaska': The Anxious Appeal of Widescreen Cinema." *Cinema Journal* 51, no. 3 (Spring 2012): 74–96.

Rogers, William, and Paul Veith. *Visual Aids in the Church*. Philadelphia: Christian Education Press, 1946.

Ross, Andrew. *No Respect: Intellectuals and Popular Culture*. New York: Routledge, 1989.

Rossell, Deac. "Amateur Film." Entry in the *Encyclopedia of Early Cinema*, edited by Richard Abel. New York: Routledge, 2005.

Rubin, Joan. "Self, Culture, and Self-Culture in Modern America: The Early History of the Book-of-the-Month Club." *Journal of American History* 71, no. 4 (March 1985).

Ruoff, Jeffrey, ed. *Virtual Voyages: Cinema and Travel*. Durham, NC: Duke University Press, 2006.

Russell, Charles, ed. *Self-Taught Art: The Culture and Aesthetics of American Vernacular Art*. Jackson: University Press of Mississippi, 2001.

Said, Edward. *Orientalism*. New York: Pantheon, 1978.

Schumacher, Alice C. *Hiram Percy Maxim*. Cortez, CO: Electric Radio Press, 1998.

Seiberling, Grace. *Amateurs, Photography, and the Mid-Victorian Imagination*. Chicago: University of Chicago Press, 1986.

Seldes, Gilbert. *The Seven Lively Arts*. New York: Harper, 1924.

Shand, Ryan. "Theorizing Amateur Cinema: Limitations and Possibilities." *Moving Image* 8, no. 2 (Fall 2008): 36–60.

Singer, Ben. "Early Home Cinema and the Edison Home Projecting Kinetoscope." *Film History* 2, no. 1. (1988).

Sitney, P. Adams. *Visionary Film: The American Avant-Garde, 1943–1978*. 2nd ed. Oxford: Oxford University Press, 1979.

Sklar, Robert. *Movie Made America*. Rev. ed. New York: Vintage, 1994.

Slide, Anthony. *Before Video*. Westport, CT: Greenwood Press, 1992.

Stebbins, Robert A. *Amateurs, Professionals, and Serious Leisure*. Montreal: McGill-Queen's University Press, 1992.

Sternberger, Paul Spencer. *Between Amateur and Aesthete: The Legitimization of Photography as Art in America, 1880–1900*. Albuquerque: University of New Mexico Press, 2001.

Stevenson, Jack. *Desperate Visions 1: Camp America—the Films of John Waters and the Kuchar Brothers*. London: Creation Books, 1996.

Stokes, Melvyn, and Richard Maltby, eds. *American Movie Audiences*. London: BFI, 1999.
Stone, Melinda. "'If It Moves, We'll Shoot It': The San Diego Amateur Movie Club." *Film History* 15, no. 2 (2003): 220–37.
———. "'If It Moves, We'll Shoot It': The San Diego Amateur Movie Club." PhD dissertation, University of California, San Diego, 2003.
Sussman, Warren. *Culture as History*. New York: Pantheon, 1984.
Swanson, Dwight. "Inventing Amateur Film: Marion Norris Gleason, Eastman Kodak and the Rochester Scene, 1921–1932." *Film History* 15, no. 2 (2003).
Tepperman, Charles. "Uncovering Canada's Amateur Film Tradition: Leslie Thatcher's Films and Contexts." In *Cinephemera: Archives, Ephemeral Cinema and New Screen Histories in Canada*, edited by Zoë Druick and Gerda Cammaer. Montreal: McGill-Queen's University Press, forthcoming.
Thompson, Emily. "Remix Redux." *Cabinet*, issue 35 (Fall 2009).
Virilio, Paul. *War and Cinema*. Translated by Patrick Camiller. London: Verso, 1989.
Waller, Gregory, ed. *Moviegoing in America*. Malden, MA: Blackwell, 2002.
Wasson, Haidee. *Museum Movies*. Berkeley: University of California, 2005.
Wheeler, Owen. *Amateur Cinematography*. London: Pitman & Sons, 1929.
Wiatr, Elizabeth. "Between Word, Image, and the Machine: Visual Education and Films of Industrial Process." *Historical Journal of Film, Radio and Television* 22, no. 3 (2002): 333–51.
Williams, Alex. "Here I Am Taking My Own Picture." *New York Times*, February 19, 2006, section 9, 1.
Williamson, Samuel H. "Seven Ways to Compute the Relative Value of a U.S. Dollar Amount, 1774 to present." MeasuringWorth, www.measuringworth.com/uscompare/, accessed April 2013.
Winkopp, C.G. *How to Write a Photoplay*. 6th ed. New York: Winkopp, 1915.
Wolfe, Charles. "The Poetics and Politics of Nonfiction: Documentary Film." In *Grand Design: Hollywood as a Modern Business Enterprise, 1930–1939*, edited by Tino Balio. Berkeley: University of California Press, 1995.
Zimmermann, Patricia R. "Morphing History into Histories." *Moving Image* 1, no. 1 (2001).
———. *Reel Families: A Social History of Amateur Film*. Bloomington: Indiana University Press, 1995.
———. "Startling Angles: Amateur Film and the Early Avant-Garde." In *Lovers of Cinema: The First American Film Avant-Garde, 1919–1945*, edited by Jan-Christopher Horak. Madison: University of Wisconsin Press, 1995.

Index

abstract films, 57, 110, 180, 194, 201–7, 214, 232
African Americans, 37, 210, 233, 235, 236–37, 299n53, 333n43
Aldrich, Clarence, 135, 136
Allen, James L., 236–37, 334n48
alternative vs. popular film public, 272–73
Amateur Cine Club, Los Angeles, 66, 69
Amateur Cine Clubs of Southern California, 72
Amateur Cinema League (ACL): affluent membership of, 20, 37, 296n3, 299n57; African Americans and, 233, 299n53; Amateur Cinema Dramatic Division, 334n3; bulletins, 243–44; on color, 107; contests, 70, 85, 218; Continuity Department, 242; demise of, 157, 159, 215, 321n89, 322n96; demographic shifts, 40–41; Depression and, 80–81; diverse constituency and, 20, 38–39; experimentalism and, 193–94, 195, 216; film distribution circuit, 75; film exchanges, 25, 37, 39–41, 218; film library, 75, 135, 176, 199, 244; formation of, 19, 20–21, 23, 43, 296n3; internationalism and, 72, 86, 149; logo and leader, 257*fig.*; membership, 37, 38–39, 58–59, 233, 305n79; merger with Photographic Society of America (PSA), 157, 159, 321n89, 322n96; mission, 218; mottos, 19*fig.*, 43*fig.*; phases, 43; *Photoplay* contests and, 54, 56; on photoplays, 242; politics and, 72, 194, 195, 207–8; postwar shifts, 148–157; practical films and, 223; race, nationality, ethnicity and, 37; second generation, 156–57; 16mm film and, 123–24; twentieth anniversary, 96; visions for, 29; youth and college student filmmakers, 37, 38. *See also* Maxim, Hiram Percy; movie clubs; *Movie Makers* magazine; Ten Best; Winton, Roy
Amateur Cinema Society of Thunder Bay, The, 254
Amateur Cine Society of Bombay, 73
amateur filmmakers, definitions of, 2–9, 49, 272–73. *See also* professionals vs. amateurs
amateur films: aesthetics of, 2, 26–29, 36–37, 41, 55; as broadcasting medium, 23; cinéphiles and, 26, 29–37, 39; commercial cinema vs., 4, 7, 25, 27, 98–99, 273; as communication technology, 4, 7, 25, 177, 191–92; costs of, 23, 80, 81, 82, 308n15, 314n69, 320n73; daily life and, 22, 86–88, 90, 94, 130, 171; ethnographic, 31, 32; as film art, 161; free expression and, 83–84; as

amateur films *(continued)*
interior processes recording tool, 172; internationalism and, 58, 63–64, 85, 86, 183; as pastime of the rich, 23, 37; as self-taught art, 5; technological precursors of, 22, 23. *See also* culture, film; experimentalism; film exchanges; genres, film; movie clubs; politics; postwar, film; pragmatism; professionals vs. amateurs; self-reflection, films and; technology innovations; World War II; *individual film titles*
amateur movie clubs. *See* movie clubs
Amateur Movie Makers magazine. See *Movie Makers* magazine
Amateur Radio Relay League, 25
American Cinematographer: Amateur Movies and 46, 47*fig.*, 65; on amateurs vs. professionals, 49–51, 143–44, 147–48; award-winning films circulation, 75; on Ciné-Kodak, 119; "Cinema Workshop, The," 142–43; *cinephotographers* moniker, 51, 320n26; columns, 65–66, 121, 140; contests, 46, 61–65, 68, 70, 73, 85, 134, 140–42, 304n61; description of, 10, 44–53; 8mm film and, 118, 140; film aesthetics articles, 48–49, 319n39; film exchanges, 95; film library and, 91; filmmaker support and, 45–46; film reviews, 48; Hollywood and, 47–51, 301n23; internationalism and, 72–73, 85; on Kodachrome, 104; membership and, 52; movie clubs and, 66, 69, 74, 140; *Movie Makers* and, 302n30; on music for films, 113; postwar, 137, 140; profiles, 50–51; Pyle, Edward and, 115; 16mm film and, 121, 122–23, 140; Society of Amateur Cinematographers, The (SAC), 52–53, 302n32; Stull, William, 112; 3-D and widescreen film issue, 128;

Top Ten and, 141–42; World War II and, 89, 91, 92, 93, 94–95
American Red Cross, 91, 92–93
American Society of Cinematographers, 44
Anger, Kenneth, 264–65
animation, 36, 214
Another Day (Thatcher), 180–82, 189, 212, 279
anti-war filmmaking, 85, 88
Arnold, John, 48, 50–51
Arriflex cameras, 122
art-film repertory cinemas, 29–30. *See also* Little Movie movement
art films, European, 37
Art in Cinema, San Francisco Museum of Fine Art, 215
artistic instruction films, 235
Associated Amateur Cinema Clubs of Chicago, 135–36
Associated Camera Clubs of America, 158
Astor, Mary, 50
At the Sandpits (Crawley), 173
Au, Fred, 115
Auricon Cine-Voice, 313n45
Australia, 73, 76, 89, 285
avant-garde films: Amateur Cinema League (ACL) and, 193, 326n3; amateurs as bourgeois hobbyists, 215; *Another Day* (Thatcher), 181; Brakhage, Stan, 1; Deren, Maya and, 154, 194, 214, 215, 326n2, 329n46; documentaries and, 327n16; *Life and Death of 9413—a Hollywood Extra* (Florey), 199; *Little Geezer* (Huff), 266; *Lovers of Cinema* (Horak), 6; *Movie Makers* and, 212; postwar emergence of, 134; sound experimental use and, 110; Steiner, Ralph and, 272; stereoscopic imagery in, 128–29; Ten Best and, 59, 215; venues and societies for, 214–15. *See also* abstract films; experimentalism
awards, 67, 140, 147, 155, 236. *See also* Hiram Percy Maxim Memorial Award; Ten Best

INDEX / **351**

Baby Breaks Loose, 173
Badger, Clarence, 35
Ballet Mécanique (Murphy and Léger), 35
Barrett, Wilson, 56
Barstow, Robbins, 262–63
Barton, Ralph, 54
Beach, Frederick, 130
Beauty and the Beast, 154
Becky Sharp (Mamoulian), 107, 312n17
Bell and Howell, 121, 124, 315n93
Bement, Alon, 237
Benjamin, Walter, 4, 8
Bennett, Miriam, 257–261
Berlin, Symphony of a Great City (Ruttman), 180
Black, Alexander, 21, 311n10
Blaisdell, George, 66
Blitzstein, Marc, 110
Block, Ralph, 26, 27, 30–31, 297n25
Blood, B.H., 207
Blood of Jesus, The (Williams), 234
Bloomer, Kenneth, 220
Body and Soul (Micheaux), 234
Bolex, 128
Bollinger, Vincent, 186
Borzage, Frank, 33
Boston South Shore Camera Club, 72
Bourdieu, Pierre, 5
Bourke-White, Margaret, 239*fig.*, 332n27
Boyer, Pierre, 137
Bradley, David, 143–44, 145*fig.*, 246–253, 335nn14–16
Brakhage, Stan, 1, 215
Breckinridge, Marvin, 228
Britain. *See* United Kingdom
Bronx Morning (Leyda), 208
Brooklyn Institute of Arts and Sciences, 21
Brown, Clarence, 34, 61–62
Brown, Karl, 32
Brownstein, Mina, 30–31, 39
"Building a Bakery 1930: Harvesting and Baking" (Harrison), 224, 279

burlesque films, 266
Bushman, Francis X., 54, 335n17
Bute, Mary Ellen, 214

Cabinet of Dr. Caligari, The (Wiene), 31, 198, 298n28
Cadarette, Claude, 67
Camera Club of New York, 201
Canada, 66–67, 90, 93, 244–46, 254, 285–86. *See also Another Day* (Thatcher); *Canadian Capers; Confusions of a Nazi Spy* (Movie Makers Club of Ottawa); *Highwayman, The* (Toronto Amateur Movie Club); *Mighty Niagara* (Thatcher); *Race for Ties, A* (Mitchell); *Tie that Binds, The* (Ottawa Cine Club); *Toronto's Royal Day* (Toronto Amateur Movie Club)
Canadian Capers; Confusions of a Nazi Spy (Movie Makers Club of Ottawa), 183
Canadian Film Awards, 155
Cannes Festival International du Film Amateur, 147, 149, 163
Capital Eights club, Washington's, 115
Carbonaro, Charles, 222, 239*fig.*
Caught (Ophüls), 261–62
Celestial Closeups, 75
Central Cinematographers, 163
Ceramics (Bloomer and Sansom), 220–22, 235, 279, 333n41
Chaney, Lon, 54
Chang (Cooper and Schoedsack), 32, 184
Chansky, Dorothy, 27–28
Chaplin, Charlie, 210, 227–28
Chicago, Associated Amateur Cinema Clubs of, 135–36
Chicago, Metro Movie Club of River Park, 138–39, 162–63, 164*fig.*
Chicago Cinema Club, 69, 138–39, 178
Chicago's South Side Cinema Club, 10–11
Chicago World's Fair, 69, 178–79
children, film and, 163, 172, 265–66

Childs, S. Winston, 207
Chromatic Rhapsody (Kehoe), 108
chronicle films, 171–192, 247–48
Ciné-Kodak, 117–18, 119–121, 127, 314n69
Cinema Club, Los Angeles, 66, 113, 135
Cinema League of Philadelphia, 111
CinemaScope, 124, 126
Cinema 16, 139, 154, 215, 318n24
Cinematographs, 22, 171
Ciné-Panor anamorphic system, 126
cinéphiles, filmmakers as, 26, 29–37, 39
cinephotographers moniker, 51, 302n26
Citizen Kane (Welles), 49
City, The (Steiner), 201
city films, 208, 212, 306n99, 324n17. See also city symphony films; urban montage films
"City of Harlem, The" (Allen), 236–37
city symphony films, 180, 328n41, 329n44
Clardy, Randolph B., 67, 115
Clark, Dan, 66
Clark, Earl, 146
Clarke, Charles G., 72, 141
clay animation, 214
clubs. See movie clubs
college students, 37, 38
color, film, 99–109, 188, 214, 311n4, 312n17, 312n25
Columbia Broadcasting System, 72
Columbia Cub Productions, 68, 305n98
Columbia's Camera Club (radio broadcast), 72
Columbia Studios, 68
Columbia University, 76–77
comedies, film, 91, 136, 176, 209–10, 216, 254–57
commercial cinema, 4, 7, 24, 25, 27, 33–37, 98–99, 241–42, 273
common faults, films, 47, 301n7
community chronicle films, 178–183
competitions. See contests

Confusions of a Nazi Spy (Movie Makers Club of Ottawa), 90
Conneely, Margaret, 11, 139, 162–65
contests: *American Cinematographer*, 46, 61–65, 68, 70, 73, 85, 134, 140–42, 304n61; Associated Amateur Cinema Clubs of Chicago, 136; Cannes Festival International du Film Amateur, 147, 149; International Cinema Competition, (PSA), 162; internationalism and, 70, 73, 85; Los Angeles movie clubs and, 66, 70, 135; Metro Movie Club of River Park, 138–39; movie clubs and, 53, 70; national amateur film exchange and, 95; non-film organizations and, 317n2; pan-European movie, 73; Photographic Society of America (PSA), 134, 160, 162; *Photoplay* magazine, 44, 54–57, 193, 196, 242; postwar, 134; sound use as judging criteria, 117; stereo or 3-D photography category, 129; UNICA 9th International Contest, 90; Why I Film, 169. See also Ten Best
Cook, Esther, 160
Cook, William L., 115
Cooper, Merriam, 32, 184
Cornell, Joseph, 214
Coronet Pictures, 121
costs, film and, 23, 80, 81, 82, 308n15, 314n69, 320n73
Crawford, Joan, 61–62
Crawley, F. Radford "Budge," 10, 155, 173, 186, 222
Crawley, Judith, 10, 155, 222
Crawley Films, 222
Creelman, James, 36
Crockwell, Douglas, 214
Crosby, Floyd, 75–76
Crowd, The (Vidor), 241–42
culture, film, 20–21, 25–26, 29, 34, 41, 43, 44–45, 53, 271–75. See also Amateur Cinema League (ACL); *Movie Makers* magazine
current events. See Depression, the; elections; politics; World War II

INDEX / 353

Curtiz, Michael, 35
Cushman, George, 117, 159–162

Dabblin' in Moods (Hansen), 105–7
daily life, film and, 22, 86–88, 90, 94, 130, 171
Dawley, J. Searle, 24
"Day in College, A," 200
"Dealers in Death" (Hershey), 85
Demeny, Georges, 22
DeMille, Cecil B., 34, 51, 61–62
Democracy (Hollywood), 84
Denmark in Color (Hansen), 312n25
Depression, the, 71, 79, 80–84, 208, 209–11, 230
Deren, Maya, 154, 194, 214, 215, 326n2, 329n46
DeVry, 111, 315n93
Dewey, John: on art, 182, 238, 269; on communication, 177, 230, 332n36; on experimentation, 193–94, 212; pragmatism and, 12, 170, 177, 194, 212, 218, 237, 274; *Public and Its Problems, The,* 177, 194, 324n14; on social interaction, 263
Dial, The, 298n28, 327n11
digital technologies, 274
Disney, Walt, 48
Ditmars, Raymond, 66
Doctors' and Dentists' Night, Fourth Annual, 74
documentaries, 41, 75–76, 230, 235, 315n91, 327n16, 330n4
Doerring, Ron, 125–26
Doomsday (Stuart), 64
Drifters (Grierson), 220
Dr. Kinema (pseudonym), 38, 41–42. See also Maxim, Hiram Percy
Duck Soup (Lawlers), 175–76, 177, 189, 279
Dunne, Irene, 61–62

Edison, Thomas, 24, 25, 183, 219
Edison Home Kinetoscope (EHK), 22, 296n12, 296n12
educational films, 28, 146–47, 218–19, 220–22, 235

Educational Screen magazine, 220
Education for Life (Garner), 237
8mm Club, New York, 74
8mm film: Canon and, 316n99; contests and, 141–42, 162; emergence of, 67–68, 80, 81–82, 117–19, 124; Kodachrome and, 104; movie clubs and, 67–68; "16mm and 8mm Section," *American Cinematographer,* 140; vs. 16mm film debate, 151–53, 162, 314n75; sound and, 111; Super 8mm film, 13; technical accomplishment and, 120–21; widescreen filmmaking and, 124
Eisenstein, Sergei, 34, 173, 266
elections, 82, 84
Elgeet 3-D lens attachment, 128
Ells, Fred C., 88, 231–33, 234
Elsaesser, Thomas, 128–29
England. See Britain
Ervin, Russell, 55–56, 302n38
ethnographic films, 31, 32. See also quasi-ethnographic films
Eumig camera, 316n99
Europe: aesthetic inspiration for *Movie Makers,* 30; vs. American amateur filmmaking, 147, 318n18; *American Cinematographer* films travel tour, 63; art films and, 37; experimentalism and, 36; fascism and films in, 96–97; moviemaking culture of, 73; postwar, film and, 134, 137, 149; Union International du Cinema d'Amateur (UNICA), 90, 149, 320n59; World War II and, 89. See also France; Germany; Holland; United Kingdom
Ewald, Arthur, 169
Experimental Cinema magazine, 208, 213, 328n30
experimentalism, 195–216; Amateur Cinema League (ACL) and, 193–94, 195, 216; in amateur films, 26–28; Cinema 16 and, 139; Conneely, Margaret and, 163–64; decrease of, 213–14; documentaries and,

experimentalism *(continued)*
200–207, 327n16; European films and, 36; Flaherty, Robert and, 31; Huff, Theodore and, 337n36; Jacobs, Lewis and, 37; Little Theatre movement and, 27–28; *Movie Makers* and, 154, 193, 195–96, 199–200, 206–7, 211, 212–13; Murphy, Dudley and, 35; Philadelphia Movie Crafters and, 37;
Photoplay magazine and, 193; Ten Best and, 59; waste work and, 195–96; Watson, James Sibley and, 54, 298n28. *See also* abstract films; avant-garde films; *individual film titles*
Eyes of Science, The (Watson and Webber), 225–27, 279

Faillace, Gaetano, 135
Fairy Princess (Conneely), 163fig., 280
Fall of the House of Usher, The (Watson and Webber), 54, 75, 194, 197–200, 280
family films, 171–77
Farmer's Daughter, The (Aldrich), 135, 136
Farrebique (Rouquier), 154
fascism, films and, 96–97
festivals, 128, 130, 142, 147, 149, 163
fiction films. *See* photoplays
Film and Photo League (New York), 71–72, 201
Film Comment, 154
film exchanges, 25, 37, 39–41, 75, 95, 136, 159, 218. *See also* "SWAPS" column
Film Forum, 74, 307n123
film gauges. *See* gauges, film
film libraries, 75, 91, 176, 199, 244
Filmorama widescreen lens, 125, 126, 128
Filmorama Travels (Doerring and Ives), 125, 127fig.
film schools, 9–10, 147–48
Film Society (New York), 74, 307n123
Fishers of Grande Anse (Thatcher), 186

Fitzmaurice, George, 34
Flaherty, Robert, 30–32, 36–37, 54, 59–60, 185, 282
Fleming, Victor, 35
Flesh and the Devil (Brown), 34
Florey, Robert, 6, 199
Flory, John, 59, 208, 209, 215, 328n41, 329n44, 337n36
Fly Low Jack and the Game (Gleason), 39, 253, 280
Footnote to Fact, A (Jacobs), 208, 280
Forbes, John, 124
Forgotten Frontier, The (Breckinridge), 58, 228–230, 280, 332n34
Fox Studios, 24, 55
France: *American Cinematographer* and, 63–64; Cannes Festival International du Film Amateur, 147, 149, 163; ciné-clubs, 38, 41; Flaherty's films and, 32; French Film d'Art films, 244, 245; Lumière brothers, 22, 171, 172, 183; pan-European Third International Contest, 73; Pathé Kok, 22; postwar, film and, 137; stereotypes of amateurs and, 306n118; Union International du Cinema d'Amateur (UNICA), 90, 149, 320n59
French Film d'Art films, 244, 245
Furia (Alessandrini), 154

Gable, Clark, 51, 61–62
Gale, Arthur, 41, 43, 155, 223, 224, 243–44
Garner, Ray, 235, 237, 334n49
Garner, Virginia, 237, 334n49
Garrison Films, 85
gauges, film, 117–124. *See also* 8mm film; 9.5mm film; 16mm film; Super 8mm film; 35mm film; 28mm film; 22mm film
genres, films, 40–41, 297n14. *See also* documentaries; home movies; practical films; travel films
Germany, 32, 73, 76, 89, 90, 97, 180, 286, 306n118
Gerstein, Evelyn, 33

Ghrist, O. E., 128
Gibbs, C. W., 204
Gist, Eloyce and James, 37, 233–34
Gleason, Marion, 39, 172, 253, 327n9
Goetz, Othon, 261, 263
Goetz, William, 143
Gold Rush, The (Chaplin), 160–61
Gray, Ralph, 143–44, 151
Great Depression, the. *See* Depression, the
Gregory, Carl Louis, 66
Grierson, John, 171, 220, 230, 315n91, 323n36, 327n16, 330n4, 330n12
Griffith, D. W., 54, 173, 245, 266, 267
group productions, 69–70, 72, 253, 306n99, 324n17
Gunning, Tom, 7–8, 22, 264–65, 325n28

Hacker, Alan S., 84
Hall, J. Belmar, 48
Haller, Ernest, 141
Hamid, Alexander, 214
Hansen, John V., 102–4, 105, 149–150, 155, 156, 186, 188–89, 312n25
Hansen, Miriam, 8, 335n4, 336n27
Harmon Foundation, 235–39, 333n41, 333n43, 333n46, 334n48
Harris, Neil, 107, 330n13, 338n4
Harrison, Dent, 224, 225, 331n25
Hartford Amateur Movie Club, 208
Hartshorn, George F., 151–52, 320n73
Hearts of the West (Huff), 264, 265–66, 281
Heaven Bound Travelers (Gists), 233
Heffernan, Leo, 186
Hell Bound Train (Gists), 233–34, 281
Her Heart's Desire (Goetz, Othon), 261–62, 263, 281
Heston, Charlton, 144, 248, 249*fig.*
High Hat (Creelman), 36
Highwayman, The (Noyes), 244–45
Highwayman, The (Toronto Amateur Movie Club), 244–46, 281
Hillhouse Highlights (New Haven High School club), 71

Hiram Percy Maxim Memorial Award, 60, 136, 151
Holland, 73, 89, 286
Hollywood, 50–51, 68, 143–44, 146–47, 158, 262–63, 266, 268, 273, 305n98
Hollywood, Joseph P., 84, 91
Hollywood Quarterly, 154
Holmes, Burton, 184, 185
Holslag, Russell, 228
home movies 6, 23, 25, 43, 111, 118–19, 130, 133
Hood, Thomas, 54
Horak, Jan-Christopher, 6, 264
Howard, Leslie, 61–62
H_2O (Steiner), 57, 75, 110, 193, 200–203, 232, 281
Huff, Theodore, 6, 10, 59, 62, 264–67, 268, 337n36, 337n44

Ibsen, Henrik, 248, 250, 251
I'd Be Delighted To! (Childs), 63, 75, 207, 281
Ince, Thomas, 50
independent producers, 145–46
India, 73, 89, 286
Indianapolis Movie Club, 95
industrial films, 28, 146–47, 218–19, 222–27, 264
Institute of Amateur Cinematography, 72–73, 149, 320n59
International Amateur Movie Show, 76
internationalism: Amateur Cinema League (ACL) and, 72, 86, 149; contests and, 63–64, 70, 73, 85; exchanges and, 85; films and promotion of, 86, 88–90, 188; foreign movie organizations and, 72–73; International Cinema Competition, (PSA), 162; movie clubs and, 72–73, 320n59; movie parties and, 76, 77; Ten Best and, 58; travel films and, 183
International Show of Amateur Motion Pictures, Eleventh Annual, 77
In the Beginning (Ells), 231–33, 234, 235, 281, 333n41

It (Little Screen Players of Boston), 39
Ivens, Joris, 232
Ives, George, 125

Jacobs, Lewis, 161, 208, 216
James, William, 19–20
Japan, 35, 64, 73, 76, 88, 89, 135, 286
Jewish film societies, 65, 305n78
Jones, Hamilton, 60–61, 113–14
Jones, Michael Owen, 5
Julius Caesar (Bradley), 143–44, 145fig., 252–53, 281

Kaleidoscopio (Machado), 214
Kattelle, Alan, 7, 10
Kehoe, Robert, 108
Kentucky Nursing Service, 228–230
Keratoplasty, 312n30
Kerr, Marion, 42–43
King of Kings (DeMille), 34
Klein, Charles, 199
Kleinhans, Chuck, 264, 265
Kodachrome, 100, 104–9, 311n4, 312n25
Kodacolor, 59, 100–107, 109, 188, 311n4, 311nn8–10
Kodak: advertisements, 19; Ciné-Kodak, 117–18, 119–121, 127, 314n69; Great Hall of Color, 108–9; non-flammable safety film, 22; panchromatic film, 172–73; on postwar camera use, 140; Rochester movie club and, 327n9; 16mm film, 39, 101. *See also* Kodachrome; Kodacolor
Kuchar brothers, 215–16

Lady Lumberjack, The (Mitchell), 254, 336n24
Lampert, Andrew, 264, 337n36
Lang, Fritz, 34
Lang, Herbert, 39
Last Laugh, The (Murnau), 160–61
La Varre, André, 185–87
Lawler, Delores, 175, 176
Lawler, Timothy, 175, 176, 177
Lears, Jackson, 224–25

Léger, Fernand, 35
Leyda, Jay, 180, 208
Life and Death of 9413—a Hollywood Extra (Florey), 199
Lightman, Herb, 144
Lippmann, Walter, 230, 323n36, 324n14
Liszt, Max, 48
literary adaptations, 243, 246–253
Little, Duncan MacD., 76–78, 85, 115
Little Cinema movement, 26–27, 54, 269
little cinemas, 36, 55, 74
Little Geezer (Huff), 62, 264, 265, 266–67, 281
Little Magazines, 298n28
Little Movie movement, 23, 27, 30, 297n25, 298n28
Little Movie parties, 45
Little Screen Players of Boston, 34, 38–39
Little Theatre movement, 23, 27–28, 54, 298n28
Lives Wasted (New Film Group), 71, 85
Lloyd, Harold, 316n112
Locke, Alain, 236, 237, 334n48
Long Beach (CA) Cinema Club, 69–70, 75–76, 92, 135, 138
Loon's Necklace, The (Crawley Films), 155
Lorenz, Pare, 201, 330n4
Los Angeles Amateur Cine Club, 66, 69
Los Angeles Cinema Club, 66, 113, 135
Los Angeles 8mm Club, 67–68, 70
Lot in Sodom (Watson and Webber), 194, 207, 225, 226, 281
Loves of Sunya, The (Parker), 35
Lucky Piece (Columbia Cub Productions), 68
Lullaby (Okamoto), 63
Lumière brothers, 22, 171, 172, 183

Macbeth (Bradley), 252, 282
Machado, Roberto, 214

machines as film subjects, 35, 203–4, 205, 332n27
Mag the Hag (Maxim), 17–19, 30, 40, 282, 295n1
Malthouse, Gordon, 139
Manhatta (Sheeler and Strand), 23, 282
Man of Aran (Flaherty), 185–86
Man Power (Badger), 35
Man with a Movie Camera (Vertov), 180
Marey, Étienne-Jules, 22
mass culture, film and, 98, 241–42, 263, 271–72
Maxim, Hiram Percy: Amateur Cinema League (ACL) formation, 2, 19, 20, 21; Amateur Radio Relay League founder, 25; on color film, 100, 105, 107–8; on communication and films, 7, 170, 171–72, 272; death of, 155; Dr. Kinema (pseudonym), 38, 41–42; on experimentation, 213; on films as creative pursuit, 4; Hiram Percy Maxim Memorial Award, 60, 136, 151; on internationalism, 85, 86; inventor, 24; Kodachrome and, 105; Maxim's manifesto, 171–72, 177; on movie clubs structure, 38; *Photoplay* contests and, 54, 57; screen writer, 24; *Virgin Paradise, A* and, 24; visions for amateur film, 24, 25, 29, 73
McKay, Herbert C., 66
McPhee, Colin, 110
Mechanical Principles (Steiner), 110, 203, 332n27
Méliès, Georges, 18
melodramas, 17–19, 90
Mencken, H. L., 54, 80
Meshes of the Afternoon (Deren), 214
Metro Movie Club of River Park, 138–39, 162–63, 164fig.
Metro News, 138fig.
Metropolis (Lang), 34
Metropolitan Motion Picture Club of New York (MMPC), 66, 136, 201
Metropolitan Motion Picture Council (New York), 222

MGM (Metro-Goldwyn-Mayer), 143–44, 145fig., 253
Micheaux, Oscar, 234
middle-class, film and the, 173–74, 176, 271, 272–73, 274
Mighty Niagara (Thatcher), 183–84, 282
Miller, Arthur C., 118, 141
M.I.T (Massachusetts Institute of Technology), 24
Mitchell, Dorothea, 254–57, 336n24
Mitchell, R. Fawn, 178–79
Mitchell Camera Corporation, 122
Mogensen, Allan, 39
Mohr, Hal, 141
montage, 173, 180, 181–82, 198, 204–5, 231, 266
Moon of Israel (Curtiz), 35
Moore, James W., 133, 156, 177, 191, 267–68, 321n84
Moore, J. Kinney, 126–27
Moorhouse, Alan, 245–46
Morton, Al, 152
Mount Kisco Cinemat Club, 74, 220
movie clubs, 37–41, 65–73; aggregate meetings, 72; "Amateur Clubs," *Movie Makers*, 38, 41, 65, 73; as amateur film development phase, 43; "Amateur Movie Clubs—What They Offer," 44; *American Cinematographer* and, 46, 65–66; "Among the Movie Clubs," 140; ciné-clubs, 38, 41; contests and, 53, 70; Cushman, George on, 159–160; directory of 285–291; film exchanges, 95, 136; government films and, 75–76; group productions, 69–70, 72, 253, 306n99, 324n17; high school, 65, 71; internationalism and, 72–73, 320n59; membership and, 38–39, 65, 299n57; organization of, 65; postwar, 134–140; race, nationality, ethnicity and, 37, 65; regional gatherings of, 135–36; research on, 6; roles of, 45; as social vs. service organizations, 139–140; Stone, Melinda and, 6; structure

movie clubs *(continued)* recommendations for, 38; topical films and, 74; as venues, 74–78, 96; women's participation in, 70; World War II and, 94–95. *See also individual movie clubs*

movie contests. *See* contests

Movie Makers Club of Chicago, The, 299n57

Movie Makers Club of Ottawa, 90

Movie Makers magazine: abstract films and, 208; aesthetic philosophy of, 36, 41; "Amateur Clubs," 38, 41, 65, 73; on amateurs vs. professionals, 263–64; *American Cinematographer* and, 302n30; on the American election (1932), 82; on cine craftsman, 268; Ciné-Kodak advertisement, 120*fig.*; on color, 100; columns, 35, 36, 41–42, 75, 150–51, 154–55, 218, 219; on commercial vs. amateur films, 30; on Crawleys, 155; "Critical Focusing: Reviews to aid the amateur," 33–37, 264, 266, 337n47; demise of, 159; on Depression and film, 81, 82–83, 209; description of, 10; editorials, 2, 86–87, 240; on education films, 220; 8mm vs. 16mm debate, 152–53; on experimentalism, 206–7; on expression vs. repression, 83–84; on film exchanges, 75; on films as peace vehicles, 90; on films worthy of emulation, 30; "gospel of expression," 213; on Hansen's color film artistry, 102–4; on historiography and film, 182; Huff, Theodore on silent films, 267; inaugural editorial, 2; on industrial films, 223; internationalism and, 72–73, 149; on Kodachrome, 104–5; on Kodacolor, 100–101; on Kodak's Great Hall of Color, 108–9; Maxim, Hiram Percy and 2, 20, 24, 171–72; on moderate path for filmmakers, 209; on montage, 173; mottos, 19*fig.*, 43*fig.*; on music and film, 113; New York World's Fair issue, 179; on organization of amateur cinematography, 20; on *Photoplay* contest, 55, 56; photoplay to chronicle films ratio, 269; politics and, 84–85, 87, 208, 209, 212–13, 260; postwar format and changes, 149–150; on practical films, 218, 219; on pragmatic vs. theoretical filmmaking, 149; profiles, 28–29, 30–32; quasi-ethnographic films and, 32, 184; race, nationality, ethnicity and, 37; on right of expression, 271–72; on Rochester, 39; second generation, 156–57; on 16mm film, 122–23; on Steiner, Ralph, 201; "SWAPS" column, 40*fig.*, 75, 218; techniques advice, 41–42, 228; on television, 130; on technical proficiency, 59; as venue for Amateur Cinema League (ACL), 20; on what makes a film interesting, 42; Vorhees, Stephen on Amateur Cinema League (ACL) as apolitical, 87; on waste work, 195–96; Winton, Roy and, 55, 196–197, 155; World War II and, 91, 92, 95

movie parties, 75, 76–78, 85. *See also* movie clubs

Movie Party and International Show of Amateur Motion Pictures, Tenth Annual, 76

Mr. Hitler Never Loses (Hollywood), 91

Mr. Motorboat's Last Stand: A Comedy of the Depression (Flory), 208, 209–12, 264, 282, 337n36

Muray, Nickolas, 54

Murnau, F.W., 33

Murphy, Dudley, 35

Museum of Modern Art (MoMA), 76, 77

music, film and, 63, 110, 112–15, 214, 248

NAACP (National Association for the Advancement of Colored People), 233, 237

Nagel, Conrad, 61–62
narrative short films, 41
National Alliance of Art and Industry, 237
National Board of Review of Motion Pictures, 25, 222
Nation Builders (Sherlock), 64
Naval Reserve Aviation Squadron, 91
New Film Group, 48, 71, 85
New Haven High School club, 71
New York: city films and, 306n99; Film and Photo League, 71–72, 201; Film Society, 74, 307n123; *Her Heart's Desire* (Goetz, Othon) and, 261; Metropolitan Motion Picture Council, 222; movie clubs, 290; Rochester, 39, 197, 253, 327n9
New York Camera Club, 201
New York City, 31–32, 72, 261
New York 8mm Club, 74, 135, 215–16;
New York Metropolitan Motion Picture Club (MMPC), 66, 136, 201
New York University (NYU), 71, 76–77, 331n20
New York World's Fair (1939), 108, 179
Niblo, Fred, 50
Nickelodeon Nights, 136
Night of Love, The (Fitzmaurice), 34
9.5mm film, 304n61, 304n75, 314n68
No Credit (Tregillus), 214
Nord 3-D converters, 128, 129*fig.*
Noyes, Alfred, 244

Oakland Camera Club, 324n17
Okamoto, Tatsuichi, 63
O'Neill, Eugene, 298n28
On the Farm (Garners), 334n49
Ophüls, Max, 261–62
Ottawa Cine Club, 93
Our Hero (Naval Reserve Aviation Squadron), 91

Pablito's Playground, 130
Pabst, G. W., 33
Page, Ernest W., 62
Palmer, William A., 62

Paramount Club, 68
Parker, Albert, 35
Parker, Robert Allerton, 23
Pathé, 22, 314n68
Pathé Kok. See Pathéscope
Pathéscope, 22, 296n12
Peer Gynt (Bradley), 248–252, 282
Pellegrini, Tullio, 125, 126
Perry, Bliss, 3–4, 24, 217
Philadelphia Movie Crafters, 37
Phonoscope, 22
Photographic Society of America (PSA), 134, 140, 157–162, 215, 273, 316n112, 321n89, 322nn96–97, 323n120
Photographic Society of America Journal (PSA Journal), 10, 158, 159–161
Photoplay magazine, 10, 44, 54–57, 193, 196, 201–2, 242
photoplays, 242–269. See also Huff, Theodore; literary adaptations, photoplays
Pizzo, Nadine, 109, 160, 319n39
Pizzo, Sal, 160
Plow That Broke the Plains, The (Lorenz), 75–76, 201
Polan, Dana, 76–77
politics: Amateur Cinema League (ACL) and, 72, 194, 195, 207–8, 216, 326n3; amateurs and, 79–80, 82, 85, 272, 327n16; art vs., 208; "Can We Hate?" editorial, 86–87; Ells, Fred C. on, 88; *Experimental Cinema* magazine and, 328n30; experimentalism and, 213; expression vs. repression, 83–84; Workers' Film and Photo League and, 72; film history and, 308n2; Harmon Foundation and, 236; *Lives Wasted* (New Film Group), 71; *Movie Makers* and, 209, 212–13; *Study in Reds, A* (Bennett), 258; UNICA International Contest and, 90; Zimmermann, Patricia R. on, 308n3
Portland Cine Club, 69

Portrait of a Young Man (Rodakiewicz), 62, 200, 204–7, 283, 328n23
postwar, film, 133–166; Amateur Cinema League (ACL) and, 96–97, 148–157; chronicle films interest, 214; color film and, 109; contests and, 133; dual-turntable systems, 112; education films and, 222; ethos changes, 133–34; filmmakers increase, 214; Kodak and, 140; magnetic sound and, 116; movie clubs, 96, 134–140; *Movie Makers* and, 149–150, 153–54; Photographic Society of America (PSA) and, 140, 157–58; practical films shift, 240; 16mm film and, 122; television and, 130–31; Ten Best and, 134, 150, 153–54, 157, 227; utopian visions and, 85–86, 90, 148–49, 171; World War II film exhibitions, 135
Potamkin, Harry Alan, 180, 181–82, 203–4, 208, 216
Potemkin (Eisenstein), 34, 160–61
Power and the Land (Ivens), 75–76
practical films, 28, 146–147, 217–240, 331n20, 330n5
pragmatism: Amateur Cinema League (ACL) and, 157, 271; amateurs and, 182, 213, 243; American, 12–13, 170–71, 295n25; *Movie Makers* and, 149; Williams, James on, 19–20; Winton, Roy on, 87, 156, 204. *See also* Dewey, John, pragmatism and
Preps in Action (Bradley), 247–48
Proem (Tregillus), 214
professional amateurs, 50–51
professionals vs. amateurs: cinematography and, 52; differences between, 3, 142–47, 159–160, 263–64, 296n11; *Photoplay* magazine and, 56; relationship between, 49–50; transition between, 130, 155, 158
PSA. *See* Photographic Society of America (PSA)

Public and Its Problems, The (Dewey), 177, 194, 324n14
Pyle, Edward, 115

quasi-ethnographic films, 32, 184, 185–86. *See also* ethnographic films
queer cinema, 264–65
Quirk, James, 56

Race for Ties, A (Mitchell), 254–57, 283, 336n24
racism, films and, 37, 65, 183, 184. *See also* African Americans
radio, 72
Ramsaye, Terry, 122
Randall, John Herman, 217, 218
Raven, The (Clouzot), 154
record vs. story films, 189–191
Red Cross, 91, 92–93
religious films, 28, 146–47, 218–19, 230–34, 235
Religious Motion Picture Foundation, 235
Rennahan, Ray, 141
Rice, Sue, 172
River, The (Lorentz), 75–76
Roach, Hal, 264, 266
Rochester amateur club (unnamed), 197, 327n9
Rochester Community Players, The, 39, 253
Rodakiewicz, Henwar, 59, 62, 200, 204, 328n25
Roscher, Charles, 141
Rothapfel, Samuel "Roxy," 54
Roundhouse to Roadbed (Beach), 130
Russell Sage Foundation, The (Huff), 264
Ruttman, Walter, 180

Saki, 252
San Diego movie club, 6
San Francisco (Pellegrini), 125*fig.*, 127*fig.*
San Francisco Cinema Club, 135
Sansom, Elizabeth, 220
satire films, 266

scenic films, 41
Schoedsack, Ernest, 32, 184
Screen Producers Guild Intercollegiate Film Award, 147
Sea, The (Maxim), 57
Secrets of a Soul (Pabst), 33
Seldes, Gilbert, 30–31
self-reflection, films and, 19–20, 21, 23–24, 42–43, 200, 207, 243, 251
Seventh Heaven (Borzage), 33
Shannon, William J., 44
Sheeler, Charles, 23
shelter shows, 94
Sherlock, James, 64, 73
Shots and Angles newsletter, 67
silent films, amateur: aesthetics and, 193, 194, 264; *Another Day* (Thatcher), 180–82; "Building a Bakery 1930: Harvesting and Baking" (Harrison), 224; *Ceramics* (Bloomer and Sansom), 220; *Forgotten Frontier, The* (Breckinridge), 228; *Her Heart's Desire* (Goetz, Othon), 262; Huff, Theodore on, 267; movie clubs and, 136; practical films and, 331n14; *Race for Ties, A* (Mitchell), 255; *Study in Reds, A* (Bennett), 257–261; techniques and, 267–68; Winton, Roy on, 101, 196–97, 264
silent films, commercial, 33–35, 101, 241–42
16mm film: camera technology development and, 39; contests and, 141–42, 162, 304n61; as decisive development, 19, 22, 23; editorial on, *Movie Makers*, 123; vs. 8mm film debate, 151–52, 162, 314n75; evolution of, 117–124; invention of, 22, 327n9; Kodachrome and, 104; postwar and, 133–34; "16mm and 8mm Section," *American Cinematographer*, 140; sound and, 111; 3-D filmmaking and, 126–28, 129*fig.*; widescreen filmmaking and, 125; World War II and, 85, 96, 133–34
Skelton, Red, 154, 320n76

Smith, Jack, 264–65
social problem films, 218–19, 227–230
social progress films, 235
social welfare films, 81, 84
Society of Amateur Cinematographers, the (SAC), 52–53, 302n32
sound, film and, 63, 101, 110–17, 142, 252, 313n45, 323n118, 331n14, 314n64. *See also* music, film and
Southern Tenant Farmers' Union, 84
Space, Kenneth, 222, 238–39
Spoongle, Francis, 152
Sprungman, Ormal, 114–15
Sredni Vashtar (Bradley), 252, 283
Starewitsch, W., 36
Stark Love (Brown), 32
Steichen, Edward, 28–29, 221–22
Steiner, Ralph, 208, 272. *See also* H_2O (Steiner)
stereoscopic filmmaking, 126–29
Stieglitz, Alfred, 4–5, 328n23
St. Louis club, 95
Stone, Melinda, 6
Stone Flower, The (Ptushko), 154
stop-motion animation, 163
story films, 189–191. *See also* photoplays
Story of Bamba, The (Garner), 235–36, 283, 333n46
Stout, Paul R., 154
Strand, Paul, 23
Struss, Karl, 48
Stuart, Ruth, 64
students, 37, 38, 71, 147, 200, 244
Studies in Blue and Chartres Cathedral (Hansen), 102, 188–89, 283
Study in Reds, A (Bennett), 257–261, 273, 283
Stull, William, 48, 49–50, 62, 63, 64, 66, 68, 112–13, 118–19
Sturrup, Leonard "Motorboat," 210
Summer, The (Maxim), 57
Summer Olympics (1932), 69
Sunrise (Murnau), 33, 36
Super 8mm film, 13

Surf and Seaweed (Steiner), 110, 203, 283
Susie Steps Out (Doerring and Ives), 125–26, 283
Swanson, Dwight, 39
"SWAPS" column, 40*fig.*, 75, 218
Syracuse Movie Makers, 94

Tarzan and the Rocky Gorge (Barstow), 262–63, 268
Tarzan Jr. (Palmer and Page), 62–63
Technicolor, 107
technology innovations, 8–9, 22–23, 24, 67, 98–132, 296n12. *See also* gauges, film; Kodachrome; Kodacolor
television, 129–132, 134, 139, 317n121
Telltale Heart, The (Klein), 75, 199, 284
Ten Best: Amateur Cinema League (ACL) and, 75; Britain and, 162; "Choosing the Ten Best," 61; color film and, 102, 105; competitions and, 41; criteria, 11, 57–60; education films and, 220; experimentalism and, 207, 212; films awarded, 108, 163, 188, 200, 204, 211, 214, 239, 252, 266; Harmon Foundation and, 235; Huff, Theodore and, 264; internationalism and, 58, 70; Kattelle, Alan and, 7, 10; *Movie Makers* and, 57–61; "New Ten Best," 60; Photographic Society of America (PSA) and, 159, 162; postwar, 134, 150, 153–54, 157, 227; public exhibitions of, 136; record films vs. story films and, 189–191; social problem films and, 228; sound and, 116; travel films and, 183; World War II and, 93
Thatcher, Leslie, 67, 155, 180–82, 183, 186, 212, 325n28
theatrical productions, 297n14
These Bloomin' Plants, 108
35mm film, 23, 39, 119, 120, 122, 230
Thrasher, Frederick, 71, 222
3-D filmmaking, 124–29, 316n112

Three Episodes, 56
Tie that Binds, The (Ottawa Cine Club), 93
time-lapse photography, 108
Time magazine, 63
Toland, Gregg, 49
Tombs of the Nobles (Hansen), 102, 189, 190*fig.*, 284
Tom Jones (Yale University student group), 244
To Om by Omnibus (Cinema League of Philadelphia), 111
Toronto Amateur Movie Club, 66–67, 90, 244–46
Toronto's Royal Day (Toronto Amateur Movie Club), 178, 284
Traffic in Souls (Tucker), 228
travel films: amateur to professional and, 146; *American Cinematographer* and, 62, 64; chronicle films and, 169–170, 171, 183–192; color and, 102–3; contests and, 64; as film genre, 32, 33, 40; "Filming with Flaherty: From Arctic to Antipodes with the Famous Amateur who made *Nanook* and *Moana*," 30–32; Kerr, Marion on, 42; qualities of, 325n32; as sensational films, 325n28; widescreen filmmaking and, 125–26
travelogues. *See* travel films
Tregillus, Leonard, 214, 215
Tuttle, Harris, 39, 158, 323n120
28 mm film, 22, 23, 297n14
24 Dollar Island (Flaherty), 32, 284
22 mm film, 22

underground cinema, 9–10
UNICA (Union International du Cinema d'Amateur), 90, 149, 320n59
United Kingdom: Amateur Cinema League (ACL) and, 75; *American Cinematographer* and, 63; British Cine Organization, 306n116; clubs and film exhibitions, 139; Institute of Amateur Cinematography, 72–73,

149, 320n59; International Amateur Movie Show, 76; international contests and, 73; movie clubs, 286; postwar, film, 137–38; shelter shows, 94; Ten Best selections, 162; Widescreen Association, 126; World War II, filmmaking and, 89, 90
United States Film Registry list, 228
University of Southern California (USC), 147
Urban, Charles, 219
urban montage films, 208. *See also* city films; city symphony films
USO (United Service Organizations), 91, 94
Utah Cine Arts Club, 135
utopian visions: amateurs and, 338n7; cinema's potential and, 13; communication technologies and, 177; Little Screen Players of Boston and, 38–39; loss of, 133; Maxim, Hiram Percy and, 7, 73; postwar, 85–86, 90, 148–49, 171; travel films and, 183, 188; World War II and, 78

Venice (Hansen), 102
Verdict: Not Guilty at the Judgment Day (Gists), 233
VerHalen, Charles, 66
vernacular modernism, 8, 335n4
Vertov, Dziga, 180
Vidor, King, 56, 241, 242, 334n2
Virginia Conservation Commission, 105, 106*fig.*
Virgin Paradise, A (Dawley), 24
Visit to Peek Frean & Co.'s Biscuit Works, A (Cricks and Martin), 222–27
visual techniques, film, 33–37
Volkmar, Leon, 220–21
Vorhees, Stephen, 56, 87, 89, 149–150, 155, 179

war effort and film, 91–92, 93–94, 309n49
Washington, D.C., movie club, 105
Wasson, Haidee, 30, 76
Watch the Birdy (Donohue), 154
Water (Blood), 207
Watson, James Sibley: "Amateur Takes Leadership: How Experimenters, in Circumventing Production Difficulties, Have Achieved the Greatest Cinematic Advance since *The Cabinet of Dr. Caligari, The*," 198; avant-garde filmmaker, 6, 59; Cinema 16 and, 215; *Dial, The* and, 298n28, 327n11; as experimental filmmaker, 194, 304n64; *Eyes of Science, The*, 225–27; *Fall of the House of Usher, The*, 54, 197; new film visual language and, 327n11; practical films and, 218; Rochester movie club and, 327n9; Ten Best and, 10; 35mm film and, 120
Way of All Flesh, The (Fleming), 34–35
We Are All Artists (Bement), 237–38, 284, 334n51
Webber, Melville: avant-garde filmmaker, 6, 59; Cinema 16 and, 215; as experimental filmmaker, 194; *Eyes of Science, The*, 225–27; *Fall of the House of Usher, The*, 54, 197; new film visual language and, 327n11; practical films and, 218; Ten Best and, 10; 35mm film and, 120
Welsh, Helen, 151–52
Western Holiday (Jones), 60–61
White, Pearl, 24
Widescreen Association, 126
widescreen filmmaking, 124–28
Wild Rice, 75
Williams, Spencer, 234
Winkopp, C.G., 253
Winton, Roy: on aesthetics, 193, 196–97, 272; Amateur Cinema League (ACL) and, 96–97, 321n89; on amateurs 25–27, 264; on artistic expression, 23–24, 169–170; "Can We Hate?" editorial, 86–87; on education films, 219–220, 221; experimentalism and, 204; Hartford Amateur Movie Club address,

Winton, Roy *(continued)*
208–9; on industrial applications of films, 28; on Little Theatre movement, 27; obituary, 155–56; *Photoplay* contest and, 55, 56; on photoplays, 268–69; popular film criticism and, 30; Red Cross films and, 92; on silent films, amateur, 101; on "talkies," 326n8; Ten Best and, 61; vision for Amateur Cinema League (ACL) and, 29

Woman Distressed, A (Kuchar, George), 216

women filmmakers, 70, 160, 164, 305n98. *See also* Bennett, Miriam; Breckinridge, Marvin; Conneely, Margaret; Crawley, Judith; Deren, Maya; Garner, Virginia; Gist, Eloyce; Kerr, Marion; Lawler, Delores; Mitchell, Dorothea

Workers' Film and Photo League, 71–72, 85, 201, 208, 230

World's Fairs, 69, 108, 178, 179

World War II, 77–78, 79, 85–97, 121–22, 135, 240, 309n49

Yale University student group, 244

Yamashina, Prince, 73

You Can Make Good Movies! (Space), 238–39

Youthful Ecstasy (Starewitsch), 36

Zimmermann, Patricia R., 6, 176, 262, 308n3

www.ingramcontent.com/pod-product-compliance
Lightning Source LLC
Chambersburg PA
CBHW020635230426
43665CB00008B/178